Extraordinary Celebrations for Extraordinary Catholics

Ideas for Inclusive Catholic Communities
during the Year of Matthew 2023

Hon. Rev. Dr. Jayme Mathias

Extraordinary Catholics Press
Austin, Texas

Extraordinary Catholics Press
P.O. Box 2386
Austin, Texas 78768

Printed in the United States of America

ISBN   979-8-36-089695-1

Table of Contents

FIRST SUNDAY OF ADVENT

(blue or violet)

Advent has arrived! Be sure to share a brief lesson on this **season of joyful hope**—and to speak of **Christ's three comings**: in the flesh 2,000 years ago, at the end of time, and in the liturgies we celebrate!

Now that Thanksgiving is over, some radio stations are already playing Christmas music 24/7. Challenge congregants to **respect the integrity of the Advent season** and to **"fast" from Christmas music and decorations until December 24**. For more ideas on how congregants might honor the Advent season, visit https://adventconspiracy.org!

Think about your worship environment!

- The beginning of a new liturgical year might be an ideal time to try out a **new placement for your liturgical furniture**.
- In place of the penitential color of violet (*violaceus*), **consider using blue this year**—a beautiful winter color that calls to mind Mary during these weeks leading up to the birth of her son! If you stick with violet, consider a shade that's toward the blue end of the spectrum, reminiscent of the night sky before the dawn, and use complementary violets that vary, like the shades of the sky. If you have green plants in your worship space, these might be less prominent during the Advent season.
- Be sure to steam or iron your **Advent vestments**—and to coordinate the color of your vestments with any other touches of blue or violet in your worship space!
- Plan how you might tie the **Advent décor** of your worship environment to the décor of the Christmas season, so as to lessen the load of Christmas decorating on December 24 and to show a more seamless joining of the Advent and Christmas seasons! While being mindful of the temptation to "deck the hall," consider pulling out the **garland and Christmas trees** and decorating them with touches of your Advent color, which can be replaced with touches of Christmas color on December 24.
- Bring a touch of **Advent color and/or accents** to other places outside your worship space: to outdoor areas, the entrance into your worship space, your Blessed Sacrament chapel, your parish hall and/or classrooms, etc. Try an outdoor banner and/or place an evergreen wreath on the front door!

- Dust off your **Advent wreath**, or create a new arrangement this year—perhaps even a "deconstructed wreath" consisting of four candles in four places. If you have a smaller space and are open to a more contemporary look, try adding a floating candle to a large glass bowl of water on each Sunday of Advent. Want to try a vintage look? Suspend a wagon wheel from the ceiling: Early American pioneers hung their wagon wheels indoors during the winter (to keep them from warping), and they decorated them with evergreens and lights to ward off the winter darkness. Instead of colored candles, consider colored glass globes that can be placed over candles; the globes can be replaced with clear globes or taken off at Christmas to expose white candles. Be sure the Advent wreath is a focal point during prayer—but that it doesn't overshadow or overpower the primary liturgical objects of the altar and ambo. Consider placing it in the spot where you'll have your creche on Christmas (to make the connection of Christ coming as the Light of the world), or consider keeping the wreath throughout the Christmas season, but with white candles and white/gold ribbon. Always consider placing the Advent wreath and/or creche in a place where people can be drawn into prayer—a "shrine" within your worship space—perhaps in a place where parents and grandparents can conveniently share a lesson with their children or grandchildren.
- Do you have any large icons of **St. John the Baptist** and/or of the **Visitation of Mary**? Consider incorporating them into the worship environment when the scriptures speak of them.
- Consider whether you'll keep the nativity scene out of the worship space until Christmas (which many liturgists recommend), or whether you'll **heighten the anticipation with a gradual addition of figures to the creche** over the four weeks of Advent. Remember: If you place the nativity scene in your worship space, **the manger is left empty until Christmas!**

Need help decorating your worship space? Don't be bashful: **Ask for volunteers!** Take leadership. Assign tasks and responsibilities. Play appropriate Advent music while you decorate. Then show your gratitude with hot chocolate and cookies, or some other appropriate winter food and drink!

The Advent wreath is an important liturgical symbol. **Bless your Advent wreath** on this first Sunday of Advent. **Involve a parish family by inviting it to carry the first, lighted, blue or violet candle in procession, or to light it at the appropriate moment.** Be sure to speak of the symbolism of the increasing light that we'll see during these four Sundays! Consider selling Advent wreaths as a parish fundraiser. Send congregants home with a prayer of blessing for their own Advent wreaths and with ideas on how they might pray as a family during this season — perhaps before a daily family meal!

In some places, the **Jesse Tree** is a popular tradition that features symbols from the story of our salvation. Consider a Jesse Tree this year, or encourage families to create their own Jesse trees and/or Advent calendars at home!

Thinking of helping those in need at a time when much of the world is focused on consumerism? Create a **"giving tree"** with tags listing gift items that might be used by the homeless or desired by families and/or senior adults in need, and/or have a coat drive and invite families to donate gently-used coats, hats, gloves, boots and blankets. A local homeless shelter will surely welcome your generosity.

Consider **restrained music** during Advent, building to a crescendo with the splendid music of the Christmas season!

To honor the penitential nature of Advent, consider singing the **Penitential Rite** and or using **Eucharistic Prayers for Reconciliation**. Think, too, of how you might better incorporate **moments of silence** into the liturgies of these dark, winter days — perhaps with longer pauses after the proclamations of scripture and/or after reception of the eucharist.

Light one blue or violet candle of the Advent wreath!

Remember: **The *Gloria* is *not* sung during the Advent season!**

The thread in today's scriptures: Proto-Isaiah and the psalmist envisioned salvation as a joyous, light-filled day (Ps. 122:1, Is. 2:5) of peace and prosperity (Is. 2:4, Ps. 122:6-8), when all nations would be gathered into the Lord's house (Is. 2:2, Ps. 122:1). The Quelle Jesus (common to Matthew & Luke) warns us to be prepared for the parousia (Mt. 24:42-44, Lk. 12:35-40), since that event will determine who is "taken" to the Lord's house or to the mountain of the Lord, and who is "left" (Mt. 24:40-41). Noting the nearness of salvation (Rom. 13:11), Paul encourages us to "throw off the works of darkness and put on the armor of light" (Rom. 13:13), so that we, too, might share in that joyous day!

Holy humor: Today we light our Advent wreath! Some churches say that each candle is symbolic. I recall the story of one pastor, who was asking the children in [his/her] community what each candle of the Advent wreath stands for. [S/he] said, "Who can tell me what the four candles of the Advent wreath represent?" Since there was a small banner hanging from each candle, one little boy raised his hand and eagerly read three of the four banners: "Love, joy, peace, and…" Seeing the boy stumble, the pastor asked, "Love, joy, peace and…what?" Love, joy, peace and…what? And you could hear the little boy's mother utter under her breath: "Love, joy, peace and quiet!" [Then segue to the progressively-increasing light of the Advent wreath and/or to the Advent theme of peace in today's scriptures.]

Looking for a visual aid for your homily or object lesson? Point to the light of the first candle of the Advent wreath! The candles and lights in our churches are symbols of the light of Christ. Are we putting on the "armor of light" (Rom. 13:13), walking in the light of the Lord (Is. 2:5), and sharing the light of Christ, so as to bring increased light to this world?

For the intellectually-curious, consider sharing a lesson on the symbolism of the Advent wreath, its historical roots in sixteenth-century Germany, and the popular tradition of lighting the wreath before family meals in the "domestic church!"

It's Advent: Encourage congregants to find a way to **make this Advent special**! Here are a few ideas:

- Challenge congregants to commit themselves to a **special act of charity** during this Advent season.

- Invite them to consider the Advent tradition of choosing a **secret Christkindl** ("Christ Child"), a person for whom they might pray and/or secretly perform small acts of kindness during this Advent season!

- Host an activity in which families can create **Advent wreaths** and/or invite families to begin this season with **an empty manger in the home into which each member of the family can place a piece of straw for every good work performed in honor of the Baby Jesus** during these four weeks, so as to welcome the Christ Child at Christmas with a padded crib. Depending on the size of your congregation, consider doing this activity as a community in or outside of your worship space.

- Looking for other activities for children? Many children write letters to Santa during these weeks; encourage them to observe the Austrian tradition exercised by the von Trapp children of writing their own *"Christkindl* **brief,"** a letter to the Baby Jesus that's placed on the window sill for their Guardian Angel to read to the Christ Child!

The First Sunday of Advent was traditionally known as **"Stir-up Sunday,"** due to the fact that the collect (or opening prayer) spoke of stirring up God's might. Many traditional Advent prayers contain the words: "Stir up your might, we beg you, and come...." Consider incorporating these words into your prayer today. Better yet, involve congregants in stirring up a salad or a dessert—like a plum pudding—after Mass!

Host a community-building event this holiday season, like a parish trip to a local holiday light display and/or live nativity. Alternatively, you could host a party in which parish families create Advent wreaths and/or holiday wreaths for their homes.

Social media is a great way to evangelize: Be sure to take advantage of social media for spreading word of the themes of this season! Think of creative ways to engage your congregants, perhaps through hashtags (#AdventLight #AdventHope #AdventJoy) and/or by inviting congregants to post photos and/or videos from their day to a **"digital Advent calendar"** of daily Advent themes!

On **November 27**, we remember the assassination of **Harvey Milk** (1930-1978), the pioneering LGBTQIA+ rights activist and most famous gay elected official in California. His birthday (May 22) is a state holiday in California, and he is memorialized in two Oscar-winning movies. A martyr for LGBTQ and human rights, he is remembered for his words: "Hope will never be silent."

On **November 27**, we remember the passing of **Louie Crew Clay** (1936-2019), the American Rutgers professor emeritus of English who campaigned for the acceptance of LGBTQ people by Christians and founded Integrity, the national Episcopal LGBTQ organization. He included more than 1,000 people and events in his "Today in LGBTQ History" calendar. In his memory, consider how you might help others to better understand others unlike themselves!

On **November 27**, we celebrate the birth in 1942 of **Robert M. Nemkovich**, the American clergyman who served as the sixth prime bishop of the Polish National Catholic Church. In his honor, pray for him and for our sisters and brothers of the Polish National Catholic Church!

On **November 28**, we remember the passing of **Adrian Johann Broekman** (1724-1800), the Dutch priest and seminary rector who served as the fifth Dutch Old Catholic bishop of Haarlem for over 20 years. His consecration by the archbishop of Utrecht, who was consecrated by the former bishop of Haarlem, brought a full circle to the shared apostolic succession that the two dioceses have since shared. In his memory, consider the ways in which you fail to reciprocate the kindness of others!

On **November 28**, we remember the passing of **Antonina Maria Izabela Wiłucka-Kowalska** (1890-1946), the first Polish woman to receive the sacrament of Holy Orders. The wife of Michał Kowalski, who was consecrated by the archbishop of Utrecht, she served as bishop and high priestess of the Mariavite Catholic Church in Poland. She led the church after her husband's imprisonment in a concentration camp, until her death in 1946. In her memory, pray for all who lead in difficult circumstances!

On **November 28**, we celebrate the birth in 1978 of **Pavel Benedikt Stránský**, the Czech bishop who leads the Old Catholic Church in the Czech Republic. In his honor, pray for him and for our sisters and brothers of the Old Catholic Church in the Czech Republic!

On **November 29**, the Church celebrates **Bl. Bernardo Francisco de Hoyos** (1711-1735), the young Spanish Jesuit priest who vividly wrote of his mystical marriage to Jesus. At age 18, he had a vision of marrying Jesus, where Jesus put a gold ring on his finger and said, "You are mine, and I am yours....You are Bernardo de Jesús and I am Jesús de Bernardo....You and I are one!" In icons, Jesus' sacred heart burns in Bernardo, a patron saint of same-sex marriage. In his memory, lift up all whose love and unity mirror our mystical marriage with Christ!

On **November 29**, we remember the passing of **Dorothy Day** (1897-1980), the American journalist and activist who maintained her social activism after converting to Catholicism. Imprisoned for being a suffragette, she later co-founded the Catholic Worker Movement and edited its newspaper. Pope Francis referred to her as one of four exemplary Americans who built a better future for our world. In her memory, pray for all whose faith calls them to advocate for civil rights!

November 29 is also **International Day of Solidarity with the Palestinian People**. In honor of this day, deepen your knowledge of the post-World War II "Palestine problem" which led to the commemoration of this day!

On **November 30**, we celebrate **St. Andrew** (c. 5-60), referred to as one of Jesus' first disciples (Mt 4:18) and, in another place, as a disciple of John the Baptist who introduced his brother, Peter, to Jesus (Jn 1:40-42). Pause to celebrate the patron saint of those who fish and sing, and consider how you are bringing others to Jesus!

On **November 30**, we remember the passing of **Oscar Wilde** (1854-1900), the Irish poet, novelist and playwright who was one of the most prominent LGBTQIA+ Catholics in his day. Sentenced to two years of prison and forced labor, he wrote of his spiritual journey in a lengthy letter that was posthumously published. In his memory, be inspired by one of the several biographies that celebrate this inaugural honoree of San Francisco's Rainbow Honor Walk!

On **November 30**, we remember the passing of **Johann Josef Demmel** (1890-1972), the sixth bishop of the Old Catholic Church of Germany. His ministry was interrupted by his military service during World War I. He published German works on the sacrament of reconciliation and Old Catholicism. In his memory, pray for our sisters and brothers of the German Old Catholic Church!

On **December 1**, we celebrate the birth in 1954 of **Medha Patkar**, the Indian social activist who fights for justice for the farmers, laborers and women of India. In her honor, consider how you are bringing God's justice to this world!

December 1 is also **World AIDS Day**. Pray for all who suffer from HIV/AIDS — and for all who care for them!

On **December 2**, we remember the passing of **Jan van Ruysbroeck** (1294-1381), the Augustinian priest and prominent Flemish mystic who penned 12 books on the spiritual life. Pause to consider where you are on the "spiritual ladder" — and what you might do to achieve the next "rung"!

On **December 2**, we remember the passing of **Pasquier Quesnel** (1634-1719), the French theologian banished from Paris for his Jansenist sympathies. The Roman church published a papal bull, *Unigenitus*, to condemn 101 sentences in his devotional commentary on the New Testament. In his memory, pray for all who continue to write and publish in an attempt to foster the devotion of others — and for all who are persecuted by the people they love!

On **December 2**, we remember the passing of **Thomas Forsyth "T.F." Torrance** (1913-2007), the Scottish Protestant theologian who was a pioneer in the study of science and theology and who edited the translations of hundreds of theological writings into English, including Karl Barth's six-million-word *Church Dogmatics*. Torrance was instrumental in drafting a joint statement on the doctrine of the Trinity for an historical agreement between the Reformed and Eastern Orthodox churches. In his memory, consider how generously you are sharing the gifts God has given you for the upbuilding of God's reign in this world!

December 2 is also **World Day for Slavery Abolition**. Deepen your knowledge of the various forms of slavery that persist in our world, and pray for the 150 million children who are still subject to child labor!

On **December 3**, the Church celebrates **St. Francis Xavier** (1506-1552), the Jesuit ordained with St. Ignatius of Loyola and later sent to evangelize India. Often portrayed as a young, bearded Jesuit with a torch or flaming heart, he's the patron saint of navigators, missionaries, foreign missions and parish missions. If you have any connection to the Jesuits and/or a desire to support the Church's missions, pray the Litany of St. Francis Xavier and/or meditate on the words of scripture shared with him by St. Ignatius: "What does it profit you to gain the whole world if you lose your soul?"

On **December 3**, we remember the passing of **Leon Chechemian** (1848-1920), the Armenian Catholic priest who founded the United Armenian Catholic Church and the Free Protestant Episcopal Church of England. After a dubious consecration chronicled by Peter Anson, he was conditionally consecrated by Alfred Spencer Richardson of the Reformed Episcopal Church of England. In his memory, pray for all who feel inspired to give birth to new promptings of the Spirit!

On **December 3**, we remember the passing of **Freda Smith** (1935-2019), the American LGBTQ activist who was the first woman ordained by Metropolitan Community Churches. Raised with Nazarene and Salvation Army influences, she struggled to reconcile her faith with her self-identity as a lesbian—until she realized that God doesn't call us to change our sexual orientation. In her memory, pray for all who struggle to accept themselves as the beautiful creations of God they are!

On **December 3**, we celebrate the birth in 1942 of **Roy Gomez**, the American Independent Catholic priest who co-founded Holy Family Catholic Church in Austin, Texas. Once a very active lay leader in the Roman Catholic Church, he retired from active presbyteral ministry at the end of 2020 but continues to advocate for immigrants and against domestic violence and to generously share of himself with God's people. Consider the social issues in which you might involve yourself and make a difference in the lives of others!

December 3 is also **International Day of Persons with Disabilities**. Consider your own actions toward making our world more inclusive and accessible!

Sunday, December 4, 2022

SECOND SUNDAY OF ADVENT

(blue or violet)

Light two blue or violet candles of the Advent wreath!

Remember: **The *Gloria* is *not* sung during the Advent season!**

The thread in today's scriptures: Proto-Isaiah continues his vision of the harmony and peace that will characterize God's reign, where those once viewed as enemies will live in harmony (Is. 11:6-8). Himself a Jew, Paul shared a similar vision through his ministry to non-Jews (Rom. 15:8), encouraging all to "think in harmony with one another, in keeping with Christ Jesus, [and]…with one accord" (Rom. 15:5-6). Rather than focus on harmony, the Matthean Baptist called out the vipers (Mt. 3:7) who co-existed among those who produce good fruits (Mt. 3:8). In the end, our ability (or lack thereof) to live in harmony and peace with one another might be one factor that aligns us more closely with the "wheat" (or with the "chaff"; Mt. 3:12)!

Holy humor: American author and publisher Elbert Hubbart was once quoted by Bugs Bunny, when Bugs Bunny said, "Don't take life too seriously. You'll never get out of it alive!" Elbert Hubbard was also famous for his definition of editors. We're all familiar with editors, right? Editors are the people who decide what is printed in certain publications, like newspapers and magazines, and how those things are said. Elbert Hubbard once defined editors as the people who work for newspapers and whose job it is to separate the wheat from the chaff — and to make sure the chaff is printed! [Segue into the gospel theme of separating wheat from chaff — and Proto-Isaiah's and Paul's (and Jesus') vision of building bridges with those traditionally regarded as "chaff"!

Looking for a visual aid for your homily or object lesson? Consider an ax or a hatchet and/or a lawn rake! Proto-Isaiah speaks of the stump of Jesse, which resulted when Israel was cut down (Is. 11:1), and the Quelle Jesus (common to Matthew & Luke) speaks of the ax being at the root of the tree (Mt. 3:10, Lk. 3:9). Fortunately, if we heed Paul's exhortations in today's letter to the Romans, we need not fear "the ax"! The Quelle Jesus speaks of the winnowing fan or fork (Mt. 3:12, Lk. 3:17), which resembled a modern-day lawn rake. Just as a lawn rake separates the leaves from your yard, the winnowing fan separates the wheat from the chaff!

Looking for a new tradition? Consider sharing bags of blessed straw for parishioners to add to their home nativity sets, as well as a card containing a prayer for the blessing of the family nativity set! You might also consider sharing a blessing for Christmas trees!

On **December 4**, when it does not fall on a Sunday, the Church celebrates **St. Barbara**, the legendary 3rd-century saint beheaded for proclaiming the Christian faith — by her own pagan father, who was subsequently struck by lightning. Though removed from the canon of Roman Catholic saints, she is one of the 140 colonnade saints at St. Peter Basilica in Vatican City. Pray for all who courageously proclaim the Good News!

On **December 4**, when it does not fall on a Sunday, the Church celebrates **St. John of Damascus** (c. 675-749), the first Christian Aristotelian, the last Greek Father, and the "Doctor of Christian Art." John was known for transmitting the teachings of the Greek Fathers and defending the veneration of images. In his memory, read of the iconoclasm that sprang up as a result of Christianity's interaction with Islam, host a religious art appreciation party, and/or reflect on the visual sacramentals of our Catholic tradition, which include statues, paintings and other images!

On **December 4**, we remember the passing of **Engelbert Sterckx** (1792-1867), the Roman Catholic archbishop of Mechelen, Belgium whose consecration was delayed due to rumors of his liberalism. When Belgium achieved its independence, he took advantages of the nation's new educational freedom to establish schools, colleges and seminaries, and to reopen the closed University of Leuven. He hosted a series of Catholic congresses to discuss the social, cultural and political engagement of the Church. In his memory, consider your own engagement in the most pressing social, cultural and political of today!

On **December 5**, the Church celebrates **St. Sabbas** (439-532), the fifth-century abbot, "Star of the Desert" and "Patriarch of Monks" who defended the faith at the Council of Chalcedon. Venerated by the Eastern Church, he's depicted as an abbot with an apple, since he overcame the temptation to eat an apple outside of prescribed meal times — and he vowed never to eat apples again. In Texas, he has a river, city, county and Spanish mission named for him. Take a moment to reflect on the greatest temptations you face in life — and the ways in which you might better overcome them!

On **December 5**, we remember the passing of **Thomas Gallus of Vercelli** (c. 1200-1246), the French theologian and member of the School of St. Victor known for his commentaries on Pseudo-Dionysius. His schema for the relationship between love and knowledge in mystical ascent influenced Bonaventure and *The Cloud of Unknowing*. Reread one of

Thomas' works and contemplate your own perspective on love and knowledge in achieving union with God!

On **December 5**, we remember the passing of **John Robinson** (1919-1983) the English Anglican bishop and New Testament scholar who was a major force in shaping liberal Christian theology. In his memory, explore one of his many writings!

On **December 5**, we remember the passing of **Nelson Mandela** (1918-2013), the South African revolutionary who became the first Black head of state in South Africa. After serving 27 years in prison, he tackled institutional racism and dismantled apartheid. In his memory, pray for all who patiently struggle to create change in our world!

On **December 5**, we remember the passing of **John Alan Lee** (1933-2013), the Canadian writer and LGBTQ activist known for his research on the sociological and psychological aspects of love and sexuality. The author of over 300 books and articles, he turned his attention later in life to the issues of assisted suicide and the right to die. In his memory, pray for "the flying boy [or girl]" you know, who might be addicted to such things as sex, work, pain and/or failure!

December 5 is **International Volunteer Day**. Consider how you're sharing of your time and talent with individuals and organizations in need!

December 5 is also **World Soil Day**, an opportunity to focus on the biodiversity of the ancient basic element that feeds and protects plants and makes earthly life possible!

On **December 6**, the Church celebrates **St. Nicholas** (c. 275-343), the fourth-century Turkish bishop whose generosity made him the protagonist in numerous folktales. Often depicted as a bishop holding three bags of gold (or three golden balls), with three children in a tub at his feet, he's invoked as the patron saint of brides and brewers, fishermen and pharmacists, maidens, mariners, merchants and murderers, pilgrims and prisoners, and scholars and schoolchildren. In his memory, research how his day is celebrated in different countries, bake some *speculaas* (Dutch spice "Kris Kringle cookies"), share one of the many charming stories of St. Nick or *Sinterklaas*, or perform a secret act of charity!

- Do you lead a community with children? Share a brief lesson on the saint's generosity, then, while all sing "Jolly Old St. Nicholas," invite a congregant to enter dressed as the saint, with small gifts for each child—perhaps candy canes in the shape of St. Nicholas' crozier!

On **December 7**, the Church celebrates **St. Ambrose** (339-397), the fourth-century "honey-tongued" bishop who played a role in the conversion of St. Augustine. Often depicted with a beehive, or holding a church in his hand, he's a patron saint of bees, beekeepers, wax melters and candlemakers. In light of the Roman Church's penchant for erecting barriers to the sacraments of the Church — condemned as the heresy of semi-Pelagianism — share a brief lesson on this unbaptized-catechumen-turned-bishop and/or try creating a Christ Candle for Christmas!

On **December 7**, we remember the passing of **Gabriel Biel** (c. 1420-1495), the German priest, philosopher and member of the Windesheim Community, whose writings as the "monarch of theologians" were repeatedly referenced at the Council of Trent. He won the pope's affection by siding against an archbishop who failed to pay required annates, by advocating that all ecclesiastical jurisdiction derives from the pope, and by arguing that clergy can withhold absolution. Pray for all who similarly feel the need to curry favor with those in power!

On **December 7**, we celebrate the birth in 1941 of **Sr. Elizabeth A. Johnson**, the Roman Catholic feminist theologian, professor and author of various works. Her book, *Quest for the Living God*, expounds new ways of thinking about God within the context of traditional Catholic beliefs; it garnered criticism by the Roman Church's hierarchy, fraying the already-strained relationship between Roman Catholic bishops and theologians. In her honor, pray for all who help us to understand traditional Catholic beliefs in new ways!

December 7 is also **U.S. Pearl Harbor Remembrance Day**. Reflect on the tragic events of this day, which pulled the U.S. into World War II.

On **December 8**, the Roman church celebrates its "holyday of obligation" of the **Immaculate Conception**, a papal pronouncement that irreparably split the Roman church in 1854 and led to the dogmatization of the novel ideas of the Roman's bishop's universal jurisdiction and purported "infallibility" in 1870. It was exactly these new ideas that led many to refer to themselves as Old Catholics, indicating their desire to return to the beliefs and practices of the ancient Church, rather than fall prey to the novelties pushed by the Roman papacracy. Whether you celebrate the Immaculate Conception or not, this could be a tremendous teaching moment for those who celebrate with you and wish to understand the differences between Independent Catholicism and the teachings of the Roman church. If you celebrate the "Patroness of the United States of America," choose Marian hymns, place white lilies near her image, and consider praying a decade (or more) of the joyful mysteries of the rosary. This is also the traditional day for baking gingerbread Moravian spritz cookies: Plan a family activity of assembling a gingerbread house or of baking holiday cookies!

On **December 8**, we remember the murder of **Tibira do Maranhão** (+1614), the first documented man to be executed in Brazil due to homosexuality. Two years after the arrival of French colonizers, Tibira, whose name means "homosexual" in the Tupi language, was sentenced to death for sodomy by a Capuchin friar. After fleeing into the woods for several days, he was captured, baptized Dismas, then strapped to the front of a cannon that blew him to pieces. In 2016, a monument was erected to him in Maranhão, Brazil, during the State Week of Human Rights. Pray for all who use religion in evil ways—and for all who suffer as a result!

On **December 8**, we remember the execution of **Pavel Florensky** (1882-1937), the Russian Orthodox theologian, priest, philosopher, mathematician, physicist, electrical engineer, inventor, polymath and neo-martyr. He wrote a groundbreaking theology of same-sex love in 1914 Moscow. As part of the 1930s Soviet anti-religious purge, he was sent to a forced labor camp and executed on false charges. In his memory, pray for all who suffer as a result of their religious beliefs!

On **December 8**, we remember the passing of **Santiago Fonacier** (1885-1977), the Filipino journalist, translator and senator who was ordained at age 18 and later served as second Supreme Bishop of the Philippine Independent Church, which was estimated to have two million adherents at the time. He led the church during the archipelago's occupation by the Japanese (1942-1945), and his cathedral was destroyed during the indiscriminate bombing of Manila by U.S. forces. Removed from leadership in 1946, he sued the church in a lawsuit that lasted nine years and led to his founding of the Independent Church of Filipino Christians, which was welcomed back into the Philippine Independent Church nearly 20 years later. In his memory, consider how well you are weathering the challenges you face!

December 9 is the Feast of **St. Juan Diego Cuauhtlatoatzin** (1474-1548), the indigenous man to whom Our Lady of Guadalupe appeared in 1531, according to the legend written about those events in 1648. A patron of Mexico, he's often pictured with roses and with an image of Our Lady of Guadalupe on his *tilma* (outer cloak). Though seemingly frightened and confused by the mandate he was given, Juan Diego obeyed and courageously sought an audience with Fray Juan de Zumárraga, the bishop of New Spain. In his honor, pray for and/or find a way to support those whose faces and courage are mirrored in this saint—including the many migrant workers who help to sustain our economy!

On **December 9**, we remember the passing of **Fulton John Sheen** (1895-1979), the American bishop known for his preaching on television and radio. For 20 years, he hosted a night-time radio program, "The Catholic Hour," before moving to television and sharing "Life is Worth Living" and "The Fulton Sheen Program." Often referred to as one of the first televangelists, Sheen was the winner of two Emmys for Most Outstanding Television Personality. In his memory, consider how you are using modern technologies to expand your reach!

On **December 9**, we remember the passing of **Casimir J. Grotnik** (1935-2005), the Polish-American bishop of the Polish National Catholic Church. In his memory, pray for our sisters and brothers of the Polish National Catholic Church!

December 9 is also **International Day of Commemoration & Dignity of the Victims of the Crime of Genocide and of the Prevention of this Crime**. Recalling the Catholic Church's historic complicity in genocide, pray for all national, ethnical, racial and religious groups that continue to be targeted and harmed by others.

On **December 10**, the Church celebrates **Our Lady of Loreto**, a commemoration of the image of Mary found inside the house venerated as her birthplace and the site of the Annunciation, which, according to tradition, was miraculously transported to Dalmatia in 1291, then to Recanati, Italy in 1294, then to Loreto. She is a matron saint of aviators and air forces (for obvious reasons), builders, construction workers and Italy. Pray for all who are flying today and throughout the upcoming holiday season!

On **December 10**, the Church celebrates **St. Melchiades** (+314), the African pope who led the Church during the last persecution before freedom was granted to Christians by Constantine. Because Melchiades helped usher in a new era of peace, St. Augustine called him "the true child of the peace of Jesus Christ." Pause today to pray for all who are persecuted, for their persecutors, and for all who are instruments of peace in our world!

On **December 10**, we remember the passing of **Karl Barth** (1886-1968), the Swiss Reformed theologian referred to by Pope Pius XII as the greatest theologian since Thomas Aquinas. How much do you know about him? Take a moment today to increase your knowledge of Karl Barth and his works!

On **December 10**, we remember the passing of **Thomas Merton** (1915-1968), the Trappist monk, theologian, mystic and social activist who dedicated the latter years of his life to the study of comparative religions.

His bestselling autobiography, *The Seven Story Mountain*, inspired countless students and veterans to enter religious life. In his memory, pull one of his works from the shelf and reacquaint yourself with his timeless wisdom!

On **December 10**, we remember the passing of **Adele Starr** (1920-2010), who overcame prejudices and served as the first national president of the support group Parents and Friends of Lesbians and Gays (PFLAG), which quickly grew to 400 chapters with 200,000 members. An unflagging champion of LGBTQ rights, she hosted the first meeting of the Los Angeles PFLAG chapter in her home. In her memory, consider the prejudices you have yet to overcome!

On **December 10**, we remember the passing of **Marek Kordzik** (1955-2016), the Polish priest and bishop who led the Old Catholic Church in Poland. In his memory, pray for our sisters and brothers of the Old Catholic Church in Poland!

December 10 is also **Human Right Day**. Familiarize yourself with the UN's Universal Declaration of Human Rights, which proclaims the inalienable rights of all persons, regardless of race, color, religion, sex, language, political or other opinion, national or social origin, property, birth or other status!

Sunday, December 11, 2022

THIRD SUNDAY OF ADVENT

(rose or blue or violet)

It's *Gaudete* **Sunday**: Share a brief lesson on the joy of this day and its tie to Paul's words: "*Gaudete in Domino semper*" [Rejoice in the Lord always] (Phil 4:4)!

Do you have **rose vestments**? Today's the day to pull them out! Aim for a shade of rose that resembles the sky at dawn—and *not* a shocking, Pepto Bismol® pink. Be sure to coordinate the color of your vestments with any other touches of rose in your worship space, and be sure to iron or steam any wrinkles!

Light three blue or violet candles—or two such candles and the rose candle—of the Advent wreath!

Remember: **The *Gloria* is *not* sung during the Advent season!**

The thread in today's scriptures: The prayer of the ancient Church was maranatha, "Come, Lord Jesus!" Clearly, the Quelle Jesus was seen as proleptically fulfilling Proto-Isaiah's vision, coming to save us (Is. 35:4, repeated as the response for our responsorial psalm today), giving sight to the blind (Is. 35:5, Ps. 146:8, Mt. 11:5, Lk. 7:21-22), causing the deaf to hear (Is. 35:5, Mt. 11:5, Lk. 7:22) making the lame to walk (Is. 35:5, Mt. 11:5, Lk. 7:22), and ransoming the captives (Is. 35:10, Ps. 146:7). James uses the words "patient" and "patience" four times (James 5:7-10): Until the risen Christ comes again in glory, we need to patient!

Holy humor: Have you heard my pink-candle-Advent-wreath story before? One year, I gathered all the children of the parish around the Advent wreath, and I was telling them about the symbolism of the candles and the evergreens and the colors of the candles. Since I was speaking with kids, I didn't refer to the candles as "violet" or "rose" — the names of our liturgical colors; instead I used colors the kids would understand: purple and pink. I asked the children what they thought the three purple candles stood for, and I explained that purple was an ancient color of penitence — of being sorry for the things that we've said and done that have hurt other people. Then I asked the children what they thought the pink candle was for. I'll never forget: One girl shot her hand into the air. I asked her: "What do you think the pink candles stands for?" With wide eyes and without hesitation, she shouted: "The pink candle means…we're going to have a baby girl!"

Looking for a visual aid for your homily or object lesson? Consider the mathematical signs for "greater than" and "less than"! Early on, kids learn that certain things (and certain people) are "greater" or "less" than others — often associating those mathematical signs with the "alligator" that eats the highest number of the two. We all know it: Our kids are programmed to think that some people are "less" than others (e.g., children, women, minorities, the elderly, those with less ability and/or resources). Proto-Isaiah had the vision that the coming messiah would make people "greater" than they might otherwise be. They'll enjoy greater health and freedom, the "valleys" in their lives will be filled, and they will be made whole! Interestingly, the Quelle Jesus points out that John the Baptist was "greater" than a prophet (Mt. 11:9); he says, "there has been none greater than John the Baptist; yet the least in the kingdom of heaven is greater than he" (Mt. 11:11, Lk. 7:28)! Like mother, like son: the Quelle Jesus shared his mother's vision (Lk. 1:51-53) that the "lesser" will be deemed the "greater"!

Christmas is drawing near: Consider hosting a **holiday party** for clergy, lay leaders and/or volunteers! Prepare holiday party games or a White Elephant gift exchange, and share Advent-colored Santa hats!

If your congregation is of Italian descent, invite them to bring their Christ Child figures to church for a special *Bambinelli* **Sunday** blessing, which always occurs on the Third Sunday of Advent!

This is *Gaudete* Sunday, but we also recognize that the holidays aren't necessarily a jolly time for all. **Share the joy of your community with the homebound and/or with those who might enjoy your visit at a local hospital, nursing home, or senior center**! Such activities can involve congregants of all ages: the children can create handmade holiday cards, the teens can bake cookies and sing carols, the adults can prepare to spend a little extra time listening to those whom you visit. Take with you prayer resources and news from your community!

On **December 11**, when it does not fall on a Sunday, the Church celebrates **St. Damasus I** (c. 304-384), the fourth-century pope who commissioned Jerome's Vulgate translation of the scriptures. He's the patron saint of archaeologists. Learn about the biblical canon approved at his Council of Rome (382 A.D.), and make a commitment to better familiarize yourself with the rich fare of scripture!

On **December 11**, we remember the passing of **Hieronymus de Bock** (+1744), the second Dutch Old Catholic bishop of Haarlem from 1742 to 1744. After the Haarlem cathedral chapter's hesitance to act, he was elected by the Utrecht cathedral chapter and consecrated by Archbishop of Utrecht Peter Johann Meindaerts. In his memory, pray for all whose hesitations cost some and benefit others!

On **December 11**, the Armenian Apostolic Church celebrates the anniversary of the installation in 2019 of Sahag Maşalyan as **Patriarch Sahak Mashalyan of Constantinople**. In his honor, pray for him and for the nine million people he serves!

On **December 11**, we remember the passing in 2021 of **Anne Rice**, the bestselling American author of vampire fiction and Christian literature, including *The Vampire Chronicles* and *Christ the Lord: Out of Egypt*. Raised Catholic, she attended Catholic schools, but left the Church at age 18. After decades of atheism, she returned to the Catholic Church in 1998—though not with a full embrace of the Church's stances on gay marriage, abortion rights, and birth control. In her honor, reach out to someone who has a similarly complex relationship with the church of his/her upbringing!

December 11 is also **International Mountain Day**. Thank God for the purple-mountain majesties traditionally seen as places of encounter with the Divine!

On **December 12**, the Church celebrates **Our Lady of Guadalupe** (1531), the Empress of the Americas, the Patroness of Latin American, and the Mother of all Mexicans!

- If you want to celebrate Our Lady of Guadalupe on December 12, remember that **the most popular celebrations of her by Mexicans occur at midnight and/or at a very early hour of the morning** (e.g., 6:00 a.m.), beginning with the singing of *"Las mañanitas."*
- If you have a Mexican community that might not gather to celebrate on December 12, consider a nod to **Our Lady of Guadalupe** during the Sunday liturgy and/or a celebration of her after your Sunday Mass.
- Invite congregants to **decorate an image of her**, perhaps with large paper flowers of the colors of the Mexican flag; you might also invite people to bring **roses and/or candles** in her honor!
- Before you begin your celebration of the eucharist, sing *"Las mañanitas"* in her honor!
- Incorporate traditional dances by *matlachines* and/or *concheros* into your liturgy and/or your gathering after Mass!
- **Share a gift** with each person present—perhaps a prayer card, pin or bookmark containing her image.
- In this Advent season of increasing light, be sure to reference the fact that she is clothed with the sun and standing on the moon. Also, note the black band around her waist—a symbol of her pregnancy: In the same way that she carried the Christ Child inside her, we are called to carry Christ within us and to share Christ with others!
- If you have the talent, organize a **dramatic reenactment of the appearance of Our Lady of Guadalupe to St. Juan Diego**! These *obras* are usually performed by children or teens, but consider involving adults: Juan Diego was some 57 years old at the time of the apparition—much older than most images of the saint!
- **For the intellectually-curious**, consider sharing a lesson on the *Nican mopohua*, the tale that was penned 118 years after the purported apparition, and/or on the incredible syncretism that we find in the image of the Aztec goddess *Tonantzín*—a now venerated by Catholics as the mother of Christ!

- If devotion to Our Lady of Guadalupe runs especially deep in your community, invite lay leaders to host a **novena** in her honor, with the nightly praying of the rosary and singing of songs in her honor, beginning on December 3.

On **December 12**, the Church also celebrates **Bl. Bartolo Buonpedoni** (1260-1320), the Italian Franciscan priest famous for being "joined in holy friendship" with Bl. Vivaldo Stricchi, the lay Franciscan 32 years his junior. When Bartolo contracted leprosy, Vivaldo moved into the leper hospital with him, thus becoming a trailblazer of same-sex fidelity. Vivaldo accompanied Bartolo through 20 years of suffering. Pray for all who accompany others through dark valleys!

On **December 12**, we remember the passing of **Avery Robert Dulles** (1918-2008), the Jesuit priest, theologian and non-bishop cardinal who penned over 20 books and 700 articles, largely on ecclesiology. Raised Presbyterian, he became agnostic, then Roman Catholic, later serving as president of the Catholic Theological Society of America and of the American Theological Society. Dulles served on the International Theological Commission and worked in Lutheran/Catholic dialogue. In his memory, consider the ways in which you might more significantly contribute to theology, ecclesiology and/or to ecumenical dialogue!

On **December 12**, we celebrate the birth in 1930 of **César Virata**, a prominent Independent Catholic and member of the Philippine Independent Church who served as finance minister (1970-1986) and succeeded Ferdinand Marcos as prime minister of the Philippines (1981-1986). A business leader and technocrat, he was the grandnephew of the first Philippine President, Emilio Aguinaldo—also an Independent Catholic. He currently chairs the Rizal Commercial Banking Corporation. In his honor, learn something new in the fields of finance and/or technology!

On **December 12**, we celebrate the anniversary of the presbyteral ordination in 2015 of Father **Roy Gomez**, co-founder and vicar emeritus of Holy Family Catholic Church in Austin, Texas. Happy anniversary!

On **December 13**, the Church celebrates **St. Lucy** (c. 283-303), the third-century Greek noblewoman whose vow of virginity infuriated the young man to whom she was unwillingly wedded. The patroness of eye problems, blindness, the blind, authors, laborers, salespeople and hemorrhages, Lucy is often depicted hitched to a yoke of oxen or holding two eyes on a dish. In Croatia, Christmas wheat is planted today; plant some wheat seeds in a small pot of soil, and you'll have fresh, green wheat about eight inches tall for your manger scene by Christmas! In honor of St. Lucy's intervention in a 1582 famine, Italians abstain from grain, bread and pasta today, eating *cuccia* instead. In Lombardy, goose is eaten today, and St. Lucy brings gifts today to the children who leave hay, carrots and bowls of milk for her donkey. In Sweden, the oldest daughter of the household dons a white dress, a crimson sash and stockings, and a crown/wreath with lighted candles—don't try this at home!—to wake family members on *Luciadagen* (Lucy's Day) with hot coffee and *Lussekatter* (saffron buns). Pray Eucharistic Prayer I, which mentions her, and reflect on her life and its application to respect for women and support for all who stand with the #MeToo movement and against sexual abuse. Remember to tie her name (from the Latin root *lux, lucis*, meaning "light") to the increasing light that we see during Advent—and to pray for those who are physically and/or spiritually blind!

On **December 13**, we remember the passing of **Pierre Martin Ngô Đình Thục** (1897-1984), the Vietnamese Roman Catholic archbishop who lived in exile after the murder of his younger brother, Ngô Đình Diệm, the president of South Vietnam. Thục was excommunicated by the Roman church for consecrating a number of bishops without the Vatican's approval during the last ten years of his life. In his memory, pray for all who continue to share his valid lines of apostolic succession with others in the Independent Catholic tradition!

On **December 13**, we remember the passing of **Léon Gauthier** (1912-2003), the Swiss priest and theologian who served as the fourth Old Catholic bishop in Switzerland for 14 years. He greatly promoted ecumenism and wrote several articles in theological journals. In his memory, pray for our sisters and brothers of the Swiss Old Catholic Church!

On **December 14**, we remember the passing of **Guillaume Briçonnet, Sr.** (1445-1514), the French cardinal and statesman who served as secretary of Louis XI's treasury. The father of Bishop Guillaume Briçonnet, Jr., he was excommunicated by Julius II for assembling cardinals to speak of the reformation of the Church, but, after Julius' death, Leo X restored him to the College of Cardinals. In his memory, pray for all who encounter resistance in their attempts to bring reform to the Church!

On **December 14**, the Church celebrates **St. John of the Cross** (1542-1591) the 16th-century Spanish Carmelite priest who helped St. Teresa of Avila to reform the Carmelite Order. Because he described his relationship with Christ in erotic terms, he is a special patron saint of same-sex marriages. He is also the patron saint of mystics, mystical theology, contemplatives and contemplative life. Share an acknowledgement that not all people are rejoicing during this holiday season. Say a prayer of blessing for those passing through "the dark night of the soul" during what might otherwise be a season of joy!

On **December 14**, we remember the passing of **Paul Melchers** (1813-1895), the German cardinal and archbishop of Cologne who wrote to Pius IX with 13 other bishops to express their concern that the definition of purported papal infallibility was untimely. Melchers played a prominent role at the First Vatican Council and counseled against a definition of papal infallibility. Faithful to the Roman papacracy, he later excommunicated professors who refused to accept the novel dogma, as well as two priests who joined the Old Catholic movement. In his memory, pray for all who, against their best judgment, heap burdens on others rather than risk the loss of the power and privileges they enjoy!

On **December 14**, we celebrate the birth in 1938 of **Leonardo Boff**, the Brazilian theologian known for his support of the early Latin American liberation theology movement. A sharp critic of the "fundamentalist" Roman papacracy and of American foreign policy, he was silenced by "religious terrorist" Joseph Ratzinger. After being silenced again and barred by the Roman church from attending the Eco-92 Earth Summit, he departed his Franciscan order and abandoned his priestly ministry. In Boff's honor, reacquaint yourself with any one of his liberating works!

On **December 14**, we celebrate the birth in 1944 of Bishop **Ronald Stephenson**, diocesan bishop of the Holy Trinity Diocese. Pray for him and for the people he serves!

On **December 15**, the Church celebrates **St. Virginia Bracelli** (1587-1651), the 17th-century Italian noblewoman who, after bearing two daughters, was widowed at age 20, professed a vow of chastity, and spent the remainder of her life helping the sick, the poor, and abandoned children during times of plague and famine. Pray today for all who are bringing light and life to others during this Advent season!

On **December 15**, we remember the passing of **John Churchill Sibley** (1858-1939), the English organist and teacher who was consecrated an Independent Catholic bishop by Frederick Ebenezer Lloyd of the American Catholic Church. As archbishop metropolitan of the Orthodox Catholic Church in the British Empire, he attracted enemies, remaining a gentleman despite the gutter press and agent provocateurs that wore on his wife. He established Intercollegiate University for the training of Independent Catholic clergy. In his memory, pray for your enemies— and for those who suffer the attacks of others!

On **December 15**, we remember the passing of **Marko Kalogjera** (1877-1956), the Croatian bishop who led the Croatian Old Catholic Church. In his memory, pray for our sisters and brothers of the Croatian Old Catholic Church!

December 15 is also **U.S. Bill of Rights Day**, the day on which we celebrate the individual rights contained in the first ten amendments to the U.S. Constitution. Reacquaint yourself with the U.S. Bill of Rights!

On **December 16**, the Church celebrates **Shadrach, Meshach and Abednego**, the three Hebrew eunuchs thrown into an oven for refusing to stop worshiping God (Dan. 3). Patron saints of sexual minorities, they were part of the corps of castrated men, homosexual men, and intersex folk who served the royal court. In their memory, pray for all who courageously face difficulties!

On **December 16**, we remember the passing of **Johann van Stiphout** (+1777), who served as the fourth Dutch Old Catholic bishop of Haarlem for nearly 30 years. Together with the bishop of Deventer, he ensured the continuance of apostolic succession for the future Dutch Old Catholic Church, co-consecrating Michael van Nieuwenhuizen as archbishop of Utrecht in 1768. In his memory, consider how generously you share your gifts with others!

On **December 16**, we remember the passing of **Maude Petre** (1863-1942), the English Roman Catholic nun and prolific writer who was swept up in the modernist controversy when she provided housing to expelled Jesuit George Tyrell. Her two-volume biography of Tyrell was placed on the Holy See's *Index of Forbidden Books*, and her bishop refused to allow a priest to officiate at her burial. In her memory, pray for all who live the corporal works of mercy — despite the consequences!

In the Latino culture, **December 16** is the first day of *las posadas*, the nine-day reenactment of Mary and Joseph's search for lodging in Bethlehem. Here are a few ideas on how to celebrate:

- Organize a parish *posada* at your worship space, complete with candles, food and drink, a *piñata*, gifts for the kids, and maybe even a visit from Santa!
- Better yet, find nine families who are willing to open their homes for parish *posadas* — one on each night from December 16 to 24 — so that you can get out and visit them at their homes. Publish the date, time and address of each *posada*, so that parishioners can join the fun!

- Remember to incorporate a lesson on how we're all called to open the "doors" of our hearts to those around us during this holiday season — and throughout the coming year.

- If there's a *piñata*, be sure to speak to the symbolism of beating the capital sins in our lives (represented by the seven "horns" of a traditional *piñata*), so that the grace of God might spill into our lives (as symbolized by the candy)! Note: The *piñata* can be an extremely dangerous tradition. Have adults hold back eager children with a large rope circle, until a whistle is blown — which is the signal for the child with the stick to stop swinging. Take time to explain these rules and obtain understanding from children *before* the excitement begins!

In the Filipino culture, **December 16** is the first day of ***Simbang Gabi***, the nine-day ritual popular in the Philippine Independent Church of holding early morning Masses with candlelight and centuries-old music. Hosted in the dark, before agricultural workers traditionally went off to work on rice, coconut and sugarcane plantations, these liturgies are celebrated as great solemnities (with the wearing of white vestments and the singing of the *Gloria*), and conclude with the sharing of *bibingka* (rice cakes) and *puto bumbong* (steamed purple rice pastries), with *tsokolate* (hot chocolate from local cacao) and *salabát* (ginger tea).

December 17 is the first day for the seven daily **O Antiphons**, which are based on fourth-century titles for the Messiah. Found in the hymn "O Come, O Come Emmanuel," they are: *O Sapientia* (Wisdom), *O Adonai* (Lord and Ruler), *O Radix Jesse* (Root of Jesse), *O Clavis David* (Key of David), *O Oriens* (Dayspring), *O Rex Gentium* (King of the Gentiles), *and O Emmanuel* (God With Us). When ordered in reverse (*Emmanuel, Rex, Oriens, Clavis, Radix, Adonai,* and *Sapientia*), they form the Latin acrostic *ero cras*, which means, "I will come tomorrow." Pray today's O Antiphon and invite the Lord to come!

On **December 17**, the old *Roman Martyrology* celebrated **St. Lazarus of Bethany**, the brother of Ss. Martha and Mary of Bethany, whom the Johannine Jesus raised from the dead (Jn. 11:1-44). According to one tradition, he went on to become a missionary to Gaul (in modern-day France), the first bishop of Marseilles, and a martyr during the persecutions of Domitian. A patron saint of the gay community, he formed a non-traditional family as the bachelor brother of his spinster sisters (sometimes portrayed as a lesbian couple) and has been suggested as "the beloved disciple" of the Johannine Jesus and as the nude young man running away from the Marcan Jesus in Gethsemane (Mk. 14:51-52).

Incorporate into your prayer today a meditation on John's story of Lazarus' rising from the dead!

On **December 17**, the Church also celebrates **St. Olympias**, the fourth-century deaconess and Roman noblewoman of Greek descent who, after the death of her husband — the prefect of Constantinople — dedicated her life to the Church. She built a hospital and orphanage and became a friend of St. John Chrysostom, which led to the seizure of her house and to her exile for the last four years of her life. Olympias is one of 140 colonnade saints at St. Peter Basilica in Vatican City. In her memory, consider how you are sharing your life with those in need!

On **December 17**, we remember the passing of **Rumi** (1207-1273), the Persian poet, Islamic scholar and Sufi mystic whose spiritual legacy has spanned seven centuries. An LGBTQ icon, he allowed his love for the whirling dervish Shams of Tabriz, the goldsmith Saladin Zarkub, and his scribe Husan Chelebi to inspire some of the world's greatest poems. In his memory, discover his poetry!

On **December 17**, the Church celebrates **St. Joseph Manyanet y Vives** (1833-1901), the 19th-century "Apostle of the Holy Family" who founded the Congregation of the Sons of the Holy Family and of the Missionary Daughters of the Holy Family of Nazareth, two congregations dedicated to parish ministry, teaching children, and serving families. Joseph encouraged devotion to the Holy Family, and he published the magazine, *La Sagrada Familia*. Pause today to consider how you might better serve your family and the families you encounter each week!

On **December 17**, we remember the passing of **Benedykt Sęk** (1932-1978), the Polish Old Catholic priest who served as administrator of the Krakow-Częstochowa diocese of the Polish Catholic Church in Poland. In his memory, pray for our sisters and brothers of the Polish Catholic Church in Poland!

On **December 17**, the Roman Catholic Church celebrates the birth in 1936 of **Jorge Mario Bergoglio**, who became Pope Francis. In a spirit of ecumenism, pray for him and for the 1.3 billion Roman Catholics he serves!

Sunday, December 18, 2022
FOURTH SUNDAY OF ADVENT
(blue or violet)

Light all four candles of the Advent wreath!

Remember: **The *Gloria* is *not* sung during the Advent season!**

The thread in today's scriptures: As we prepare our hearts for the coming of Christ at Christmas, we sing with the psalmist: "Let the Lord enter" (Ps. 24:7)! Proto-Isaiah had a vision that "God-with-us" would enter the world through a young girl (Is. 7:14, too often mistranslated as "virgin"). Matthew suggests that the young girl was Miryam, the wife of Yossef, who was a descendant of King David (Rom. 1:3), that Miryam "was found with child through the Holy Spirit" (Mt. 1:18), and that Yossef, in line with Proto-Isaiah's prophecy (Is. 7:14, Mt. 1:23), was to name the boy Yeshua (Mt. 1:21).

Holy humor: One day, when Jesus was a child, he heard his name shouted from the family's carpentry shop, by his stepfather, Joseph. Jesus ran to Joseph in the carpentry shop and asked, "Did you call me?" And you know where this joke is going: Joseph looked at Jesus and said, "Did I call you? No. I just hit my thumb with the hammer!" ("Jesus Christ!") [Segue into Matthew's story of Joseph giving Jesus his name, trusting that the child's conception was really due to supernatural reasons, and welcoming Jesus into his heart and into his home, in the same way that we're called to welcome Christ into our hearts.]

Looking for a visual aid for your homily or object lesson? Consider an image of St. Joseph with the child Jesus! We've all seen the tender, serene images of Joseph holding his wife's child, but imagine for a moment the leap of faith required for Joseph to take Mary into his home and to raise her son, believing it was "through the Holy Spirit that this child has been conceived in her" (Mt. 1:20). It is for this reason that Joseph, a simple tekton (handyman), is a model of faith for all generations! As we approach Christmas, ask yourself how you're opening your heart and your life to welcome the Christ Child!

Looking to start a new tradition? Consider sharing *Oplatki* (Polish Christmas wafers) with blessings after Mass!

On **December 18**, we remember the passing of **Michael Wadding** (1591-1644), the Irish Jesuit known as Miguel Godínez. He spent over 20 years of his life as a missionary in present-day Mexico. In his memory, pray for the missionaries of the Church—especially for those who continue to minister to the needs of Spanish-speaking persons in the U.S. and abroad!

On **December 18**, we remember the passing of **Pieter Codde** (1648-1710), who served for 16 years as the Roman Catholic archbishop of Utrecht before being suspended in 1704 for his Jansenist sympathies and his refusal to sign the formulary required by *Unigenitus*. His see sat empty for nearly 20 years, until the Chapter of Utrecht elected Cornelius Steenoven as his successor. In his memory, pray for all who are willing to risk the loss of titles and positions due to uncompromising beliefs!

On **December 18**, we remember the passing of **Hans Vaihinger** (1852-1933), the German Kantian philosopher known for his "as if" philosophy. He stated that humans construct systems of thought to match their understanding of reality—then assume patently false fictions to be true. In his memory, reacquaint yourself with his philosophy!

On **December 18**, we celebrate the birth in 1961 of Bishop **David Strong**, bishop of the Missionaries of the Incarnation and pastor of Spirit of Christ Catholic Community in Tacoma, Washington. Pray for him and for the people he serves!

On **December 18**, we celebrate the birth in 1974 of **Marek Bożek**, the Polish Roman Catholic priest famously excommunicated for his intervention on behalf of a parish abandoned by its priests and archbishop. Intimidated and alienated for over ten years, his community finally prevailed in a court of law, and St. Stanislaus Polish Catholic Church in St. Louis, Missouri became a vibrant, inclusive Catholic community known for its multilingual liturgies, Polish hospitality and social ministry. Pray for him and reflect on how your words and actions enflesh the Polish adage, "When guests arrive, God arrives"!

On **December 18**, we celebrate the anniversary of the presbyteral ordination in 2002 of Father **Marek Bożek**, former pastor of St. Stanislaus Polish Catholic Church in St. Louis, Missouri. Happy anniversary!

December 18 is also **International Migrants Day**, a day to reflect on the challenges and difficulties of international migration. Pray for our 270 million sisters and brothers who face life's challenges as migrants!

For our Jewish sisters and brothers, **Chanukah** begins on the evening of December 18. Read about this Festival of Lights, which celebrates the liberation of Israel from the Greeks and the subsequent purification of the Temple, in 1Maccabees, and learn about the various Chanukah traditions, including the lighting of the menorah (or hanukkah), the singing of Hanukkah songs, the playing of games (like dreidel), and the eating of oil-based foods, like *latkes* and *sufganiyot*.

On **December 19**, the Church celebrates **St. Fausta of Sirmium**, the mother of St. Anastasia of Sirmium. A model mother for having raised such a saintly daughter, she is one of the 140 colonnade saints at St. Peter Basilica in Vatican City. In her memory, pray for all saintly parents!

On **December 19**, we remember the passing of **Johann Friedrich von Schulte** (1827-1914), the German canonist and historian who opposed the First Vatican Council and was the architect for the canon law of the German Old Catholic Church. He served as President of the Old Catholic Congress from 1871 to 1890. In his memory, pray for all who follow in his footsteps, leading and guiding Independent Catholic movements at the national and international levels!

On **December 19**, we remember the passing of **Arnold Harris Mathew** (1852-1919), the founder of Old Catholicism in England. Born Arnoldo Girolamo Povoleri, he served as a Roman Catholic priest until he lost faith in scripture and the divinity of Christ. Later consecrated by the Archbishop of Utrecht, who believed Mathew's assertions on the number of Old Catholics in England, Mathew shared apostolic succession with other men in the hope of cementing his legacy. Ironically, he died a lonely man. In his memory, pray for all in our movement who struggle to lead and nourish others—particularly those who feel a need to consecrate others who may be ill-equipped to fulfill the *triplex munus* of the episcopacy.

On **December 19**, we celebrate the birth in 1950 of **Maria Ludwik Jabłoński**, the Polish Old Catholic bishop who led the Old Catholic Mariavite Church and currently serves as the ordinary of the Lublin-Podlasie diocese. In his honor, pray for him and for our sisters and brothers of the Old Catholic Mariavite Church in Poland!

On **December 20**, the Church celebrates **St. Dominic of Silos** (1000-1073), the 11th-century Spanish Benedictine abbot who was exiled for not surrendering his monastery's land to the king. A beloved saint in Spain, he rescued Christian slaves from the Moors, and his shrine was the site where St. Dominic de Guzmán's mother prayed for a child. He's a patron saint of prisoners and pregnant women and is invoked against insects, rabies, and rabid dogs. Find a way today to show your solidarity and support for those praying for a child during this Advent season!

On **December 20**, the Church also celebrates **Ruth and Naomi**, the biblical women whose love for one another (Ruth 1) has made them matron saints of the lesbian community. Ruth's famous vow to Naomi is often repeated at weddings: ""Where you go, I will go, and where you stay, I will stay. Your people will be my people and your God my God" (Ruth 1:6). In their memory, pray for all who share similar vows, bringing God's love and light to our world!

On **December 20**, we remember the passing of **Henry of Kalkar** (1328-1408), who inspired his friend and classmate, Geert Groote, to found the Brothers of the Common Life. An organizer of the Catholic Renaissance that found its expression in the Council of Trent, Henry's spiritual writings were distributed by Groote's Windesheim communities. Consider how you are following in Henry's footsteps and inspiring others to do great things!

On **December 20**, we remember the passing of "*die Lutherin*," Martin Luther's wife, **Katharina von Bora** (1499-1552), who was an important part of the Reformation due to her role in helping to define Protestant family life and in setting the tone for married clergy. A former nun dissatisfied with monastic life and interested in the growing reform movement, Katharina married Martin, who concluded that "his marriage would please his father, rile the pope, cause the angels to laugh and the devils to weep." She managed their brewery and cattle business to support their family as well as the students and visitors who boarded with them — and the hospital she operated on site in times of widespread illness. In her memory, pray for the spouses who so generously support the ministries of our clergy!

On **December 20**, we remember the passing of **Samuel Cotton** (1947-2003), the American activist who fought against modern-day slavery in Mauritania and Sudan. In his memory, pray for all who suffer the yoke of slavery — and for all who seek to liberate them!

On **December 20**, we celebrate the birth in 1958 of **Dick Jan Schoon**, who has served as the eighteenth Dutch Old Catholic bishop of Haarlem since 2008. He has written on various themes of pastoral spirituality and the church in the Netherlands. His episcopal motto is "God is Just and Liberating." In his honor, consider how you are bringing God's justice and liberation to our world!

December 20 is also **International Human Solidarity Day**, a day to celebrate our unity in diversity, and to raise public awareness of the importance of solidarity. Lift up and celebrate this fundamental 21-century value!

On **December 21**, the Church celebrates **St. Peter Canisius** (1521-1597), the 16th-century Dutch Jesuit priest who defended the Church by preaching, writing, founding colleges and seminaries, and contributing to the Council of Trent. Peter authored several catechisms that were translated into twelve languages during his lifetime, and he penned 1,400 letters in support of Church reform. As we celebrate this patron saint of catechism writers, consider how you're helping others to grow in their knowledge of our faith!

On **December 21**, we remember the passing of **John Newton** (1725-1807), the English Anglican abolitionist known for composing "Amazing Grace." A sailor in the Royal Navy and a captain of slave ships, he worked in the slave trade for several years until a storm at sea caused the conversion experience that propelled him to become an Anglican priest. He renounced the slave trade, became a prominent supporter of abolitionism, and he saw Britain's abolition of the African slave trade only days before his death. In his memory, pray for those who are enslaved—and for the "lost" and "blind" whose words and actions impinge on the freedom of others!

On **December 21**, we remember the passing of **F. Scott Fitzgerald** (1896-1940), the Catholic author regarded as one of the greatest American writers of the 20th century. He was raised Roman Catholic and attended Catholic schools, but, for 25 years, the Roman church denied his family's request that he be buried in the family's plot at St. Mary's Cemetery in Rockville, Maryland. In his memory, pray for all who have been marginalized in life and/or in death by misguided "representatives" of God and/or the Church!

On **December 21**, we celebrate the birth in 1940 of **Matthew Fox**, the American Episcopal priest and theologian who was an early exponent of creation spirituality. The author of 35 books that have been read by millions, Fox has sought to align contemporary ecological and environmental movements with various spiritual traditions. In his honor, consider how you employ scripture and tradition to honor God's creation!

On **December 21**, we celebrate the birth in 1951 of **Jan Michael Joncas**, the priest, liturgical theologian and composer of contemporary Catholic music, known for such songs as "On Eagle's Wings," "I Have Loved You," and "Take and Eat." In his honor, incorporate a tune or two of his into your prayer today!

December 21 is the **Winter Solstice**, the day of the year with the least amount of sunlight in the northern hemisphere. Reflect on the Roman celebration of *Sol Invictus*, and enjoy a moment of prayerful silence as we prepare to welcome the Light of the World!

On **December 22**, we remember the passing of **Giles of Rome** (c. 1243-1316), the French archbishop and prior general of the Augustinian order, who wrote a guide for princes as well as the major text on 14th-century papism. The "Best-grounded Doctor" took an active part in ending the controversy concerning the validity of Boniface VIII's election to the papacy. In his memory, pray for all who dedicate their lives to the defense of the Church!

On **December 22**, we remember the passing of **Isaac Hecker** (1819-1888), the American priest and founder of the Paulist Fathers, who sought to evangelize America through preaching and publication. He believed that the American political culture of small government, property rights, civil society and liberal democracy could be reconciled with Catholic teachings. Known as "the Yellow Dart" by conservatives, he empowered laypeople and encouraged individual initiative. In his memory, consider how you empower others and equip them to take initiative!

On **December 22**, we remember the passing of **Lucy Burns** (1879-1966), the American suffragette who co-founded the National Woman's Party. In her memory, pray for all who continue the fight for women's rights!

On **December 22**, the Autocephalous Turkish Orthodox Church celebrates the anniversary of the installation in 2002 of Paşa Ümit Erenerol as **Turkish Orthodox Patriarch Papa Efrim IV**. In a spirit of ecumenism, pray for him and for the people he serves!

On **December 23**, we remember the passing of **St. Ivo of Chartres** (c. 1040-1115), the bishop of Chartres involved in the investiture crisis, who opposed simony and was imprisoned for opposing King Philip's decision to dismiss his wife and marry another woman. He authored three extensive canonical works that influenced Hugh of St. Victor, Peter Abelard and Gratian. In his memory, pause today to reach out and thank some of the influences in your life!

On **December 23**, we remember the passing of **Sarah Moore Grimké** (1792-1873), the American abolitionist considered the mother of the women's suffrage movement. In her memory, pray for all who fight for the rights of others!

On **December 23**, we remember the passing of **Maurice de Wulf** (1867-1947), the Belgian Thomist philosopher at Louvain who distinguished medieval philosophy from Scholasticism, highlighting the "anti-Scholastic" thought of Scotus Erigena, the Cathars, the Albigenses, and the Pantheistic schools. In his memory, explore some of the counter movements that have enriched our world, our faith and our theology!

On **December 23**, we remember the passing of **Abraham Joshua Heschel** (1907-1972), the Polish-born American rabbi who was one of the leading Jewish philosophers and theologians of the 20th century. He was active in the civil rights movement and authored a number of widely-read books on Jewish philosophy and mysticism. In his memory, seek out a spiritual friend with whom you might share an insight or two from his works!

On **December 23**, we remember the passing of **Edward Schillebeeckx** (1914-2009), the Belgian Dominican theologian whose contributions to the Second Vatican Council made him known throughout the world. Schillebeeckx's innovative thought (including his attempt to overcome the Aristotelian categories of transubstantiation with a fresher thought of "transignification") were sometimes viewed with suspect, though never condemned by the Vatican. In his memory, consider the space that you allow the Spirit in your own theology and thought!

On **December 23**, we celebrate the birth in 1980 of **Wael Ghonim**, the Egyptian activist who created the Facebook page that helped spark the 2011 Arab Spring. In his honor, pray for all who bravely stand up against authoritarian oppression!

On **December 24**, we remember the passing of **Bastiaan Abraham van Kleef** (1889-1965), the theologian, seminary rector and first married priest of the Dutch Old Catholic Church. After declaring his intention to marry, he was released from the Haarlem diocese and served the German Old Catholic Church in Baden for four years, until the mandate of clerical celibacy in Haarlem was lifted in 1923. Van Kleef served as mayor of Egmond, and a as professor of New Testament and pastoral theology at the Amersfoort seminary. He served on the Utrecht cathedral chapter for 20 years, and as dean of the chapter for nearly ten years. He edited *De Oud-Katholiek* magazine and the *International Ecclesiastical Journal*, and he was the founder of the Old Catholic Trade Union Association and the International Old Catholic Theological Conference. His son, Gerhard, later served as bishop of Haarlem. Pastoor van Kleefstraat Street in Egmond, Netherlands is named for him. In his memory, pray for the many married persons who so generously share of themselves with the Church — and for the many family members who support them in their ministry!

On **December 24**, we remember the passing of **John Boswell** (1947-1994), the American historian and Yale professor who wrote several works on Christianity, homosexuality and those at the margins of society. An openly-gay Roman Catholic, he attended daily mass despite disagreeing with his church's teachings on sexuality. He noted that the Roman

Church did not condemn homosexuality until the 12th century. He is buried beside his lifelong partner, and his headstone reads, "He was not a tame lion," a reference to the *Chronicles of Narnia*. In his memory, share with someone close to you the words that might best characterize you one day on your headstone!

On **December 24**, we remember the passing of **Joseph Augustine Fitzmyer** (1920-2016), the Jesuit priest and professor emeritus at The Catholic University of America, who specialized in the study of the New Testament but who also made contributions to the study of the Dead Sea Scrolls and early Jewish literature. In his memory, thumb through one of his commentaries and see what new insights you might gain!

On **December 24**, we celebrate the founding in 2004 of **Ss. Francis & Clare Catholic Community** in Wilton Manors, Florida, currently led by Fathers Joseph C. Spina and Vincent Treglio. Happy anniversary, Ss. Francis & Clare!

Sunday, December 25, 2022
THE NATIVITY OF OUR LORD
(white)

Christmas is here: Let's decorate!

- Break out the **Christmas décor**—or, even better, smoothly transition from your Advent décor to Christmas décor by replacing the touches of Advent color with Christmas color. Avoid the temptation of extravagant displays of trees and decorations that might overpower your worship space and eclipse your spring celebration of Christ's resurrection. You're decorating a liturgical space, not a shopping mall!

- Remember: Red, white and green may be the traditional colors of Christmas in the secular world, but **white is the liturgical color for the Church's Christmas season**, often with touches of gold that bring to mind the newborn King!

- Be sure to steam or iron your **Christmas vestments**—and to coordinate the color of your vestments with other decorative details in your worship space!

- This is a high solemnity: Be sure to cover the altar with your loveliest white and/or gold altar cloth!

- Consider appropriate places for **evergreen** decorations—perhaps with wreaths on the end of pews and/or with garland that accents the architecture of your worship space. Try making your garland extraordinary with touches of boxwood, seeded eucalyptus, wax flowers, white hypernicum, pine cones, and/or other ideas you find online or at your local florist.

- Try making your **creche** extraordinary: Instead of simply placing it on a table or on the floor, nestle it in a fitting devotional space where congregants can pray and where parents and grandparents can explain the figures to their children and grandchildren. Be sure that adequate light shines on the figures—but not in the eyes of those gazing on it. Unless the placement of the Christ Child in the manger is part of your liturgy, **be sure to place the Christ Child in the manger before the Mass begins**! Remember: The magi will not arrive at the nativity scene until January 6; **find a place for the magi that suggests that they are** *en route* but still a distance away.

- Be cautious *not* to impede liturgical movement with a forest of trees in the sanctuary.

- Be prepared to leave the Christmas décor up through the end of the Christmas season (which concludes with the Baptism of the Lord)—or, if you lead a *Latino* community, consider leaving touches of Christmas in the worship space for the entire 40 days of Christmas in the *Latino* culture, which concludes February 2.

- **Continue the decoration** into the entrance to your worship space, outdoors, and into other spaces on the grounds, including your Blessed Sacrament chapel, parish hall and classrooms! Be especially sure to **communicate "the reason for the season" outside your worship space** to passersby, perhaps with outdoor banners, wreaths, an outdoor nativity set, *luminarias* (candles in paper bags), and/or tasteful inflatables.

Christmas Eve Masses are famous for their **reenactments by children of the birth of Jesus**; this is an especially dear memory for parents and grandparents! If you have a liturgy with a child-friendly focus, be sure children leave knowing the key figures in the Christmas story!

For the intellectually-curious, find time outside the Mass to share a brief lesson on the **differences between the two nativity stories** in the gospels of Matthew and Luke—and the **lack of nativity stories in Mark and John!** Take two cans of spray paint to an old nativity set, so that adult learners can easily distinguish the elements highlighted in Matthew (Joseph, magi, camels, star) from the elements highlighted in Luke

(Mary, stable, manger, ox, donkey, sheep, shepherds, the angel of the Lord). Also consider sharing the story of **the origin of the Christmas creche** and its attribution to St. Francis of Assisi! Other possible lessons might include the reason for the date for Christmas, the theology of the incarnation, and the two natures of Christ.

The most common question for Catholic parishes on Christmas Eve Day is, "What time is your midnight mass?" Consider celebrating a liturgy *at midnight*, complete with a **candlelight service**!

- Ring a bell at midnight, begin your service in the dark with soft music in the background, and share a brief lesson on Christ's coming as the Light of the world!
- Be sure to test the environment you've created before the Mass: Some church electrical outlets might be tied to light switches!
- Before the liturgy, be sure all liturgical ministers understand the importance of the dark, quiet environment you're attempting to create; they need to know not to talk loudly and/or open doors that will allow light to flood the space.

Be sure that **hospitality ministers** are aware that holiday visitors may be joining you for this Mass; visitors should be welcomed with joy. Christmas is no time for impatience, judgment, or criticism. It's Christmas; don't be a scrooge or a grinch!

Bless your parish nativity scene during your first Christmas Mass, and incense it during the singing of the *Gloria*!

After four Sundays of "fasting" from it, **bring the *Gloria* back with gusto!** Consider asking someone to ring the church bell and/or other bells in the church to highlight the solemnity of this song!

Also, consider the use of hypoallergenic **incense** — presuming you and your thurifer have practiced how you'll handle the thurible and boat. Be sure to remind your altar server(s) when incense will be used and that the *lavabo* (handwashing) will occur *after* the incensation of the altar and gifts! If you're swinging the thurible, remember that the closer you place your fingers to the thurible, the more control you'll have over it. Finally, if you have a skilled thurifer, work with him/her in advance to perfect a 360-degree vertical swing of the thurible with a simple flick of his/her wrist (forward, back, circle, forward, back, circle, etc.) as s/he leads the procession down the aisle!

Homily Help: Remember that there are four sets of scriptures for today, based on when you celebrate Mass. Your worship environment is likely very special today; for the sake of the 65% of your listeners who are visual, tie your message to the visuals in your space!

Looking for a visual aid for your homily or object lesson? Look around your now-decorated worship environment for symbols to incorporate into your message: The **lights** on the trees and the **candles** remind us of Christ's coming as the Light of the world. The **evergreens** remind us of God's enduring love for us. The shape of the **poinsettias** remind us of the star leading people to Christ, and the story of the poinsettia's purported origin links to a drummer-boy-like story of a poor girl with nothing to offer the newborn King. The **creche** reminds us of the ordinary circumstances of the Lucan Jesus' birth and God's choice to come to the poor and marginalized, rather than to the rich and powerful of that time. We display these symbols at Christmas; how will we continue to proclaim the message of these symbols in our daily lives throughout the year ahead?

If you have a Latino community, consider incorporating **the last** *posada*, the traditional *arrullo*, the traditional **veneration of an image of the Child Jesus**, and/or a *pastorela*!

- Before Mass, the antiphonal singing of the traditional song for *las posadas* might be sung by congregants inside and outside your worship space, with those outside being welcomed in for mass.

- In the Mexican culture, the image of the Child Jesus is taken from its upright position on the home altar, "rocked to sleep" with a lullaby (the *arrullo*), and placed in the manger; consider incorporating this rite into the liturgy.

- When Mexican families celebrate *las posadas*, they often place an image of the Christ Child in a basket or on a platter filled with candies; individuals then come forward to venerate the image of the Christ Child with a kiss and to take a piece of candy from the basket or tray. Looking to involve young people? Invite two teens to hold the basket or platter as people come to venerate the image and take a piece of candy!

- *Pastorelas* are traditional Christmas plays portraying the journey of the shepherds to the place where the Christ Child lay; *pastorelas* involve more planning and work, but can be an extremely memorable experience for all involved!

Send congregants home with a copy of a **prayer of blessing for their creche and/or Christmas tree**!

If you begin Mass with a candlelight service (reminiscent of the Easter vigil and common in non-Catholic congregations), have hospitality ministers prepared to distribute the taper candles before Mass — and prepared to collect the taper candles after Mass.

On **December 25**, we remember the passing of **Jean Soanen** (1647-1740), the French bishop who opposed the papal bull *Unigenitus*, calling for a general council of the Church to discuss the matter. After sharing a letter with his congregation, urging the reading of Pasquier Quesnel, his archbishop exiled him from his own diocese at age 81 and imprisoned him at the Abbey of Chaise Dieu in Auvergne, where he died 14 years later. In his memory, pray for all senior adults who are mistreated or taken advantage of by others!

On **December 25**, we celebrate the birth in 1968 of Bishop **John Plummer**, author of *The Many Paths of the Independent Sacramental Movement*. Reacquaint yourself with his work, and pray for our many sisters and brothers who tread the many paths of the ISM!

On **December 25**, the Georgian Orthodox Church (recognized by the Ecumenical Patriarch of Constantinople) celebrates the anniversary of the installation in 1977 of Irakli Ghudushauri-Shiolashvili as **Catholicos-Patriarch Ilia II of Georgia**. In a spirit of ecumenism, pray for him and for the 3.5 million Georgian Orthodox Catholics he serves!

On **December 26**, the Church celebrates **St. Stephen** (c. 5 – c. 33-36): Be sure to recognize and bless your deacon(s) as we celebrate their patron saint! Consider sharing with your deacon(s) a seasonal gift, perhaps a Christmas ornament with a personalized message of gratitude for their ministry to the Church. Also, don't forget to recognize those who are preparing for diaconal ministry!

On **December 26**, we remember the passing of **Bernhard Word Anderson** (1916-2007), the American United Methodist pastor and Old Testament scholar. His *Understanding the Old Testament* is a classic textbook. In his memory, thumb through one of his works and expand your knowledge of the Old Testament world!

On **December 26**, we remember the passing in 2021 of **Desmond Mpilo Tutu**, the South African Anglican archbishop, theologian, and Nobel Peace Prize winner known for his stand on human rights issues and against the racial segregation of apartheid. As the first Black archbishop of Cape Town, he oversaw the introduction of women priests and led negotiations to end apartheid and institute a multi-racial democracy. In his honor, consider how you are using your influence to address the most pressing human rights abuses around you!

December 26 is also the beginning of **Kwanzaa**, a six-day celebration of African-American culture culminating with the communal feast of *Karamu* on January 1!

December 26 is **Boxing Day** in many countries, a traditional day of generosity to the poor but now largely viewed as a "second Christmas Day" of holiday shopping.

December 26 is also the last day of **Chanukah**, the Jewish Festival of Lights!

On **December 27**, the Church celebrates **St. John the Evangelist** (c. 6 – c. 100. Known as the Beloved Disciple, he placed his head on the Johannine Jesus' breast during the Last Supper (Jn. 13:23). The apocryphal Acts of John states that he broke off his engagement to a woman to "bind himself" to Jesus, and one medieval European tradition even stated that he and Jesus were the couple married at Cana (Jn. 2:1-12). A 12th-century miniature shares two scenes: of Jesus coaxing John to leave his bride and follow him, and of John resting his head on Jesus' chest, with Jesus cupping John's chin, an indication of romantic intimacy. Reacquaint yourself with John's high Christology (his emphasis on the divine nature of Christ), why his gospel is symbolized by an eagle, his poetry and symbolic language, and/or some of the many differences between this gospel and the synoptic gospels!

On **December 27**, the Church celebrates **St. Fabiola** (+399), the Roman noblewoman who gave up her immense wealth to devote herself to the poor and sick. She is one of the 140 colonnade saints at St. Peter Basilica in Vatican City. In her memory, consider how you might more generously share of yourself and of your time, talent and treasure!

On **December 27**, we remember the passing of **Józef Rokita** (1911-1995), the Polish bishop who was archbishop of the Old Catholic Church in the People's Republic of Poland. In his memory, pray for our sisters and brothers of the Old Catholic Church in Poland!

On **December 27**, we remember the passing of **Sir Michael Anthony Eardley Dummett** (1925-2011), the English philosopher who has been described as "among the most significant British philosophers of the last century and a leading campaigner for racial tolerance and equality." He wrote that opposition to immigration is largely based on racism, and his work, *On Immigration and Refugees*, detailed the demands of justice for nations with respect to the movement of people between them. A convert to the Roman church, he sparked controversy in 1987 by writing that "from the earliest times, the Catholic Church, claiming to have a mission from God to safeguard divinely-revealed truth, has taught and insisted on the acceptance of falsehoods." In his memory, reflect on how you are bringing greater credibility to the Independent Catholic movement, so that it might not become, in Dummett's characterization of the Roman church, "a laughing-stock in the eyes of the world"!

On **December 27**, we celebrate the birth in 1938 of **Jon Sobrino**, the Spanish Jesuit theologian and co-founder of the University of Central America, known for his contributions to liberation theology. Sobrino narrowly escaped the targeted assassinations that occurred at his rectory during the El Salvador civil war, and he continues to be an outspoken advocate for peace and against the U.S. training of Latin American military officers in torture techniques at the School of the Americas. The Vatican has criticized his works for their emphasis on Jesus' human nature and purported downplaying of Jesus' divinity. In his honor, consider how you are esteeming and serving "the Church of the poor"!

On **December 28**, the Church celebrates the Memorial of the **Holy Innocents**, a purported event mentioned by Matthew (Mt. 2:16-18) but not supported by historical evidence. Pray for those who, like the fabled Herod, try to stamp out the Word of God. If you have a Mexican community, and if you have a parish gathering on December 28, prepare a prank in honor of *el día de los santos inocentes* — the equivalent of April Fool's Day in Mexico — and be ready to shout the traditional "April Fool's" line: "*¡Inocente palomita!*"

On **December 28**, we remember the passing of **Franz Xaver Kraus** (1840-1901), the German priest and historian whose association with Liberal Catholics acquainted him with those who opposed purported papal infallibility. His growing dissatisfaction with the Church led him to publish sensational articles under the pseudonym "Spectator." He is credited with the distinction between "religious Catholicism" and "political Catholicism." In his memory, reflect on the religious and political elements of your own church and ministry!

On **December 28**, we remember the passing of **John Gritenas** (1884-1928), the Russian bishop who led the Lithuanian National Catholic Church in Scranton, Pennsylvania. In his memory, pray for our sisters and brothers of the Lithuanian National Catholic Church!

On **December 28**, we remember the passing of **Georg Moog** (1863-1934), the fourth bishop of the German Old Catholic Church who served during much of World War I. A professor of New Testament at the Old Catholic seminary in Bonn, he represented his church at the 1931 Bonn conference that resulted in full union between the Anglican Church and the Old

Catholic Church. In his memory, consider how you are working to bring greater unity to our world!

On **December 28**, we remember the passing of **Jacques Dupuis** (1923-2004), the Belgian Jesuit theologian who spent several decades in India before teaching non-Christian religions at the Gregorian University in Rome. The Roman Curia censured his book, *Toward a Christian Theology of Religious Pluralism*, due to its suggestion that non-Christian religions might possess "the seeds of truth and goodness." Regardless, Dupuis' work was praised as a pioneering effort to esteem "God's plan of salvation" in other religions. In his memory, pause to consider how God's plan of salvation might be unfolding in religions quite unlike ours!

On **December 28**, we celebrate the anniversary of the ordination in 1970 of **Ludmila Javorová** (1932-), the Czech Roman Catholic woman who helped organize the underground church of Czechoslovakia during communist rule. She and some five other women were ordained by their Roman Catholic bishop to serve women who were imprisoned and tortured but who had no access to male priests. In her honor, lift up all the women who have bravely shared of their lives and ordained ministries with our Catholic Church!

On **December 29**, the Church celebrates **St. Thomas Becket** (1118-1170): In a special way, we pray for those who, like Henry VIII, wish to rid the world—or at least some of our communities—of the "meddlesome priest[s]" of the Independent Catholic movement!

On **December 29**, the LGBTQIA+ community celebrates **David and Jonathan**, the heroes in Hebrew scriptures known for their intimate relationship. Jonathan "loved [David] as his own soul" (1Sam. 18:3), and the Bible traces their tears and kisses over 15 years. In David's famous lament for Jonathan, David cried, "Your love to me was wonderful, surpassing the love of women" (2Sam. 1:26). Their love was brought to life in the 2020 musical, "Beloved King." In their memory, lift up and celebrate the love of those who enflesh the spirit of David and Jonathan in our world!

On **December 29**, we remember the passing of **Rainer Maria Rilke** (1875-1926), the German poet and novelist whose mystical works focus on the difficulty of communion with the Ineffable in an age of disbelief, solitude and profound anxiety. As we wind down this year, dust off his *Notebooks of Malte Laurids Brigge* and ponder his reflections on the quest for individuality, the significance of death, and the experience of time as death approaches!

On **December 29**, we celebrate the birth in 1960 of **James J. Martin**, the American Jesuit priest and writer who has written and edited various books, many of which are largely about his own experiences as a Catholic. He is a frequent commentator on national news outlets. When Glenn Beck suggested that Catholics run away from priests who preach social justice, Martin noted that "Christ asked us to work with the poor…He says that the way that we're going to be judged at the end of our lives is not what church we prayed in, or how we prayed, but really…how we treated the poor." His recent work on welcoming LGBTQ Catholics has drawn the ire of conservatives in the Roman church. In his honor, pause to share with him a few words of encouragement!

Friday, December 30, 2022
HOLY FAMILY OF JESUS, MARY AND JOSEPH
(white)

Like most people, Jesus of Nazareth was born into a family! Point to the **model of holiness** of the Holy Family of Jesus, Mary and Joseph; draw the connection between your community's families and the Holy Family; but also, in a spirit of inclusivity, acknowledge that **families come in different forms**!

We're still in the Christmas Octave: **Sing the *Gloria* with gusto!**

Choose the first reading you'll proclaim: Sirach's admonition to honor and care for parents, or God's promise in Genesis that the aged Abram and Sara would have descendants numbering like the stars in the sky. If you choose the former, beware of the exclusive language that can easily be remedied by changing the reading to the second person: "When you honor your parents, you atone for sins and preserve yourself from them. When you pray, you are heard….My children take care of your parents."

Select the psalm you'll sing: Psalm 128 (a traditional wedding psalm) or Psalm 105's reflection on God's covenant. If you choose the former, beware the traditional references to "man" and "wife." The latter is riddled with problematic, exclusive language: Consider changing the response to the second person, "You, Lord, remember your covenant forever," and include the names of Sarah and Rebecca, the wives of Abraham and Isaac.

Choose the second reading as well: Colossians' extended discourse with its outdated admonition of wives submitting to their husbands, or the shorter version without those controversial lines, or Hebrews' recounting of the inheritance received by Abraham and Sarah.

Holy humor: Perhaps you've seen the cartoon that depicts the first-ever rosary. We're all familiar with the rosary, right? The rosary is a set of prayers through which we repeatedly call upon Mary, the mother of our Lord. So, in the cartoon of the first-ever rosary, we see the young child Jesus pulling at his mother's dress and yelling, "Mom! Mom! Mom! Mom! Mom! Mom! Mom! Mom! Mom! Mom!" The first-ever rosary! (Segue to today's gospel where an adolescent Jesus is no longer calling on his mother, but instead is so focused on his God that he neglects to think of his mother for days on end!)

Looking for a visual aid for your homily or object lesson? Consider an image of your own family and/or an image of the Holy Family. So many images of the Holy Family abound, idealizing persons who seem so unlike us—until we read stories like today's gospel and other more humanized accounts of Jesus and his family!

On **December 30**, we remember the passing of **Alfred North Whitehead** (1861-1947), the English mathematician and philosopher who was a defining figure of process philosophy and an inspiration for process theology. Critiquing traditional monotheistic notions of God as a divine king who imposes his will and power on the world, Whitehead envisioned a God not necessarily tied to religion, "the unlimited conceptual realization of the absolute wealth of potentiality." In his memory, reacquaint yourself with Whitehead's views of God and religion!

On **December 30**, we remember the passing of **Huston Cummings Smith** (1919-2016), the American scholar regarded as one of the world's most influential figures in religious studies. Cumming's work, *The World's Religions*, remains a popular text on comparative religion. In his memory, spend a few minutes today broadening your perspective on other world religions!

On **December 31**, the Church celebrates **St. Columba of Sens** (c. 257 - 273), the Iberian nun who was beheaded for refusing to marry the son of Roman Emperor Aurelian. She is one of the 140 colonnade saints at St. Peter Basilica in Vatican City. In her memory, pray for all lack of self-esteem leads them to harm others!

On **December 31**, we remember the passing of **John Wycliffe** (c. 1320s-1384), the English priest, philosopher, theologian and reformer who became an important dissident within Roman Catholicism. Wycliffe translated the gospels and questioned monasticism, transubstantiation, *requiem* masses, veneration of the saints, caesaropapism, and the privileged status of clergy. In his memory, pray for all who respectfully and courageously question the traditions of our Catholic tradition, causing us to think more deeply about our beliefs and practices!

On **December 31**, we remember the passing of **Domenico Agostini** (1825-1891) , the Italian Roman Catholic cardinal and patriarch of Venice who secretly consecrated bishops for the Order of Corporate Reunion in 1877. In his memory, pause to thank God for our allies in other churches who have shared with us the gifts of the Spirit and valid lines of apostolic succession!

Sunday, January 1, 2023
MARY THE MOTHER OF GOD
(white)

How's your devotion to Mary? This is a day for you to share your love for your Mother with others! Think how you might be able to **make this celebration special** for the people with whom you celebrate. Remember: Mass attendance on New Year's Day can be extremely challenging, particularly for those who rang in the New Year at midnight!

For the intellectually-curious, provide a brief lesson on the history of Mary's designation as the *theotokos* (the God-bearer), and the very recent renaming of this eighth-day feast from the **Feast of the Circumcision**, to the **Solemnity of Mary the Mother of God**!

The Christmas Octave concludes today: **Sing the *Gloria* with gusto!**

Be mindful of the exclusive language in the second reading: If you begin "Brothers and sisters," as you should, you'll need to rephrase the two instances of "son" to "son or daughter" and the two instances of "sons" to "sons and daughters."

The thread in today's scriptures: In this new year, we pray for God's blessing (Num. 6:22-27 & Ps 67:2), calling upon God as father/mother (Gal 4:6) and upon Mary as mother. Her son was born "under the law" (Gal 4:4), and she showed her devotion to God and to God's law by submitting her son to circumcision (Lk 2:21). How are we manifesting our devotion? Are we striking an active/contemplative balance in our lives this holiday season, as captured by the active response of the shepherds (Lk 2:16-17) and the contemplative response of Mary (Lk 2:19) — both of which are good!

Holy humor: We made it through Christmas! Did you hear the story of what happened at one church's Christmas pageant? All the little kids were dressed up for their roles as shepherds, magi and angels in the Nativity story, and the older kids, the eight-year-olds, simply had to memorize one line each, so that they could tell the Nativity story together. One boy had his line memorized: All he had to say was, "And the Virgin Mary was with Child." What did he have to say? "And the Virgin Mary was with Child!" How could that go wrong, right? At every rehearsal, he perfectly delivered his one line: "And the Virgin Mary was with Child!" But on Christmas Eve, stage fright got the best of him, and, while all the other children flawlessly recited their lines, when it came time for him to share his line, "And the Virgin Mary was with Child," what came out of his mouth was — are you ready for this? — "And the Viking Mary was with Child"! Imagine that for a moment: "the Viking Mary," as if Mary were some Norse personality, with a horned helmet and Thor at her side! (Segue into an even more incredible image: of a young woman chosen to be the mother of…God!)

Looking for a visual aid for your homily or object lesson? Point to Mary and the shepherds in your Christmas creche, and/or draw an invisible triangle connecting you and your listeners through the common divine father/mother figures (i.e., God & Mary) that we share! We are not strangers, but sisters and brothers (Gal 4:7), daughters and sons of Mary our Mother!

As we honor the Mother of God, consider having a **blessing for mothers of all types** (birth mothers, step mothers, mothers-in-law, mother figures, etc.)!

No plans for ringing in the New Year? Invite others to join you at midnight, to ring in the New Year with prayer and a **midnight Mass**!

- Ring a bell at midnight, then begin the service. Or, time your Mass to conclude just before midnight.
- In addition to anything that you say about Mary, speak of the important liminal moment of this celebration — even referencing **New Year's resolutions** and the two-faced, forward/backward-facing Roman god, **Janus**, after whom January is named.
- If you find yourself ministering within the context of the *Latino* culture, invite someone to bring along enough **grapes**, so that each

44

person in attendance can enjoy the tradition of eating 12 grapes, one for each of 12 wishes s/he makes for the new year.

- End with a sampling of traditional New Year foods and/or a **toast** to the New Year with sparkling juice in plastic flute glasses!
- Conclude the night with firecrackers, traditionally used in Asia to scare away demons. You will have created a memory!

It's the New Year, and many people are making resolutions. Suggest a few **spiritual resolutions** for the new year!

On **January 1**, the Greek Orthodox Church of Antioch (recognized by the Ecumenical Patriarch of Constantinople) celebrates the birth in 1955 of **John Yazigi**, who became Patriarch John X of Antioch. In a spirit of ecumenism, pray for him and for the 1.8 million Greek Orthodox Catholics he serves!

On **January 1**, the Church of God in Christ celebrates the birth in 1959 of **Presiding Bishop John Drew Sheard, Sr**. In a spirit of ecumenism, pray for him and for the 6.5 Christians he serves!

January 1 is also the **World Day of Prayer for Peace**: Consider incorporating themes of peace into the intercessions, and pray for peace in the world and in all families!

January is **National Mentoring Month** in the United States. Prayerfully consider whether you might share of your time and experience this year with any number of organizations that work with young people!

On **January 2**, the Church celebrates **Ss. Basil the Great** (329-379) **and Gregory Nazianzen** (329-390), two Cappadocian Fathers who defended the divinity of Christ (against the Arian heresy). Gregory wrote that they were "two bodies with a single spirit," and, due to their intimate relationship, they are patron saints of the gay community. Reflect on Basil's famous words: "When someone steals another's clothes, we call him/her a thief. Should we not give the same name to one who could clothe the naked and does not? The bread in your cupboard belongs to the hungry; the coat unused in your closet belongs to the one who needs it; the shoes rotting in your closet belong to the one who has no shoes; the money which you hoard up belongs to the poor." Challenging words, indeed!

On **January 2**, we celebrate the birth in 1937 of **Maria Włodzimierz Jaworski,** the Polish Old Catholic Mariavite bishop who served as presiding bishop of the Old Catholic Mariavite Church in Poland. In his honor, pray for him and for our sisters and brothers of the Old Catholic Mariavite Church!

On **January 2**, we celebrate the founding in 1994 of the **Apostolic Catholic Church in America**, currently led by Bishop David Strong. Happy anniversary!

January 3 is the Optional Memorial of the **Holy Name of Jesus**. Remember: His name was *not* "Jesus," and he *didn't* speak English! [Try telling that to those who say, "If English was good enough for Jesus, it's good enough for me"!] Learn about the history and meaning of the name *Yehoshua* and what the scriptures say about that name (e.g., Mt. 1:21, Jn. 14:13, Phil. 2:9-11)!

On **January 3**, we remember the passing of **Mary Daly** (1928-2010), the feminist philosopher and theologian who taught at Boston College for 33 years, refusing to allow male students into her advanced Women's Studies classes. Her book, *Beyond God the Father*, is considered a foundational work in feminist theology for its attempt to overcome androcentrism in Western religion. She focused her scholarship on ways in which men have attempted to suppress women through the "religion" of patriarchy. In her memory, consider the ways in which your own words and actions might reinforce patriarchy and/or androcentrism!

On **January 3**, we celebrate the birth in 1952 of Bishop **Thomas Abel**, bishop of the Catholic Church of America and pastor of Santo Niño Catholic Church in Las Vegas, Nevada. Pray for him and for the people he serves!

On **January 4**, the Church celebrates **St. Elizabeth Ann Seton** (1774-1821), the first native-born American saint: If the Sisters of Charity have a ministry in your area, be sure to include a brief lesson on Seton's contribution to the schools and hospital systems that bear her name!

On **January 4**, we remember the passing of **Joseph-Antoine Boullan** (1824-1893), the French Roman Catholic priest who was dismissed after being forced to defend himself against accusations of being a Satanist. He inspired French novelist Joris-Karl Huysmans, who defended him against occultists. In his memory, pray for all who are misunderstood or who suffer persecution from others!

On **January 4**, we remember the passing of **Joseph Hubert Reinkens** (1821-1896), the first German Old Catholic bishop. A professor of theology, Reinkens was known for his writings on the early Church Fathers, including his renowned *Cyprian and the Unity of the Church*. As a Roman Catholic priest, he wrote various pamphlets against purported papal infallibility and on the proceedings of the First Vatican Council. When Old Catholics separated from the Roman Church in 1873, they chose Reinkens as their bishop. It was due to his efforts that the Old

Catholic movement crystallized into an organized church, with status in various German states. He consecrated Eduard Herzog as Old Catholic bishop of Switzerland, and he advocated for the validity of Anglican orders to the Old Catholic Church of the Netherlands. In his memory, pray for the pioneers and founders of the various Old Catholic churches throughout the world — and for all who continue their great work!

On **January 4**, we remember the passing of **Thomas Stearns "T.S." Eliot** (1888-1965), the epic essayist and poet whose post-conversion Christian poems discomfited the secular *literati* of his day. In his memory, savor a few hope-filled lines from his conversion poem "Ash-Wednesday"!

On **January 4**, the Georgian Orthodox Church (recognized by the Ecumenical Patriarch of Constantinople) celebrates the birth in 1933 of **Irakli Ghudushauri-Shiolashvili**, who became Catholicos-Patriarch Ilia II of Georgia. In a spirit of ecumenism, pray for him and for the 3.5 million Georgian Orthodox Catholics he serves!

On **January 5**, the Church celebrates **St. John Neumann** (1811-1860), an early missionary who was named bishop of the largest diocese in the U.S. at that time. If your community has a place in its heart for our immigrant sisters and brothers, illuminate Neumann's love for those he served!

On **January 5**, the Church also celebrates **St. Apollinaria**, the fifth-century Egyptian saint and transvestite icon known for dressing as a man and entering a monastery with the assumed identity of a (male) eunuch named Dorotheos. In her memory, pray for all who choose not to conform to the gender binary!

On **January 6**, the Church remembers **St. André Bessette** (1845-1937), the charismatic brother of the Congregation of Holy Cross to whom many miracles were attributed during his life at the St. Joseph Oratory in Montreal. Consider your own charism and your ability to attract others to God and the Church!

On **January 6**, we remember the passing of **Sigisbert Kraft** (1927-2006), who served as the eighth bishop of the German Old Catholic Church for ten years. A Roman Catholic priest for over ten years, he continued his priestly ministry after incardinating into the Old Catholic tradition, publishing a handful of hymnals and works on congregational singing. In his memory, sing a song of praise for the ways God is blessing you!

On **January 6**, we celebrate the birth in 1939 of **David Tracy**, the theologian and priest who was teaching at The Catholic University of America in 1968 when he joined other professors there in rejecting Paul VI's encyclical *Humanae vitae*. He and others were tried by the faculty senate and fired. He subsequently taught at the University of Chicago Divinity School until his retirement and is best known for his works of systematic theology. In his honor, enjoy one of his works!

On **January 6**, the Church of England celebrates the birth in 1956 of **Archbishop Justin Portal Welby of Canterbury**, the Primate of England and *primus inter pares* of the worldwide Anglican Communion. In a spirit of ecumenism, pray for him and for the 85 million Anglicans he serves!

On **January 6**, the Polish National Catholic Church celebrates the birth in 1966 of **Prime Bishop Anthony Mikovsky**. In a spirit of ecumenism, pray for him and for the 26,000 people he serves!

On **January 6**, we celebrate the anniversary of the episcopal consecration in 2019 of Bishop **Kenneth von Folmar**, presiding bishop of the Convergent Christian Communion and pastor of Solomon's Porch in Phoenix, Arizona. Happy anniversary!

January 7 is **Christmas Day** for our sisters and brothers of Eastern Orthodox traditions. Merry Christmas to them!

On **January 7**, the Church celebrates **St. Raymond of Peñafort** (1185-1275), the patron saint of lawyers, known for his leadership of the Dominican Order, his collection of Church law, and his manual for confessors. Consider how you're growing in your own pastoral skills, particularly with respect to those who come to you in confidence!

On **January 7**, we remember the passing of **Hugo von Hohenlandenberg** (c. 1457-1532), the German bishop who unsuccessfully tried to reform the Roman church. He spoke against Lenten fasting and the sale of indulgences, but, despite his romantic relationship with the mayor's daughter, he opposed the abolition of clerical celibacy. In his memory, prayerfully consider how your actions might not match your words!

On **January 7**, we remember the passing of **Jacob van der Oord** (1882-1973), the Dutch priest who served as the fourteenth Dutch Old Catholic bishop of Haarlem for 22 years. After 14 years of priestly ministry, he married shortly after compulsory celibacy was eliminated by the Old Catholic Church. He managed the diocesan treasury for 30 years and served as president of the Willibrord Society, which strengthened the relationship between the Anglican and Old Catholic churches. Elected to the episcopacy the same month that World War II ended, he set himself to rebuilding a church in Den Helder that had been destroyed during the German occupation. He laid the cornerstone for a new church in Ijmuiden, and he installed a new altar and stained glass windows in the

Cathedral of Ss. Anna and Mary in Haarlem. In his memory, consider how you help to "build up" the Church!

On **January 7**, we remember the passing of **Augustin Podolák** (1912-1991), the Czech bishop who led the Old Catholic Church in the Czech Republic through many years of persecution, from 1950 until his death in 1991. In his memory, pray for our sisters and brothers of the Old Catholic Church in the Czech Republic!

On **January 7**, we remember the passing of **Nikolaus Hummel** (1924-2006), the Romanian-Austrian priest who served as the fourth bishop of the Austrian Old Catholic Church for 20 years. In his memory, pray for all our sisters and brothers of the Austrian Old Catholic Church!

Sunday, January 8, 2023

THE EPIPHANY OF OUR LORD

(white)

Do you have a creche in your worship space? Be sure to **set out the figures of the *magi* (and any accompanying animals)** before Mass!

Note: The introductory line of today's second reading is misleading. The Letter to the Ephesians is a pseudonymous letter, written in Paul's name and spirit, but not written by Paul. Rather than confuse your listeners, begin with, "A reading from the Letter to the Ephesians" — and avoid the mistake of saying, "In today's second reading, Paul tells us…" Paul didn't write those words!

The thread in today's scriptures: Today's scriptures feature rich fare for inclusive Catholic communities! The mystery of God is made known to all people (Eph. 3:3), and people from distant lands (Is 60:6 & Ps 72:10-11) recognize the Light (Is 60:1). Now, "every nation on earth will adore [God]" (Ps 72:17) — and even the Gentiles will inherit God's kingdom (Col 3:6)! The magi — Gentiles from distant lands — recognize the presence of Emmanuel (Mt 2:10-11). Do we?

Holy humor: There are all sorts of cartoons about the people in today's gospel: of the magi's visit to the Christ Child. You've likely seen the cartoon where the magi arrive on the scene, not with gold, frankincense and myrrh, but with gold, myrrh and…Frankenstein! My favorites, though, are those that imagine what it would have been like if the magi were women. If they were women, would the magi have given such impractical gifts as frankincense and myrrh? No, they would have come with talc, bottles, diapers and lots of motherly advice! (Segue into the nature of epiphanies causing us to open our eyes and see things differently—in the same way that the magi opened their eyes and recognized the presence of Emmanuel!)

Looking for a visual aid for your homily or object lesson? Point to the magi in your creche, and/or consider buying or making a king cake (then sharing it after Mass): In the same way that the figurine of the Christ child is hidden inside the bread or cake, the magi recognized the divine in the Christ child. Are we able to recognize the presence of Christ hidden in the "dough" of others' lives?

Today is the traditional day for the **proclamation of the dates of the moveable feasts for the coming year**. Have a deacon or cantor sing the traditional text. Remember: Traditionally, this proclamation is *not* made by a priest, and it is omitted if not chanted!

For the intellectually-curious, there are various possible lessons today.

- Share a brief lesson on the three manifestations of Christ: the epiphany, the baptism of Jesus, and Jesus' first miracle at the wedding in Cana.
- Explain the spiritual significance of the three gifts listed in scripture: gold, frankincense and myrrh.
- Help congregants to separate fact from fiction (e.g., scripture says neither that they were "three" nor that they were "kings"; traditional names were later appended to the *magi* in some cultures [e.g., Balthazar, Caspar and Melchior], some cultures even assign a different animal [e.g., a horse, elephant and camel] to each *magus* to show the universality of the magi who respectively came from Europe, Africa and Asia!)
- Speak of various traditions of this day, including extractions, house blessings, and the *rosca de reyes*!

If you minister in a Latino context, you'll definitely want to purchase enough **rosca de reyes** (a ring-shaped king cake) to go around. Use the *rosca* as a visual in your homily, and explain how Christ is often hidden in the "dough" of others' lives in such a way that, even though we can't see him, he's there! While at the bakery, buy extra plastic figurines of the Christ child, to be inserted into the bottom of the bread. Those who find these figurines in their piece of the *rosca* are tasked with providing the *tamales* (filled corn-dough, wrapped in corn husks or banana leaves) and *atole* (a hot chocolate drink) for the traditional celebration of *el día de la candelaria* (the Presentation of the Lord) on February 2!

Remember: This is the **traditional gift-giving day** (more so than Christmas) in some parts of the world, including parts of Latin America, where the magi visit children in the night and bring them gifts! If you minister to congregants from such contexts, **have three persons dress as the traditional *magi* and come bearing gifts for the children and/or for all**!

Epiphany is a traditional day of **house blessing** in some cultures. At the end of Mass, share small pieces of chalk and slips of paper with the traditional "20+C+B+M+22" inscription for the year and the names of the traditional names of the magi (viz., Caspar, Melchior and Balthasar). Lead all present in blessing your worship space, then invite up to nine people to chalk the lintel with those characters!

Some religious orders have the tradition of **"extractions"** on this day: Sing a prayer to the Holy Spirit (e.g., "Come, Holy Ghost"), then have all present pull a piece of paper from a basket containing patron and matron saint for the year, a bible verse for the year, and/or words of wisdom for the year. Encourage each person present to research his/her patron saint for the year, to learn about the saint's life, and to discern why the Spirit might have "assigned" him/her that saint for the year. Encourage congregants to keep these slips of paper in a place (e.g., inside the front cover of their bible, on a bathroom mirror, or on their nightstand) where they can be reminded of them throughout the coming year!

Everyone knows **"The Twelve Days of Christmas"**! Epiphany is the 12th day of Christmas: Consider singing the song during your post-Mass activity, perhaps with as many as 12 groups of people acting out the gift of each day, or with the alternate lyrics you've created (perhaps even with visuals), or with earlier versions of the song's lyrics (11 badgers baiting and eight hares a-running, in England, or 10 cocks a-crowing, nine bears a-beating, eight hounds a-running, etc., in early America). Or, find your favorite video version of it (perhaps the Muppets), or have a contest to see who can remember the gift of each day! Or, explain that the song was originally a memory game for kids, and have your own memory game using the names of all present!

Now that a new calendar year has begun and kids are back in school, these weeks of January might be an ideal time for the **formation of your liturgical ministers**. Consider providing them a time of formation and/or retreat, where you can lead them in reflecting on their ministry during the past year and help them envision where the Lord might be leading them and their ministries in this new calendar year!

After Mass today, there's likely a lot of **Christmas décor that needs to come down**: Don't be bashful about asking for volunteers! Take leadership. Assign tasks and responsibilities. Then show your gratitude with hot chocolate and holiday cookies, or some other appropriate food and drink!

On **January 8**, when it doesn't fall on a Sunday, we remember the passing of **Johann Heÿkamp** (1824-1892), the Dutch priest who served as the sixteenth archbishop of Utrecht. A learned theologian, he wrote an 1870 attack on papal infallibility under the pseudonym Adulfus, and he argued that the valid marriage of Catholics can exist outside the sacrament. Johann convened and chaired the conference that drafted the Declaration of Utrecht, asserting that the Council of Trent had no infallible authority except insofar as its teachings represented the ancient Church—thus clearing a path to union for the Union of Utrecht of Old Catholic Churches with the Orthodox Catholic Church and the Anglican Communion. In his memory, pause to consider the extent to which your beliefs and practices might be rooted in the ancient Church!

On **January 8**, we remember the passing of **Richard John Neuhaus** (1936-2009, an advisor to President George W. Bush on bioethical issues and a leading advocate for denying communion to Roman Catholic politicians who voted against the Roman church's positions on women's reproductive health. He brought the conservative views of his Missouri Synod Lutheran upbringing to his ministry as a "Bushism-made-Catholic" priest, and he was named one of the 25 most influential evangelicals in America at that time. In his memory, pray for all who continue to take hardline stances on issues of conscience and who seek to exclude God's holy people from the sacraments of the Church!

On **January 8**, we remember the passing of **Jeanne Manford** (1920-2013), the American schoolteacher and activist who, after a 1972 attack on her gay son, co-founded the support group Parents and Friends of Lesbians and Gays (PFLAG), which has grown to 400 chapters with 200,000 members. In her memory, consider how you might better be an ally of those who feel marginalized or attacked by others!

Monday, January 9, 2023
THE BAPTISM OF OUR LORD
(white)

If you have any baptisms, this is an appropriate day to **celebrate the sacrament of Baptism** during Sunday Mass! We are baptized into Christ! If you have no baptisms today, use a **sprinkling rite** as part of the introductory rite, or consider having a **renewal of baptismal vows** in place of the creed, complete with the sprinkling of holy water (as we do at the Easter Vigil)! If you want to more closely tie this action to the Easter Vigil, share **taper candles** (with bobaches) with all, and have congregants light them before the renewal of baptismal vows, and/or, even better, **invite congregants to bring their own baptismal candles** from home, to be lit on this special day as a reminder of their own baptism in Christ!

If you have a sprinkling rite and/or baptism during the Mass, be sure to prominently feature the **paschal candle** and a **large glass bowl of water** (perhaps on a stand covered with a white cloth) as part of your worship environment!

For the intellectually-curious, include a lesson on why the synoptic Jesus underwent John's "baptism of repentance," the manifestation of the Trinity in the story, and/or the differences between the various gospel tellings of the story!

The thread in today's scriptures: Our baptism manifests that we, like Jesus (Mt. 3:17), are daughters and sons of God! In the synoptic gospels, Jesus' baptism initiated his public ministry—when he set about being a light for the nations, opening the eyes of the blind and freeing the oppressed (Is. 42:6-7). Does our own impartial, inclusive love (Acts 10:34-35) show that the glory of the Lord is revealed in us (Is 40:5), and/or that we follow in the footsteps of the "light of the nations" (Is 42:6)? Are we being instruments of peace, allowing God to bless all people with peace (Ps. 29:11) through us?

Holy humor: The story is told of little Johnny, who used to enjoy "playing church." When he was four or five years old, he would pretend to be a priest—which was usually O.K. One day, Johnny's mother looked out the window and saw Johnny playing church in the backyard with the family's cat, Whiskers. Johnny was preaching to Whiskers, and Whiskers seemed to be quietly listening, and Johnny's mother smiled as she went about her work. And then, a few minutes later, she heard the cat scream! Johnny's mother ran to the open window and saw him trying to dunk the cat in a tub of water: As part of his playing church, Johnny was trying to baptize Whiskers, who was now hissing at him! The mother yelled, "Johnny, stop!!!" Then, quickly thinking how to explain to Johnny that this was not O.K., she said, "Whiskers is afraid of water!" Johnny looked at his mother, and, with all the self-righteousness he could muster, he replied, "Whiskers is afraid of water? He should have thought about that before he joined my church!" [Segue into the silly idea of any person referring to any church as his/her own. We are all baptized into the Body of Christ, which is larger than any single church. Does our parochial sense of "church" keep us from being a light to the nations, from being instruments of peace, from acknowledging that "Jesus Christ…is Lord of all," and/or from sharing God's inclusive love with all?]

Looking for a visual aid for your homily or object lesson? Consider water and/or light, two of the primary symbols of the sacrament of baptism! Having passed through the "bath of rebirth" (Tit 3:5), we are called to be a light to the nations (Is 42:6)!

On **January 9**, the Church celebrates **St. Basilissa**, the 4th-century woman who, forced to marry, established a convent for women and a hospital in her home. She is one of the 140 colonnade saints at St. Peter Basilica in Vatican City. In her memory, consider how you share of your gifts and blessings with others!

On **January 9**, we remember the passing of **Alessandro Gavazzi** (1809-1889), the Italian Barnabite monk and professor of rhetoric who left Roman Catholicism and toured Europe and the U.S. as a provocative speaker against the Roman Church. A protest against him in Quebec resulted in 10 deaths as part of the 1853 Gavazzi Riots. Returning to Italy, he founded the Free Church of Italy and the theological college of the Free Church in Rome. In his memory, reflect on the ways in which your words and actions might contribute to violence!

On **January 9**, we remember the passing of **Michel de Certeau** (1925-1986), the French Jesuit priest who worked to synthesize history, philosophy, psychoanalysis and the social sciences. His most renowned work, *The Practice of Everyday Life*, studied the way in which we unconsciously navigate the repetitive tasks of daily life. In his memory, reflect on some of the repetitive tasks that fill your "everyday life"!

On **January 9**, we remember the passing of **Anscar Chupungco** (1939-2013), the Filipino Benedictine monk and liturgical theologian known for his work on the inculturation of local customs and traditions into the Catholic mass. He wrote against "the reform of the reform," which he saw as having "an agenda that can have a regrettable impact on the liturgical gains of the [Second Vatican] council." In his memory, consider your own views toward the liturgical reforms of the Church and the ways in which you push the liturgy forward and/or pull it backward!

On **January 9**, we celebrate the birth in 1941 of **Joan Baez**, the American folk singer and activist who has used her music to spread messages of civil rights, women's rights, LGBTQ rights and other causes. In her honor, pray for all who use their gifts to champion social causes!

On **January 10**, we remember the passing of **William Dool Killen** (1806-1902), the Irish Presbyterian minister and church historian who wrote various works on the ancient Church, the Ignatian epistles and the Old Catholic Church. In his memory, acquaint yourself with his works!

On **January 10**, we remember the passing of **Jeanne Cordova** (1948-2016), the pioneering lesbian feminist activist and ex-nun who shook the world by revealing lesbian life in the convent. The founder of *Lesbian Tide* magazine and the *Gay & Lesbian Community Yellow Pages,* she led protests that helped decriminalize homosexuality and protect the jobs of openly lesbian and gay teachers. In her memory, consider the areas in which you might be a real pioneer!

On **January 11**, we remember the passing of **Carmel Henry Carfora** (1878-1958), the Italian Roman Catholic priest who immigrated to New York, then founded St. Rocco's Independent National Catholic Church in Youngstown, Ohio to serve a large group of former Roman Catholics. Known for forming mission congregations to serve ethnic groups not well served by the Roman church, Carfora was consecrated by Bishop Rudolph de Landas Berghes and headed the North American Old Roman Catholic Church, which focused on a non-papal, pre-Vatican I Roman Catholic theology and practice. In his memory, consider how you might better contribute to the upbuilding of Independent Catholicism in our world!

On **January 12**, the Church celebrates **St. Aelred of Rievaulx** (1110-1167), the English Cistercian monk and abbot of Rievaulx. Known for his great work, *On Spiritual Friendship*, in which he spoke of "friend cleaving to friend in the spirit of Christ," he is considered a gay saint of friendship and a patron saint of same-sex intimacy. In his memory, find a way to reach out to spiritual friends and let them know how much you love and appreciate them!

On **January 12**, we remember the passing of **Theodor Hubert Weber** (1836-1906), the German theologian and professor of philosophy who served as vicar general of the first bishop of the German Old Catholic Church—and was later named his successor. He was an important follower and defender of Anton Günther and his philosophy. In his memory, pray for our sisters and brothers of the German Old Catholic Church!

On **January 12**, we celebrate the birth in 1929 of **Alasdair Chalmers MacIntyre**, the Scottish philosopher known for his virtue ethics, as well as for his work in the history of philosophy and theology. He writes that good judgment emanates from good character, such that being a good person is not about following rules or fulfilling obligations. He explained his conversion to Catholicism by suggesting that people don't choose their religious traditions; their religious traditions choose them! In his memory, reflect on your own virtue and/or how and why you were *chosen* by the Independent Catholic tradition!

On **January 13**, the Church celebrates **St. Hilary of Poitiers** (c. 315 – c. 367), who, exiled from his bishopric, dedicated his life to study and writing. He "chanced upon" and was drawn to the Christian religion as a result of reading about the God of Exodus ("I AM Who I AM"). Reflect today on the scriptural verses that best describe God for you!

On **January 13**, we remember the passing of **James Joyce** (1882-1941), the Irish novelist, short story writer and poet who is regarded as one of the most influential authors of the 20th century. Having lapsed from the Roman church, he wrote, "Now I make open war upon it by what I write and say and do." His later works, *Ulysses* and *Finnegans Wake*, are nonetheless essentially Catholic, suggesting a reconciliation within himself with the Catholic traditions he loved, despite resisting the oppressive power of those who led the church. When he died, a Roman Catholic priest offered to celebrate Joyce's funeral, but his wife declined, saying, "I couldn't do that to him." In his memory, pray for all who have a complex relationship with—and conflicting emotions for—the church they once loved!

On **January 14**, we remember the passing of **Johann Nieuwenhuis** (1739-1810), the Dutch priest who served as the sixth Dutch Old Catholic bishop of Haarlem. Pius VII immediately excommunicated him and all who participated in his consecration. In his memory, pray for all who persevere despite the obstacles placed in front of them by others!

On **January 14**, we remember the passing of **Johann Joseph Ignaz von Döllinger** (1799-1890), the German priest, church historian and theologian whose reverence for tradition annoyed liberals and whose criticism of the papacy and its power antagonized Ultramontanes. Considered an important contributor to the doctrine, growth and development of the Old Catholic Church, Döllinger derided the dogma of purported papal infallibility as intellectually indefensible. After its proclamation, he convened 44 professors in Munich to issue a declaration to resist the Council's resolutions—and he was excommunicated by the Roman church. In his memory, recommit yourself to positively contributing to the doctrine, growth and development of Independent Catholicism!

On **January 14**, the Church of Jesus Christ of Latter-day Saints celebrates the anniversary of the installation in 2018 of President **Russell Marion Nelson**. In a spirit of ecumenism, pray for him and for the 16 million Mormons he serves!

January 14 is also **Orthodox New Year**. Happy New Year to our sisters and brothers of Eastern Christian traditions!

Sunday, January 15, 2023

SECOND SUNDAY IN ORDINARY TIME

(green)

Winter Ordinary Time is here: Invite congregants to **wear green today**!

We're jumping into Ordinary Time for seven weeks: This is an ideal time to **try out a new musical setting of a few acclamations**!

Looking for **a new touch for your worship environment**: Instead of storing the Book of the Gospels on a shelf, display it opened, on a lectern, in the entrance to your worship space, and with the ribbon across the page opposite where the gospel of the coming Sunday is located (thus drawing attention to the evangelist's words), so that anyone who passes by can glance at it!

Think through **the décor for this season**.

- Try a **darker shade of green** for Winter Ordinary Time.
- Be sure that the colors of all fabrics in the worship space are coordinated—including the color of vestments. Be sure to steam or iron your **Ordinary Time vestments**!
- Fill the space with **green plants**, to which you can add accents of white (and/or other colors) for such celebrations as the Presentation of the Lord.
- Sprinkle the décor with **objects you find outdoors** at this time of year (e.g., pine cones and/or dried, seemingly-dead branches).

- **Continue the decoration** into the entrance to your worship space, outdoors, and into other spaces on the grounds, including your Blessed Sacrament chapel, parish hall and classrooms!

For the intellectually-curious, there is an abundance of possible lessons!

- Share a refresher on the **Year of Matthew**. Encourage congregants to find time this year to read and familiarize themselves with the entire gospel — and to incorporate Matthew's gospel into their personal prayer!

- Share a lesson on **how the dates of Ordinary Time are determined** (viz., beginning on the first Monday after the first Sunday after January 6, and concluding on the Tuesday before Ash Wednesday).

- Explain why **the "first" Sunday in Ordinary Time is actually the Second Sunday in Ordinary Time** (because it kicks off the second full week of the season).

- Note that **the word "ordinary" in Ordinary Time refers to the ordering of weeks with ordinal numbers** (and in no ways suggests that these weeks are not extra-ordinary).

- Let community members know that **Winter Ordinary Time consists this year of the Second through Eighth Sundays in Ordinary Time**. After that, the next Sunday of Ordinary Time, after the Lent/Easter season, will fall on June 26, with our celebration of the Thirteenth Sunday in Ordinary Time. Explain what will happen to the Ninth week in Ordinary Time (viz., the Church always omits one week that would otherwise precede the resumption of Ordinary Time following Pentecost Sunday, so as to always have a total of 33 or 34 weeks [rather than 32 or 33 weeks] of Ordinary Time). Explain, too, why we won't celebrate the Tenth, Eleventh and Twelfth Sundays of Ordinary Time (which is when we'll celebrate the Solemnity of Pentecost, the Solemnity of the Most Holy Trinity, and the Solemnity of the Body and Blood of Christ).

- Note that the second reading will come from the Paul's First Letter to the Corinthians on Sundays through Lent. Share a lesson on the history and context of this letter, and note the misnomer of the book as the "first letter" to the Corinthians (1Cor. 5:9): It's the first extant or canonical letter that Paul wrote to that community.

The thread in today's scriptures: In the gospel of John, the Baptist testifies that Jesus is the son of God (Jn. 1:34), and we who are baptized into the Body of Christ are also "sanctified in Christ Jesus [and] called to be holy" (1Cor. 1:2). Like Israel, we are called to be "a light to the nations, that [God's] salvation may reach to the ends of the earth" (Is. 49:6, echoing the words of Deutero-Isaiah in last Sunday's first reading). Are we willing to say, "Here I am, Lord; I come to do your will"?

Holy humor: Last Sunday, we heard the story of Jesus' baptism in the Jordan River, and today's gospel continues the story of John the Baptist testifying that Jesus is the son of God. All these stories of John the Baptist and of Jesus' baptism make me think of the story of the drunk man who was baptized down in the river by the Pentecostal pastor. The man was walking along the river one Sunday afternoon when he stumbled into the Pentecostal baptismal service. The preacher called to him from the water, "Are you ready to find Jesus?" The man thought this was odd, but he decided to join the people in the river. As the drunk man approached the preacher, the preacher asked him again, "Are you ready to find Jesus?" And the man replied, "Yes, I am!" The pastor immersed the man's head under the water, then pulled him up again. The preacher asked him, "Have you found Jesus?" The man replied, "No, I haven't." The preacher dunked him again, this time longer, then brought him up and asked him, "Brother, have you found Jesus?" And the man replied, "No, I haven't." And, yes, you know where this is going. Becoming exasperated, the preacher plunged the man's head under the water, this time for nearly 30 seconds, then he brought the man up and asked, "My God, tell me, brother: Have you found Jesus yet?" And the drunk man wiped his eyes and coughed and asked, "Preacher, are you sure this is where he fell in?" [Segue into the way in which the "baptism" opened the man's eyes; have our eyes been opened as a result of our baptism into the Body of Christ?]

Looking for a visual aid for your homily or object lesson? Consider a big sign saying, WEIRD (or, if in Austin, a sign saying, "Keep Austin Weird")! Think about it: Some people are just plain weird! In fact, take a moment, and think about the weirdest people you know? What makes them weird? Now, do you know the origins of the English word "weird"? The English word, weird, W-E-I-R-D, comes from an Old English word, WYRD [pronounced the same way], W-Y-R-D, which meant "not like us" or "not of this world." That's really what it means to be…holy! In the ancient sense of the word, to be "holy" was to be "set apart," not like the rest of people. Sure, maybe other people ate porkchops or shrimp or catfish, or played football, or wore cotton-poly blends—all outlawed by the Bible (Lev. 11:7, 11:12, 11:8, 19:19), but we, Jews, were going to be different. We were going to be "holy," a nation set apart. In the eyes of others, we were going to be weird! Paul says we're called to be holy (1Cor. 1:2). Deutero-Isaiah imagined that we'd be "weird" or "holy" as God's servants (Is. 49:6). In the fourth gospel, John the Baptist pointed out that there was something different (or "weird") about Jesus (Jn. 1:29-34). Perhaps we should take seriously today's scriptures and commit ourselves to being "weird" — to being God's holy people! [Let's "keep [insert the name of your city] weird"; let's keep [insert the name of your city]…holy!]

This weekend, the U.S. celebrates a prominent voice for civil rights, **Martin Luther King, Jr.,** who is considered a saint in some Independent Catholic churches. Intertwine his message with the Christian message of a "discipleship of equals," and share with all a bookmark or image of him!

With the holidays now fading from memory, these **dark, winter months can be a lonely and/or depressing time for some**: Encourage families to "adopt a grandparent." Create homemade cards and promote visits to the homebound and those in nursing homes. Host a canned food drive for the hungry and homeless. Find a way to enflesh the corporal works of mercy that distinguish the "sheep" from the "goats" (Mt. 25:31-46)!

On **January 15**, when it doesn't fall on a Sunday, we remember the passing of **St. Maurus** (c. 512-584), the Roman and first disciple of St. Benedict often depicted as the ideal Benedictine monk. The blessing of Saint Mauer for the restoration of health was traditionally made with relics of the "true cross," which have been replaced by the St. Benedict medal. In his honor, share a special prayer for all who are ill!

On **January 15**, the Church celebrates **St. Francis Fernández de Capillas** (1607-1648), the Spanish Dominican friar beheaded in China for disseminating "false doctrines" and inciting people against the Chinese emperor. Pray for all who find themselves surrounded by hostile people!

On **January 15**, we celebrate the birth in 1942 of **Maria Norbert Szuwart**, the German bishop who leads the Mariavite Church in Germany. In his honor, pray for him and for our sisters and brothers of the German Mariavite Church!

On **January 15**, we celebrate the birth in 1972 of **Artur Tadeusz Miłański**, the Polish auxiliary bishop of the Polish diocese of the National Catholic Church in Germany. In his honor, pray for him and for our sisters and brothers of the National Catholic Church in Germany!

January 15 is also **World Religion Day**, a day to recall the "many paths up the mountain" and to pray for and manifest an interreligious spirit toward our sisters and brothers of other spiritual traditions.

On **January 16**, we remember the passing of **Charles Chiniquy** (1809-1899), the Canadian Roman Catholic priest who denounced the treatment of French Canadians by the Roman Catholic bishop of Chicago and became a Presbyterian minister known for his fiery preaching and attacks on the anti-Christian and pagan elements of the Roman Church. One of Canada's all-time bestselling authors, he penned *Fifty Years in the Church of Rome* and *The Priest, the Woman & the Confessional*. When his congregation was excommunicated by the Roman Catholic Church, he proclaimed, "You can exclude us from the Catholic Church of Rome—but not from the Catholic Church of Christ!" In his memory, consider your own faithful service to the Catholic Church of Christ!

On **January 16**, we celebrate the birth in 1951 of **Antoni Norman**, the Polish Old Catholic bishop who led the Kraków-Częstochowa diocese of the Polish Catholic Church in the Republic of Poland. In his honor, pray for him and for our sisters and brothers of the Polish Catholic Church in Poland!

On **January 17**, the Church celebrates **St. Anthony the Abbot** (251-356): Challenge listeners often caught up in the busyness of the world to focus on a better active/contemplative balance and to strive for a bit of silence, solitude, and contemplative prayer today!

On **January 17**, we remember the passing of **Juan Luis Segundo** (1925-1996), the Uruguayan Jesuit theologian who played a leading role in the Latin American liberation theology movement. A physician by training, he penned numerous works on theology, ideology, faith, hermeneutics and social justice. He was also an outspoken critic of the Roman church's deafness with respect to the oppression and suffering of the poor. In his memory, pause to consider how deaf you might be to the plight and cries of the poor—and commit yourself to at least one concrete way in which you might better be the hands and heart of Christ to them!

On **January 17**, we remember the passing of **Joseph M. Champlin** (1930-2008), the American Roman Catholic priest and author of numerous paperbacks on the Roman Catholic faith, including the popular *Together for Life* marriage preparation guide. In his memory, consider how you help to prepare young couples for the covenantal life of marriage!

On **January 17**, we remember the passing of **Mary Oliver** (1935-2019), the American lesbian poet who won the National Book Award and Pulitzer Prize for her nature-inspired, Christian works. Often compared to Hildegard of Bingen, she drunk deeply of the *Via Positiva* but did not self-identify with any church. In her memory, discover her life and works!

On **January 18**, we remember the passing of **Guillaume de Champeaux** (c. 1070-1121), the French philosopher, theologian and bishop of Châlons-en-Champagne, whose renowned viticultural chart gave rise to the modern-day Champagne wine region. The theology teacher of the arrogant, young Peter Abelard (who later replaced him), Guillaume is known for nursing his friend, Bernard of Clairvaux, back to health, and for having Bernard's *Apologia* dedicated to him. In his memory, enjoy a glass of bubbly and consider how you are caring for your friends!

On **January 18**, the Coptic Catholic Church (in union with Rome) celebrates the anniversary of the installation in 2013 of **Ibrahim Isaac Sidrak** as Patriarch of Alexandria. In a spirit of ecumenism, pray for him and for the 175,000 Coptic Catholics he serves!

It's the beginning of the **Week of Prayer for Christian Unity** (January 18-25)! Historical divisions have rent the Body of Christ: Reflect on the Johannine Jesus' prayer for unity (Jn. 17:22-23), and pray for those—particularly those church leaders and people of faith—who continue to divide people, rather than create the inclusive community that Jesus imagined. Participate in a local ecumenical gathering or prayer service—or invite a pastor from another faith tradition to breakfast, coffee, lunch or dinner. Use social media to raise awareness of this important week!

On **January 19**, we remember the passing of **George Errington** (1804-1886), the English Roman Catholic coadjutor bishop of Westminster whose estrangement from the provost of Westminster led to his being deprived of his coadjutorship by Pius IX in favor of the provost. Errington then declined the Vatican's invitation to travel to Scotland and restore the Roman church's hierarchy there. At the First Vatican Council, Errington opposed the neo-Ultramontanism of his rival, the new bishop of Westminster. In his memory, pray for all who suffer the personal and political attacks of their rivals!

On **January 19**, we remember the passing of **Charles Lindley Wood** (1839-1934), the British ecumenist who served as president of the English Church Union and promoted dialogue between the Anglican Church and the Roman Catholic Church. His efforts were quashed when Leo XIII declared Anglican orders "absolutely null and utterly void." In his memory, pray for all whose efforts are stymied by others!

On **January 19**, we remember the passing of **Tadeusz Stanisław Pepłowski** (1936-2018), the Polish-American bishop who led the Polish National Catholic Church in the United States and Canada. In his memory, pray for our sisters and brothers of the Polish National Catholic Church!

On **January 19**, we remember the passing of **Hans Gerny** (1937-2021), the Swiss priest who served as the fifth Old Catholic bishop in Switzerland for 15 years. He maintained unity while leading his church to approve the ordination of women. In his memory, pray for all who help to restore our sisters to the ministries they rightfully enjoyed in the early Church!

On **January 19**, we remember the passing of **Augustín Bačinský** (1940-2021), the Slovak priest who served as archbishop of the Old Catholic Church in Slovakia. A victim of the COVID-19 pandemic, he previously chaired the World Council of National Catholic Churches. In his memory, pray for our sisters and brothers of the Old Catholic Church in Slovakia!

On **January 20**, the Church celebrates **St. Fabian** (+250), the farmer who was proclaimed pope when a dove landed on his head! Reflect today on your own incredible stories of the presence and activity of God's Spirit in your life and in the lives of those around you!

On **January 20**, the Church celebrates **St. Sebastian** (256-288), the martyr shot with arrows and rescued by St. Irene of Rome, who was clubbed to death after warning Diocletian of his sins. Referred to as the world's first gay icon, due to the homoerotic portrayal of his pierced body and similar suffering endured by members of the LGBTQIA+ community, he is considered a patron saint of homosexuality—as well as of soldiers, athletes and archers. In the Middle Ages, his intercession was sought to protect from plagues. Lift up in prayer all who identify with his suffering and seek his patronage!

On **January 20**, we remember the passing of **Milan "Emilio" Komar** (1921-2006), the Slovene Argentinian philosopher, essayist and polyglot who spoke eight languages and whose works were more influential in Latin America, Spain and Italy, than in his homeland, where his writings were banned by the Communist regime of Slovenia. As a young man, he was involved in Slovenian Catholic Action, and he established journals, publishing houses and schools in Slovenia before emigrating to Argentina, where he taught philosophy and pedagogy to the "Komar School" that developed around him. In his memory, consider your own willingness to be a prophet in places other than your homeland!

On **January 20**, we remember the passing of **Anton Jan Glazemaker** (1931-2018), the Dutch priest who served as the twenty-first archbishop of Utrecht for nearly 20 years. Under his leadership, the Dutch Old Catholic Church first permitted remarriage after divorce and ordained its first woman priest in 1999. In his memory, consider how you are creating an ever-widening circle of love and inclusion!

On **January 20**, the Roman Catholic Church celebrates the birth in 1953 of **Filipe Neri António Sebastião do Rosário Ferrão**, the Latin Patriarch of the East Indies. In a spirit of ecumenism, pray for him and for the Roman Catholics he serves!

On **January 20**, we celebrate the birth in 1965 of **John L. Allen, Jr.**, the CNN, NPR and National Catholic Reporter journalist who, as "America's leading Vaticanist," writes on "All Things Catholic." He has authored several books, including the inside story of how Joseph Ratzinger became Pope Benedict XVI, and a work on the controversial *Opus Dei*. *Newsweek* once remarked, "Outside of the North Korean government in Pyongyang, no bureaucracy is harder for a journalist to crack than the Vatican's. And no one does it better than John L. Allen, Jr." In his honor, indulge yourself with a quick internet search of his latest writings!

On **January 21**, the Church celebrates **St. Agnes** (c. 291 – c. 304), who was martyred at age 12 for refusing to marry a prefect's son. 650 million women in our world today were married as children, largely as a result of tradition, poverty and/or insecurity: Learn more at girlsnotbrides.org, and use this day to advocate for all affected by the issue of child marriage!

Sunday, January 22, 2023
THIRD SUNDAY IN ORDINARY TIME
(green)

The thread in today's scriptures: For the third Sunday in a row, we're hearing of light—but this time from Proto-Isaiah (Is. 8:22—9:1), the psalmist (Ps. 27:1) and the Matthean Jesus (Mt. 4:16). In the long form of today's gospel, Peter, Andrew, James and John follow the Light. If indeed we're walking in the light, then we're working for unity (1Cor. 1:10) and ecumenism!

Holy humor: Creation can be exhausting: Just ask God! The story is told in Genesis, the first book of the Bible, of how God created the world. Do you remember the story? This is the way I imagine it took place. Before the earth was created, God was in heaven, talking to one of the angels and telling the angel about God's first day of creation. And God says to the angel, "Do you know what I just did? I just separated darkness from light, and I created a 24-hour period of alternating light and darkness! Isn't that great?" With enthusiasm, the angel replies, "That's great…but what will you do now?" And God replies, "I think I'll call it...a day!" [Insert a "ba-dum tss" drum-and-cymbal sting, then segue into how we're called to bring light to this world!

Looking for a visual aid for your homily or object lesson? Consider a source of light: perhaps a lamp or a flashlight, or the flashlight of your smart phone! The message of today's scripture is clear: We're called to be a light and to bring light to the darkness of this world!

On **January 22**, we remember the passing of **Jan van Schoonhoven** (c. 1356-1432), the Flemish theologian and writer who, as a member of the Windesheim Community, defended his friend, Jan van Ruysbroeck, against critics. He played an important role in the spiritual evolution from van Ruysbroeck and Geert Groote, to Desiderius Erasmus. Consider how you come to the defense of others and your own role in the spiritual evolution of your community!

On **January 22**, we remember the passing of **Frederick George Lee** (1832-1902), the English Anglican priest and prolific author who co-founded the clandestine Order of Corporate Reunion to restore unity and apostolic succession through reordinations. Secretly consecrated by two Roman Catholic bishops, he performed various ordinations within the Independent Catholic movement before being received into the Roman church shortly before his death. In his memory, pray for all who work for unity in our church and in our world!

On **January 22**, we remember the passing of **Adam Jurgielewicz** (1895-1959), the Polish army officer who served as a Polish Old Catholic bishop. He came into many conflicts with the Roman Church of his upbringing, which accused him of inciting riots. After a conflict with the Old Catholic Church, he joined the Polish National Catholic Church. Before his death, he returned to the Polish Old Catholic Church. In his memory, pray for all whose personalities keep them from finding a home in various faith communities!

On **January 22**, we remember the passing of **Henryk Tymoteusz Marciniak** (1947-2018), the Polish Catholic bishop of the underground Old Catholic Church in Poland. In his memory, pray for all who are not able to openly profess and celebrate their faith!

For the Roman Church of the U.S., **January 22** is the **Day of Prayer for the Legal Protection of Unborn Children**. Explain the pastoral challenge of such a commemoration: While we esteem a "womb-to-tomb" ethic of life, we also recognize that women and men have found themselves in extremely difficult situations where they made what they, inspired by the Spirit, believed to be the best choice at that time and in those circumstances. Rather than judge and condemn them, we want to be the loving, healing and forgiving face of Christ: Widen your prayer today to include those who've suffered such circumstances, those who are considering abortion, and those who call themselves "pro-life" but are unable to take strong pro-life stands against the death penalty and/or on such life issues as gun control, homelessness, hunger, incarceration, care for immigrants/refugees, and support for public education!

January 22 is also the beginning of the **Chinese New Year**. Happy year of the Rabbit!

On **January 23**, the Church celebrates **St. Vincent of Saragosa** (+304), who inspired others with his heroic witness of faith. We also celebrate **St. Marianne Cope** (1838-1918), who cared for the sick and continued St. Damien of Moloka'i's ministry to Hawaiian patients infected with leprosy. Lift them up as models and mirrors of holiness!

On **January 23**, we remember the passing of **Otfrid of Weissenburg** (c. 800 - after 870), the German monk and first-named German poet known for his *Evangelienbuch*, a gospel written in 7,104 couplets—the first use of rhyme in German literature. In his memory, engage in a "right-brain" activity today—perhaps even writing your own rhyme or poem!

On **January 23**, the Serbian Orthodox Church (recognized by the Ecumenical Patriarch of Constantinople) celebrates the anniversary of the installation in 2010 of Miroslav Gavrilović as **Patriarch Irinej of Serbia**. In a spirit of ecumenism, pray for him and for the 12 million Serbian Orthodox Catholics he serves!

January 23 is also **World Leprosy Day**, an annual opportunity to pray for and support the 200,000 people who will be diagnosed with Hansen's disease this year.

On **January 24**, we remember the passing of **Guillaume Briçonnet, Jr.** (1472-1534), the French bishop who worked to reform his diocese in Meaux, improving clergy training and monastic discipline, and advocating for a return to the theology and practices of the early Church. In his memory, consider your own role in reclaiming the riches of the ancient Church!

On **January 24**, the Church celebrates **St. Francis de Sales** (1567-1622), the Swiss bishop who inspired the development of lay spirituality with his first-of-its-kind book written for laity (and not for clerics), *An Introduction to the Devout Life*. In his honor, lift up the holiness of the laity—who are the backbone of the Church and who share in the universal priesthood of Christ—and, in your own time of prayer and contemplation, meditate on de Sales' words: "The measure of love is to love without measure"!

On **January 24**, we remember the passing of **William "Bill" Wilson** (1895-1971), the co-founder of Alcoholics Anonymous, the twelve-step spiritual program that helps two million people in some 10,000 groups to achieve and maintain sobriety. AA focuses on belief in a higher power, incorporates prayer into its gatherings, and assists members with the task of reconciliation. In Bill's memory, perform some small act that might benefit those suffering from any number of addictions!

On **January 24**, we remember the passing of **William Barclay** (1907-1978), the Scottish professor and Church of Scotland minister whose popular biblical commentaries sold 1.5 million copies during his lifetime. A pacifist and believer in universal salvation, he was reticent to speak on the inspiration of scripture, virgin birth, miracles or other matters that conservatives might find imprecise or heretical. In his memory, consider how you help to make the bible more accessible to persons of varying levels of education!

On **January 25**, the Church celebrates the **Conversion of Paul** (c. 31-36) — proof that no one is outside of God's grace, that even the hardest of hearts can melt, and that "with God all things are possible" (Mt. 19:26). Some voices speculate that Paul's homosexual desires within an intolerant society caused him to write on inclusivity and unconditional love — as well as a few "clobber passages" used against the LGBTQIA+ community. In light of John Shelby Spong's case for Paul's homosexuality, many have reluctantly claimed Paul as a queer saint. Pray for all whose inability to accept themselves as the marvelous creations they are leads them to persecute others!

On **January 25**, we remember the passing of **Bl. Henry Suso** (1296-1366), the German Dominican friar considered the most popular German writer of the fourteenth century. An acclaimed preacher and spiritual director, Henry famously defended Meister Eckhart, who was posthumously condemned as a heretic. In his memory, consider how you might hone your own gifts for writing, preaching and/or spiritual direction!

On **January 25**, we remember the passing of **Richard Peter McBrien** (1936-2015), the Catholic priest and Notre Dame professor who authored 25 books, including his popular *Catholicism*, which was criticized by the U.S. Conference of Catholic Bishops. He garnered the ire of conservatives for singling out "single-issue, anti-abortion Catholics," criticizing church policy on obligatory celibacy and the ordination of women, and for suggesting in 1991 that "ecclesiastical hardliners" were engaged in a "prolonged, slow-motion coup...attempting to reverse the new, progressive course set by Pope John XXIII." In his memory, consider concrete ways in which you might further the "new, progressive course" of the Church!

On **January 25**, we celebrate the birth in 1958 of **James C. "Jim" Collins**, the American author, lecturer and executive coach known for his study of organizations. His bestselling work, *Good to Great*, chronicles the lessons of organizations that went from good to great—many of which are now gone. In his honor, consider the lessons from his works that might help to ensure that your ministry is "built to last"!

We've reached the end of the **Week of Prayer for Christian Unity** (January 18-25). Mark the occasion with a prayer for unity!

On **January 26**, the Church celebrates **Ss. Timothy** (+97) **and Titus** (+c. 96-107), Paul's associates who are a study in contrasts with the Apostle: Paul circumcised Timothy, so that Timothy would be accepted by Jewish Christians, but he refused to circumcise Titus after coming to believe that the gospel freed Gentiles from the Jewish Law. Are you the Paul of Timothy, hoping to fit in, or the Paul of Titus, taking a stand? Both Timothy and Titus were considered important enough by early Christian communities that pseudonymous letters were penned to them in Paul's name and spirit; be sure to clarify that these Pastoral Letters were *not* penned by Paul!

On **January 26**, we remember the passing of **Katharine Bushnell** (1855-1946), the American missionary, medical doctor and biblical scholar who affirmed biblical views on gender equality. Considered a forerunner of feminist theology, she published *God's Word to Women* as a correction to the many mistranslations and misinterpretations of the bible. In her honor, reacquaint yourself with her life and works!

On **January 26**, we remember the passing of **Dietrich Richard Alfred von Hildebrand** (1889-1977), the German Catholic philosopher and theologian deemed "the 20th-century Doctor of the Church" by Pius XII. A vocal critic of Vatican II reforms, he especially resented the Council's liturgical reforms, stating: "Truly, if one of the devils in C.S. Lewis' *The Screwtape Letters* had been entrusted with the ruin of the liturgy, he could not have done it better." In his memory, pray for all who block the full and active participation of God's holy people in the Church and/or who resist attempts to make the Body of Christ more loving, inclusive, accessible, and true to the traditions of the ancient Church!

On **January 26**, we remember the death of **David Kato Kisule** (c. 1964-2011), the Ugandan teacher and LGBTQ activist considered the father of the gay rights movement in Uganda. Many blame conservative religious rhetoric for his murder. In his memory, pray for all who continues to contribute to the deaths of modern-day martyrs!

On **January 26**, we celebrate the anniversary of the episcopal consecration in 2011 of Bishop **Christopher Carpenter**, presiding bishop of the Reformed Catholic Church. Happy anniversary!

January 26 is **International Customs Day**, a day to celebrate all who facilitate the flow of goods across world borders.

January 26 is also **Australia Day**. Happy day to our friends "down under"!

On **January 27**, the Church celebrates **St. Angela Merici** (1474-1540), who was moved by the plight of uneducated girls and laid the foundation for the Order of the Ursulines. Share her story and inspire those for whom she is a matron saint: the ill, the disabled, the physically-challenged, and those grieving the loss of a parent!

On **January 27**, we remember the passing of **Scipione de' Ricci** (1741-1810), the Italian bishop of Pistoia with Jansenist sympathies whose diocesan reforms were opposed by the pope. He championed improvised liturgies, founded a Jansenist press, discouraged the veneration of relics and images, and condemned devotion to the Sacred Heart. His posthumous memoirs were immediately placed on the *Index of Forbidden Books*. Pray for all whose zeal for reform is dampened by the reactions of others!

On **January 27**, we remember the passing of **Friedrich von Hügel** (1852-1925), the Austrian baron and Roman Catholic modernist theologian who enjoyed the help of Anchile Ratti (Pius XI) in writing *The Mystical Element of Religion*, deemed the most important theological work of the late 19th century. As a modernist, he believed that science raised new questions regarding faith, which undermine dogmatic authority as a source of truth. In his memory, discover his works and his philosophy of mysticism!

On **January 27**, we remember the passing of Old Catholic Mariavite bishop **Wacław Maria Bartłomiej Przysiecki** (1878-1961). Previously an atheist, he was one of the first six priests ordained for the Mariavite Church. A promoter of ecumenism, he served on the Polish Ecumenical Council. In his memory, pray for all who build bridges and bring people together!

January 27 is also **World Holocaust Victims Remembrance Day**, the anniversary of the liberation of Auschwitz-Birkenau and a somber day of reflection on the six million Jewish lights that were extinguished as the result of the genocide that occurred during World War II.

On **January 28**, we remember the passing of **Charlemagne** (748-814), the king of the Franks and Lombards who was crowned on Christmas Day 800 as Holy Roman Emperor by the assaulted Leo III. Charlemagne alienated Eastern Christians not only through his acceptance of the *filioque*, but also through the symbol of the new empire's unwillingness to recognize the legitimacy of Empress Irene of Constantinople. Considered the "Father of Europe," he was the first to rule the empire from Western Europe since the fall of Rome four centuries earlier, and his rule spurred the Carolingian Renaissance, a period of great intellectual activity in the Western Church. In his memory, pause to consider the politics that are part of any religious institution!

On **January 28**, the Church celebrates **St. Thomas Aquinas** (1225-1274), whose thought was used to bring uniformity to the nascent seminary system of a fortress church: In honor of his day, take a break from his "straw" and indulge in some good post-scholastic philosophy and/or theology!

Sunday, January 29, 2023

FOURTH SUNDAY IN ORDINARY TIME

(green)

The thread in today's scriptures: Zephaniah speaks of "humble and lowly" people (Zeph. 2:3) who "seek justice, seek humility (Zeph. 3:12), a theme echoed in the beatitudes of the Matthean Jesus (Mt. 5:1-12). The refrain of today's responsorial psalm is taken from the latter (Mt. 5:3), and the psalm speaks of God's preferential option for the oppressed and hungry (Ps. 146:7). The good news for those who aren't powerful or "wise by human standards" (1Cor. 1:26): God chooses the foolish, weak, lowly and despised (1Cor. 1:27-28)!

Holy humor: Mother Anabel was visiting the parish's Sunday school classes. When she entered the first-grade room, the teacher was talking about how we get into heaven. Mother Anabel greeted the children and asked them: "If I sell my house and car, and if I sell everything I have in a garage sale and give the money to the church, will that get me into heaven?" Together the children shouted, "No!!!" She asked, "What do I

70

have to do to get into heaven?" Little Juanita shouted, "First you have to die!" (Segue into the Quelle Jesus' "recipes" for experiencing happiness and entering into eternal life.)

Looking for a visual aid for your homily or object lesson? Consider a few recipe cards with extremely simple recipes! Tell listeners that you'll play a game: You'll read the recipes on the old recipe cards you found, and they have to guess what each is a recipe for. Example: "Preheat the oven to 350°. Mash the bananas with a fork. Stir in the melted butter, baking soda, salt, sugar, egg, vanilla extract and flour. Pour batter into a buttered loaf pan and bake for 50 minutes." What's that a recipe for? Banana bread! After you try two or three recipes, read the following recipe: "Be poor. Be hungry. Weep. Let people insult and exclude you." What's that a recipe for? Happiness! (Segue into the beatitudes as the Quelle Jesus' "recipe" for happiness or blessedness. Recall that many preachers riff on the beatitudes as the Quelle Jesus' "attitudes" for how to "be" in the world! You might also play off such puns as the "bee" attitudes (for children) or the "me attitudes"!

On **January 29**, we remember the passing of **Angélique de Saint Jean Arnauld d'Andilly** (1624-1684), the French Jansenist nun of Port-Royal-des-Champs who opposed the *Formulary of Submission for the Jansenists*. Arrested and imprisoned at the Annonciades convent, she wrote an account of her captivity, reflections and conferences, and a necrology of the nuns of Port-Royal-des-Champs. In her honor, consider how you are recording and sharing your own experiences and reflections!

On **January 29**, we remember the passing of **Ralph Matthew McInerny** (1929-2010), the Notre Dame professor known for his Father Dowling mystery series, which was the basis for the 1980's television series. After nearly 20 works of philosophy and theology, he wrote more than 60 works of fiction using five pseudonyms. In his memory, consider the creative ways in which you might interest others in our Catholic faith!

On **January 29**, we celebrate the birth in 1954 of **Oprah Gail Winfrey**, the American media executive, actress, talk show host and philanthropist sometimes ranked as the most influential woman in the world. The longtime host of *The Oprah Winfrey Show*, she broke taboos and allowed LGBTQ people to enter the mainstream of television appearances, and she later reinvented her show with a focus on literature, self-improvement, mindfulness and spirituality. In her honor, consider how you might reinvent your ministry to reach more minds, hearts and souls!

U.S. Catholic Schools Week begins today. Find a way to support the students in your community who enjoy this longtime Catholic ministry!

On **January 30**, the Church celebrates **St. Martina of Rome** (+c. 228), the Roman woman who was martyred for refusing to return to idolatry. She is one of the 140 colonnade saints at St. Peter Basilica in Vatican City. In her memory, pray for all who are experience persecution for their faith!

On **January 30**, we remember the passing of **Mohandas "Mahatma" Gandhi** (1869-1948), the Indian activist who inspired nonviolent movements for freedom and civil rights throughout the world. His vision of religious pluralism was especially important in a nation torn by Hindu, Sikh and Muslim factions. In his memory, reflect on how you are championing the Catholic values of social justice and peace in our world!

On **January 30**, we remember the passing of **Donald Attwater** (1892-1977), the British author, editor and translator who lectured at Notre Dame University and co-founded the Pax Catholic peace movement. He edited the 1931 *Catholic Encyclopedia Dictionary* and the four-volume *Butler's Lives of the Saints*, and he touched on themes connected to Independent Catholicism in his biography of Ignatius of Llanthony and *The Dissident Eastern Churches*. In his memory, thumb through one of his works, and consider how you might honor his legacy in the 21st century!

On **January 30**, we remember the passing of **Coretta Scott King** (1927-2006), the American civil rights leader and wife of Martin Luther King Jr. After her husband's assassination, she advocated for civil, women's and LGBTQ rights. In her memory, pray for all those using their influence to advocate for the rights of others!

On **January 31**, the Church celebrates **St. John Bosco** (1815-1888), the patron saint of schoolchildren, magicians, disadvantaged youths, and juvenile delinquents. Host a children's celebration in his honor. Stop by a local magic store and learn a gospel trick or two. Provide simple, kid-friendly food and drink. Invite a clown, balloon artist and/or magician!

On **January 31**, the Chaldean Catholic Church (in union with Rome) celebrates the anniversary of the installation in 2013 of **Louis Raphaël Sako** as Catholicos-Patriarch of Babylon. In a spirit of ecumenism, pray for him and for the 640,000 Chaldean Catholics he serves!

On **February 1**, the Church celebrates **Ss. Brigid and Darlughdach**, the sixth-century Irish nuns who brought art, education and spirituality to early medieval Ireland. Soul friends who shared the same bed, they are considered special saints of the lesbian community. Brigid died on February 1, 525, and her younger soul mate died exactly one year later. In their memory, pray for all women who, together with their soul mates, mirror God's love to our world!

On **February 1**, we remember the passing of **Henri van Caelen** (1583-1653), the Dutch archpriest and diocesan censor who approved and glowingly recommended Jansen's *Augustinus*. Henri was named bishop of Roermond, but the pope refused to confirm his appointment. In his memory, reach out to those who have experienced a recent disappointment — and be the hands and heart of Christ to them!

On **February 1**, we remember the passing of **Ernst Melzer** (1835-1899), the German philosopher and educator who was a prominent supporter of Güntherianism, became part of the German Old Catholic Church, and wrote a biography of theologian Johann Baptista Baltzer. In his memory, consider your own stance toward those with novel ideas — even with respect to theology and religion!

On **February 1**, we remember the passing of **Ernst Troeltsch** (1865-1923), the German politician and liberal Protestant theologian best known for his seminal work, *The Social Teachings of the Christian Church*. Unlike the many scholars who equated the start of modernity with the rise of Protestantism, he viewed the Reformation as "simply a modification of Catholicism." He saw all history as revisable and without absolute truth, since the narratives of all historians apply anachronism to the past. In his memory, consider the ways in which you might apply anachronisms to the past!

On **February 1**, we celebrate the birth in 1947 of Bishop **Robert Ortega**, archbishop of the Charismatic Old Catholic Church. Pray for him and for the people he serves!

On **February 1**, we celebrate the birth in 1972 of **Leymah Gbowee**, the Liberian activist who helped lead the Women of Liberia Mass Action for Peace, which helped bring an end to the second Liberian civil war. In her honor, pray for her and for all peacemakers!

On **February 1**, the Russian Orthodox Church (recognized by the Ecumenical Patriarch of Constantinople) celebrates the anniversary of the installation in 2009 of Vladimir Mikhailovich Gundyayev as **Patriarch Kirill of Moscow**. In a spirit of ecumenism, pray for him and for the Russian Orthodox Catholics he serves!

February 1 is **U.S. National Freedom Day**, a commemoration of Abraham Lincoln's abolition of slavery in 1865. Find a way to celebrate Black History Day!

On **February 2**, the Church celebrates the **Presentation of the Lord** (or "Candlemass")!

- It's the 40th day of Christmas, the day on which Mary and Joseph appeared in the temple for Mary's "purification." **Pull touches of white into your décor** (perhaps with white flowers among your Ordinary Time greenery).

- In honor of the traditional celebration of Candlemass on this day, consider **blessing all the candles you'll use during the next year**, and invite congregants to bring candles to be blessed as well, for use in their prayer at home. Share **taper candles** (with bobaches) before the hymn of gathering, bless all candles and sprinkle them with holy water, then light the candles for a **procession** into your worship space — to symbolize entering the temple with Jesus, Mary and Joseph. Have your thurifer (with incense and boat), crucifer (with cross) and lucifers (with candles) lead the procession. Place a large container of sand in the sanctuary, where congregants can leave their candles burning during the liturgy.

- **For the intellectually-curious**, note that, for farmers in an age before Groundhog Day, the weather on this day purportedly forecasted whether spring was on its way. The ancients believed that if it was sunny on Candlemass (similar to the groundhog seeing its shadow!), winter would return, and farmers would say: "When the wind's in the East on Candlemass Day, there it will stick 'til the second of May!"

- This is a big day in the *Latino* culture! For *Latinos*, it's *el día de la candelaria*, the traditional day for taking down the Christmas creche and bringing the image of the Child Jesus (along with candles) to church, to be blessed. Upon returning home from Mass, rather than pack the image of the Child Jesus in a box for the year, *Latino* families sit their images of the Christ Child upright on their home altars. If you have a *Latino* community, **invite congregants to bring their images of the Child Jesus to church for a special blessing**, then share with them a copy of the prayer for the traditional *levantar el Niño Dios*, the rite of placing the image upright on their home altar.

- If you're celebrating at night, illuminate the path to your worship space with *luminarias* (candles inside paper bags).

- Looking for a great community-building activity? **Invite those who found the image of the Child Jesus in their *rosca de reyes* on Epiphany, to bring the *tamales* and *atole* for a post-Mass gathering!**

- Do you have a relationship with a religious order and/or congregation? The Feast of the Presentation is also **World Day for**

Consecrated Life! Honor those who have given their lives to religious life, invite them to renew their vows on this day, and challenge congregants of all ages to reflect on whether God might be calling them to such a life!

On **February 2**, we remember the passing of **Charles Isaac Stevens** (1835-1917), the English priest and organist of the Reformed Episcopal Church who was consecrated Mar Theophilus I and served as the second patriarch of the Ancient British Church and as primus of the Free Protestant Episcopal Church of England. In his memory, pray for all who have courageously embraced new life experiences and ministries!

February 2 is also **World Wetlands Day**. If you live near a wetland, consider hosting an educational gathering, complete with hike and blessing!

On **February 3**, the Church celebrates **St. Blaise** (+c. 316), the fourth-century bishop credited with saving a boy who was choking on a fishbone. Hence, the traditional blessing of throats on this day!

On **February 3**, the Church also celebrates **St. Ansgar** (801-865), the "apostle to the north" who brought Christianity to Denmark and Sweden during the tumultuous period following Charlemagne's death. Pray for our sisters and brothers in Scandinavia!

On **February 3**, we remember the passing of **Cornelius Loos** (1546-1595), the first Roman Catholic priest and theologian to write against the witch trials that raged in Europe during the 1580's and 1590's. He was imprisoned and forced to recant, and his work was confiscated and suppressed by his church, only to be discovered 300 years later. In his memory, pray for all whose words, works and contributions are not always appreciated during their lifetimes!

On **February 3**, we remember the passing of **Frederick Charles Copleston** (1907-1994), the Jesuit priest, philosopher and historian of philosophy most known for his eleven-volume work, *A History of Philosophy*. He achieved popularity by debating atheist Bertrand Russell on the BBC in 1948. In his memory, wrestle with a paragraph or two of his history of philosophy!

On **February 3**, we also celebrate **Four Chaplains Day**, a day to honor Methodist minister George L. Fox, Reformed Church in America minister Clark V. Poling, Reform Rabbi Alexander D. Goode, and Roman Catholic priest John P. Washington, who sacrificed their lives during World War II for the troops they served. Pray for all military chaplains!

February 3 is **National Wear Red Day** in the U.S., a day to raise awareness of heart disease and stroke in women.

On **February 4,** we remember the passing of **Baldomero Aguinaldo y Baloy** (1869-1915), a prominent Independent Catholic and member of the Philippine Independent Church who served as a general during the Philippine revolution. The first cousin of general Emilio Aguinaldo and the grandfather of Philippine prime minister César Virata, he served as president of the Philippine Independent Church's Men's Committee. In his memory, consider new ways in which you might be called to leadership in society and in the Church!

On **February 4**, we remember the passing of **Betty Friedan** (1921-2006), the American feminist writer and activist whose book, *The Feminine Mystique*, sparked a second wave of American feminism. In her memory, pray for all who advocate for and defend women's rights!

On **February 4**, we celebrate the birth in 1975 of **Waldemar Maj**, the Polish Old Catholic bishop who has led the Old Catholic Church in the Republic of Poland since 2019. In his honor, pray for him and for the 250 people he serves!

February 4 is **World Cancer Day**. Pray for the 17 million people worldwide who contract cancer each year and for the 9.5 million who yearly lose their lives to cancer—and for all who love and care for them.

Sunday, February 5, 2023

FIFTH SUNDAY IN ORDINARY TIME

(green)

February is here! **For the intellectually-curious**, incorporate the etymology of this month's name into your words at some point during this month! "February" comes from the Latin root, *februa*, "to cleanse." *Februalia* was the month during which the ancient Romans celebrated their annual festival of purification and atonement. This year, Lent begins on February 22!

Note the exclusive language in today's responsorial psalm: "The just man is a light" can just as easily be rephrased, "The just are a light," and all male pronouns in the psalm can easily be recast in the third person plural (they/them/their)!

The thread in today's scriptures: Are you salt and light (Mt. 5:13-16)? Can others "taste and see" the goodness of the Lord in you (Ps. 34:8)? Being salt and light has less to do with human strength, courage or wisdom (1Cor. 2:3-5) and more to do with the light we produce when we act with justice (Is. 58:7-8, Ps. 112:4)!

Holy humor: Hold up a light bulb, and loosen up your listeners with a few light bulb jokes. Hundreds are available online. Try three or four of the following, highlight how, despite the humor of these jokes, all the people contained therein are bringing light to their world...through the changing of a lightbulb. Then segue into the theme of light in today's scriptures!

- How many psychotherapists does it take to change a light bulb? One, but the light bulb really has to want to change!
- How many chiropractors does it take to change a light bulb? One, but it takes six visits!
- How many graduate students does it take to change a light bulb? One, but it takes him five years to do it!
- How many college football players does it take to change a light bulb? One, and he gets three credits for it!
- How many police officers does it take to change a light bulb? None. It turned itself in.
- How many folk singers does it take to change a light bulb? Two. One to change the bulb, and the other to write a song about how good the old bulb was!
- How many vertically-challenged people does it take to change a light bulb? One — with a ladder. They're short, not dumb!
- How many gorillas does it take to change a light bulb? Only but, but it takes a lot of lightbulbs!
- How many lawyers does it take to change a light bulb? How many can you afford?
- How many magicians does it take to change a light bulb? It depends on what you want to change it into!
- How many men does it take to change a light bulb or a roll of toilet paper? No one knows; it's never happened!

Looking for a visual aid for your homily or object lesson? Yes, this is the fourth Sunday in a row in which the scriptures speak of light. This Sunday, light a pillar candle on the altar (be sure the flame can be seen by all!), and invite listeners to imagine the difference the candle would make if the room were dark. Explain that the candle represents the light of Christ that all of us receive in baptism. Now take an empty tin can — large enough to fit over the candle, but not too large, so that the candle will quickly burn out if the can is placed over it. Talk about how we sometimes tend to hide our light—while quickly covering and uncovering the candle. (Be careful not to let the can be there long enough for the flame to extinguish yet.) Then place the can over the candle (allowing the candle to be snuffed out by the lack of oxygen) and talk about how it is that some people attempt to entirely hide the light of Christ that they received at baptism. What happens? Take the can off the candle to reveal that the flame is extinguished. This is what happens when we attempt to hide the light of Christ, or when the flavor goes out of the salt. Yikes! Relight the candle, hold it high, and speak to the gospel admonition to let your light shine!

On this first Sunday of February—which is Black History Month—U.S. Roman Catholic bishops invite their faithful to mark the **National Day of Prayer for the African American Family**. Consider your own honoring of **Black History Month**, perhaps even inviting a pastor from a local African-American congregation to preach to your community!

On **February 5**, when it doesn't fall on a Sunday, the Church celebrates **St. Agatha** (c. 231 – c. 251), who was tortured and killed for spurning a senator's wish to marry her. Pray Eucharistic Prayer I, which mentions her. Agatha is the matron saint of breast cancer patients: Pause to learn and share with loved ones how to detect various common forms of cancer!

On **February 5**, we remember the passing of **Rabanus Maurus** (c. 780-856), the Frankish Benedictine monk, theologian, poet, encyclopedist and military writer known as "the teacher of Germany." The archbishop of Mainz, he authored several works, many of which are only now being translated to English. In his memory, consider how you help to make the works of others available to those thirsting to learn more about their faith!

On **February 5**, we celebrate the birth in 1928 of **Martin Emil Marty**, the American Lutheran religious scholar who has written extensively on religion in the U.S. He has written more than 5,000 articles and encyclopedia entries—in addition to the two books that he authored and edited each year of his professorship. In his honor, consider what you're writing—or not—about our faith!

February 5 is the **National Day of Prayer for the African American & African Family**. Pray for and find a way to better support the families around you!

February 5 is also **Scout Sunday** in the U.S., an opportunity to involve and celebrate the energy and volunteerism of the scouts in your community!

On **February 6**, we remember the passing of **Franjo Petriš** or Franciscus Patricius (1529-1597), the Venetian philosopher and scientist of Croatian descent, who undertook a comprehensive study of contemporary science and defended Platonism against followers of Aristotle. He advanced that, whereas Plato foreshadowed Christian revelation, Aristotle's teaching was in direct opposition to Christianity. In his memory, consider the Aristotelian notions — like transubstantiation — of your own theology and spirituality!

On **February 6**, the Church celebrates **St. Paul Miki** (c. 1562-1597) **and his 25 companions**, missionaries to Japan who were forced to march 600 miles to their crucifixion in Nagasaki. Share prayers for modern-day martyrs who are persecuted for their faith!

On **February 6**, we remember the passing of **Auguste Gratry** (1805-1872), the French priest and gifted academic who held the seat formerly occupied by Voltaire and who advocated for modern scientific exploration in tandem with theology. He helped to reconstitute the French Oratory, a society of priests dedicated to education. Most notably, he was one of the principal opponents of the dogma of purported papal infallibility at the First Vatican Council. In his memory, pray for all who have the courage to question the thoughts and beliefs that are imposed on them by others!

On **February 6**, we remember the passing of **Felipe Buencamino, Sr.** (1848-1929), a prominent Independent Catholic and co-founder of the Philippine Independent Church. A composer and member of the Malolos Congress, he co-authored the Constitution of the Philippine Republic at Malolos. In his memory, consider how you share of your gifts for the upbuilding of God's reign in our world!

On **February 6,** we remember the passing of **Emilio Aguinaldo y Famy** (1869-1964), a prominent Independent Catholic and member of the Philippine Independent Church who served as the first president of the Philippines. Together with other Caviteño revolutionary generals and officers, he cleared the way for the province of Cavite to become a stronghold of the Philippine Independent Church. In his memory, consider how you might enhance your own leadership skills!

On **February 7**, we remember the passing of **Daniel J. Harrington** (1940-2014), the Jesuit New Testament professor who edited the 18-volume *Sacra Pagina* series of New Testament commentaries. His writing interests included biblical interpretation, Second Temple Judaism, the Dead Sea Scrolls, biblical language and theology, the synoptic gospels, and Pauline theology. In his memory, choose a volume of *Sacra Pagina*, and see what you can learn from a quick read of a paragraph or two!

On **February 7**, we remember the passing of **Emmanuel Milingo** (1930-2021), the former Roman Catholic archbishop of Lusaka, Zambia, who shared valid lines of apostolic succession with persons outside the Roman church. Take a moment today to thank God for his courage — and for the courage of so many former Roman Catholic bishops and priests who continue to share the Church's sacraments outside the structures and strictures of Rome!

On **February 7**, we remember the passing of **Mary Lou Piña** (1932-2021), the co-founder of Holy Family Catholic Church in Austin, Texas. An active lay leader in the Roman Catholic Church, she led over 1,000 funeral rosaries as part of a ministry to the elderly, homebound and bereaved. Known for her joyful spirit, effusive hospitality, delicious foods and selfless spirit, she was often found in the parish kitchen — beginning on the day of the parish's founding. Pause to consider how well you are serving the servants of God!

On **February 7**, we remember the passing of **John Hubert "Canica" Limon** (1944-2021), a longtime faithful deacon at Holy Family Catholic Church in Austin, Texas. Known as "Friar Tuck" for his extreme involvement as a lay minister in the Roman Catholic Church, he was unable to fulfill his call to ordained ministry there and found a home in Independent Catholicism. As a minister of God's people, he joyfully and selflessly shared of himself, opened his home to clergy, summoned the generosity of others, and was ever willing to visit those in need at any hour of the day or night. Pause to consider the nicknames that people might give you as a result of their perceptions of your ministry to God's people!

On **February 8**, the Church celebrates **St. Jerome Emiliani** (1486-1537) and **St. Josephine Bakhita** (c. 1869-1947). Jerome was dedicated to the poor and disadvantaged; visits a hospital or orphanage in his honor. Josephine was enslaved for more than 15 years; bring a spotlight to the various slave trades that persist in our world!

On **February 8**, we remember the passing of **Matthias Tanner** (1630-1693), the Bohemian Jesuit who served as rector of the imperial university and as superior of his province. He fostered devotion to the mass and dedicated his leisure time to sharing the heroic deeds of prominent Jesuits. In his memory, consider how you're sharing your leisure time!

On **February 8**, we celebrate the birth in 1948 of **Antonio José da Costa Raposo**, the Portuguese bishop who serves as archbishop primate of the Old Catholic Church in Portugal. In his honor, pray for him and for our sisters and brothers of the Old Catholic Church in Portugal!

On **February 9**, the Church celebrates **St. Apollonia** (+249), the Egyptian woman murdered after an uprising against Christians in Alexandria. Tortured through the violent removal of her teeth, she is a matron saint of dentistry and is one of the 140 colonnade saints at St. Peter Basilica in Vatican City. In her memory, pray for all who are persecuted!

On **February 9**, we remember the passing of **Charles Hyacinthe Loyson** (1827-1912), the French Carmelite priest and provincial known for his eloquent sermons and his desire to reconcile Catholicism with modern ideas. He was excommunicated for stating that Catholicism was one of the three great religions of civilized peoples (together with Judaism and Protestantism) and for publicly opposing the manner in which the First Vatican Council was called for the purpose of ratifying purported papal infallibility. His manifesto against abuses by the Roman church attracted great attention. He urged European nations to establish national Old Catholic churches that would unite in an international confederation. For nearly 40 years, he sought to establish Old Catholicism in France. In his memory, pray for all who spread the gospel message of unity!

On **February 9**, we remember the passing of **Gerard Gul** (1847-1920), the seventeenth archbishop of Utrecht, known for assisting the establishment of the Polish National Catholic Church in the United States. Gul also consecrated Arnold Mathew Harris, the founder of the Old Catholic Church in Great Britain whose split from the church birthed a new movement of "Old Catholic" clergy not affiliated with the Old Catholic Church. Pray today for all who so courageously act to establish new communities and ministries to serve the people of God in new and diverse ways!

On **February 9**, we remember the passing of **John Harwood Hick** (1922-2012), the English theologian and philosopher of religion who contributed to theodicy, eschatology, Christology and religious pluralism. He is known for comparing the "Ptolemaic view of religion" — that Christianity is the only way to true salvation and knowledge of God — with "Copernican" views of religious pluralism. In his memory, reflect on how your view of religion might be like the parable of "the blind men and the elephant" — and consider your stance toward the many spiritual paths that lead up the mountain of the Most High!

On **February 9**, we remember the passing of **Ibrahim Abdurrahman Farajajé** (1952-2016), the American HIV/AIDS activist, queer theologian and self-described "scholartivist" — scholar, artist and activist. A professor at Howard University and Starr King School for the Ministry, he spoke 16 languages and wrote on such themes as heteronormativity, multireligiosity, transphobia, 'earthodoxy,' immigration policies, hasidic/sufi overlaps, colonization, gynophobia, abolition of the death penalty, and Buddhist/Muslim intersections. In his memory, consider how you use your knowledge and life experiences to better our world!

On **February 9**, we celebrate the birth in 1925 of **John Boswell Cobb, Jr.**, the American theologian, philosopher and environmentalist often referred to as the preeminent scholar in the fields of process philosophy and theology. The author of more than 50 books, he has written on religious pluralism, interfaith dialogue, the need to reconcile religion and science, and our need to preserve the world on which we depend. In his honor, consider your own stances toward these important issues!

On **February 9**, we celebrate the birth in 1944 of **Alice Walker**, the first African-American woman to win the Pulitzer Prize for fiction for her novel, *The Color Purple*. In her honor, pray for her and for those who break down barriers!

On **February 10**, the Church celebrates **St. Scholastica** (c. 480-543), the twin sister of St. Benedict, who invoked a storm to keep him from leaving her deathbed. Consider ways to spend a bit more time with those you love!

On **February 10**, we remember the passing of **Francis Kenninck** (+1937), the 18th archbishop of Utrecht, who abolished compulsory clerical celibacy in the Old Catholic Church and cleared the path to restored communion between the Old Catholic Church and the Anglican Church. Perform a small act today that might lead to greater unity in the beautifully-diverse body that is the Church!

On **February 10**, the Greek Orthodox Church of Antioch (recognized by the Ecumenical Patriarch of Constantinople) celebrates the anniversary of the installation in 2013 of John Yazigi as **Patriarch John X of Antioch**. In a spirit of ecumenism, pray for him and for the 1.8 million Greek Orthodox Catholics he serves!

On **February 11**, we remember the passing of **Hugh of Saint Victor** (c. 1096-1141), the Saxon canon and mystical theologian who wrote several significant philosophical and theological works that influenced St. Bonaventure and the "School of St. Victor." He expounded on a theology of love, embraced science and philosophy as tools for approaching God, and viewed the sacraments as God's divine gifts for our redemption. Take a moment today to reacquaint yourself with one of his works!

On **February 11**, we remember the passing of **René Descartes** (1596-1650), the French philosopher, mathematician and scientist who laid the foundation for 17th-century rationalism and is considered one of the most notable intellectual figures of the Dutch Golden Age and of the Scientific Revolution. Known for his *cogito ergo sum* ("I think, therefore I am"), he rejected the splitting of corporeal substance into the Aristotelian categories of matter and form, and he insisted on the absolute freedom of God's act of creation. In his memory, consider other possible eucharistic theologies than the outdated Aristotelian categories contained in "transubstantiation"!

On **February 11**, we remember the passing of **Adrian Fortescue** (1874-1923), the English Roman Catholic priest, liturgist, polyglot, composer and calligrapher who wrote *The Lesser Eastern Churches*, which focused on smaller, more obscure churches of the ancient East. In his memory, increase your own knowledge of the many smaller churches of the East and West!

On **February 11**, we celebrate the birth in 1939 of **Fritz-René Müller,** the Swiss priest who served as the sixth bishop of the Swiss Old Catholic Church for seven years. He enjoyed increasing responsibilities, from parish priest, to editor of the national church newspaper, to secretary of the national synod. Upon reaching the mandatory retirement age of 70, he retired as bishop in 2009, though he continues to oversee Old Catholic missions in France and Italy for the International Bishops' Conference. In his honor, consider how you empower others through increasing roles of responsibility!

On **February 11**, the Roman church celebrates **Our Lady of Lourdes**, the 1858 apparition in which Mary self-identified under the recently-proclaimed (1854) title of the Immaculate Conception and to whom many miracles of healing have been attributed. John Paul II declared February 11 the **World Day of the Sick** and encouraged prayers for those in need of healing. Call or visit family members and friends who might be ill, and pray for all who work in healing professions!

Sunday, February 12, 2023

SIXTH SUNDAY IN ORDINARY TIME

(green)

Note the exclusive language in today's scriptures: In the first reading, "God understands man's every deed" can just as easily be rephrased, "God understands our every deed," and the four references to "brother" in the gospel might just as easily be "brother or sister"!

You'll need to **choose whether you'll proclaim the short form of today's gospel or the longer form**, which includes an introductory three verses to note that Jesus came to fulfill the law, and an additional ten verses interspersed among the words of the short form. For the sake of your listeners, don't decide lightly to opt for the longer form!

The thread in today's scriptures: "Blessed are they who follow the law of the Lord" (Ps. 119:1) and keep God's commandments (Sir. 15:15)! The Matthean Jesus expands on the Law of Moses: If you get angry, you're guilty of murder (Mt. 5:22), and if you look lustfully at another person, you're committing adultery (Mt. 5:28)! Paul foreshadows Jesus' great commandment of love for God in the synoptic gospels (Mt. 22:37, Mk. 12:30, Lk. 10:27): We can't even begin to imagine what God has in store for those who love God (1Cor. 2:9)!

Holy humor: Have you read the Bible? If so, you probably know the answer to this simple question: Who was the most flagrant lawbreaker in the whole, entire Bible? Adam and Eve, who disobeyed God? No, they weren't the most flagrant lawbreakers in the Bible. Saul, who persecuted the early Christians before becoming Paul? No, he wasn't the most flagrant lawbreaker in the Bible. King David, who killed a man, just to have the man's wife? No, he wasn't the most flagrant lawbreaker in the Bible. The most flagrant lawbreaker in the Bible was...Moses: He broke all Ten Commandments at once! [Segue to an explanation of Moses breaking the tablets on which the Law was written (Ex. 32:19), then to how it is that we, too, break God's commandments.]

Looking for a visual aid for your homily or object lesson? Consider a lit candle and a clear container of water! Sirach 15:16 warns us that our choice to follow God's commandments—or not—is like choosing refreshing, life-giving water—or destructive fire! He continues: "Whatever you choose, stretch out your hand. Before everyone are life and death, whichever they choose will be given them" (Sir. 15:16-17). That's a powerful image! Which will you choose? Are you burning others

84

with the "fire" of anger and/or playing with the "fire" of lust? Oh, that we would all have the wisdom (1Cor. 2:6) to realize what we're doing!

Today is **World Marriage Day**! Consider floral arrangements in your worship space to honor and celebrate married couples. Invite couples to stand and renew their vows to one another. Cue couples to stand, invite each person standing to take the hands of his/her spouse, and decide who will recite the vows first. You'll also need to cue them to insert appropriate names after the words "I" and "you." Be conscious of the fact that some couples may be same-sex couples: To be inclusive, consider using the words: "I, ___, take you, ___, to be my spouse" or "...as my beloved." Immediately after the renewal, invite all who are seated to extend their hands for a prayer of blessing, then lead all in a round of applause for all who renewed their vows!

Valentine's Day is here! Secure a volunteer to set up a Valentine's Day photo booth or photo wall, so that couples can get their photos after mass. Avoid schmaltzy cupids, and be sure the photographer is thinking about how the photos will look when cropped. Looking to score a few points? Print copies of the photos and share them next Sunday with those in the photos!

On **February 12**, we remember the passing of **Friedrich Daniel Ernst Schleiermacher** (1768-1834), the German theologian, philosopher, and biblical scholar known for his attempt to reconcile the criticisms of the Enlightenment with traditional Christianity. Known as the "Father of Modern Liberal Theology," he played an important role in modern biblical hermeneutics. Karl Barth's neo-orthodoxy was largely an attempt to challenge Schleiermacher's "liberal Christianity." In his memory, take a moment today to reacquaint yourself with his life and works!

On **February 12**, we remember the passing of **Richard A. McCormick** (1922-2000), the Jesuit theologian who helped reshape Catholic thought in the U.S. by his writings on moral theory and social teachings. An expert in Catholic medical ethics, he was one of five moral theologians who crafted in 1964 a political position that would permit abortion in U.S. law. He wrote that the prohibition of discussion of *Humanae vitae* led to "a debilitating malaise that has undermined the credibility of the [Roman Catholic] magisterium in other areas." In his memory, familiarize yourself with his works and/or send up a prayer for the brave moral theologians who continue to explore positions that may not be accepted by more conservative voices!

On **February 12**, the Indian Orthodox Church celebrates the birth in 1949 of **Catholicos Baselios Marthoma Mathews III**. In a spirit of ecumenism, pray for him and for the 2.5 million people he serves!

On **February 13**, the Church celebrates **St. Apollos**, the first-century Alexandrian Jewish-Christian and colleague of Paul who was instrumental in the early churches of Ephesus and Corinth. One of four factions in Corinth apparently identified with him, and Martin Luther suggested that Apollos was the author of the Letter to the Hebrews. In Apollos' memory, pray for all who labor to establish new Christian communities!

On **February 13**, the Church celebrates **St. Polyeuct**, the third-century Roman soldier in Armenia known with St. Nearchus as "brothers by affection." Polyeuct, who converted to Nearchus' Christianity, zealously attacked a pagan procession and was beheaded for the crime. He spoke his last words to Nearchus: "Remember our secret vow," making St. Polyeuct the protector of vows and the avenger of broken promises. Polyeuct and Nearchus are portrayed together as patron saints of the gay community. In their memory, pray for all who make vows to others — and for all who suffer when such vows are broken!

On **February 13**, we remember the passing of **Roman Maria Jakub Próchniewski** (1872-1954), who served as bishop of the Mariavite Old Catholic Church for eight years. A popular preacher, confessor and seminary professor, he wrote a renowned work on the life and revelations of Maria Franciszka Kozłowska. In his memory, pray for our sisters and brothers of the Mariavite tradition!

On **February 13**, we celebrate the birth in 1943 of **Elaine Pagels**, the American religious historian and Princeton professor who wrote widely on early Christianity and the Gnostic gospels. Her works highlight the ways in which women have been viewed throughout Jewish and Christian history. In her honor, perform your own brief study of a Gnostic gospel that didn't "make the cut" in the scriptural canon, so as to enrich your preaching and storytelling!

On **February 14**, the Church formerly celebrated **St. Valentine**, the third-century Roman priest who defied restrictive marriage laws to bless couples forbidden to marry. The patron saint of love, couples, and happy marriages, he is also an icon in the same-sex marriage movement due to his willingness to perform outlawed marriages and to put love over laws. In his memory, pray for all lovers and couples!

On **February 14**, the Church celebrates the brother-saints **Cyril** (c. 826-869) **and Methodius** (815-885), the "Apostles to the Slavs"! They were a "bridge" between the West and the East: In their honor, learn about Eastern cultures and/or reach out to persons of other language groups!

On **February 15**, the Syriac Catholic Church (in union with Rome) celebrates the anniversary of the installation in 2009 of **Ignatius Ephrem Joseph III Yonan** as Patriarch of Antioch. In a spirit of ecumenism, pray for him and for the 205,000 Syriac Catholics he serves!

On **February 16**, the Church celebrates **St. Juliana** of Nicomedia (+304), the Greek woman who converted to Christianity and was tortured and beheaded for refusing to marry a pagan governor. Often depicted fighting a dragon or enslaving a winged devil, she is one of the 140 colonnade saints at St. Peter Basilica in Vatican City. In her memory, pray for all who fight "demons"!

On **February 16**, we remember the passing of **Francis Hodur** (1866-1953), the founder and first prime bishop of the Polish National Catholic Church. A Roman Catholic priest for five years, he was excommunicated for his rejection of purported papal infallibility and the universal jurisdiction of the pope. He founded St. Stanislaus Parish in Scranton, New York, where he celebrated the mass in Polish — an uncommon act in an era of Latin masses. Within ten years, he was consecrated by Dutch Old Catholic bishop Gerard Gul. He expanded the church to nearly 250 parishes in the U.S. and Poland. In his memory, pray for all who actively work to expand God's reign in our world!

On **February 16**, we celebrate the birth in 1948 of **Ulrich Leonard "Eckhart" Tölle**, the German-Canadian spiritual teacher and bestselling author referred to as "the most spiritually influential person in the world." After struggling with depression for the first 29 years of his life, he experienced a transformation and penned *The Power of Now* and *A New Earth*. In his honor, be inspired by his works and/or reach out to a loved one who might be suffering from depression!

On **February 17**, the Church celebrates the **Seven Founders of the Servite Order** (died over nearly 50 years, 1266-1310), seven prominent men of Florence who withdrew to monastic life while finding ways to support their wives and widows. Pause today to consider the active/contemplative balance in your life!

On **February 17**, we remember the passing of **Juan de Mariana** (1536-1624), the Spanish Jesuit scholastic and historian who, due to ill health, retired to Toledo and wrote a 30-volume history of the Iberian peninsula. A Monarchomach, he opposed monarchy and helped paved the way to social contract theories of "popular sovereignty." In his memory, consider the ways in which you are—or are not—helping to capture history!

On **February 17**, we remember the brutal execution in 1872 of **GomBurZa**, the three Filipino priests—Mariano Gómez, José Burgos, and Jacinto Zamora—accused of mutiny against Spain, which claimed sovereignty over the Philippines. Their controversial deaths, for their role in the purported Cavite Mutiny, contributed to the birth of Filipino nationalism, resulting in the overthrow of the Spanish government in 1898. In their memory, pray for all who suffer the scapegoating of others!

On **February 17**, we remember the passing of **Frances Willard** (1839-1898), the American educator and suffragette who used scripture to call for the equality of women. The president of the Woman's Christian Temperance Union, she was influential during the passing of the 18th and 19th Amendments on prohibition and women's suffrage. She advocated for raising the age of consent in many states, limiting the work day to eight hours, and expanding women's rights throughout the globe. In her memory, reacquaint yourself with her life and works!

On **February 17**, we celebrate the birth in 1934 of **John Dominic Crossan**, the Irish-American New Testament scholar and historian of early Christianity known for both his scholarly and popular works. A former Catholic priest, he has focused his research on the historical Jesus and the cultural anthropology of the New Testament world. Crossan's work has garnered controversy due to his suggestions that Jesus' divinity is metaphorical and that the second coming of Christ is a late corruption of Jesus' message. In his honor, enjoy some time reading up on the historical Jesus and his message!

On **February 17**, we celebrate the birth in 1938 of **Mary Frances Berry**, the American historian and activist who served as president of the Civil Rights Commission. In her honor, pray for her and for all who continue the fight for civil rights!

On **February 17-18**, our Islamic spiritual siblings celebrate **Isra and Mi'raj**, the "night journey" of Mohammad from Mecca to Jerusalem (the *Isra*), then to heaven (the *Mi'raj*). Light a candle and pray for greater unity with our 1.9 billion spiritual siblings of the Islamic tradition, with whom we share common spiritual ancestors!

On **February 18**, the Church celebrates **St. Constance** (c. 317 - 354), the daughter of the Roman emperor Constantine the Great. She dedicated her wealth to Christian works and is one of the 140 colonnade saints at St. Peter Basilica in Vatican City. In her memory, pray for all who share of their resources for the upbuilding of God's reign in our world!

On **February 18**, we remember the passing of **Martin Luther** (1483-1546), the German Roman Catholic priest who dared to question the teachings and practices of his church, including indulgences and salvation through works. He translated the Bible to the vernacular, esteemed scripture as the only source of divinely-revealed knowledge, and brought attention to the priesthood of all the baptized. A composer and professor of theology, Martin refused to renounce his views and was excommunicated by Leo X and condemned as an outlaw by Emperor Charles V. In his memory, pray for all who are ostracized by those whom they love!

Sunday, February 19, 2023

SEVENTH SUNDAY IN ORDINARY TIME

(green)

Note the exclusive language in today's scriptures: The reference to "brothers" in the gospel might just as easily be rephrased "brothers and sisters"!

This is the last Sunday that we'll sing the Alleluia until the Easter Vigil: Sing it with gusto!

The thread in today's scriptures: Last Sunday, we heard Paul speak of the need for us to love God; this week, we turn our attention to loving others (Lev. 19:18)—even our enemies (Mt. 5:44)! In this way, we model the compassion of God, who is kind and merciful (Ps. 103:8), and we respect the fact that others are temples of God (1Cor. 3:16-17)!

Holy humor: The story is told of the priest who was preaching on the need to love and forgive our enemies. She asked her listeners to raise their hands if they had forgiven all their enemies. Many hands went up, but there was one old, gray-haired woman in the back of the church who didn't raise her hand. The priest asked her: "Are you denying forgiveness to your enemies?" "Oh no, dear," the grey-haired woman said. "I just have no enemies. None whatsoever!" "What a blessing!" the priest responded. "What a wonderful life you must life! Now, for those of us who feel that we have enemies, tell us your secret: How is it that you don't have any enemies?" The woman paused thoughtfully and replied, "I'm 98 years old. Fortunately, I outlived them, and all my goll-darned enemies are...dead!" [Segue to today's message that we're called to share God's love, kindness and compassion with all people—yes, even with our enemies!]

Looking for a visual aid for your homily or object lesson? Make a visual of the famous phrase attributed to Gandhi: "An eye for an eye makes the whole world blind." Many images online contain Gandhi's image, but perhaps the image will hit closer to home if it contains a blind person or the Three Stooges (known for hitting one another back) or someone from the news who recently suffered tragic loss at the hands of others. Remember the compassion that John Paul II showed to the young man who tried to assassinate him in 1981? How might we similarly reflect God's love and forgiveness to others?

If you haven't already given a nod to **Black History Month**, this might be an ideal Sunday for hosting an African-American preacher with all the energy and enthusiasm s/he might bring!

In the U.S, we celebrate **President's Day** tomorrow: Be sure to pray in a special way today for our President and for all world leaders!

On **February 19**, we remember the passing of **Jeanne-Catherine-Agnès Arnauld** (1593-1671), the Cistercian abbess known as "Mother Agnes," who led Port-Royal-des-Champs at the height of the anti-Jansenist movement. The sister of Antoine Arnauld, she was confronted by the Archbishop of Paris for organizing resistance to the *Formulary of Submission for the Jansenists*. In her honor, consider your own courage in standing for your beliefs and convictions!

On **February 19**, we remember the passing of **Melchora Aquino de Ramos** (1812-1919), a prominent Independent Catholic of the Philippine Independent Church who was known as "Elder Sora" (due to her age during the Philippine revolution), the "Grand Woman of the Revolution" and the "Mother of Balintawak." The mother of six children whose father died when the youngest was seven, she hosted secret meetings of revolutionaries in her home, and was later arrested and deported to Guam. She appeared on the Philippines 100 peso bill (1951-1967) and is the namesake of Tandang Sora National Shrine, a national monument and memorial park in Quezon City, Manila, Philippines. In her memory, consider how you enflesh the courage and hospitality that she modeled!

On **February 19**, we remember the passing of **Zygmunt Szypold** (1909-1964), who served as bishop of the Polish Old Catholic Church for 16 years. Many clergy and laity resisted his leadership, accusing him of a number of crimes and scandals. After his death, his successor failed to obtain government consent to operate the church, which was subsequently banned and went underground. In his memory, pray for all who encounter resistance and persecution!

On **February 19**, we remember the passing of **Sylvia Ray Rivera** (1951-2002), the American gay liberation and transgender rights activist credited with throwing the bottle that incited to action the "Saints of Stonewall" in New York City on June 28, 1969. The co-founder of a ministry to homeless drag queens, gay youth and trans women, she is considered a matron saint of the trans community. In her memory, consider how you are stirring others to action and caring for the most marginalized in our society!

On **February 20**, we remember the passing of **Marcella Althaus-Reid** (1952-2009), the Argentinian pioneer in queer theology and first woman chair at the School of Divinity of Edinburgh University in Scotland. Known for her work in the slums of Buenos Aires, she applied the principles of Latin American liberation theology to women and sexual minorities, and she sparked controversy with her books *Indecent Theology* and *The Queer of God*. In her memory, consider your own liberating message for those who have historically been marginalized or oppressed!

On **February 20**, we celebrate the birth in 1947 of **John Maxwell**, the American pastor, speaker and author whose many books primarily focus on leadership. Considered by many to be the #1 author on leadership, he shares stories of the struggles he faced as a young pastor attempting to build congregations. In his honor, prayerfully consider how you are developing the leader within you — and the leaders around you!

February 20 is also **World Day of Social Justice**, a day to focus on the eradication of poverty and full employment and social integration for those in need. Pray and advocate for today's motto: "Social justice and decent life for all"!

On **February 21**, the Church celebrates **St. Peter Damian** (1007-1072), the gifted scholar and Doctor of the Church who spoke out against clerical abuses and challenged bishops to recommit themselves to their vocation. When is the last time that you spoke out against clerical abuse(s)? If you are a bishop, recommit yourself today to your vocation of leading, teaching and sanctifying God's people — with a special focus on leading, since you can't teach and sanctify others if you're walking alone!

On **February 21**, we remember the passing of **Malcolm X** (1925-1965), the American civil rights activist who worked for Black empowerment and racial justice. He famously criticized Martin Luther King Jr. and the civil rights movement for emphasizing nonviolence and racial integration, and his impatience for justice led him to preach racism and violence. In his memory, pray for all who grow weary thirsting for justice!

On **February 21**, we remember the passing of **William Franklin "Billy" Graham, Jr.** (1918-2018), the prominent Southern Baptist evangelist and advisor to U.S. presidents whose annual "crusades" and sermons helped some 2.2 billion people during his lifetime to explore the Bible and its connection to daily life. He encouraged new converts to become members of the Protestant and Catholic churches near them. In his memory, consider what you're doing to expand and multiply your efforts to evangelize!

February 21 is also **International Mother Language Day**, an annual opportunity to recall that many of our ancestors spoke languages other than English — and to work toward inclusion through multilingualism. Consider your own attitudes toward others of different languages!

Wednesday, February 22, 2023
ASH WEDNESDAY
(purple)

Catholics are famous for wanting their ashes and their palms: Be sure to **schedule your Ash Wednesday Mass(es) and/or service(s) at times that are convenient** for those who have families and/or other responsibilities, like work or school!

Be sure that **your worship environment** expresses the starkness of Lent.
- **Strip the altar and ambo**.
- **Remove all flowers, green plants, and unnecessary furnishings**.
- Simplicity is crucial during Lent. Draw attention to the items most essential during this season: ambo, altar, cross and font. Avoid duplicating crosses on vestments and banners.
- **Use fabric sparingly**, remembering that deep purple is used to mark the season, not to decorate it.
- Consider incorporating **decorative accents**, like, burlap, ashes, rocks, sand, broken pottery and cacti.
- **Decorate the entrance to your worship space** with wood or metal crosses and/or wreaths of dried grapevines.

- Be sure to steam or iron your **Lenten vestments** — and to coordinate the color of your vestments with any other touches of purple in your worship space!

Think through **the details of this day**:

- Do you have ashes?
- How, when and by whom will they be blessed? [Remember: Ashes are only blessed once.]
- Will you share them after the homily, or outside the mass?
- Will you need other ministers (clergy and/or laity) to assist with the distribution? When/how will you train them? Which formula will they use for the imposition of ashes? Do they know how they will clean the sacramental from their fingers, perhaps with premoistened towelettes that are later burned?
- Do you have a song or instrumental music to accompany the distribution of ashes?
- Try something different: Because the Church's rite doesn't mandate pushing ashes into the pores of a person's forehead, designate (and announce) a minister who will be happy to assist with the more ancient symbol of sprinkling ashes on the heads of those who, in line with the gospel mandate (Mt. 6:16-18), would like a different experience of Ash Wednesday!

Remember: The Penitential Rite is *not* used due to the distribution of ashes, the Creed is omitted, and the *Gloria* and Alleluia are *not* sung today; lead the congregation in another, easy-to-sing gospel acclamation!

The thread in today's scriptures: The Matthean Jesus speaks of what we now know as the three traditional Lenten practices of prayer, fasting & almsgiving (Mt. 6:1-6 & 16-18). The first reading (Jl. 2:12-18) and psalm (Ps. 51) are acknowledgements of our sinfulness (Ps. 51:4-6) — but more importantly of God's mercy and compassion (Jl. 2:13 & Ps 51:3). "Reconciled to God" during this Lenten season, may we be worthy "ambassadors of Christ" (2Cor. 5:20)!

Holy humor: The story is told of the youth minister who was a bit of a prankster. He was invited to be an ash minister on Ash Wednesday, and to share ashes with some of the young people who were known to pull pranks on him from time to time. So when the young man who often instigated the most pranks stepped up to him for ashes, the youth minister traced a cross of ashes on the young man's forehead [trace a cross in the air with your right thumb, as if sharing ashes with an invisible person], reverently saying, "Repent and believe the good news." And then he quickly swiped his ash-filled thumb over the young man's upper lip [make a small arc with your thumb, as though marking the person with a big ash moustache]. The youth minister flashed a wry smile, thinking revenge is so sweet, and you know what he said, right? "Happy 'Stache Wednesday!" [Segue into a lesson on the symbolism of the ashes and why we don't wear the ashes like a moustache, but instead have them sprinkled on our heads or marked on our foreheads in the shape of a cross.]

Looking for a visual aid for your homily or object lesson? Consider the ashes! Congregants will leave with the ashes on their forehead: Tie a strong message to that visual! As your "hook" (to pique interest), invite congregants to sing with you "Ring around the rosie," then draw attention to the imagery of "ashes, ashes" and note how "we all fall down" in death—hence, the symbolism of the ashes, which come from a plant that has died and been burned! Speak to the ancient connection of ashes with repentance.

Congregants will likely default to the thinking with which they were programmed: that they should "give up something" for Lent (e.g., candy, desserts, soda, coffee, smoking, social media). Explain that these are forms of fasting. Encourage them to consider instead **a Lent of service** as a sacrifice that might *help others*: assisting an elderly neighbor, serving a meal at a soup kitchen, visiting the homebound, etc.

Encourage congregants to go deeper in their exploration of all three traditional Lenten practices. For those on social media, suggest a **"virtual" Lenten journey**:

- *Pray* by sharing scripture, prayers and reflections on social media;

- *Fast* from mean comments, mean-spirited memes, and rigid views on religion and/or politics, fast by spending less time on social media and/or by abstaining from sites that may detract from holiness; and

- Engage in *almsgiving* by raising awareness of and contributing to worthy online campaigns for persons and organizations in need!

Ash Wednesday, like Good Friday, is one of two days of fasting and abstinence in the Western Church: Invite congregants to participate in this ancient ritual! Even better, note the connection between going meatless and protecting the environment. Search for internet resources (e.g., https://www.downtoearth.org/go-veggie/top-10-reasons).

For the intellectually-curious, share a history of Lent, how the first day of Lent is determined, how the 40 days are counted, and how Sundays are not numbered among the 40 days of Lent!

If you're thinking ahead to Easter, this may be an opportunity to share giving envelopes with those wishing to help buy **Easter lilies**, to decorate your worship space for the Triduum! Tell them what the suggested donation is for each lily, and tell them that they'll be able to take their lilies home with them at the conclusion of the Easter Mass they attend. These lilies can be shared with loved ones on Easter and/or planted outside!

On **February 22**, when it doesn't fall on Ash Wednesday, the Roman church celebrates the **Chair of St. Peter**, the foundational teaching *cathedra* presumed to have been passed by Peter to his purported successors. The feast traces to the fourth-century celebration of *Parentalia*, a winter commemoration of deceased family members and friends when a chair (*cathedra*) was left empty in memory of the deceased. Pray in a special way today for the bishops and church leaders who influenced you. If you celebrate mass, draw attention to an empty chair as a symbol of their abiding presence with us!

On **February 22**, we remember the passing of **Hendrik Herp** (c. 1400-1477), the Dutch mystical writer who founded and led a community of the Brothers of the Common Life before becoming a Capuchin Franciscan. His writings, including the *Mirror of Perfection*, were widely translated and distributed, influencing future mystics throughout Europe. His work, *On Mystical Theology*, dedicated to Ignatius of Loyola, however, was assigned to the *Index of Forbidden Books*. Pause to consider how you are gazing into the Mirror of Perfection and encouraging others to do likewise!

On **February 22**, we remember the elevation in 1940 of **Tenzin Gyatso** as the Dalai Lama, the foremost spiritual leader of the Buddhist people of Tibet. An ecumenical figure holding together disparate religious and regional groups, the Dalai Lama actively models and promotes Buddhist values and traditions to the world. In his honor, consider your own stance toward our sisters and brothers of diverse religious traditions!

On **February 22**, we celebrate the birth in 1963 of **Matthias Ring**, who has served as the tenth bishop of the German Old Catholic Church since 2010. With a doctorate in theology, he edited his diocesan newspaper, chaired the diocesan finance council, and chaired the Bavarian regional synod. In his honor, pray for him and for all our sisters and brothers of the German Old Catholic Church!

On **February 23**, the Church celebrates **St. Polycarp** (c. 65-155), the presumed friend of various eyewitnesses of Jesus' ministry. The Romans tried to burn him at the stake — and failed. Pray today for those members of the Roman Church whose fixations and lack of psychological and/or emotional health continue to affect our ministries in the Independent Catholic tradition!

On **February 24**, we remember the passing of **Franz Jacob Clemens** (1815-1862), the German philosopher and Catholic layman who defended the theological stances of the Church. He was so popular that 70 students followed him when he was transferred from the University of Bonn to the University of Münster. In his memory, consider your own defense of our liberating faith!

On **February 24**, we remember the passing of **Anton Günther** (1783-1863), the Czech-Austrian priest whose "liberal Catholic" Hegelian ideas of the Trinity, of the person of Christ, and of creation as the "non-ego" of God were condemned by scholastic theologians of his day. After the First Vatican Council, many adherents of Güntherianism joined the Old Catholic Church. In his memory, pray for all who attempt to enrich theology with ideas and perspectives from other disciplines!

On **February 24**, the Bulgarian Orthodox Church (recognized by the Ecumenical Patriarch of Constantinople) celebrates the anniversary of the installation in 2013 of Simeon Nikolov Dimitrov as **Patriarch Neophyte of Bulgaria**. In a spirit of ecumenism, pray for him and for the 11 million Bulgarian Orthodox Catholics he serves!

On **February 25**, the Church celebrates **St. Avertanus and Bl. Romeo**, the 14th-century French monks and traveling companions whose tales of their travels and miracles became extremely popular after their death. They died of the plague, shared the same coffin, and were invoked as patron saints of the AIDS pandemic. Their love was memorialized by William Shakespeare, who named one of his protagonists for Romeo. The inscription on their sarcophagus reads, "The two bodies were placed together, so that these who dwell in the same house in heaven may be united in the honor of one same urn." In their memory, pray for all victims of AIDS and for all who model love and unity to our world!

On **February 25**, we remember the passing of **Walter Walsh** (1847-1912), the English author and journalist best known for exposing the Jesuit and Vatican infiltration of Oxford University and the Church of England in his work, *The Secret History of the Oxford Movement*. He presented well-known Tractarians like John Henry Newman, Edward Pusey and John

Keble as turncoats. In his memory, consider how your characterizations of others might be impacting your relationships with them!

On **February 25**, we celebrate the birth in 1939 of **Paul Francis Knitter**, the theology professor known for his writings on religious pluralism. Criticized by Joseph Ratzinger, he was one of 97 Catholic theologians and leaders in 1984 who signed a statement calling for pluralism in the Roman church's conversations on its myopic position on abortion. In his honor, consider the place of pluralism in your own views and theology!

On **February 25**, the Maronite Catholic Church (in union with Rome) celebrates the birth in 1940 of **Cardinal Patriarch Bechara Boutros al-Rahi**. In a spirit of ecumenism, pray for him and for the 3.5 million Maronite Catholics he serves!

Sunday, February 26, 2023

FIRST SUNDAY OF LENT

(purple)

Remember: The *Gloria* and Alleluia are *not* sung today. Lead the congregation in another, easy-to-sing gospel acclamation!

You'll need to **choose whether you'll proclaim the shorter form of today's second reading, or the longer one**, which suggests that Adam was "the type of the one who was to come" and intersperses additional verses throughout the shorter form.

Be mindful of the exclusive language in today's scriptures: In the first reading, the creation of "man" is really the story of the creation of the human person, and the second reading can easily be rephrased, "death came to all people, inasmuch as all sinned." Note also the three problematic uses of "one man."

The thread in today's scriptures: Paul tells us that "through one man, sin entered the world" (Rom. 5:12), and that story is shared by the Yahwist author of Genesis (Gen. 3:1-7). Like Adam and Eve, all of us have sinned and are in need of God's mercy (Ps. 51:3). In contract, the Quelle Jesus was able to resist sin and temptation (Mt. 4:1-11).

Holy humor: The story is told of how Adam and Eve were wandering in the Garden of Eden, now in their new, makeshift clothes, since they tasted the forbidden fruit and realized that they were naked. Suddenly,

God comes into the garden, and, seeing the clothes, God begins to yell with a thunderous voice: "Why?!? How could you do this?!? Were all the other fruits of the garden not enough?!? Why are you wearing those clothes?!?" Scared and surprised, Adam looked at Eve and realized it was no using lying to God. Shaking, he said with a trembling voice: "We…we just…we just…we just updated our privacy policy!" [Segue into the story of Adam & Eve's sin, which led to their new "privacy policy."]

Looking for a visual aid for your homily or object lesson? Consider a fig, pomegranate and/or citron! Because the same Latin word (malum) can mean "apple" or "evil," Western Europeans invented the notion that the forbidden fruit of Genesis 3:6 was an apple. Blow your congregants' minds with the suggestion, rooted in scholarship, that it wasn't an apple! Rabbi Nechemia is credited with suggesting that the forbidden fruit was a fig, since Adam and Eve purportedly clothed themselves with fig leaves. The ancient Greeks associated Persephone's pomegranate—a fruit indigenous to the Middle East—with knowledge of the underworld. Other scholars suggest it was a citron. Regardless, the problem wasn't the apple, fig, pomegranate or citron in the tree; the problem was the pair (the "pear") on the ground!

If you have **catechumens** who will receive sacraments at the Easter Vigil, consider hosting the **Rite of Election** as part of your Mass today, with your catechumens' bishop in attendance! Prepare lovely copies of the Creed and Lord's Prayer, to be shared with them. Provide catechesis on the elements of the rite, including the *ephphetha*.

On **February 27**, we remember the passing of **Félicité Robert de Lamennais** (1782-1854), the French priest, philosopher and political theorist who is considered a forerunner of liberal and social Catholicism. In response to Rome's reactionary absolutism, he renounced his priesthood and published a polemic against the Roman Church and its conspiring with rulers against the people. Gregory XVI condemned the work, calling it "small in size, but immense in perversity"—an act largely seen as squelching open expression of modernist ideas in Catholic circles. Lamennais' views on religion and government softened, giving way to staunch Ultramontane views. In his memory, pause to consider how your own views and beliefs have changed over time!

On **February 27**, we remember the passing of **Fred McFeely Rogers** (1928-2003), the Presbyterian minister, musician and writer who became the beloved American television personality in "Mr. Rogers' Neighborhood." Known as a kind, neighborly educator of kids, he was famous for saying, "You've made this day a special day, by just your being you. There's no person in the whole world like you, and I like you just the way you are." In his memory, take a moment today to let as many people as possible know that…you love them just the way they are!

On **February 27**, we remember the passing of **Malcolm Boyd** (1923-2015), the American Episcopal priest, Freedom Rider, author and gay rights advocate. His 1965 bestseller, *Are You Running with Me, Jesus?*, shared conversational prayer-poems. He famously noted, "Through history, gays have always dominated religious life and churches." In his memory, try your own hand at creating a conversational prayer-poem to God!

On **February 27**, we celebrate the birth in 1971 of **Bernd Wallet**, who was installed as Archbishop of Utrecht in 2020, thus becoming the 84th successor to St. Willibrord as Old Catholic Archbishop of Utrecht. Pray today for Archbishop Wallet and his flock in the Old Catholic tradition!

On **February 28**, we remember the passing of **Martin Bucer** (1491-1551), the German Dominican friar who renounced his vows to champion Church reform. Excommunicated by the Roman church, he attempted to reconcile Martin Luther and Ulrich Zwingli, who differed on Eucharistic theology. An early pioneer of ecumenism, he later brought reformers together to agree to the Tetrapolitan Confession and the Wittenberg Concord, and he attempted to unite Roman Catholics and Protestants into a national German church separate from Rome. In his memory, pray for all who use their gifts to build bridges and bring together people of differing perspectives!

On **February 28**, we remember the passing of **Willibrord van Os** (+1825), the Dutch priest who served as the thirteenth archbishop of Utrecht. The story is told that, after the poisoning of his predecessor, Willibrord met with Napoleon and resisted his plan to confiscate the revenues of the church of Utrecht. Church historian John Neale writes, "He boldly and resolutely withstood the man to whose iron will Pius VII had yielded." In his memory, consider how you stand up to and challenge those who attempt to take what rightfully belongs to others!

On **February 28**, we remember the passing of **Hugh George de Willmott Newman** (1905-1979), the Independent Catholic bishop known as Mar Georgius I, whose conditional "cross-consecration" with bishops from 1945 to 1955 resulted in the consolidation of several lines of apostolic succession that were subsequently shared with hundreds of bishops around the world. In his memory, share a prayer of thanksgiving for all who have allowed Independent Catholics throughout the world to enjoy the Church's sacraments!

On **February 28**, we remember the passing of **Peter Gomes** (1942-2011), the American Baptist minister, Harvard professor and prominent spiritual voice for tolerance. A man of many contradictions, he shared the benediction at Ronald Reagan's second inauguration, preached at the inauguration of George H.W. Bush, then later became a Democrat. At a 1991 student rally, after a Harvard student magazine published a condemnation of homosexuality, he came out publicly as "a Christian who happens as well to be gay." He later said, "I will devote the rest of my life to addressing the 'religious case' against gays." In his memory, consider how you are helping to dismantle the "religious case" against various persons!

On **February 28**, the Ethiopian Orthodox Tewahedo Church celebrates the anniversary of the appointment in 2013 of Teklemariam Asrat as **Catholicos and Co-Patriarch Abune Mathias I**. In a spirit of ecumenism, pray for him and for the people he serves!

On **February 29**, the Church celebrates **St. Auguste Chapdelaine** (1814-1856), the French missionary whose beating, hanging and beheading in China sparked the Second Opium War, which concluded with a treaty allowing Christian missionaries to spread their faith and own property in China. Pray for all whose suffering paved the path for others to enjoy the lives they live!

On **February 29**, we remember the passing of **Roman Maria Jakub Próchniewski** (1872-1954), the Polish bishop who led the Old Catholic Mariavite Church. He wrote a book on the visions revealed to the Blessed Maria Franciszka Kozłowska. In his memory, pray for our sisters and brothers of the Old Catholic Mariavite Church!

On **February 29**, we remember the passing of **Jan Wirix** (1946-2008), the Dutch priest and seminary professor who served as the seventeenth Dutch Old Catholic bishop of Haarlem for 14 years. A research fellow at the University of Ghent, he wrote his doctoral dissertation on the Christian rites and symbols of dying and burial. In addition to his research publications, he wrote a prayer book and a work of poetry, both of which he illustrated himself. His episcopal motto was "Mercy and Truth." In his memory, consider how you model mercy and truth to our world!

On **February 29**, the Eastern Orthodox Church celebrates the birth in 1940 of **Dimitrios Arhondonis**, who became Ecumenical Patriarch Bartholomew I of Constantinople. In a spirit of ecumenism, pray for him and for the 260 million Eastern Orthodox Catholics he serves!

In **March**, we remember the passing of **Jacques Lefèvre d'Étaples** (c. 1455-1536), the French theologian and biblical translator who attempted to reform the Roman church from within. Though he enjoyed the friendship and protection of King Francis I of France, many of his ideas were condemned as heretical — including his suggestion that Mary Magdalene, Mary the sister of Lazarus, and the woman who anointed Jesus' feet were different women. In his memory, expand your knowledge of contemporary insights into our Christian scriptures!

On **March 1**, the Church celebrates **St. David of Wales** (+589), the national patron of Wales and founder of 12 monasteries there. Welsh traditions include the wearing of traditional dress and the eating of cawl (vegetable soup) and rarebit (cheese bread). Pray for all who celebrate "the Saint Patrick of Wales"!

On **March 1**, we celebrate the birth in 1942 of **Bernhard Heitz**, the German-Austrian Roman Catholic Redemptorist priest who served as the fourth bishop of the Austrian Old Catholic Church for 13 years. In his honor, pray for all our sisters and brothers of the Austrian Old Catholic Church!

March 1 is **Zero Discrimination Day**, an opportunity to celebrate the right of everyone to live a full and productive life with dignity!

March 1 is also **Self-injury Awareness Day**, an annual day to raise awareness of self-injury behaviors and to provide resources for those who suffer from the emotional roller coaster of self-deprivation, relief, emotional release, shame and guilt surrounding such behaviors. 50-85% of those who self-injure have a history of suicidal attempt. Raise your awareness of the warning signs and find new ways to support those suffering the stigma of self-harm!

March 2 is **Read Across America Day**, a day to encourage children to read. When was the last time you read to a child? Gather the kids or grandkids today, or use social media to share a children's story!

On **March 3**, we remember the passing of **Franz Heinrich Reusch** (1823-1900), the Roman Catholic priest excommunicated for his stance against purported papal infallibility. He went on to exercise his priestly ministry in the Old Catholic Church, serving as vicar general for Old Catholic Bishop Joseph Reinkens — a position he resigned when the German Old Catholic Church allowed clergy to marry. A prolific writer, he served on the Old Catholic theological faculty at the University of Bonn and was the official reporter of the reunion conferences held in Bonn during those years. In his memory, pray for all who struggle to find a home in the various manifestations of the Catholic Church!

On **March 3**, the Church celebrates **St. Katharine Drexel** (1858-1955), the American heiress-turned-educator who dedicated her life to Native

Americans west of the Mississippi. Consider how you are working for racial justice, and inspire philanthropists with stories of their matron saint!

On **March 3**, we remember the passing of **Julian Pękala** (1904-1977), the Polish Old Catholic bishop who organized a secret meeting of clergy to oust his predecessor and clear the way for his leadership of the church. He pastored Holy Spirit Cathedral in Warsaw. In his memory, pray for all whose ambitions negatively impact others!

On **March 3**, the Russian Old Orthodox Church celebrates the anniversary of the installation in 2003 of Alexander Kalinin as **Patriarch Alexander of Moscow and all Russia**. In a spirit of ecumenism, pray for him and for the people he serves!

March 3 is **Employee Appreciation Day**, an opportunity to honor contributions and achievements by those who work alongside us. Find new ways to show your gratitude for others!

March 3 is also **World Wildlife Day**, an annual opportunity to raise awareness of wild animals and plants. Contemporary "creature comforts" protect us from the world experienced by our ancestors: Take a hike today and enjoy a bit more of our planet's biodiversity!

On **March 4**, we remember the passing of **Rupert of Deutz** (c. 1075-1129), the Benedictine exegete who wrote widely on liturgy and music. He was criticized for his support of impanation, the belief that the bread and wine are united to Christ's divine person. Consider how you encourage alternate expressions of the great mystery that is the Eucharist!

On **March 4**, the Church celebrates **St. Casimir** (1458-1484), the Polish prince renowned for his piety and devotion. He was made weak from fasting, and he died of a lung disease. Pray for and/or reach out today to those who might be growing weak under the burdens of life!

On **March 4**, we remember the passing of **Peter Richard Kenrick** (1806-1896), the Roman Catholic archbishop of St. Louis, Missouri, who courageously stood against American Ultramontane bishops and opposed the definition of purported papal infallibility at the First Vatican Council. He wrote, "We think it most inopportune to define as a dogma of faith an opinion which seems to us a novelty in the Church, destitute of solid foundation in Scripture and Tradition, and contradicted by indisputable evidence." Subsequent harassment caused him to turn over his archdiocese to his coadjutor. In his memory, pray for all who take courageous stands on issues, knowing that such strong stands may result in unexpected consequences!

On **March 4**, we celebrate the birth in 1938 of **Kazimierz Fonfara**, the Polish priest who administered the Kraków-Częstochowa diocese of the Polish Catholic Church in Poland. In his honor, pray for him and for our sisters and brothers of the Polish Catholic Church in Poland!

On **March 4**, we celebrate the birth in 1976 of **Leonard Beg**, the Croatian Old Catholic bishop who serves as vicar general of the Old Catholic General Vicariate of St. Methodius in Croatia. In his honor, pray for him and for our sisters and brothers of the Old Catholic Church in Croatia!

Sunday, March 5, 2023
SECOND SUNDAY OF LENT
(purple)

Remember: The *Gloria* and Alleluia are *not* sung today. Lead the congregation in another, easy-to-sing gospel acclamation!

Note: The introductory line of today's second reading is misleading. The Second Letter to Timothy is a pseudonymous letter, written in Paul's name and spirit, but not written by Paul. Rather than confuse your listeners, begin the proclamation with, "A reading from the Second Letter to Timothy"!

The thread in today's scriptures: As our Lenten journey continues, we journey with the faithful Abraham, who trusted the God who called him and his family to a foreign land (Gen. 12:1-4). We can imagine Abraham and his family saying with the psalmist: "Lord, …we place our trust in you" (Ps. 33:22)! We also journey up a mountain with Peter, James and John, who enjoy an "appearance of our savior Christ Jesus" (2Tim. 1:10) — the transfiguration of the Lord (Mt. 17:1-9)!

Holy humor: Four weeks ago, on February 9, we had a number of lightbulb jokes that focused on light. This Sunday, try three or four of the following lightbulb jokes, culminating in those that speak of resistance to change, then segue to Abraham's willingness to place his trust in a God who called him to change his address, then to the story of Jesus' friends who witnessed the change of his transfiguration — in which he became brighter than any lightbulb imaginable: "His face shone like the sun, and his clothes became white as light" (Mt. 17:2)! As we undertake our own Lenten journey, how willing are we to change, so as to bring more light into this world?

- How many Pentecostals does it take to change a light bulb? Only one, but 99 more to cast out the spirit of darkness!

- How many Fundamentalists does it take to change a light bulb? None. The Bible doesn't mention light bulbs!

- How many Southern Baptists does it take to change a light bulb? One to change the bulb, and 16 million to boycott the company that made the old bulb—for bringing darkness into the church!

- How many TV evangelists does it take to change a light bulb? One, but, for the message of light to continue, please donate today!

- How many Lutherans does it take to change a light bulb? Change? Lutherans don't do change!

- How many Catholics does it take to change a light bulb? What? Change the lightbulb? My grandparents donated that lightbulb!

Looking for a visual aid for your homily or object lesson? Consider the yellow tape used at crime scenes and construction sites! You can buy it at any home improvement store. Why are crime scenes and construction sites cordoned off, so that no one can walk through them? That's the same reason that Peter suggested setting up three tents: to cordon off and keep people from trespassing the "holy ground" where the transfigured Christ appeared with Moses and Elijah! Retreats are sometimes referred to as "mountaintop experiences," from which we eventually have to descend: During these 40 special days of Lent, how are you "cordoning" off a bit more time and space, to retreat to and ascend the "mountain" with our transfigured Lord?

Will you be sharing any **Easter cards** this year with those who support the ministries of your community? If so, you might begin thinking now about the design and printing of Easter cards!

March is here! **For the intellectually-curious**, share a lesson on the etymology of this month! Named after Mars, the Roman god of war, March was the month to resume military campaigns interrupted by the winter. As the outside world thaws, reflect on those "frozen" aspects of your life that might benefit from a bit of thawing!

Daylight Saving Time begins next Sunday: Be sure to remind people to "spring forward"—or they'll arrive an hour late for Mass!

On **March 5**, we remember the passing of **Ambrose Phillipps de Lisle** (1809-1878), the English founder of the Trappist abbey at Mount St. Bernard, who spurred a Catholic revival in England and co-founded the

Association for the Promotion of the Unity of Christendom. His calls for Catholics, Anglicans and Orthodox to pray for the unity of the Body of Christ were condemned by Rome, and he was forced to recant his belief that all three churches possessed "the one Lord, the one faith and the one baptism." In his memory, consider what you are doing to overcome the divisions in the Body of Christ!

On **March 5**, we celebrate the birth in 1933 of **Walter Kasper**, the German Roman Catholic cardinal and theologian who built bridges between various denominations as president of the Pontifical Council for Promoting Christian Unity. For 10 years, he met with like-minded cardinals to discuss reforms of the Roman church with respect to such issues as collegiality, the appointment of bishops, the primacy of the papacy, and the Church's approach to sexual morality. He is known for his proposal to admit divorced and remarried couples to communion — but also for his criticism of the Anglican Church, for its allowance of female clergy and same-sex marriage. In his honor, pray for all who esteem and work to strengthen ecumenical relations!

On **March 5**, we celebrate the birth in 1963 of **Joel Scott Osteen**, the American televangelist and author whose sermons are viewed by seven million viewers each week. He has written ten books that have been ranked #1 on *The New York Times* bestseller list. In his honor, listen to one of his sermons and/or read a chapter from one of his books, to see what you might learn and apply to your own style of preaching, teaching and community building!

On **March 5**, the Syro-Malankara Catholic Church (in union with Rome) celebrates the anniversary of the installation in 2007 of Isaac Thottumkal as **Moran Mor Baselios Cleemis, Major Archbishop-Catholicos of Trivandrum**. In a spirit of ecumenism, pray for him and for the 500,000 Syro-Malankara Catholics he serves!

On **March 6,** we remember the passing of **Hilaria del Rosario Aguinaldo** (1877-1921), a prominent Independent Catholic and member of the Philippine Independent Church who served as the inaugural First Lady of the Philippines. She married her husband Emilio Aguinaldo on New Year's Day 1896, the same day that he joined the secret society that initiated the Philippine revolution. She complemented his military campaigns by caring for wounded soldiers and their families. She organized the Daughters of the Revolution, a precursor of the Philippine National Red Cross. She later served as an officer of the Philippine Independent Church's Women's Commission. In her memory, consider how your work and ministry complement the work and ministries of those around you!

On **March 6**, we remember the passing of **Pearl Buck** (1892-1973), the American author, missionary, and activist who advocated for the rights of women and minorities. In her memory, pray for those who follow in her footsteps!

On **March 6**, we remember the passing of **Jan Dawidziuk** (1937-2012), the Polish-American bishop who led the Polish National Catholic Church in the United States and Canada. In his memory, pray for our sisters and brothers of the Polish National Catholic Church!

On the evening of **March 6**, our Jewish spiritual siblings celebrate **Purim**, the joyful celebration of their survival after being marked for death by their Persian rulers. Read the story in Esther 3-7, and pray for all who are persecuted!

On **March 7**, the Church celebrates **Ss. Perpetua and Felicity** (+c. 203), the wealthy, North African 22-year-old noblewoman and her slave girl who were united through their martyrdom. Both were mothers of very young children. They are considered matron saints of lesbians and same-sex couples, and, because of her dream of being transformed into a man, Perpetua is also seen as a transgender saint. Pray Eucharistic Prayer I, which mentions them, and find a way to acknowledge the many sacrifices parents make as they "lay down their lives" for their children!

On **March 7**, we remember the passing of **Wilhelm Vet** (1781-1853), the fourth Dutch Old Catholic bishop of Deventer for nearly 30 years. A resident of Amsterdam for over 50 years, he, like his predecessors, served as a titular bishop with no jurisdiction in Deventer. In his memory, consider the ways in which you may not be living up to some of the titles and responsibilities you bear!

On **March 7**, we remember the passing of **Antonio Fogazzaro** (1842-1911), the Italian novelist and proponent of Liberal Catholicism who was nominated for the Nobel Prize in Literature seven times. He attempted to reconcile Christianity with Darwin's theory of evolution, leading the Roman Catholic Church to ban two of his novels. In his memory, consider your own attitude toward scientific theories that might impact our faith!

On **March 7**, we celebrate the birth in 1946 of **Daniel Goleman**, the journalist and author best known for his longtime bestseller, *Emotional Intelligence*. He has written on a wide variety of topics, including self-deception, creativity, transparency, meditation, and the ecological crisis. In his honor, consider how you might enhance your own EQ—and that of those around you!

106

On **March 8**, the Church celebrates **St. John of God** (1495-1550), who suffered temporary insanity, was sobered by life inside the mental institutions of his day, and dedicated the rest of his life to ministering to those living in such places. Take advantage of this day to raise awareness of the mental illnesses that afflict one in every four to five American adults!

On **March 8**, we remember the passing of **Mariano Marcos y Rubio** (1897-1945), a prominent Independent Catholic and member of the Philippine Independent Church. A lawyer and Philippine Congressman, he was best known as the father of former president and dictator Ferdinand Marcos. A militant follower of Gregorio Aglipay, the first supreme bishop of the Philippine Independent Church, he insisted on baptizing and raising his four children in the church. He suffered an excruciating death at the hands of guerilla forces who suspected him of collaborating with Japan during its occupation of the archipelago. Two universities and a town are named for him. In his memory, consider your own commitment to our Independent Catholic ideals!

On **March 8**, the Armenian Apostolic Church celebrates the birth in 1947 of **Pedros Keshishian**, who became Catholicos Aram I of Cilicia. In his honor, pray for him and for the 9 million people he serves!

March 8 is **International Women's Day**, a global day celebrating the social, economic, cultural and political achievements of women. Pray and advocate for the acceleration of parity and equality for women!

On **March 9**, the Church celebrates **St. Frances of Rome** (1384-1440), who inspired the wealthy of her day to visit the poor and to care for the sick. In a spirit of Lenten almsgiving, share of your time, talent and/or treasure with the poor and the sick in your community!

On **March 9**, we remember the passing of **Carrie Chapman Catt** (1859-1947), the American suffragette who campaigned for passage of the 19th Amendment, giving women the right to vote. In her memory, pray for all who continue to fight for women's rights throughout the world!

On **March 9**, we remember the passing of **Josef Fuchs** (1912-2005), the German Jesuit theologian credited with achieving in moral theology what Karl Rahner had accomplished in systematic theology. He chaired the Pontifical Commission on Population, Family and Birth, whose report on artificial birth control within marriage was rejected by Paul VI. In his memory, pray for all who struggle with the very real conundrum of differing with those who hold power over them!

On **March 9**, we remember the passing of **Sir John Charlton Polkinghorne** (1930-2021), the English Anglican priest, physicist and theologian who has authored over 25 books on the relationship between science and religion. In his honor, reacquaint yourself with any one of his works!

On **March 10**, we remember the passing of **Richard of Saint Victor** (+1173), the Scottish philosopher and mystical theologian known for his dogmatic theology on the Trinity and his psychological analysis of the contemplative experience. Pause today to reacquaint yourself with his works!

On **March 10**, we celebrate the anniversary of the presbyteral ordination in 2001 of Father **Jayme Mathias**, pastor of Holy Family Catholic Church in Austin, Texas. Happy anniversary!

On **March 11**, we celebrate the birth in 1933 of **Walter Brueggemann**, the American Protestant theologian widely considered one of the most influential Old Testament scholars of the 20th century. His research has focused on the Hebrew prophetic tradition and the sociopolitical imagination of the Church. In his honor, consider how prophetic your stances really are toward consumerism, militarism and nationalism!

On **March 11**, we celebrate the founding in 2012 of **Holy Family Catholic Church** in Austin, Texas, currently led by Father Jayme Mathias, Father Roy Gomez, Deacon Elsa Nelligan and Deacon Stephen Rodriguez. Happy anniversary, Holy Family!

Sunday, March 12, 2023
THIRD SUNDAY OF LENT
(purple)

Remember: The *Gloria* and Alleluia are *not* sung today. Lead the congregation in another, easy-to-sing gospel acclamation!

You'll need to **choose which gospel you'll proclaim today**: the shorter form, or the longer form, which includes an additional 16 verses that could just as easily be summarized in your homily!

Be mindful of the exclusive language in today's psalm: Is there any reason a person should proclaim God's Word by saying anything less inclusive than, "where your ancestors tempted me"? Remember: Even the Samaritan woman speaks of "our ancestors" — rather than "our fathers" — in today's gospel!

The thread in today's scriptures: The thirsty Israelites grumbled (Ex. 17:3-7), and their grumble was forever memorialized by the psalmist (Ps. 95:8-9)! The woman at the well realized the thirst she had for the living waters that the Johannine Jesus could provide (Jn. 4:15). We pray during these weeks of Lent that our thirst might be quenched by the love that God pours into our hearts (Rom. 5:5)!

Holy humor: The story is told of the Hollywood star who was shopping on Rodeo Drive when she came across a man begging on a street corner. The man held out his cupped hand and pleaded, "I haven't eaten in four days." She paused, looked at him over her sunglasses, and replied, "I wish I had your willpower!" [Segue into the fact that food and water are essential for life, then to how it is that many of us, like the Israelites and the Samaritan woman, are focused on the things of this world, while our spiritual lives languish for lack of "living water" and spiritual nourishment!]

Looking for a visual aid for your homily or object lesson? Consider a clear pitcher of water and a glass! Water is essential for life — which is why the Israelites were so concerned with finding water in the wilderness! As you pour the water into the glass, refer to the second reading, on how "the love of God has been poured out into our hearts" (Rom. 5:5). The Johannine Jesus promised the Samaritan woman "living water" (Jn. 4:10) — not stagnant water at the bottom of a well, but the life and love that he would pour into her heart!

On **March 12**, when it doesn't' fall on a Sunday, the Church celebrates **Symeon the New Theologian** (949-1022), the Galatian monk who was the most important Byzantine theologian between John of Damascus in the 8th century and Gregory Palamas in the 14th century. He employed homoerotic imagery to describe salvation as a heavenly marriage with God, thus making him a patron saint of the LGBTQIA+ community. In his memory, consider how you communicate the great mysteries of our faith!

On **March 12**, we remember the passing of **Denis the Carthusian** (1402-1471), the Limburgish theologian, mystic and "Ecstatic Doctor" who divided each day between prayer and his study and writing. He detailed the purgative, illuminative and unitive stages of the path to supernatural wisdom, and was consulted as an oracle by bishops and princes. In his memory, consider where you are on the path to wisdom — and possible actions for taking a step in the direction of union with God!

On **March 12**, we celebrate the birth in 1936 of **Michał Kazimierz Heller**, the Polish priest and professor of philosophy and science who has authored more than 50 books and who received the Templeton Prize for his attempts to reconcile the "known scientific world with the unknowable dimensions of God." His current research provides new perspectives on quantum entanglement and the EPR paradox. In his honor, consider your own attempts to simultaneously honor what science tells us about our world, and "the root of all possible causes" that forms the foundation of our faith tradition!

On **March 13**, we remember the passing of **Johann Gropper** (1503-1559), the Westphalian cardinal whose "most detailed and most important pre-Tridentine dogmatic of the Reformation period" was placed on the *Index of Forbidden Books*. A student of Erasmus, he rooted his writings in scripture and the Church Fathers. Gropper was denounced to the Inquisition and died in poverty. In his memory, pray for all who faithfully serve institutions that later disappoint them!

On **March 13**, we remember the passing of **Charles de Montalembert** (1810-1870), the French historian and count whose advocacy for the freedom of Ireland and Poland — and of education by church and state — made enemies among Ultramontanists. In 1863, he delivered two long addresses on freedom of religion and thought at the Catholic Congress in Malines, Belgium. In his later years, he wrote on Western monasticism. In his memory, consider your own views on the constraints that are often placed on truth!

On **March 13**, we remember the passing of **Susan B. Anthony** (1820-1906), the American activist who became one of the most well-known suffragettes. In her memory, pray for all who continue the fight for women's rights throughout the world!

On **March 13**, we remember the passing of **Engelbert Lagerwey** (1880-1959), who served as the ninth Dutch Old Catholic bishop of Deventer for 18 years. As a priest, he served as pastor of the newly-constructed St. Gertrude Cathedral in Utrecht. Ten years later, he was named to the metropolitan chapter. In 1941, largely due to his resistance to German occupation, he was consecrated titular bishop of Deventer, with no jurisdiction. His episcopal motto was "We work for eternity." In his memory, consider how you are working for eternity!

On **March 13**, we remember the passing of **Milan Dobrovoljac** (1879-1966), the Croatian Old Catholic bishop of the Old Catholic Church in Serbia. In his memory, pray for our sisters and brothers of the Old Catholic Church in Serbia!

On **March 13**, the Roman Catholic Church celebrates the anniversary of the installation in 2013 of Jorge Mario Bergoglio as **Pope Francis**. In a spirit of ecumenism, pray for him and for the 1.3 billion Roman Catholics he serves!

On **March 14**, we remember the passing of **Virgilio P. Elizondo** (1935-2016), the Mexican-American Roman Catholic priest and activist who was a leading scholar of Hispanic theology and Latin American liberation theology. Widely regarded as "the father of U.S. Latino religious thought," he examined the similarities between Jesus' Galilean background and the *mestizo* experience. He viewed Our Lady of Guadalupe as the ultimate symbol and product of *mestizaje*, the mixing of people of different backgrounds. In his memory, reacquaint yourself with any one of his many works!

On **March 14**, we remember the assassination of **Marielle Franco** (1979-2018), the Brazilian feminist, politician and human rights activist who, as a city councilmember in Rio de Janeiro, spoke against police brutality and extrajudicial killings. A bisexual Afro-Latina, she was known for saying, "To be a black woman is to resist and survive all the time." In her memory, pray for contemporary prophets who continue to advocate for the human and civil rights of others!

On **March 15**, we celebrate the anniversary of the presbyteral ordination in 1982 of Bishop **Edmund N. Cass**, a longtime bishop in the Independent Catholic movement. Happy anniversary!

On **March 16**, we remember the passing of **Christoph von Utenheim** (1450-1527), the Swiss bishop who unsuccessfully advocated for reform of the Roman church. His attempts to reform abuses in his diocese were resisted by his cathedral chapter. Pray for all who whose innovative spirits are opposed by others!

On **March 16**, we celebrate the birth in 1950 of **Karen Furr**, the sacramental minister of Our Lady of the Angels Catholic Community in Kingman, Arizona. Pray for her and for the people she serves!

On **March 16**, we celebrate the birth in 1955 of **Tina Beattie**, the English professor of Catholic Studies who has raised awareness of social justice, non-violence, women's rights, same-sex marriage and women's ordination. Beattie has challenged the Roman church's teachings on contraception and has advocated for a more-nuanced ethical approach to the question of early abortion. In her honor, consider how you are raising awareness of the key social justice issues that intersect with theology!

On **March 17**, the Church celebrates **St. Patrick** (c. 415-493), the Romano/British missionary and "Apostle of Ireland." Reflect on his analogy of the shamrock for the mystery of the Trinity and/or note that the color originally associated with St. Patrick was…blue!

On **March 17**, we remember the passing of **Józef Maria Rafael Wojciechowski** (1917-2005), the Polish bishop who helped lead the Catholic Mariavite Church in Poland. In his memory, pray for our sisters and brothers of the Catholic Mariavite Church in Poland!

On **March 17**, we celebrate the birth in 1948 of **George Augustus Stalling, Jr.,** the Roman Catholic priest excommunicated after announcing on the Phil Donahue Show his renouncement of papal authority and the Roman church's teachings on contraception, abortion, homosexuality and divorce. Known as the first Independent Catholic in the U.S. to gather together a vibrant Black community, he founded the Imani Temple African American Catholic Congregation in Washington, D.C. In his honor, consider how you might better esteem and lift up our Black sisters and brothers!

On **March 17**, the Armenian Apostolic Church celebrates the birth in 1962 of **Sahag Maşalyan**, who became Patriarch Sahag II Mashalian of Constantinople. Pray for him and for the 9 million people he serves!

On **March 18**, the Church celebrates **St. Cyril of Jerusalem** (c. 315 - c. 386), the early Church theologian thrice-exiled for teaching that Jesus was fully divine. He sold his gifts from the emperor, to raise money for the poor. Consider your own support for those in need!

Sunday, March 19, 2023
FOURTH SUNDAY OF LENT
(rose or purple)

It's *Laetare* **Sunday**:
- Pull out the **rose vestments,** if you have them; make sure they're ironed or steamed!
- Incorporate **small touches of rose** into your otherwise-stark worship environment!

Remember: The *Gloria* and Alleluia are *not* sung today. Lead the congregation in another, easy-to-sing gospel acclamation!

You'll need to **choose which gospel you'll proclaim**: the shorter form, or the longer form, which adds 26 verses that you could just as easily summarize in your homily!

Note: The introductory line of today's second reading is misleading. The Letter to the Ephesians is a pseudonymous letter, written in Paul's name and spirit, but not written by Paul. Rather than confuse your listeners, begin the proclamation with, "A reading from the Letter to the Ephesians"!

The thread in today's scriptures: The pseudonymous author of the Letter to the Ephesians admonishes us to "live as children of the light" (Eph. 5:8), thus preparing us for the gospel irony: The blind man sees, and those with eyes (viz., the Pharisees) are blind! Jesse and his family were blind, too: They didn't see that God was shepherding (Ps. 23:1) the shepherd-king in their midst (1Sam. 16:6-13)!

Holy humor: The story is told of the nun who knocked on the bathroom door of the convent and told her mother superior, who was showering, that there was a blind man there to see her. The mother superior replied, "Well, if he's a blind man, it doesn't matter if I'm in the shower, so send him in." So the blind man walked into the bathroom where the mother superior was showering, and she began to share her gratitude with the blind man. He interrupted her, "That's nice and all, ma'am, but when you get out of the shower, could you tell me where to put these blinds?" [Summarize that not all "blind" people are blind, segue to the blind man in today's gospel, then tie back to the mother superior when you talk about how it is that not all people with eyes can "see"!]

Looking for a visual aid for your homily or object lesson? Consider a blindfold! The blindfold keeps those with eyes from seeing. In what ways are you "blind"? What are you not "seeing"? Maybe it's time to take off the "blindfold"!

On **March 19**, we remember the passing of **Péter Pázmány** (1570-1637), the Hungarian Jesuit who was a noted statesman, philosopher, theologian and cardinal. An important figure in the Counter-Reformation of Hungary, he created the Hungarian literary language. In his memory, pray for the people of Hungary who continue to benefit from his legacy!

On **March 20**, the Church celebrates the **Solemnity of St. Joseph**, Jesus' stepfather and the patron saint of workers and of the Universal Church!

• Wear white—and the *Gloria* may be sung today.

- Pray the **Litany of St. Joseph** and consider **cultural celebrations**, like the St. Joseph Blessing of Bread, the blessing of the St. Joseph Table (a Sicilian tradition of blessing food principally intended for the poor) and/or the sharing of ravioli (another Italian tradition) on this day! If you're in New Orleans, build your three-tiered St. Joseph altar and bake your *pupa cu l'ova*! Recalling the legacy of St. Cyril, whom we celebrated yesterday, consider giving the bread from your St. Joseph altar to those in need! As an alternative to the St. Joseph Table, consider hosting a **Lenten auction** of donated breads and homemade pastas, with the income designated for a Lenten alms project.

- **For the intellectually-curious**, share a lesson on what the scriptures say (and don't say) about today's saint. Note that he was a *tekton* (literally, a handyman — and *not* a carpenter, as mistranslation and popular imagination suggest), that he protected Jesus from the slaughter of the Innocents, and that there is no mention of him after Luke's story of the child Jesus in the temple. Explain that we infer that he died prior to Jesus' public ministry, and certainly before Jesus' death (or else he would have claimed Jesus' body from the cross). Share the tradition of him dying in the arms of Jesus and Mary, and thus being known today as the patron of a happy death. Also, speak to the superstitions and shamanistic rituals related to this saint (e.g., burying a statue of St. Joseph upside-down to sell your home, stealing a lemon from the St. Joseph altar to find a spouse, the carrying of blessed fava beans as a talisman, and freezing bread to ward off hurricanes).

On **March 20**, we remember the passing of **Johann Nepomuk Huber** (1830-1879), the German philosopher and theologian who opposed purported papal infallibility and was an early leader in the Old Catholic Church. He attracted attention by pseudonymously co-authoring *The Pope and the Council*, which challenged Ultramontane promoters of the First Vatican Council. He also pseudonymously published *Roman Letters*, a redaction of secret reports leaked from Rome during the Council. In his memory, pray for all who lack the freedoms we take for granted — including freedom of the press!

On **March 20**, we remember the passing of **Christopher Wordsworth** (1807-1885), the English Anglican bishop who wrote several books and hymns, including "Songs of Thankfulness and Praise." He represented the Anglican Church at the Reunion Conferences of 1874 and 1875, where Old Catholic, Anglican and Orthodox clergy convened to discuss possible paths to unification. In his memory, pray for all who continue to open their hearts to and build relationships with persons of different backgrounds!

On **March 20**, we remember the passing of **Leon Maria Andrzej Gołębiowski** (1867-1933), the Polish Old Catholic Mariavite bishop who was the first Mariavite bishop of the Silesian-Łódź diocese. He remained firm despite persecution for his Marianite beliefs. In his memory, pray for all who are persecuted!

On **March 20**, we remember the passing of **Anthony Rysz** (1924-2015), the Polish-American bishop of the central diocese of the Polish Catholic Church. In his memory, pray for our sisters and brothers of the Polish Catholic Church!

On **March 20**, we celebrate the birthday in 1943 of **Richard Rohr**, the prolific Franciscan spiritual writer who founded the New Jerusalem Community in Cincinnati and the Center for Action and Contemplation in Albuquerque. Emphasizing an "alternative orthodoxy" that allows for advocacy against such issues as religious-based oppression of LGBTQ persons, Father Richard has inspired millions of readers and listeners. In his honor, ruminate on a few paragraphs of his wisdom!

On **March 20**, the Church of God in Christ celebrates the anniversary of the installation in 2021 of **Presiding Bishop John Drew Sheard, Sr**. In a spirit of ecumenism, pray for him and for the 6.5 Christians he serves!

On **March 20**, we celebrate the anniversary of the founding in 2005 of the nursing home ministry of Father **Bruce Douglas** in Hartford, Connecticut. Happy anniversary, Father Bruce!

March 20 is the **spring equinox**, the day when the sun crosses the equator and continues its journey north. Recall the historical significance of this day: Easter is always celebrated on the first Sunday after the first full moon after the spring equinox!

March 20 is also **International Day of Happiness**, an annual day to remind us that happiness and well-being should take precedence over economic gain. Pause to pray for all whose priorities are "upside-down"!

On **March 21**, we remember the passing of **Jean Guitton** (1901-1999), the French philosopher and theologian who was the first lay person invited to be an observer of the Second Vatican Council. During the course of 60 years, he authored some 50 books on a wide range of philosophical and theological topics. In his memory, pause to consider the great gifts of the lay persons who enrich the Church!

On **March 21**, we remember the passing of **Vekoslav Grmič** (1923-2005), the Slovenian bishop and theologian known as "the red bishop" for his strong Socialist leanings. A supporter of liberation theology, of the political-religious thought of Swiss reformer Hans Küng, and of the collaboration of the Catholic Church with Marxism in Yugoslavia, Grmič was removed from his bishopric by John Paul II. He was the author of more than 40 books and several translations. In his memory, pray for all who champion the apostolic ideals of shared ownership of resources and the equitable distribution of goods and services in our world!

On **March 21**, the Roman Catholic Church celebrates the anniversary of the installation in 2003 of **Filipe Neri António Sebastião do Rosário Ferrão** as Latin Patriarch of the East Indies. In a spirit of ecumenism, pray for him and for the Roman Catholics he serves!

On **March 21**, the Church of England celebrates the anniversary of the installation in 2013 of **Archbishop Justin Portal Welby of Canterbury**. In a spirit of ecumenism, pray for him and for the 85 million Anglicans he serves!

March 21 is **World Day to Eliminate Racial Discrimination**, a day to focus on the social sins of racism and discrimination. Marking the day in 1960 when police in Sharpeville, South Africa killed 69 demonstrators against Apartheid, today is a day to reflect on—and work toward dismantling—racist laws and practices!

March 21 is also **International Day of Forests**, an opportunity to reflect on the woodlands that house 80% of our planet's biodiversity and over 60,000 species of trees. Each year our world loses 10 million hectares of forest—the equivalent of Iceland—contributing to a 12-20% increase in the greenhouse gas emissions that accelerate climate change. Plant a tree and help to raise awareness of these issues!

On **March 22**, we remember the passing of **Clemente Domínguez y Gómez** (1946-2005), one of the more bizarre stories in the Independent Catholic! Domínguez y Gómez was a blind Palmarian bishop (consecrated by Roman Catholic archbishop Pierre Martin Ngô Đình Thục) who claimed to enjoy apparitions and the stigmata, and who proclaimed himself the successor of Pope Paul VI, took the name Pope Gregory XVII, and reigned for only 11 days less than his "rival," Pope John Paul II. He admitted sexual improprieties with several priests and nuns, and was satirized in the Spanish film "*Manuel y Clemente.*" In his memory, pray for all whose eccentricities and questionable words and actions cast long shadows over the Independent Catholic Movement!

On **March 22**, we celebrate the birth in 1930 of **Joseph Bracken**, the American Jesuit philosopher and theologian who has attempted to synthesize Christian trinitarian doctrine with the process theology of

Alfred North Whitehead and Charles Hartshorne. In his honor, reacquaint yourself with Bracken's works and/or with the works of process theology!

March 22 is the first day of **Ramadan**, the month-long Islamic holiday of fasting from sunrise to sunset. We pray for our Muslim spiritual siblings!

March 22 is **World Water Day**, an annual reminder that 2.2 billion people live without access to safe drinking water. Consider how you might better raise awareness of this issue and take action to tackle our global water crisis!

On **March 23**, the Church celebrates **St. Turibius of Mogrovejo** (1538-1606), the Spanish nobleman who traveled all of Peru as bishop there. He is most known for baptizing St. Rose of Lima (the first saint of the Americas) and St. Martin de Porres, and for his defense of the native peoples against the injustices of the Spanish government. In his honor, commit to doing a better job of visiting those entrusted to your spiritual care, and consider how you might better advocate for those who suffer injustice in our world!

On **March 23**, we remember the passing of **Henry Nutcombe Oxenham** (1829-1888), the English Anglican priest who converted to the Roman church, traveled to Germany, and began a friendship with Döllinger, whose work he translated to English. He also translated Hefele's *History of the Councils of the Church*, and he published several pamphlets on the reunion of Christian churches. In his memory, pray in a special way for all who support us in our ministry and in our efforts to bring unity to the Body of Christ!

On **March 24**, the Church celebrates **St. Óscar Arnulfo Romero y Galdámez** (1917-1980), the archbishop of San Salvador who spoke out against poverty and violence during the civil war in El Salvador. Hailed as a hero by social activists and liberation theologians, Romero actively denounced violations of human rights, particularly against the most vulnerable. As a result, the United Nations has proclaimed March 24 as International Day for the Right to the Truth Concerning Gross Human Rights Violations and for the Dignity of Victims. In Romero's memory, pause to consider how you are defending human rights and promoting the dignity of those who suffer violence!

On **March 24**, we celebrate the birth in 1936 of **David Suzuki**, the Canadian academic and longtime environmental activist who advocates for clean energy and the reversal of climate change. In his honor, consider ways in which you might lessen your impact on Mother Earth!

On **March 24**, we celebrate the birth in 1939 of **Wiktor Wysoczański**, the bishop of the Polish Old Catholic Church since 1995. A co-editor of the *International Church Journal*, he has served as rector of the Christian Theological Academy in Warsaw for nearly 20 years. In his honor, pray for him and for all our sisters and brothers of the Polish Old Catholic Church!

On **March 24**, we celebrate the founding in 2005 of the **Orthodox-Catholic Church of America**, currently led by Bishop Lynn "Elizabeth" Walker. Happy anniversary!

On **March 25**, the Church celebrates the **Annunciation**—the archangel Gabriel's appearance to Mary of Nazareth with the incredible news that she would conceive and bear God's Son!

- If you want to place **an image of the Annunciation** in your worship space, search for one that portrays Mary as something other than a literate, Italian noblewoman. Decorate the image with **candles and lilies** or other white flowers.
- Invite an art historian to talk about the **iconography of Mary**.
- Find time to pray the Joyful Mysteries of the Rosary—or at least **the first Joyful Mystery**.
- Wear white, and the *Gloria* can be sung today.
- **For the intellectually-curious**, explain the timing of this solemnity (exactly nine months before the celebration of Jesus' birth), and the different annunciation stories in Matthew and Luke.
- Many **women's religious communities** celebrate this day with great festivity: Take a moment to pray a rosary for the religious sisters who have touched your life, and consider gathering together those who might be open to discerning their own vocation to religious life and/or ordained ministry in the Church!

On **March 25**, we remember the passing of **Andreas Rinkel** (1889-1979), the Dutch priest and seminary professor who served as nineteenth archbishop of Utrecht for over 30 years. He was part of the Old Catholic commission that worked toward reconciliation with the Anglican Church. In his memory, pray for all who work for reconciliation in our church and in our world!

On **March 25**, we remember the passing of **Marcel Lefebvre** (1905-1991), the Roman Catholic bishop who was a leading conservative voice at Vatican II. Lefebvre founded the Society of Saint Pius X for seminarians, then consecrated four bishops in 1988 against the expressed prohibition of Pope John Paul II, who excommunicated him and the four bishops he had consecrated. In his memory, pray for persons of all theological stripes who seek to live their Catholic faith outside the structures and strictures of Rome!

On **March 25**, we remember the passing of **Theodore "Ted" Jennings** (1942-2020), the American Methodist minister and Chicago Theological Seminary professor who wrote *The Man Jesus Loved* and other landmark books affirming queer people in the Bible. In his memory, consider how you confront homophobia in the Church!

On **March 25**, we celebrate the birth in 1934 of **Gloria Steinem**, the American activist and feminist leader who co-founded *Ms.* magazine and wrote several articles on women's rights. In her honor, pray for her and for all who continue to fight for women's rights!

On **March 25**, the Maronite Catholic Church (in union with Rome) celebrates the anniversary of the installation in 2011 of **Bechara Boutros al-Rahi** as Cardinal Patriarch of Antioch. In a spirit of ecumenism, pray for him and for the 3.5 million Maronite Catholics he serves!

On **March 25**, the Roman Catholic Church celebrates the anniversary of the installation in 2012 of **Francesco Moraglia** as Latin Patriarch of Venice. In a spirit of ecumenism, pray for him and for the Roman Catholics he serves!

March 25 is **International Day of Remembrance of the Victims of Slaver and of the Transatlantic Slave Trade**, an opportunity to honor those who suffered and died as a result of brutal slavery. Consider our global imperative to end slavery's legacy of racism!

March 25 is also **World Solidarity Day for Detained and Missing Workers**, a day to protect world peacekeepers who risk their lives as instruments of peace in our world. Pray for and raise awareness of those who are attacked and abducted!

On **March 25**, we celebrate **Earth Hour**, an opportunity at 8:30 p.m. (your local time) to turn off your house lights and draw attention to nature loss and the climate crisis. For resources to mark this day, visit earthhour.org.

Sunday, March 26, 2023
FIFTH SUNDAY OF LENT
(purple)

Remember: The *Gloria* and Alleluia are *not* sung today. Lead the congregation in another, easy-to-sing gospel acclamation!

You'll need to **choose which gospel you'll proclaim today**: the shorter form, or the longer form, which adds 18 verses that you could just as easily summarize in your homily!

The thread in today's scriptures: Ezekiel's prophecy of opened graves (Ez. 37:12) is realized with the raising of Lazarus (Jn. 11:1-45), which foreshadows the resurrection of the risen Christ! We trust that the "fullness of redemption" (Ps. 130:7) awaits us as well, and that, since "the Spirit of the one who raised Jesus from the dead dwells in [us], the one who raised Christ from the dead will give life to [our] mortal bodies also" (Rom. 8:11)!

Holy humor: The Sunday school teacher asked her students if they knew any of Jesus' miracles. Terry raised her hand: "Yes," she said. "Jesus raised Lazarus from the dead!" The teacher encouraged her: "And what can you tell us about that miracle?" Terry's eyes widened, as she said, "Jesus said, 'Lazarus, come out!' And it's a good thing that Jesus said his name, 'Lazarus,' because otherwise it would have been like a zombie apocalypse, with all the dead people stampeding out of that tomb!" [Segue to the images of zombies that listeners see in countless movies and television series, then to Ezekiel's prophecy of God's ability to raise an entire stampede of dead people. Because of God's life-giving power, we live with the hope that God "will give life to [our] mortal bodies also" (Rom. 8:11)!

Looking for a visual aid for your homily or object lesson? Consider a plastic skull! The skull is a symbol of death, and all four gospels state that Jesus was crucified at the "place of the skull" (Mt. 27:33, Mk. 15:22, Lk. 23:33, Jn. 19:17). Physical death awaits all our mortal bodies—but today's scriptures suggest that death is not the end of the story: The resurrections of Lazarus and of the risen Christ give us the hope that "the one who raised Christ from the dead will give life to [our] mortal bodies also" (Rom. 8:11)!

If you have Elect (a.k.a., catechumens who have celebrated the Rite of Election and are preparing to receive sacraments at the Easter Vigil), celebrate the **Third (and final) Scrutiny** during Mass today!

Have you hosted a **Lenten reconciliation service** already? If not, consider a communal celebration of the sacrament today!

On **March 26**, we remember the passing of **Eduard Herzog** (1841-1924), the Swiss priest and theologian who became the first Old Catholic bishop in Switzerland. After the First Vatican Council, he expressed his opposition to purported papal infallibility at the Old Catholic Congress of 1872 and began serving as an Old Catholic priest and professor. He was consecrated by Joseph Reinkens of the German Old Catholic Church and was subsequently excommunicated by Pius IX. In his memory, pray for all who have the courage to step outside the institutions they love, in order to faithfully follow the promptings of the Spirit!

On **March 26**, we remember the passing on Palm Sunday in 1961 of **Carlos Duarte Costa** (1888-1961), the Roman Catholic bishop who shared valid lines of apostolic succession without the permission of the Roman papacracy. Known by many as St. Carlos of Brazil, a patron saint of Independent Catholicism, he was a vocal critic of the Brazilian government's mistreatment of the poor, of papal encyclicals, and of clergy and popes with loyalties to Nazi and Fascist regimes. Honor his memory by considering how courageous you are in denouncing mistruths and mistreatment!

On **March 26**, we remember the passing of **Joseph Blenkinsopp** (1927-2022), the Old Testament scholar who wrote widely on the Pentateuch, the prophets, and Ezra-Nehemiah. In his memory, explore more deeply the prophetic tradition of the Hebrew scriptures!

On **March 27**, we remember the passing of **Friedrich zu Schwarzenberg** (1809-1885), the Austrian prince who became archbishop of Salzburg at age 26 and a cardinal at age 33. He was sympathetic to the adversities suffered by Reformers and their families as a result of being expelled from the empire. He zealously defended his teacher, Anton Günther, repeatedly appealing to Rome to prevent the condemnation of Günther's writings. In his memory, pray for all our friends and advocates in other churches—including the Roman Church—who courageously speak up for and defend us!

On **March 27**, we remember the passing of **Adrienne Rich** (1929-2012), the American feminist and essayist regarded as one of the most widely-read poets of the second half of the 20th century. Credited with bringing the oppression of women to the forefront of poetic discourse, she coined the "lesbian continuum" for the female continuum of solidarity and creativity that impacts and fills women's lives. In her memory, discover her life and works!

On **March 27**, the Ukrainian Greek Catholic Church (in union with Rome) celebrates the anniversary of the installation in 2011 of **Sviatoslav Shevchuk** as Patriarch of Kyiv-Galicia. In a spirit of ecumenism, pray for him and for the 4.5 million Ukrainian Greek Catholics he serves!

On **March 28**, we remember the passing of **Ladislao Bonus** (1854-1908), a prominent Independent Catholic and member of the Philippine Independent Church known as the "Father of Filipino Opera." A composer, conductor and contrabass player, he directed the Arevalo Band, which served the revolutionary government in Malalos. In his memory, consider how you bring music and joy to the lives of others!

On **March 29**, we celebrate the birth in 1957 of **Kathryn Tanner**, the American theologian, professor at Yale Divinity School, and past president of the American Theological Society known for her systematic theology in *Christ the Key*. In her honor, reacquaint yourself with her works!

March 29 is **U.S. National Vietnam War Veterans Day**, an opportunity to celebrate the sacrifice and service of the three million Americans who served in Vietnam, many of whom are still living. Find a fitting way to honor those nearest you!

On **March 30**, we remember the passing of **Joachim of Fiore** (c. 1135-1202), the Italian theologian considered the most important apocalyptic medieval thinker. Inspiring an entire movement of "Joachimites," he prophesied the coming Age of the Holy Spirit—a new dispensation of love that would supersede the law. Though Joachim was held in high regard, all the ideas and movements around him were condemned. In his memory, consider how you contribute to the "Age of the Holy Spirit"!

On **March 30**, we remember the passing of **Karl Rahner** (1904-1984), the renowned 20th-century Jesuit philosopher and theologian. Perhaps the greatest voice on the post-conciliar understanding of the Catholic faith, Rahner was a prolific writer of voluminous—and often difficult-to-understand—works. In his memory, pull one of his works off the shelf and wrestle with a paragraph or two of his profound thought!

On **March 30**, we celebrate the birth in 1934 of **Charles E. Curran**, the Roman Catholic priest and moral theologian known for his dissenting views on contraception, his co-authoring of a response to *Humanae Vitae*, and his suggestion in 1971 that homosexual acts within committed relationships may not be morally evil. In 1986, he was removed from his faculty position at The Catholic University of America for his dissent of the Roman church's moral teaching. His views on divorce, artificial contraception, masturbation, pre-marital sex, and homosexual acts were later condemned by Joseph Ratzinger. In his honor, pray for all moral theologians and persons of faith who, while respecting the teaching office of the Church, find themselves led by the Spirt to disagree with the sometimes-myopic moral views of others!

On **March 31**, the Church celebrates **St. Balbina of Rome** (+c. 130), the Roman woman who converted to Christianity and was martyred for her faith. Her actions led to the building of St. Peter in Chains in Rome, and she is one of the 140 colonnade saints at St. Peter Basilica in Vatican City. In her memory, pray for all those who stand firm amid persecution!

On **March 31**, we remember the passing of **Francisco de Osuna** (c. 1492 – c. 1540), the Spanish Franciscan friar who authored some of the most influential spiritual works of 16th-century Spain. His *Third Spiritual Alphabet* shared an ABCs for the spiritual life. Consider how you are making our faith more accessible to persons of all levels of education!

On **March 31**, we celebrate **César Chávez** (1927-1993), the labor leader and civil rights advocate who co-founded the National Farm Workers Association. Combining leftist politics with Catholic social teachings, he organized non-violent picket and boycotts, and manifested his Catholicism in public processions, masses and fasts. An icon for organized labor, he quickly became a folk saint of Mexican Americans. In his memory, reflect on his social justice message!

On **March 31**, we remember the passing of **John Norman Davidson Kelly** (1909-1997), the British Anglican priest who specialized in biblical studies, patristics, and early Christian creeds and doctrines. For years, his *Early Christian Creeds* and *Early Christian Doctrines* were standard seminary textbooks. In his memory, thumb through his works and reacquaint yourself with the beliefs of the early Church!

On **March 31**, the Syriac Orthodox Church celebrates the anniversary of the election in 2014 of Sa'id Karim as **Patriarch Ignatius Aphrem II of Antioch and All the East**. In a spirit of ecumenism, pray for him and for the people he serves!

On **April 1**, the Church celebrates **St. Theodora** (+120), the Roman woman who assisted her brother, St. Hermes, during his imprisonment and was later executed for her faith. She is one of the 140 colonnade saints at St. Peter Basilica in Vatican City. In her memory, pray for all who minister to the imprisoned!

On **April 1**, the Church celebrates **St. Mary of Egypt** (c. 344 - c. 421), the Egyptian woman who repented of sexual impurities after an encounter with a statue of Mary at a church in Jerusalem. She is one of the 140 colonnade saints at St. Peter Basilica in Vatican City. In her memory, pray for all those struggling with sin!

On **April 1**, we remember the passing of **Władysław Marcin Faron** (1891-1965), the Roman Catholic priest and army chaplain who served as a bishop of the Polish National Catholic Church for three years before founding and leading for 17 years the Polish National Catholic Apostolic Church (which he branded as the Polish Old Catholic Church). As a Roman priest, he publicized moral scandals of the Roman Church, and the ensuing riots led to military intervention and his house arrest. As a PNCC bishop, he attempted to separate his diocese from the church in the U.S., a move that later hampered his attempts to create a union of Old Catholic churches in Poland. Frustrated, he returned to the Roman Church within 20 years, where he served as a priest for another 15 years. In his memory, pray for all who struggle to find their spiritual home!

Sunday, April 2, 2023
PALM SUNDAY
(red)

"Get your palms!" **Let people know when your Palm Sunday masses are** — and they'll show up!

Decorate your worship space!
- Decorate with **plentiful palm plants and fronds**, using them to draw attention to the altar and ambo.
- Use **red ribbon** to attach large fronds to the processional cross.
- Consider a **long red runner** hanging down over the sides of an otherwise bare altar.
- Be sure all **red vestments** are ironed or steamed — and that they match any other shades of red used in the worship space. If you'll use a **cope** for the procession, be sure to steam it as well!
- **Continue the decoration** into the entrance to your worship space, outdoors, and into other spaces on the grounds, including your Blessed Sacrament chapel, parish hall, and classrooms. Pique the curiosity of congregants and passersby with outdoor touches of palms and red ribbon!

Be sure to familiarize yourself with the details of today's rite!
- Decide whether you'll have a **solemn or simple entrance**.

- Be sure your deacon is **prepared to proclaim both gospels** today.
- Have **a bowl of holy water and an aspergillum** on hand for the blessing of palms, and think through whether your worship space permits a procession with the palms. Consider swapping out your metal aspergillum (which likely shares very few drops of water with every swing) for a natural broom sprinkler adorned with red ribbons.
- If you'll have a procession, **prepare a song to accompany the ritual action**, and be sure those leading the procession (viz., your thurifer, cross bearer & candle bearers) know the route you'll use. Looking for a familiar tune? Repeat several times the line from the *Sanctus* you sing: "Blessed is he who comes in the name of the Lord! Hosanna in the highest!"
- If you'll use **incense**, be sure the thurible, charcoals, and boat of incense are prepared.
- If processing with several people and/or a long distance, **think through how you'll sustain the singing in unison throughout the procession**. To maintain singing, place gifted vocalists at the beginning, middle and end of the procession.
- If you'll be using a **cope** during the procession, prepare your altar servers to know when to take it from you, and when to hand you your chasuble.
- Let your altar servers know that **the passion will be proclaimed without incense or candles**.
- If the passion will be proclaimed by multiple people, be sure you have sufficient copies and that all ministers are prepared.

Have hospitality ministers share palms with congregants as they arrive. Instead of skimping, order plenty of extra palms and encourage congregants to take an extra palm to share with a homebound family member, friend or neighbor. Be sure, though, to **divide your supply of palms across all your masses**, so that the last Mass won't be left without sufficient palms!

Remember: The *Gloria* and Alleluia are *not* sung today. Lead the congregation in another, easy-to-sing gospel acclamation.

Be sure the person who proclaims (or begins) **the passion** knows that there is no greeting ("The Lord be with you") before the passion, nor is the Book of the Gospels signed before proclaiming the passion. Consider dividing the proclamation of the passion among various voices, but know that only a deacon asks for the blessing of the presider before proclaiming the gospel. Or, even better, have various cantors chant the passion this year, to highlight the solemnity of this day!

During the proclamation of the passion, remember to **kneel for a prolonged period of silence after Jesus' death**. Remember: True silence begins when all shuffling, rustling and other noises end. Find a way to say this without words (e.g., in your Mass program and/or PowerPoint), so that all will know to kneel in silence to reflect on Jesus' death.

The thread in today's scriptures: The "roller coaster" of Holy Week has begun: Today's first gospel (Mt. 21:1-11) begins on an extremely high note, with the people of Jerusalem acclaiming Jesus as king. By the end of today's second gospel (Mt. 26:14 – 27:66), the same people have called for his crucifixion, and he has been executed. We'll again hear the story of his passion and death on Good Friday, but we know his descent to the dead is not the end of the story – and, at the Easter Vigil, we'll celebrate his rising to new life! We all pass through dark valleys, when we feel the buffets and beatings of life (Is. 50:6), perhaps when we even feel abandoned by God (Ps. 22:1). Paul's words (Phil. 2:6-11) gives us the hope that we, too, might one day be exalted with Christ!

Holy humor: We just heard the proclamation of Jesus' death on the cross, so skip any attempts at humor. Today's solemn celebration marks the beginning of Holy Week. Perhaps it's best to try another "hook" to grab listeners' attention today? It could be as simple as a show of hands: How many of us have ever ridden a roller coaster? How many of us love roller coasters? How many of us would never ride a roller coaster, even if we were paid to? Segue into the "roller coaster" of Holy Week, which has already left the station!

Looking for a visual aid for your homily or object lesson? Consider drawing a big circle in the air and/or appealing to the palms with which we began this liturgy! Saint Bonaventure was fond of the image of the circle: Christ started in heaven (start with your hand above your head), then came down to earth (begin drawing the circle counter-clockwise, so that it's clockwise from the vantage of your listeners, until you reach the bottommost point of the circle), and was exalted to the heavens again (complete the circle)! The palms we hold today remind us of the same polarities: They were waved to proclaim victory, and they are burned to make the ashes that recall our own deaths. Christians know that death does not have the final word – and that what goes down…must go up!

Know that many families who leave after Mass today will not return until next Sunday: **Encourage them to be part of your *Triduum* celebrations!** Be sure that everyone leaves Mass today knowing your *Triduum* schedule. Consider printing flyers or postcards for those who might be willing to help spread word of your Triduum services this week. As we enter Holy Week, encourage congregants to re-read the passion narrative later today or sometime this week.

In some places, Palm Sunday is known as **Carling Sunday**, named for carling peas. In other places, it's known as **Fig Sunday**, due to the tradition that Jesus ate figs after his entry into Jerusalem. If you're looking for appropriate dishes to share after Mass, consider split pea soup, peas porridge and/or figs!

Holy Week is the traditional time for the annual **Chrism Mass**.

- If your bishop is joining you for the Triduum, consider when you'll celebrate the Chrism Mass as a community. Know that **Tuesday is a common day** for this celebration.
- **Spread word of the celebration**, so that all can join you in this **celebration of the priesthood**—complete with the blessing of the oils that we'll use during the next year!
- Be sure to incorporate **the burning of this year's holy oils** as part of your parish mission or a Lenten night of prayer: Simply pour the oils into a flame-resistant receptacle and add a wick!

On **April 2**, when it doesn't' fall on a Sunday, the Church celebrates **St. Theodosia of Tyre** (290-307), the Lebanese teen who was tortured and killed at age 17 for refusing to sacrifice to pagan gods. She is one of the 140 colonnade saints at St. Peter Basilica in Vatican City. In her memory, pray for perseverance during times of trial!

On **April 2**, the Church celebrates **St. Francis of Paola** (1416-1507), a hermit dedicated to solitude, asceticism and the contemplative life. Lift him up as a model of Lenten prayer!

On **April 2,** we remember the passing of **Cuthbert Butler** (1858-1934), the Irish Benedictine and ecclesiastical historian who wrote on mysticism and monasticism, contributed dozens of articles to the 1911 *Encyclopedia Britannica*, and who provided an insider's view of the First Vatican Council through his publication of the correspondence of Bishop William Ullathorne. In his memory, acquaint yourself with one of his works!

On **April 2**, we remember the passing of **Brocard Sewell** (1912-2000), the British Carmelite friar who publicly opposed the Roman Catholic Church's prohibition of contraception in the 1960s and called for Paul VI's resignation as pope. A member of PAX, he opposed nuclear weapons and often found himself "at odds with a red hat." Removed from his priory, he lectured for several years in Canada, where he authored several works. In his memory, reflect on the ways in which your life has not turned out as expected but has nonetheless reflected God's grace to the world!

On **April 2**, we remember the passing of **Robert Harold Schuller** (1926-2015), the American Christian televangelist, motivational speaker and author who shared his weekly, televised "Hour of Power" from the Crystal Cathedral in Garden Grove, California. Schuller focused on the positive aspects of our Christian faith and deliberately avoided condemning people for sin, saying that Jesus "met needs before touting creeds." In his memory, consider how positive and non-judgmental your words, actions and ministry are!

On **April 2**, we celebrate the birth in 1958 of Bishop **Doreen C. Noble**, presiding bishop of the Reformed Catholic Church International. Pray for her and for the people she serves!

On **April 3**, we remember the passing of **Cornelius van Steenoven** (1661-1725), who served as the seventh archbishop of Utrecht. Consecrated by Roman Catholic bishop Dominique-Marie Varlet, he filled a bishopric left vacant for 20 years—only to die less than six months later. He wrote a manifesto explaining the principles upon which he and his clergy had acted, appealing for judgment by a future general council of the Church. In his memory, consider how you serve others despite the condemnation of others!

On **April 3**, we remember the passing of **Graham Greene** (1904-1991), the Nobel Prize-winning novelist who explored ambivalent moral and political issues through a Catholic perspective. He is best known for *The Power and the Glory*, which told the story of a renegade "whisky priest" during the government suppression of the Catholic faith in Mexico. In his memory, pray for the "whisky priests" of our world, who, like Greene's protagonist, teach high standards while manifesting signs of weakness!

On **April 3**, we celebrate the birth in 1950 of Bishop **Alan Kemp**, Chief Executive Officer of the Ascension Alliance. Happy birthday!

On **April 4,** the Church celebrates **St. Isidore of Seville** (c. 560-636, not to be confused with St. Isidore the Farmer, who is celebrated on May 15). Isidore organized the church of Spain through his theology and the hosting of councils. Consider how conciliar or authoritarian you are, and allow today's saint to challenge you toward a spirit of greater conciliarity!

On **April 4**, we remember the passing of **François Aimé Pouget** (1666-1723), the French priest, doctor of theology and seminary rector who co-authored the popular, controversial and condemned *Montpellier Catechism*. After publishing 30 editions of the work over eight years, and nearly blind, he translated it into Latin. His defenders note that his condemnation was the result of politics, and his French catechism was adopted by the Diocese of St. Pierre, Martinique a century after his death. In his memory, pray for all who risk their health advancing the gospel message!

On **April 4**, the Greek Orthodox Church of Jerusalem (recognized by the Ecumenical Patriarch of Constantinople) celebrates the birth in 1952 of **Ilias Giannopoulos**, who became Patriarch Theophilus III of Jerusalem. In a spirit of ecumenism, pray for him and for the 500,000 Greek Orthodox Catholics he serves!

April 4 is **International Mine Awareness Day**, an annual opportunity to recall that mines and explosive remnants of war constitute a serious threat to the safety, health and lives of people throughout the world, impeding social and economic development. Pray for and raise awareness of those who long for a world free of remnants of war!

On **April 5**, the Church celebrates **St. Vincent Ferrer** (c. 1350-1419), the Dominican friar who forced Spanish Jews to convert to Catholicism. Pray today for all who mistakenly believe that God's salvation could be limited to their church alone, and for all throughout history whose fervor for "evangelization" was responsible for erasing indigenous cultures and centuries of rich religious traditions!

At sunset on **April 5**, **Passover** begins for our Jewish spiritual siblings, who share a seder meal to recall their liberation from slavery in Egypt. Pray for our 15 million Jewish sisters and brothers with whom we share common spiritual ancestors!

Thursday, April 6, 2023
HOLY THURSDAY
(white)

Remember: Unless you have a Chrism Mass, **no Mass is celebrated today until the evening celebration of the Lord's Supper**. Lent officially ends when your celebration of the Lord's Supper commences, and this evening's celebration is the beginning of a **three-day liturgy** — our *Triduum*: There is no blessing and dismissal tonight or tomorrow, and there is no introductory rite for Good Friday or the Easter Vigil. We begin the Mass of the Lord's Supper with the introductory rite — and the solemn blessing and dismissal will come at the conclusion of this three-day rite, at the Easter Vigil on Saturday night!

Be sure to have an experienced photographer capture memories of your Triduum services!

Our Easter *Triduum* begins: Be sure to think through the details of your **worship environment** as we transition to white today, then to red for tomorrow, then back to white for the Easter Vigil.

- Use **flowers** in moderation, reserving a full flowering of your worship space for the Easter Vigil.
- Prepare easily-visible **footwashing stations** for the *mandatum*, perhaps even throughout the church. Have on hand **enough pitchers of warm water, basins, towels and a mop**. If using paper towels instead of towels, have baskets or small trash receptacles into which used paper towels can be placed. Designate persons to quietly clean up after the footwashing ritual, with minimal distraction. Have a means for the presider to wash his/her hands after the rite of footwashing, preferably with warm water and soap.
- Create an **altar of repose** conducive to prayer and meditation, perhaps bringing to mind the Synoptic Jesus' prayer in the Garden of Gethsemane. If necessary, place a kneeler for the presider before the altar of repose; otherwise, leave the altar unobstructed. Be sure to have enough seats for those who might wish to spend time in prayer with the Blessed Sacrament.
- Think of possible accents (e.g., candles or *luminarias*) that might **illuminate the journey from your worship space, to the altar of repose**. Beforehand, fill the space with green plants, illuminated by candlelight, and turn off any overhead lights.
- Be sure the **cope** and **humeral veil** are ironed or steamed.

Will you incorporate your **reception of the holy oils** into this Mass? If so, consider the following:

- Will you incorporate this into the introductory rite, or as part of the presentation of gifts?
- Prepare an ambry table in the sanctuary to receive the holy oils.
- Have texts that speak to the symbolism of the oils, and of the function of each.
- To emphasize the symbolism of each oil, consider having a catechist or student carry the Oil of Catechumens, a medical professional carry the Oil of the Sick, and a member of the clergy or someone who has recently received (or will receive) the sacraments of initiation carry the Sacred Chrism!

Be sure to familiarize yourself with the rite of this special day! **Think through how you'll do the washing of feet**:

- Will seats be reserved for this, or will chairs need to be discretely placed and removed?
- Choose an easy-to-sing musical setting for this ritual action, perhaps a Taizé-style refrain or a song that can be sung antiphonally between the cantor and congregation.
- Consider addressing a few pastoral words to those who might find footwashing countercultural and/or awkward.
- If you'll be washing a large number of feet, think through details like the refilling of pitchers (with warm water), the emptying of water basins, and what to do with soiled towels (or paper towels).
- If you'll be removing your chasuble for this rite, let altar servers know if you'll need their assistance with your vestments.
- Will you wash the feet of others, or have a more-inclusive gesture of inviting them to wash one another's feet—something now forbidden by the Roman Church? If you alone will be washing the feet of others, choose a representative cross-section of women and men, young and wise, healthy and less-mobile, clergy and laity, persons of different language groups, etc. Consider going to them, rather than having them come to you! Be sure your actions are highly visible, so that people are not left wondering "What's happening?"

We're celebrating a solemnity: **Consider using incense!**

- Make sure your thurifer is familiar with all his/her responsibilities and is ready with the thurible (with burning charcoals) and boat: for the hymn of gathering, gospel acclamation, preparation of gifts and the procession to the altar of repose.

- Be sure those who are leading music know that the hymn of gathering and/or preparation of the altar and presentation of gifts may be prolonged due to incensation.
- Be sure your deacon knows how to incense the Book of the Gospels prior to proclaiming the gospel. Remember: If your thurible is on a chain, the closer you hold the chain to the thurible, the more control you'll have over the swinging thurible!
- Be sure to tip off your altar server(s) to the fact that the handwashing will occur *after* the incensation of the altar and gifts!

If you have a multilingual community, **think through how you'll make a single community celebration meaningful to persons of all languages!**

- Consider music that incorporates all languages.
- Divide the scriptures between languages, and, so that all can understand them, consider printing the scriptures in the language in which they're not being proclaimed.
- Have a multilingual psalm and proclamation of the gospel.
- Be sure the presider and homilist are able to easily transition between languages for prayers and preaching, without sharing a homily that's repeated in two languages.
- Share a multilingual invitation to share the sign of peace.
- Invite people to pray the Lord's Prayer in their own languages.
- Rather than guess the language of those coming to communion, train eucharistic ministers to alternate between "The Body of Christ" (or "The Blood of Christ") and its equivalent in the other language(s).

Think through the details of your **procession to the altar of repose**.

- Will you need assistance putting on the cope?
- Will the altar be stripped while you hold the consecrated elements?
- Will incense be used?
- Does the person leading the procession know the route?
- What will you sing during the procession? Is the song easy to sing while walking in the dark? (Remember: *Pange lingua* is the traditional hymn for this in many places, but many people don't know Latin and/or don't know the lyrics well enough to sing them in the dark.) Consider a Taizé-style refrain, or, if you have a Spanish-speaking community, the refrain of "*Bendito, bendito, bendito sea Dios.*"

- To maintain the song, place gifted vocalists at the beginning, middle and end of the procession.
- Beforehand, invite people to stay as long as they wish, to pray before the altar of repose.

Be sure to prepare all ministers, so that they know their role and responsibilities for this special celebration. For the smoothest-possible liturgical experience, consider having a rehearsal!

Have the traditional **ringing of bells** during the *Gloria* — with someone ringing the church bell and/or with altar servers and congregants ringing bells. (Remember to never allow anyone to ring a bell who hasn't practiced in advance: The liturgy is never an appropriate time to practice ringing a bell!) If you have an organ, use it for the *Gloria*. Remember: After the ringing of the bells at the *Gloria* tonight, all bells will remain silent until the *Gloria* at the Easter Vigil.

Inform musicians that, after the singing of the *Gloria*, **the music becomes increasingly solemn this evening**, with musical instruments used after the *Gloria* only to support the singing.

Remember: The Alleluia is *not* sung today. Lead the congregation in another, easy-to-sing gospel acclamation!

The thread in today's scriptures: The Jewish celebration of Passover (Ex. 12:1-8 & 11-14) was an important part of Jesus' faith tradition: God led God's people to life and liberty! Indeed, how can we make a return to the Lord for all the good God has done for us (Ps. 116:12)? As Johannine Jesus prepared to celebrate the Passover with his friends, with the traditional bread and wine (1Cor. 11:23-26), he shared with them — and with us — a lesson on servant leadership (Jn. 13:1-15)!

Holy humor: A lot of work goes into planning the liturgies — the services — of Holy Week, so have you heard this one before: What's the difference between a liturgist — a person who plans Masses like this — and a terrorist? If you've been to a seminary — a place where lots of people are planning lots of masses — you know the answer. What's the difference between a liturgist and a terrorist? You can negotiate with a…terrorist! (Segue into the Johannine Peter's firm-as-a-liturgist attitude against having his feet washed, and the Johannine Jesus' line-in-the-sand statement that servant leadership is a necessary part of discipleship. "Unless I wash your feet, you will have no part with me" (Jn. 13:8) is a clear non-negotiable!)

Looking for a visual aid for your homily or object lesson? Consider an image of the Last Supper and/or a pitcher and basin! Paul provides a snapshot for the foundation of traditional images of the Last Supper — but, interestingly, John provides us a whole different picture: of Jesus stooping down to wash the dirty feet of his friends! We call ourselves followers of Jesus: How often do we humble ourselves and find ways to figuratively "wash one another's feet" (Jn. 13:14-15)?

Will you have a **collection** during this special liturgy? Let your hospitality ministers know!

Many presiders fall into a rut of always using the same eucharistic prayer: **Use a different, perhaps-lengthier eucharistic prayer today**, to bring attention to the Lord's Supper!

If the Blessed Sacrament is brought from the tabernacle before communion, have a minister **leave the tabernacle door open and extinguish the vigil light there**, so that it will be clear that **the tabernacle will remain empty** until the Blessed Sacrament is returned there at the conclusion of the Easter Vigil.

Post-Vatican II communities share the Eucharist under the forms of bread and wine. If your community doesn't ordinarily **share communion under both forms**, consider doing so tonight!

Be prepared for **the many details of the procession to the altar of repose**:

- Have all eucharistic ministers bring any remaining bread and wine to the altar after communion.
- After communion, add incense to the thurible, kneel before the Blessed Sacrament, and incense it three times.
- Put on the humeral veil and take the Blessed Sacrament.
- Remember: Tonight's procession is led by the cross bearer and candle bearers, followed by the assembly, then followed by the thurifer and presider.
- Conduct the procession to the altar of repose with reverence and noble simplicity.
- Be sure that those who lead the procession walk slowly enough that congregants stay together!
- Place the Blessed Sacrament on the altar of repose, or, if it is placed in a tabernacle, leave the door open until after the Blessed Sacrament is incensed there.
- Be sure the thurifer is ready to assist with the incensing of the Blessed Sacrament at the altar of repose.
- Let all ministers know that all (who are able) will kneel before the Blessed Sacrament, and that ministers will *not* leave the space in procession; instead, all ministers will stand, genuflect, and depart,

with no formal procession — a functional leaving of ministers, rather than a ritual departure.

- Invite congregants beforehand to remain in prayer before the Blessed Sacrament as long as they'd like.
- Be sure that those who decorate your worship space aren't immediately rushing off after this service to change the décor for Good Friday — particularly if these actions will be seen or heard by those praying at the altar of repose!

Some churches have a traditional distribution of loaves on this night: Visit your local baker and ask him/her to individually package small loaves for you, to which you can add a prayer for the breaking of bread as family!

On **April 6**, when it doesn't fall on Holy Thursday, the Church celebrates **St. Galla of Rome** (+550), the Roman widow who founded a hospital and convent. One of the 140 colonnade saints at St. Peter Basilica in Vatican City, she avoided remarriage by purportedly growing a legendary beard. She begged St. Peter to allow her to accompany her lover, Benedicta, to heaven. In her memory, pray for all who follow in the footsteps of a matron saint of those who dare to be different!

On **April 6**, we remember the passing of **John Dobree Dalgairns** (1818-1876), the English Catholic convert and friend of John Henry Newman who translated Aquinas, wrote on Cistercian saints and German mystics, and included a history of Jansenism in his *Devotion to the Sacred Heart of Jesus*. In his memory, consider your own contributions to theology and/or to the sharing of the stories of the saints whom you've known!

On **April 6**, we remember the passing of **Wilma Mankiller** (1945-2010), the American Cherokee activist who was the first woman elected chief of the Cherokee Nation. In her memory, pray for all our Native American sisters and brothers!

On **April 6**, we remember the passing of **Hans Küng** (1928-2021), the Swiss Catholic priest, theologian and author known for his rejection of purported papal infallibility. Despite not being officially allowed to share Roman Catholic theology, Küng continues to teach ecumenical theology at the University of Tübingen. In his honor, pray for all who are persecuted for following their Spirit-enlightened consciences!

Friday, April 7, 2023
GOOD FRIDAY
(red, without chasuble/dalmatic)

Good Friday is a somber day:

- We meditate on Jesus' death and entombment. The environment and lack of instrumental music should reflect this.

- Abstain from ringing bells today.

- The only sacraments that can be celebrated today are Reconciliation and Anointing of the Sick. Communion is celebrated only as viaticum (for those near or in danger of death).

- For those looking for ideas on how to pray on this day, suggest the Stations of the Cross and/or the Sorrowful Mysteries of the rosary.

- Noon is traditionally marked as the hour of Jesus' crucifixion (though Mark places it at 9:00 a.m.), and 3:00 p.m. as the hour of his death: Know that any services at these hours may be sparsely attended by those who work during the day. Some churches have a *Tre Ore* (three hours) service and/or time of prayer during this time.

Think through **the details of today's worship environment**:

- **Today's color is red, except for the veiling of the cross, which is violet**. Remember, though, that color is used today to highlight, not to decorate.

- **Remove all images and crosses** from your worship space. **Cover with red cloth those images and crosses that can't be removed**.

- **Take away all plants and candles**.

- **Strip the altar**. (Remember: There are no crosses, candles, bookstands, images or accoutrements on post-Vatican II altars; on this day, in particular, there should be nothing—*nothing*—on the altar.)

- **Empty fonts of holy water**, and consider filling them with sand instead. In this way, people aren't left wondering, "Did someone forget to fill the holy water fonts?"

- There is no need to decorate anything today—but do **cover with a violet cloth the cross that will be used for the adoration of the cross**. Be sure the cross is without a *corpus* (Jesus' body). Let the symbol speak: Find a large cross for this rite, perhaps even inviting an artist in your community to craft this. Before the liturgy, place the cross in a spot where the person carrying it will know where to find it. Have a plan for the cross after the adoration: Ideally, find a way for it to remain upright in the sanctuary.

- No Mass is celebrated today, so **the credence table is not prepared as usual**. Know, though, whether the corporal (and/or any other items) will be brought to the stripped altar during the rite, and by whom.

This is the one day each year in which **no mass is celebrated anywhere in the world**. Because the chasuble and dalmatic are worn only for the celebration of Mass, be sure to **vest only with alb and stole**—and perhaps with a cope for the presider.

Think through music for this commemoration of the Lord's suffering and death. **Totally abstain today from musical instruments**, and have *a capella* music; or, if necessary, soft accompaniment simply to sustain singing. Also, **prepare a song for the adoration of the cross**!

If the passion will be proclaimed by multiple people, be sure all ministers are prepared and that you have sufficient copies of the passion for them. There are no candles or incense during today's gospel, nor does the deacon greet people before the proclamation or sign the Book of the Gospels. Consider highlighting the solemnity of this day by chanting the passion.

Good Friday (like Ash Wednesday) is one of two days of **fasting *and* abstinence** in the Western Church: Invite congregants to participate in this ancient ritual as a way of preparing for the celebration of Christ's resurrection!

If you have a multilingual community, **think through how you'll make a single community celebration meaningful to persons of all languages!**

- Consider music that incorporates all languages.
- Divide the scriptures between languages, and, so that all can understand them, and consider printing the scriptures in the language in which they're not being proclaimed.
- Have a multilingual psalm and proclamation of the gospel.
- Be sure the presider and homilist are able to easily transition between languages for prayers and preaching, without sharing a homily that's repeated in two languages.
- Share a multilingual invitation to share the sign of peace.
- Invite people to pray the Lord's Prayer in their own languages.

- Rather than guess the language of those coming to communion, train eucharistic ministers to alternate between "The Body of Christ" (or "The Blood of Christ") and its equivalent(s) in the other language(s).

Be sure to prepare all ministers, so that they know their role and responsibilities for this special celebration. For the smoothest-possible liturgical experience, consider having a rehearsal!

The liturgy begins in the silence, with the ministers coming to the sanctuary and lying prostrate before the altar.

- The cross, candles and Book of the Gospels are not part of this procession.
- Think through whether all ministers are able to lie prostrate, or whether accommodations need to be made.
- Ideally, all congregants kneel during this action; think through a way of communicating this without speaking it—perhaps with a note in your Mass program and/or PowerPoint.
- While lying prostrate, the presider should allow for a prolonged period of true silence, which begins when all shuffling, rustling, and other noises end.

Remember: The liturgy continues with the collect (opening prayer), but without the customary "Let us pray." (This is a continuation of the liturgy that began last night, so the sign of the cross and greeting are omitted.)

The Alleluia is *not* sung today. Lead the congregation in another, easy-to-sing Gospel Acclamation!

During the proclamation of the passion, remember to **kneel for a prolonged period of silence after Jesus' death**. Remember: True silence begins when all shuffling, rustling and other noises end. Find a way to communicate this without words (e.g., in your Mass program and/or PowerPoint), so that all will know to kneel in silence to reflect on Jesus' death.

The thread in today's scriptures: Deutero-Isaiah says it well: "Who would believe what we have heard?" (Is. 53:1). Like the Lord's servant (Is. 52:13—53:12), Jesus suffered and was led to the slaughter (Jn. 18:1—19:42). We believe that "he suffered, and, when he was made perfect, he became the source of eternal salvation for all" (Heb. 5:9), and so we trust in God, saying with the Johannine Jesus: "Father, into your hands I commend my spirit" (Ps. 31:5).

Looking for a visual aid for your homily or object lesson? Consider foregoing any type of object lesson today. Today's environment is stark. Today's liturgy is somber. Keep your words brief. Let silence speak.

Today is an especially appropriate day for **periods of silence** during the liturgy. Consider a moment of prolonged silence after your homily.

Think through **how you'll bring the cross into your worship space**:

- Will the deacon retrieve it alone or be accompanied by altar servers with candles?
- Be sure the person who holds it has practiced the chant "Behold the wood."
- Instruct him/her to pause three times: inside the entrance to the church, in the middle of the church, and at the entrance to the sanctuary.

Think through **how you'll perform the adoration of the cross**:

- What will you sing, and will congregants know how to respond?
- Who will lead the adoration of the cross, and who will invite congregants to participate in this action?
- Will hospitality ministers assist the flow of people?
- Remember: We venerate the cross on this day. Encourage people to do so by genuflecting, bowing and/or kissing the cross. (Be sure to explain in simple language that "genuflecting" means touching the floor with the right knee.)
- Try something new this year: If you're wearing sandals, slip them off before you approach the cross and/or invite all to remove their shoes (a ritual gesture common in many world religions), to symbolize the holiness of the act and the "holy ground" now marked by the cross.
- In many places, there is a custom of wiping the cross with a purificator at the place at which a person kisses it. Will this be done? If so, by whom? If you fear the spread of contagion, consider using a disinfectant wipe instead of smearing germs with a purificator.
- After the adoration, is there a way to stand the cross upright in the sanctuary, perhaps flanked by the candles that accompanied it in procession?
- Know how you'll share the **solemn intercessions** on this day.
- Will you use the traditional rite, shared between the deacon and presider, with periods of silence and alternating times of kneeling and standing—or will you avoid the up-and-down movement by

inviting congregants to kneel for a prolonged time of silent prayer only once during the entire rite?

- Be sure that all assisting with this (e.g., your deacon) know how these prayers will be shared and any instructions that need to be shared with the congregation (which is part of the role of the deacon).

Will you have a **collection** during this special liturgy? Let your hospitality ministers know! It's Good Friday; you might do well to abstain from a collection today. The Roman church has the custom of taking up a collection on this day for the Holy Land; if you have a collection, consider having it for such a need, outside the operating expenses of your community.

Think through the **Rite of Communion** today:

- Plan how the Blessed Sacrament will come from the altar of repose to your worship space at the appropriate time. This might best be performed by your deacon, with a humeral veil. Ideally, have an altar server or two accompany the Blessed Sacrament with candles.
- After communion, return the Blessed Sacrament to the altar of repose without procession, then be sure to consume the consecrated bread and wine after the service, so that none is left.
- Extinguish the candle at the tabernacle, and leave the tabernacle door open, so that no one will think that the Blessed Sacrament is inside.
- Think through **the details for concluding today's rite**:
- Before dismissing, invite all to remain after the service to adore the cross—a parallel action to the adoration of the Blessed Sacrament last night.
- At the conclusion of the service, all ministers genuflect to the cross, then depart in silence.
- Be sure that those who decorate your worship space aren't immediately rushing after this service to change the décor for the Easter Vigil—particularly if these actions will be seen or heard by those spending time in prayer before the cross!

Designate persons—perhaps clergy, eucharistic ministers, and/or altar servers—to help **consume any of the Blessed Sacrament that remains** after today's commemoration. The altar of repose can be disassembled after this liturgy as well.

If you have a vibrant *Latino* community with plentiful lay leaders and creative talent, consider organizing the necessary talent to host a **Viacrucis en vivo**, the live reenactment of the Way of the Cross that is popular in Latin America. Begin the Way of the Cross in one location, with the judgment of Jesus by Pontius Pilate, then recite the rosary or sing mournful songs en route to the place of crucifixion. Various *Latino* traditions can be appended to such a celebration, including hooded penitents, the **seven last words of Jesus**, the *pésame a la Virgen* (an expression of condolence to Jesus' mother), the **veneration of an image of the entombed Jesus**, and the popular *quema de Judas* — the burning of an effigy of Judas filled with firecrackers!

On **April 7**, when it doesn't fall on Good Friday, the Church celebrates **St. John Baptist de la Salle** (1651-1719), the first to emphasize classroom teaching over individual instruction. This patron saint of teachers taught in the vernacular, rather than Latin. In his honor, lift up and pray for all teachers in your community!

On **April 7**, we remember the passing of **Macario Ga** (1913-2002), the fifth supreme bishop of the Philippine Independent Church. He served the church during the 1970 First Quarter Storm, when Filipino youth protested against Philippine president Ferdinand Marcos and against the Philippine Independent Church's support of his dictatorship. The movement resulted in increased lay involvement and democratization of the church, a national youth office, and a new constitution for a "synodically-governed" church. In his memory, reflect on the tension caused by "unholy alliances" that you and others may sometimes feel!

April 7 is **World Health Day**, an opportunity provided by the United Nations to annually highlight a global health issue. Discover and lift up this year's world health issue!

April 7 is also the **Day to Remember Rwanda Genocide Victims**, the beginning of a week of mourning to remember when no nation intervened to stop the slaughter of 1.1 million people over some 100 days in 1994. Pause today to mourn genocide and genocide ideology.

Saturday, April 8, 2023
THE EASTER VIGIL
(white)

Research online when the sun will set at your place of worship. **Plan to begin this evening's service** *after* **sunset**. Remember: Each day of the Jewish calendar begins at sunset (hence the Church's celebration of vigils). If you light the Easter fire outside, and if the hour of your service is close to sunset, invite congregants to come and watch the sunset — and to experience the dawning of a "new day" with the lighting of the Easter fire!

Transform your worship space into a proclamation of the Easter message!

- Place **the stand for the paschal candle** next to the ambo, and consider decorating it with flowers and/or ribbon.
- Locate **the symbol of baptismal water** in close proximity.
- Have a **bowl and aspergillum** ready for the sprinkling after the renewal of baptismal vows. Let the symbol speak: Consider swapping out your metal aspergillum (which likely shares very few drops of water with every swing) for a natural broom sprinkler adorned with white and gold ribbons.
- Be sure **the holy water fonts of the church are empty**, ready to be filled after the sprinkling rite. Consider ways to bring attention to the baptismal font during the Easter season, perhaps by placing flowers or plants beside it or hanging a mobile above it.
- Don't skimp on the **Easter lilies** — the traditional Easter flower that resembles the trumpets announcing Christ's resurrection! Rather than leave the lilies in plastic-wrapped pots, think about how you'll cover the pots in a way that ties them to your décor.
- Consider decorating the space with **flowering plants and floral arrangements** as well.
- Cover the altar with your **finest altar cloth**.
- Be sure to **steam or iron your Easter vestments** — and coordinate the color of your vestments with other decorative details in your worship space!
- If your worship space contains the **Stations of the Cross**, consider removing them or making it clear that they culminate in the 15th Station, the resurrection of Christ from the dead!

- Jesus is off the cross: Consider removing or replacing any crucifix that has a *corpus* (Jesus' body) on it. Drape white fabric behind the head and over the horizontal bars of every sizeable cross, to create the look of the "**Easter cross**."

- Think how you might use white cloth to **draw the eyes of congregants upwards**, perhaps with sheer, white fabric suspended over the congregation and/or between pillars.

- If you have a Latino community, have congregants create **white/gold paper flowers or *papel picado*** (cut tissue paper) that might lift eyes upward and toward the sanctuary.

- Consider **banners** with images of Easter joy, the risen Christ and/or the empty tomb.

- **Continue the decoration** into the entrance to your worship space, outdoors, and into other spaces on the grounds, including your Blessed Sacrament chapel, parish hall and classrooms!

- If you're celebrating with an outdoor **Easter fire**, gather the necessary materials: a pit, newspaper, wood, a lighter, a wick to transfer the Easter fire to the paschal candle, and a nearby fire extinguisher. Let the symbol speak: Be sure to have a skilled camper build and tend a bonfire; don't risk an inexperienced fire-builder placing a few fire starters among loosely-wadded newspaper and green twigs. In the event of inclement weather, have a "Plan B" for a smaller, indoor fire (perhaps in a small, tabletop grill).

- Prepare the necessary **taper candles (with bobaches)** and mass programs.

- Ready the **paschal candle** and its **nails**. The Roman church mandates that the paschal candle "must be made of wax, never be artificial, be renewed each year, be only one in number, and be of sufficiently large size so that it may evoke the truth that Christ is the light of the world"; reflect on how this fits with your practice, particularly if your "paschal candle" is a plastic tube with an oil canister. Traditionally, as the fire was lit, the priest carved into the candle a cross, the Greek letters alpha and omega, and the date, and inserted five grains of incense to symbolize the wounds of Christ.

- If there may be any hint of wind, be sure to have a **glass topper** on hand to protect the flame — and a "Plan B" in the event that the wind extinguishes the paschal candle while the procession is in process.

- Be sure the **thurible** is ready, that you have plenty of **charcoal**, and that the **boat is filled with incense**.
- Prepare for mass as usual, making sure to include **gluten-free hosts** in the communion bowl, if necessary.
- If it's your community's custom to bring to the altar during the Lamb of God a ciborium with the Blessed Sacrament, let the appropriate person know that **there is no Blessed Sacrament in the tabernacle this evening**, so there in nothing to be brought to the altar.
- Before the first congregant arrives, **be sure all lights in the church are turned off, no candles are lit, and that all ministers know to maintain a prayerful environment**.
- Designate someone to **share mass programs and taper candles with congregants** as they arrive; think of this as a ministerial opportunity for children and/or for the families of those who will be receiving sacraments.

If you have a multilingual community, think through how you'll make a single community celebration meaningful to persons of all languages!

- Consider music that incorporates all languages.
- Divide the scriptures between languages, and, so that all can understand them, and consider printing the scriptures in the language in which they're not being proclaimed.
- Have a multilingual psalm and proclamation of the gospel.
- Be sure the presider and homilist are able to easily transition between languages for prayers and preaching, without sharing a homily that's repeated in two languages.
- Share a multilingual invitation to share the sign of peace.
- Invite people to pray the Lord's Prayer in their own languages.
- Rather than guess the language of those coming to communion, train eucharistic ministers to alternate between "The Body of Christ" (or "The Blood of Christ") and its equivalent(s) in the other language(s).

Be sure to prepare all ministers, so that they know their role and responsibilities for this special celebration. For the smoothest-possible liturgical experience, consider having a rehearsal!

Think through the details of **the procession from the Easter fire into the worship space**:

- Be sure your thurifer is ready for his/her responsibilities tonight — including his/her leading of the procession and

144

assistance with the deacon's (or presider's) incensation of the paschal candle.

- Be sure your deacon (or the person carrying the paschal candle) knows how to chant "Light of Christ" and where s/he will stop to chant it. Have him/her consider chanting this from the same three spots from which the proclamation "Behold the wood" was chanted on Good Friday.
- Plan how you'll spread the Light of Christ quickly and reverently after the second singing of "Light of Christ."
- Have the person holding the paschal candle place it in its stand after the third singing of "Light of Christ."
- Let altar servers know when to light all candles in the sanctuary and when to turn on the lights of the church (e.g., before the *Exsultet* is proclaimed—as a symbol of the paschal candle completely illuminating everything—or during the singing of the *Gloria*, as a symbol of Light of Christ becoming flesh).
- Similarly, your deacon should know when to tell congregants to extinguish their taper candles.

The *Exsultet* is a complex chant: Today is *not* the day to begin practicing it. Weeks in advance, select the deacon or cantor who will proclaim this, so that s/he can be preparing over the course of weeks! If it is your deacon, s/he should approach the presider for a blessing, which is the same blessing as the one given before the proclamation of the gospel at mass, except that the words "paschal praise" are used instead of "gospel."

The singing of the *Gloria* returns the congregation to the **full instrumental use** that we haven't heard since the *Gloria* on Holy Thursday. Like Holy Thursday, consider the **ringing of bells** during the *Gloria*. For all other music before the *Gloria* (e.g., the responsorial psalms), use *a capella* singing or softer accompaniment.

The Alleluia returns for the first time since Winter Ordinary Time: Sing it with gusto! Consider using a **triple Alleluia** tonight, with three verses from Psalm 118. For the musically-proficient, sing each succeeding refrain a half-step higher. Remember: Candles are not used during the proclamation of the gospel on this day!

For all other songs after the Alleluia, **consider tunes that might be familiar** to those who may not attend mass very often outside of Christmas and Easter. Also, consider ways in which you might **assist them in knowing the responses of the assembly**!

This is an especially appropriate night for celebrating the Church's **sacraments of initiation**!

- Know whether you'll be celebrating sacraments this evening, and, if so, for whom.
- Be sure recipients of sacraments are prepared and that they know how you'll celebrate these sacraments and what they need to do.
- Prepare the necessary oil(s).
- Have baptismal candles and white vestments on hand.
- Have a plan for dressing the newly-baptized in these white garments after they are baptized; consider giving them a space in which they can dry off and change clothes (if necessary), while the "veteran" Catholics renew their baptismal vows.
- Consider incorporating into the Litany of Saints the patron/matron saints of the newly-baptized and also of your community.
- Make the newly-baptized feel "part of the family": Be sure to include their names in the Prayers of the Faithful.

Will you have a **collection** during this special liturgy? Let your hospitality ministers know!

Because of the complexity of this service and its various rites (e.g., for the reception of sacraments by persons of different age groups, or for celebrations in which no sacraments are received), **consider assembling your own "missal" for this Mass**, inside a beautiful binder!

We celebrate the solemnity of solemnities tonight: Consider using **hypoallergenic incense** during your liturgy—but be sure that all who touch the thurible and/or boat have practiced in advance. (We've seen far too many carpets burned by inexperienced thurifers!) Be sure to tip off your altar server(s) to the fact that the handwashing will occur *after* the incensation of the altar and gifts! Because of the high nature of this solemnity, train your thurifer to swing the thurible during the song of sending forth in a vertical circle, with his/her swinging forearm parallel to the floor and his/her elbow at his/her side. It's a simple flipping of the wrist: forward, back, loop forward, back, loop forward, back, etc. Be sure s/he understands the laws of physics: Once the thurible (with flaming charcoals) is set in motion, the centrifugal force can't be stopped when the thurible is upside-down in the air!

The thread in today's scriptures: Like people gathered around a campfire, we listen tonight to highlights from the story of our salvation: The creation of the world (Gen. 1:1−2:2), the great faith of our ancestors (Gen. 22:1-18), and God's great act of freeing us from slavery (Ex. 14:15−15:1). We hear God speaking through the prophets, telling us how God's love is everlasting (Is. 54:5-14), how God is merciful, generous and forgiving (Is. 55:1-11), and how we are called to walk in the ways of prudence, wisdom and understanding (Bar. 3:9-15 & 3:32 — 4:4), with the hope that God will replace our hearts of stone with hearts of flesh (Ez. 36:16-28). The glorified Christ was raised from the dead (Lk. 24:1-12), and Paul assures us that we, too, will "live in newness of life" (Rom. 6:4)!

Holy humor: The Sunday school teacher had prepared a lesson on Christ's resurrection on Easter Sunday. She asked her students, "What did Jesus do on Easter Sunday?" There was no response. So, she gave her students a hint: "It starts with the letter R…" And one boy blurted out, "Jesus recycled?" (Segue from "resurrection," the answer the teacher expected, to the fact that Christ's resurrection from the dead broke the cycle of sin and death, bringing us full-circle from death, back to life! It's Easter: Feel free to point to other examples of life-to-death-to-life, like the Easter lilies in your worship space, which are alive today, will eventually die, but will bloom with life again next Easter!)

Looking for a visual aid for your homily or object lesson? Consider the objects in your worship environment! The paschal candle is a symbol of the Light of Christ vanquishing the darkness, and the tapers are symbolic of our sharing in the Light of Christ! The water has returned (recall that Good Friday is the one day in which our holy water fonts are empty) and is symbolic of the new life we receive in baptism, our being cleansed from sin, and the fact that we have died with Christ in baptism and will share in his resurrection! The Easter lilies recall the trumpets that heralded Christ's resurrection! Imagine for a moment what this world would be like if we took seriously our baptismal promises and, nourished by Word and Sacrament, went forth to be heralds of Christ's light in this world!

Know how you'll celebrate **the blessing of water, the renewal of baptismal promises, and the sprinkling rite**.

- Be prepared to remove the paschal candle from its stand and lower it into the water once (or three times, depending on local custom), holding it in the water for the remainder of the prayer.

- Be sure to have a taper on hand, for relighting all tapers from the paschal candle, for the renewal of baptismal promises. Have a plan for quickly relighting the taper candles of all congregants at this moment in the rite. Consider having instrumental music to accompany this action.

- If you anticipate a large number of congregants and a generous sharing of water, consider having an altar server follow you with another pitcher or bowl of holy water.

- If, at the end of the sprinkling rite, you have only a small amount of holy water left in the bowl you're carrying, let the symbol speak: Hand the aspergillum to your altar server, and conclude the rite by tightly holding the bowl and throwing the remaining water high over the heads of all congregants!

- Before the liturgy, instruct an altar server to use a pitcher to transfer the newly-blessed water to all holy water fonts of the church after the sprinkling rite.

After communion, **the Blessed Sacrament is returned to the tabernacle**, which has remained open since Holy Thursday. Instruct the appropriate minister to lock the tabernacle and light the vigil light there.

Be sure your deacon knows how to **chant the double Alleluia of the dismissal**.

After Mass, have hospitality ministers prepared with baskets, in which they can **collect the taper candles**.

If you serve a *Latino* community, consider having **holy water bottles** for purchase: In many places in Mexico, people are accustomed to taking holy water home at the conclusion of Easter masses!

On **April 8**, we remember the passing of **Charles-Joachim Colbert de Croissy** (1667-1738), the French bishop who opposed *Unigenitus* and called for a general council of the Church to discuss the papal bull. The nephew of France's first minister of state, he edited the *Montpellier Catechism*, which was condemned by Rome. In his memory, pray for all catechists who are challenged by some of the teachings imposed on them by hierarchs in the Church!

On **April 8**, we remember the passing of **Antony Flew** (1923-2010), the English philosopher of religion and advocate for atheism known for his criticism of concepts of God, life after death, free will, and the problem of evil. Late in life, he shocked colleagues by changing his position, choosing to believe in an intelligent creator, and clarifying his own personal concept of God. In his memory, pray for all who struggle to believe the good news we daily teach and preach!

On **April 8**, we celebrate the birth in 1926 of **Jürgen Moltmann**, the German Reformed theologian who contributed to a number of areas of Christian theology. He shared his "theology of hope," a form of liberation theology predicated on a view that God suffers with humanity but that the hope of the resurrection promises us a better future. In his memory, consider the place that hope holds in your own theology and worldview—and how it is that you might be a better instrument of hope in this world!

Sunday, April 9, 2023
THE RESURRECTION OF OUR LORD
(white)

This is a high solemnity: **Keep in place all décor** from your celebration of the Easter Vigil!

Be sure your hospitality ministers are ready to **welcome the "Christmas and Easter Catholics"** who may not often come to church. Encourage ministers to make newcomers feel so welcomed that they might consider returning!

The Church shares four "great sequences" each year: Today's is the *Victimae Paschali Laudes*. Consider having a gifted cantor sing or chant a setting of this, before segueing into the gospel acclamation!

The thread in today's scriptures: Filled with Christ's Spirit, Peter (previously known for his denial of Jesus) now boldly proclaims the risen Christ (Acts 10:34a & 37-43), whose rising is told in today's gospel (Jn. 20:1-9). With the psalmist, we sing: "This is the day the Lord has made: Let us rejoice and be glad!" (Ps. 118:24).

Holy humor: Sometimes Easter can be stressful—with early-rising children eager to see what the Easter Bunny brought them, getting everyone dressed for church, preparing for family gatherings, and all the other details that fill this day. So, do you want to know how to make Easter easier? I'll tell you how to make Easter easier. How do you make Easter easier? Simply replace the "t" of Easter with an "i," and you've just made "Easter" "easier"! (Segue into the fact that while the simple change of a letter won't necessarily make Easter easier, through his resurrection, Christ changed an otherwise-ordinary Sunday into the reason for our hope and the source of our salvation! He changed our destiny from death, to life! From sin, to mercy and forgiveness! From darkness, to light! He is risen! Alleluia!)

Looking for a visual aid for your homily or object lesson? Consider a baseball! Easter signals that spring has arrived, and baseball season is right around the corner. Throw the baseball in the air, and note the physical laws of this world: What goes up...must come down! We know that God often sees this world from a very different perspective; indeed, from God's perspective, as evidenced in today's scriptures, what goes down (into the grave)…must come up!

Consider having a **sprinkling rite** this morning, with the holy water from the Easter Vigil: This could be at the beginning of Mass (in place of the Penitential Rite), or after the Renewal of Baptismal Promises (which would be in place of the Creed).

For the intellectually-curious, speak to the etymology of Easter (with Eostre, the Anglo-Saxon goddess of the dawn), explain that Easter is a moveable feast (celebrated on the first Sunday after the first full moon after the spring equinox), note that the bunny was an ancient Egyptian symbol of fertility, and/or share how eggs, a symbol of new life, were forbidden during Lent by the medieval Church!

Happy Easter! Consider engaging kids through an **Easter egg hunt** and/or a visit from the **Easter Bunny**. Photos with the Easter bunny can be extremely popular and will likely be posted by congregants to social media! Even better, print copies of photos and make them available at no cost next Sunday; they'll hang on refrigerators and be framed in homes for years to come!

Lent is over: For those who survived without meat on the Fridays of Lent, suggest a continued practice of **"Meatless Mondays"** or **"Fruit & Veggie Fridays"** as a way to address the impact we have on our environment through our consumption of meat!

If your community celebrated the *Via Crucis* (stations of the cross) during Lent, consider balancing this practice with a *Via Lucis* (way of light) throughout the Easter season, highlighting 14 post-resurrection appearances of the risen Christ to his friends.

On **April 9**, we remember the passing of **William of Ockham** (1285-1347), the English Franciscan friar and scholastic philosopher and theologian who was one of the major figures of medieval thought, standing at the center of major intellectual controversies of the 14th century. He is known for "Ockham's razor," the problem-solving principle that simpler solutions are more likely correct than complex solutions. In his memory, reflect on simpler solutions to the various challenges you face!

On **April 9**, we remember the passing of **Francis Bacon** (1561-1626), the English Anglican philosopher, statesman and pioneer of scientific method during the scientific revolution. He wrote a number of religious works, including numerous theological tracts, sacred meditations and his utopian *The New Atlantis*, which emphasized the complementary role of science and religion. In his memory, discover one of his many works!

On **April 9**, we remember the passing of **Dietrich Bonhoeffer** (1906-1945), the German pastor and theologian executed by the Nazi regime and best known for *The Cost of Discipleship* and other writings on justice, the role of faith in a "world come of age," and a "religionless Christianity" where God might be unfettered from the metaphysical constructs of the previous 1900 years. In his memory, consider ways in which you might shed a "garment" or two covering your own faith!

On **April 10**, we remember the passing of **Pierre Teilhard de Chardin** (1881-1955), the French paleontologist, idealist philosopher and Jesuit priest who popularized Vladimir Vernadsky's concept of the noosphere and conceived the vitalist idea of the Omega Point toward which the universe is evolving. In his memory, reflect on possible connections that might be made between his thought and the daily lives of your community members!

On **April 11**, the Church celebrates **St. Stanislas** (1030-1079), the patron saint of Poland, who bravely spoke out against a cruel and unjust king. In iconography, he's the bishop being cut to pieces at the foot of an altar. In his memory, listen to Franz Liszt's last and unfinished work, the *Oratorio St. Stanislaus*, and/or voice support today for the courageous prophetic women and men who, inspired by the Spirit, continue to speak out against injustices and/or unjust leaders.

On **April 12**, the Church celebrates **Julius I** (+352), the pope who defended Athanasius against Arian accusers. In his honor, pray for those who courageously stand in defense of others!

On **April 12**, we remember the passing of **Jacques-Bénigne Bossuet** (1627-1704), the French Catholic bishop who drafted Louis XIV's anti-papal declaration, declared null and void by the pope for its suggestion that the king could limit the power of the pope. At an 1882 assembly of French clergy, he drafted the Gallican Articles, asserting the king's independence from Rome in secular matters—and that the pope can never be regarded as infallible without the consent of the Church. Pause today to pray for all who blur the line between Church and State and who continue to insist on purported papal infallibility!

On **April 12**, we remember the passing of **Pierre de Langle** (1643-1724), the French bishop whose manifesto in opposition to *Unigenitus* incited a riot in his diocese. He called for a council of the Church to discuss the papal bull and opposed the 1720 compromise, which led the Duke of

Orleans to banish him from his own diocese. In his memory, pray for all exiles!

On **April 12**, we remember the passing of **Johann Adam Möhler** (1796-1838), the German priest and theologian who died at age 41 but was influential on other young minds, like Henri de Lubac and Yves Congar. A prominent exponent of liberal thought, he supported Döllinger's criticisms of the papacy and its claims of purported papal infallibility. In his memory, pray for the young people who dedicate their lives to bringing fresh thought to sometimes-stale institutions!

On **April 13**, the Church celebrates **St. Hermenegild** (+585), the Visigoth (Spanish) prince who defied his Arian father by converting to Catholicism, the religion of his devout wife, the daughter of the king of the Franks. Hermenegild was imprisoned and beheaded, which is why he's depicted in iconography as a prince in chains and/or holding an ax and being lifted to heaven above the king and bishops below him. His courage inspired his younger brother, Recared, to convert to Catholicism as well. In honor of the patron saint of converts, pray for all who have come to embrace our faith from other traditions!

On **April 13**, the Church celebrates **St. Martin I** (+655), the pope imprisoned by Emperor Constans II and who died as a consequence of the mistreatment he received from fellow Christians. In iconography, he's a pope in a prison cell or a pope holding money. In his memory, read up on the Lateran Council that he convened and the Monothelitism condemned at that council, and/or pray today for all who are persecuted by "Christians" and by our fellow Catholics — and for those "Christians" who fail to see the error of their myopic ways!

On **April 13**, we celebrate the birth in 1943 of **Roald Flemestad**, the Norwegian Old Catholic bishop of the Nordic Catholic Church. In his honor, pray for him and for our sisters and brothers of the Nordic Catholic Church!

On **April 13**, we remember the passing of **Chriton Atuhwera** (c. 1998-2021), the LGBTQ activist and Ugandan refugee who died from burn wounds sustained in a homophobic firebomb attack in Block 13 of Kenya's largest refugee camp, where 300 LGBTQ refugees lived. Known as "Trinidad Jerry," he studied business administration at a Ugandan university until he was outed and forced to flee the country. In his memory, advocate for all who continue to be persecuted due to their self-identity!

On **April 13**, we celebrate the birth in 1958 of **Heinz Georg Lederleitner**, who has served as the seventh bishop of the Austrian Old Catholic

Church since 2016. Ordained a Roman Catholic priest by the future Benedict XVI, he served the Roman Church for 20 years before incardinating into Old Catholicism. His episcopal motto is "Christ, Light of the World." In his honor, pray for our sisters and brothers of the Austrian Old Catholic Church and consider how you are sharing Christ's light in our world!

On **April 13**, we celebrate the anniversary of the presbyteral ordination in 2013 of **Karen Furr**, the sacramental minister of Our Lady of the Angels Catholic Community in Kingman, Arizona. Pray for her and for the people she serves!

On **April 14**, we remember the passing on Good Friday of **Walter van Nieuwenhuisen** (+1797), the Dutch priest who served as the eleventh archbishop of Utrecht. He received letters of communion from Roman Catholic bishops in France, Germany, Italy, and Spain, and from a large number of Roman Catholic priests who recognized his jurisdiction and orthodoxy. In his memory, consider how you are working to increase communion between people!

On **April 14**, we remember the passing of **Simone de Beauvoir** (1908-1986), the French writer known for her feminist existentialism and theory. In her memory, pray for all who contribute to the evolution of feminist ideas!

On **April 14**, we celebrate the anniversary of the episcopal consecration in 2012 of Bishop **Edmund N. Cass**, a longtime bishop in the Independent Catholic movement. Happy anniversary!

April 14 is also **Orthodox Good Friday**. We pray for our spiritual siblings of Eastern Christian rites who mourn the death of our Lord today.

April 14 is **National Library Workers' Day** in the U.S., an opportunity to celebrate the community members whose public service contributes to the transformation of our communities through education and lifelong learning. Find a suitable way to let them know of your gratitude!

On **April 15**, we remember the passing of **Charles Journet** (1891-1975), the Swiss theologian and cardinal who co-founded the theological journal *Nova et Vetera* with Jacques Maritain and was influential in the Second Vatican Council's writing of *Dignitatis humanae* and *Nostra aetate*. In his memory, reflect on your own concrete efforts to bring to flesh "the Church of the Word Incarnate"!

Sunday, April 16, 2023
SECOND SUNDAY OF EASTER
(white)

It's the Easter season: The **paschal candle** remains in close proximity to the ambo!

This Sunday was traditionally known as *dominica in albis* (White Sunday): Invite the newly-baptized to round out the Easter octave by wearing their white gowns, shirts or dresses again this Sunday! Even better, spread word a week or two in advance, and invite all congregants to wear a touch of white!

The thread in today's scriptures: We hear John's story of Easter night, when the risen Christ wished his disciples peace and shared with them the Spirit (Jn. 20:19-31). As a result, they changed their lives and began working all sorts of signs and wonders (Acts 2:42-47). Speaking of changed lives, God "gave us a new birth to a living hope through the resurrection of Jesus Christ from the dead" (1Pet. 1:3), which is a cause for rejoicing (1Pet. 1:6). Christ is risen, and we can now sing with the psalmist: "This is the day the Lord has made; let us be glad and rejoice in it" (Ps. 118:24)!

Holy humor: I couldn't make this up: Early Greek Christians referred to the Sunday after Easter as "Holy Humor Sunday"! It was a day of great joy and laughter, to celebrate the "joke" that Jesus played on Sin and Death by conquering them! So, in the spirit of the early Greek Christians, who would tell jokes on this day, I'll share with you the story of the day that Jesus and Moses played golf in heaven! So there they were, Jesus and Moses, playing golf in heaven, and darned the luck, they both hit their golf balls into the same water trap! So Jesus turned to Moses and said, "Didn't you do something with water once?" And Moses said, "I did," and he did his trick of parting the waters, and he fetched his golf ball from the water trap. Then Moses turned to Jesus and said, "Didn't you do something with water once?" And Jesus said, "I did," and he stepped out onto the water. But almost immediately, he sank into the water. Puzzled, he got out of the water and tried again, this time with a running start—but he ended up in water up to his waist. Jesus was now confused and embarrassed, so Moses asked him, "What are you trying to do?" And Jesus replied, "I used to be able to walk on water." Moses smiled and asked, "But the last time you tried it, did you have those holes in your feet?" [Acknowledge once more that it's Holy Humor Sunday, and segue into the holes in Jesus' feet and hands and side—the proof that he had died on the cross and was now raised from the dead!]

Looking for a visual aid for your homily or object lesson? Consider a large button! The English word "peace" comes from an ancient Greek root that literally mean "to fasten" or "to button." Just as a button fastens together two pieces of cloth, we are ideally united in the peace that the risen Christ wished his friends. Every time we wish one another peace—at every Mass—we show our desire to be "buttoned" to all those other members of the Body of Christ!

It's the final day of the Easter Octave: Be sure your deacon knows how to **chant the double Alleluia of the dismissal**.

It's **Divine Mercy Sunday**: Find a way to incorporate this into your preaching and/or catechesis! Many people are not familiar with the Chaplet of the Divine Mercy; consider the possibility of having a lay leader guide all present in this prayer!

On **April 16**, the Roman church celebrates the birth in 1927 of **Joseph Aloisius Ratzinger**, who headed the Roman church for eight years as Benedict XVI. Originally a liberal theologian questioning literal interpretations of the resurrection of Jesus, he adopted conservative views after Vatican II and became John Paul II's closest advisor and "Rottweiler" as head of the Congregation for the Doctrine of the Faith. Lift a prayer heavenward today for this "pope emeritus"—and for the church that will long feel his legacy of attempting a "reform of the [Vatican II] reform"!

April 16 is **Orthodox Easter**, the day on which Eastern Christians celebrate our Lord's resurrection. Pray for our 260 million Orthodox spiritual siblings on this day!

On **April 17**, we remember the passing of **Louis de Berquin** (c. 1490-1529), the French lawyer, linguist and reformer. "Providentially guided to the Bible, he was amazed to find there 'not the doctrines of Rome, but the doctrines of Luther.'" Apart from a few translations of Erasmus, all his works are lost: He was forced to watch the burning of his books, his tongue was pierced, and, refusing to recant, he was burned at the stake the next day. In his memory, pray for all who mistreat others in defense of their own fragile "truths."

On **April 17**, we remember the passing of **Juana Inés de la Cruz** (1648-1695), the Mexican writer, nun and proto-feminist who was a vocal critic of misogyny. Considered one of the greatest Latin American poets and North America's first lesbian feminist writer, she had a special relationship with Countess Maria Luisa de Paredes, who inspired Juana to write amorous love poems. Juana assembled a library of 4,000 books for women who were not allowed in Mexico's universities. A critic of her church's hierarchy, she appears on Mexico's currency but was never canonized. Pray for all who help to lift up all our sisters!

On **April 17**, we celebrate the birth in 1938 of **Elisabeth Schüssler Fiorenza**, the Romanian-born, German, Roman Catholic feminist theologian who co-founded the *Journal of Feminist Studies in Religion*. Her book, *In Memory of Her*, argued for the retrieval of the overlooked contributions of women in the early Church. In her honor, find a way today to advocate for Jesus' vision of a "discipleship of equals"!

April 18 is **International Day for Monuments and Sites**, a day dedicated to recognizing sites of historical importance, raising awareness regarding them, and stressing the need to restore and preserve them. Search the internet for the historical sites near you and plan a field trip to learn about local history!

On **April 19**, we remember the passing of **Philip Melanchton** (1497-1560), the systematic theologian who contributed to the reform of the Church through his questioning of transubstantiation, the sacrament of penance, justification through works, and the medieval Church's exaggerated cult of saints. In his memory, consider multiple perspectives on these and other theological issues!

On **April 19**, the Syro Malabar Catholic Church (in union with Rome) celebrates the birth in 1945 of **Major Archbishop George Alencherry**. In a spirit of ecumenism, pray for him and for the 5.1 million Syro Malabar Catholics he serves!

On **April 20**, we remember the passing of **Victor IV** (1095-1164), the cardinal and "antipope" supported by Emperor Frederick Barbarossa after the election of Alexander III, whom five cardinals, the priests of St. Peter's and the Roman people refused to recognize as pope. Consecrated by the dean of the College of Cardinals, Victor IV took control of Rome, causing Alexander III to flee to Sicily. A fascinating split in the Church ensued, with kings, clergy and laity forced to decide which pope they supported. After miracles were reported at Victor's tomb, Gregory VIII ordered it to be destroyed. In Victor's memory, consider the lessons learned from the instances you've witnessed of politics in the Church!

On **April 20**, we remember the passing of **Ernesto Buonaiuti** (1881-1946), the Italian priest, historian and philosopher of religion who lost his chair at the University of Rome for refusing to swear allegiance to Fascism. He studied the influence of imperial politics on the early Church, and his magazines on historical-critical research of the Church were placed on the *Index of Forbidden Books*. In his autobiography, he referred to himself as a "loyal son" of the church that excommunicated him and confirmed his excommunication several times. In his memory, pray for all who are ill-treated by their "parents"!

On **April 20**, we remember the passing of **Dorothy Height** (1912-2010), the African-American civil rights activist and feminist who was one of the first in the civil rights movement to advocate specifically for African-American women. In her memory, pray for all those who advocate for civil rights!

On **April 21**, the Church celebrates **St. Anselm** (c. 1033-1109), the archbishop of Canterbury whose metaphysical works continue to shed light on the attributes of God. He resisted his king's efforts to use the Church's money in a war against the king's brother. Consider today how you are stewarding the resources entrusted to your care!

On **April 21**, we remember the passing of **Peter Abelard** (1079-1142), the medieval French scholastic philosopher and theologian now legendary for his love affair with Héloïse d'Argenteuil. His work, *Sic et Non*, brought together opposite opinions on doctrinal points from various Fathers of the Church. In his memory, consider opposing perspectives to some of your most strongly-held thoughts and beliefs, and/or re-watch the 1988 film, "Stealing Heaven," which attempted to tell the tale of these lovers!

On **April 21**, we remember the passing of **Louis Marie Duchesne** (1843-1922), the French priest and modernist professor of Christian history and liturgy. His history of the early Church was placed on the Roman church's *Index of Forbidden Books*. After his death, the London *Tablet* wrote, "By his rigid application of scientific methods of research and judgment, by his caustic pen and tongue, Msgr. Duchesne was regarded by some as a scoffer and a vandal among pious traditions. But by those who knew him, he was regarded as a master of the sciences that are auxiliary to ecclesiastical history." In his memory, consider your own response to the caustic "pens" and tongues of others!

On **April 21**, we remember the passing of **Olga Novikoff** (1842-1925), the expatriate Russian author and journalist who financially supported the ministry of Arnold Harris Mathew in England and who introduced him to Rudolph de Landas Berghes, whom he consecrated. In her memory, pray for all whose good will supports and extends our ministries!

On **April 21**, we remember the passing of **Catharina Joanna Maria Halkes** (1920-2011), the Dutch feminist theologian who gained notoriety when she was forbidden to address John Paul II during his visit to the Netherlands in 1985. Considered the mother of feminist theology in the Netherlands, she held the first chair of Feminism and Christianity at Radboud University. In her memory, consider your own commitment to gender equality in the Body of Christ (Gal 3:28)!

On **April 21**, we celebrate the birth in 1939 of **Sr. Helen Prejean**, the American Roman Catholic sister who authored the bestseller, *Dead Man Walking,* and who became a leading advocate for the abolition of the death penalty in the U.S. Sister Helen founded support groups for the family members of murder victims. In her honor, call to mind others who have lost a family member or friend to similar tragic circumstances—and find a small way to reach out to them today, to let them know you care!

On **April 21**, the Roman Catholic Church celebrates the birth in 1965 of **Pierbattista Pizzaballa**, the Latin Patriarch of Jerusalem. In a spirit of ecumenism, pray for him and for the Roman Catholics he serves!

On **April 21**, our Muslim spiritual siblings celebrate **Eid al-Fitr**, the joyful end of their month of Ramadan fasting.

On **April 22**, the Church celebrates **St. Nearchus**, the third-century Roman soldier in Armenia known with St. Polyeuct as "brothers by affection." Polyeuct, who converted to Nearchus' Christianity, zealously attacked a pagan procession and was beheaded for the crime. He spoke his last words to Nearchus: "Remember our secret vow," making St. Polyeuct the protector of vows and the avenger of broken promises. Nearchus and Polyeuct are portrayed together as patron saints of the gay community. In their memory, pray for all who make vows to others—and for all who suffer when such vows are broken!

On **April 22**, we remember the passing of **Mircea Eliade** (1907-1986), the Romanian philosopher and religious historian who established paradigms for religious study that continue to be used today. He suggested that myths and rituals allow us to actually participate in hierophanies. In his memory, reflect on how our Catholic stories and rituals connect us with the larger spiritual motifs shared by peoples throughout our world!

April 22 is **Earth Day**: Is there anything that your community might do to mark this day? Consider planting trees, putting in place bins for recyclables (as well as a system for ensuring that objects placed there are recycled), and/or inviting a high school environmental sciences class to do an audit of the trash/recyclables/composting efforts of your community!

Sunday, April 23, 2023
THIRD SUNDAY OF EASTER
(white)

It's the Easter season: The **paschal candle** remains in close proximity to the ambo!

Also, Catholic worship spaces are famously decorated with explosions of lilies on Easter Sunday, only for those spaces to begin looking barren when the Easter lilies begin to die.

- Create a plan this year to **spread your Easter decorating budget over the 50 days of Easter**, so that, even after the Easter lilies wither, you'll have a way to brighten your worship space with color and natural beauty through Pentecost. Consider ivy and potted flowers, like calla lilies, azaleas, and begonias, which can thrive for weeks.

- Decide what to do with the Easter lilies that you cycle out of your worship space: Plant them outside (presuming there's someone to water and care for them), or give them away to congregants with a "green thumb"!

The thread in today's scriptures: As the disciples on the road to Emmaus came to see (Lk. 24:13-35), God raised Jesus from the dead (1Pet. 1:21, Acts 2:32), allowing us to sing with the psalmist: "My heart is glad and my soul rejoices; my body, too, abides in confidence because you will not abandon my soul to the netherworld, nor will you suffer your faithful one to undergo corruption" (Ps. 16:9-10)!

Holy humor: The story is told of the man who decided on Friday afternoon to stay out the entire weekend — hunting with his friends and spending his entire paycheck…without telling his wife! When he finally came home on Sunday evening, he was confronted by his angry wife. The exchange became heated, and she asked, "How would you like it if you didn't see me for two or three days?" And he made the mistake of replying, "Not see you for two or three days? That would be fine with me!" Monday went by, and he didn't see his wife. Tuesday and Wednesday came, and he didn't see her. Finally on Thursday, the swelling went down just enough, so that he could begin to see her just a little bit out of the corner of his left eye! [Note that it likely took the guy a few more days to begin to see again, then segue into how it is that the disciples on the road to Emmaus didn't "see" that they were with the risen Christ. Theirs wasn't a gradual opening of eyes, though: They immediately recognized him in the breaking of the bread — and the risen Christ was gone!]

Looking for a visual aid for your homily or object lesson? Try a hat and a gardener's spade! You may have used a blindfold on March 22, the Fourth Sunday of Lent; if not, pull out a blindfold for this homily and speak about how the disciples on the road to Emmaus were "blind" to the fact that they were speaking with the risen Christ. If you already used the blindfold, put on a hat and grab a spade instead: This is how Rembrandt painted the risen Christ, who appeared to Mary Magdalene and wasn't recognized by her. That's right: Rembrandt's imagination was seized by the thought of Mary thinking that the risen Christ was…a gardener! The risen Christ appeared to his disciples while they were fishing, and they didn't recognize him! In today's gospel, the risen Christ appears to the disciples on the road to Emmaus, and they don't recognize him! Lead your listeners in a reflection on how it is that sometimes we don't recognize the risen Christ in our daily lives!

On **April 23**, when it doesn't fall on Sunday, the Church celebrates **St. George** (+c. 303) and **St. Adalbert** (956-997). George was a soldier in the imperial guard, tortured and martyred for refusing to sacrifice to Roman gods. Portrayed in iconography as killing a dragon, George is the patron saint of England and of Boy Scouts and is venerated by Christians of the East and West — as well as by Muslims. Adalbert was the bishop of Prague who was exiled by clergy refusing to observe his clerical reforms, and exiled again after excommunicating those who violated the Church's right of sanctuary by dragging a woman accused of adultery from a church and murdering her. Consider a fitting way to honor their legacy!

On **April 23**, we remember the passing of **William Shakespeare** (1564-1616), the English playwright widely regarded as the world's greatest dramatist. His parents were Catholic at a time when practicing Catholicism in England was against the law. In his and his parents' memory, pray for those who bring beauty to our world — and to those who bravely profess their faith despite difficult circumstances!

On **April 23**, we remember the passing of **Ignacy Jan Wysoczański** (1901-1975), the Polish Old Catholic bishop appointed to lead the Polish Old Catholic Church in 1965, one year after communist authorities banned all church activities. In his memory, pray for all whose expression of their beliefs is stifled!

On **April 23**, the Palmarian Catholic Church — a small, traditionalist church — celebrates the anniversary of the installation in 2016 of Joseph

Odermatt as **Pope Peter III**. In his honor, pray for him and for the 1,000 people he serves!

On **April 24**, the *Roman Martyrology* celebrated **Ss. Salome and Mary of Clopas**, who are revered by the Orthodox tradition as two of eight "myrrh bearers." Present at Jesus' crucifixion and at the discovery of the empty tomb, they are often referred to as "followers" of Jesus, rather than as "disciples." Contemporary critiques suggest that their significance as female supporters of Jesus was historically underplayed. In their memory, pray for the countless people whose behind-the-scenes support is critical for the spread of the gospel message!

On **April 24**, we remember the passing of **St. Wilfrid** (c. 633 – c. 709), the Northumbrian abbot and bishop who reportedly introduced the Rule of St. Benedict to the Isles and chose to be consecrated in Gaul due to the lack of validly-consecrated bishops in Northumbria. Wilfrid lived ostentatiously, always traveled with a large retinue, founded a see in West Sussex, and constantly championed Roman customs over local practices. In his memory, consider your own views on the tension between local customs and the rites and practices imposed by "universal" organizations!

On **April 24**, the Church celebrates **St. Fidel of Sigmaringen** (1577-1622), the "lawyer of the poor," who divided his wealth between the poor and seminarians in need. On his day, reflect on his words: "Woe to me if I should prove myself but a halfhearted soldier in the service of my thorn-crowned Captain!"

On **April 25**, the Church celebrates **St. Mark** (+c. 68), to whom the second gospel is attributed. In his honor, thumb through his short work to see what it says about the life of Jesus!

On **April 25**, we remember the passing of **Bernard Philip Kelly** (1907-1958), the English layman who, when not working as a banker or raising his large family, penned philosophical essays and book reviews for *Blackfriars* for 25 years. He developed the social and economic theory of distributism, reflected on the poetry of Gerard Manley Hopkins, and outlined an informed, Christian approach to Eastern religions. In his memory, explore elements of an Eastern philosophy and/or religion!

On **April 25**, we remember the brutal murder in 2016 of **Xulhaz Mannan and Tanay Mojumdar**, the LGBTQ activists hacked to death in a "blessed attack" by militant Islamists of Al-Qaeda in Bangladesh. The editor of Bangladesh's first and only LGBTQ magazine, Xulhaz was prevented by government officials from organizing a Rainbow Rally for LGBTQ youth. His friend, Tanay, was visiting his apartment at the time of the attack. In their memory, consider what you might do to prevent the misuse of religion to condone violence!

On **April 26**, the Church celebrates **St. Paschasius Radbertus** (c. 785 – c. 860), the Carolingian theologian and abbot of Corbie known for his work, *On the Body and Blood of the Lord*, the first lengthy treatise on the sacrament of the Eucharist in the Western world. He affirmed that the Eucharist contains the true, historical body of Jesus — a view that was refuted by his predecessor, Ratramnus, who wrote a work with the same name and advanced that the Eucharist is strictly metaphorical. In Paschasius' memory, reacquaint yourself with that important controversy in Eucharistic theology!

On **April 26**, we remember the passing of **Yook Woo-Dang** (1984-2003), the South Korean LGBT Catholic poet and activist who committed suicide in protest against discrimination against homosexuals in South Korea. The victim of prejudice due to his sexual identity, he was involved in LGBT human rights, anti-discrimination, disability rights, and the anti-war peace movement. His death paved the way to the South Korean Youth Protection Act. In his memory, consider how you stand up for those who often confront the ugly face of the social sin of discrimination!

On **April 26**, we remember the passing of **Harry Wu** (1937-2016), the Chinese-American human rights activist who spent 19 years in a Chinese labor camp as a result of his advocacy. In his memory, pray for all who suffer the iron fist of oppressive governments!

On **April 26**, the Church celebrates the birth in 1936 of **Joan Chittister**, the Benedictine nun and theologian known for her works on virtue and monasticism and for her advocacy on feminism and women's role in society. Forbidden by the Vatican in 2001 to address the Women's Ordination Worldwide conference, she did so anyway. In her honor, pray for all women and men who bravely and boldly advocate for Jesus' and Paul's vision of a "discipleship of equals"!

April 26 is **World Intellectual Property Day**, an opportunity for us to increase our knowledge of intellectual property — and the ways in which we might be violating it!

April 26 is also **International Chernobyl Disaster Remembrance Day**, an annual commemoration of the 1986 explosion that spread contamination throughout Russia, Ukraine and Belarus. Nearly 40 years later, millions continue to suffer its effects. Pray for all affected persons and all who safeguard us from the adverse effects of modern technologies!

April 26 is **Administrative Professionals Day**: How will you recognize those who assist the administrative functions of your community, and/or how will you empower others to assist with such details?

On **April 27**, we remember the passing of **Christina Georgina Rossetti** (1830-1894), the English poet and gay mystic whose work ranged from British Christmas carols to lesbian love poetry. Her poetry inspired the homoerotic themes of Roman Catholic priest Gerard Manley Hopkins. In her memory, discover her life and works!

On **April 27**, we remember the passing of **Dorothee Steffensky-Sölle** (1929-2003), the German liberation theologian who coined the term Christofascism to describe fundamentalists. Steffensky-Sölle attempted to bridge theology to practical life, and her best-known work, *Suffering*, offered a critique of "Christian masochism" and "Christian sadism." In her memory, consider the extent to which your own theology and spirituality press against or reinforce conventional thinking on matters of religion and spirituality!

The fourth Thursday of April is also **Bring Your Child to Work Day** in the U.S., an opportunity for us to help our children and grandchildren understand how we support our families and contribute to the world!

On **April 28**, the Church celebrates **St. Peter Chanel** (1803-1841) and **St. Louis-Marie Grignion de Montfort** (1673-1716). Peter was a Marist missionary and protomartyr of the South Seas, whose death led to the conversion of the island of Futuna. Louis-Marie was an early writer in the field of Mariology, who promoted consecration to Jesus in Mary. Take a moment today to entrust the missionaries of the Church to Jesus and Mary!

On **April 28**, we remember the passing of **John Zenon Jasinski** (1887-1951), the Polish-American bishop who led the Polish National Catholic Church. In his memory, pray for our sisters and brothers of the Polish National Catholic Church!

On **April 28**, we remember the passing of **Jacques Maritain** (1882-1973), the French Catholic philosopher who revived Aquinas, authored over 60 books, and was influential in the drafting of the Universal Declaration of Human Rights. A mentor and close friend of Paul VI, who wanted to name him a cardinal, Maritain was especially interested in metaphysics, being, and the apprehension of being through intuition and sense experience. In his memory, re-read the Universal Declaration of Human Rights and/or consider the extent to which your knowledge allows you to "Thomisticize" and/or "measure [your] knowing spirit by the real"!

On **April 28**, we remember the passing of **James Hal Cone** (1938-2018), the American theologian known for his works on Black theology and Black liberation theology. Cone noted that Jesus advocated for the same ideals espoused in the Black Power movement—and that White American churches preached a gospel based on White supremacy, antithetical to the gospel of Jesus. In his memory, reflect on how your words and actions oppress and/or liberate persons of different races, cultures and socioeconomic levels!

April 28 is **World Day for Safety and Health at Work**, an annual opportunity to remind ourselves of the importance of preventing accidents and diseases in our work places. Pray and advocate for occupational safety and health!

On **April 29**, the Church celebrates **St. Catherine of Siena** (1347-1380), the 24th of 25 children, who died at the young age of 33. She's the patroness of Europe and Italy, and is often depicted holding a lily. Draw attention to her dedication to Christ from an early age (a model for children!), her care of the sick and poor, her contemplative life, and her influence in the Church!

On **April 29**, we remember the passing of **Augusta Theodosia Drane** (1823-1894), the English Dominican nun and writer who anonymously published a moral essay long attributed to John Henry Newman. Her major works included histories of St. Dominic, St. Catherine of Siena, St. Thomas More, and an overview of Christian schools and scholars. In her memory, pray for the countless anonymous women whose lives and works have inspired the Church throughout the centuries!

On **April 29**, we celebrate the birth in 1950 of **Rita Nakashima Brock**, the Japanese-American theologian, feminist and non-profit leader who has published several works on Christianity and feminism. A Huffington Post blogger on religion, she is the author of *Saving Paradise: How Christianity Traded Love of This World for Crucifixion and Empire*. In her honor, reacquaint yourself with her writings!

April 29 is also the **Day to Remember Chemical Warfare Victims**, an opportunity to highlight the need to eliminate from our world the threat of chemical weapons.

Sunday, April 30, 2023
FOURTH SUNDAY OF EASTER
(white)

It's the Easter season: The **paschal candle** remains in close proximity to the ambo!

Today is **Good Shepherd Sunday**: Point to the ancient imagery of shepherd-rulers, and challenge listeners to be good shepherds of others!

The thread in today's scriptures: On this Good Shepherd Sunday, we recall that Jesus is the shepherd (Ps. 23:1-6, 1Pet. 2:25), the lamb who takes away our sins (1Pet. 2:24), and the sheep gate (Jn. 10:1-10, remember that shepherds and shepherdesses often blocked the entrance to the sheep pen with themselves and with their herding sticks). Following in Jesus' footsteps, Peter, filled with the Spirit, also helped to shepherd others to salvation (Acts 2:36-41).

Holy humor: One day, the shepherdess told her son to go outside and count the family's sheep. A little while later, he came back in, and she asked him, "How many sheep did you count?" He replied, "40." "Forty?", she said, "That's not possible; we only had 38 to begin with!" And the boy replied, "I know. I rounded them up!" [Expect a groan, unless you have a "ba-dum tss" drum-and-cymbal sting. Segue into the responsibilities of shepherds and shepherdesses, which include "rounding up" the sheep, then to how it is that God shepherds us and how we are called to shepherd one another!]

Looking for a visual aid for your homily or object lesson? Consider a stuffed animal of a lamb! What does it mean to be a sheep? We listen to and follow the Shepherd! What does it mean to be a shepherd? We care for the "sheep"! It's easy for us to love our pets [hold the stuffed animal closely, with affection]; are we sharing the same love and affection with the many "sheep" we meet throughout the week?

On **April 30**, when it doesn't fall on Sunday, the Church celebrates **St. Pius V** (1504-1572), the pope whose white Dominican habit would change the papal wardrobe to the present day. In honor of this reformer of the Church, consider the possible reforms needed in your own celebrations of the Church's liturgies!

On **April 30**, the Romanian Greek-Catholic Church (in union with Rome) celebrates the anniversary of the installation in 2006 of **Lucian Mureşan** as Major Archbishop of Făgăraş and Alba Iulia. In a spirit of ecumenism, pray for him and for the 504,000 Romanian Greek-Catholics he serves!

April 30 is also a big day in Latin America: It's *el día del niño* (Children's Day)! If you have a *Latino* community, and if you won't be doing anything to celebrate the day on April 30, consider hosting children's games and activities after your Sunday Mass. Pull in volunteers to organize games, children's music, food and drink. If your budget allows, rent a moonwalk or contract a clown, a balloon artist and/or a magician!

On **May 1**, the Church celebrates **St. Joseph the Worker**, a recent addition to the liturgical calendar, to counteract May Day celebrations of workers in communist nations. In his honor, bring attention to the sanctity and dignity of human labor as a source of holiness!

On **May 1**, the Church also celebrates **Bl. Vivaldo Stricchi** (1260-1320), the Italian lay Franciscan famous for being "joined in holy friendship" with Bl. Bartolo Buonpedoni, the Franciscan priest 32 years his senior who served as his "mother" and mentor. When Bartolo contracted leprosy, Vivaldo moved into the leper hospital with him, a sign of his fidelity "in the beautiful flower of that age when the passions begin to boil, in the tumult of affections." A trailblazer of same-sex fidelity, Vivaldo accompanied Bartolo through 20 years of suffering before retiring in grief and depression to live another 20 years inside the "hermitage" of the trunk of a chestnut tree. In his memory, pray for all who grieve the loss of a dearly loved one!

On **May 1**, we remember the passing of **John Major** (1467-1550), the Scottish philosopher, theologian and historian known for his skeptical, logical approach to the Bible and his premise that people and councils should be placed above kings and popes. In his memory, consider the place of logic and/or skepticism in your own approach to the scriptures!

On **May 1**, we remember the passing of **Lope Santos y Canseco** (1879-1963), a prominent Independent Catholic and member of the Philippine Independent Church known for his novel, *From Early Dawn to Full Light*, and for his weekly labor magazine, *The Rebirth*. He served as governor of Rizal, governor of Nueva Vizcaya, and as a senator of a largely non-Christian district. He also created Abakada Tagalog, a now-obsolete national language for the Philippines, and was charged with translating government documents and inaugural addresses to that language. In his memory, consider how you are "translating" our Christian message in ways that may or may not make sense to others!

On **May 2**, the Church celebrates **St. Athanasius** (c. 293-373), whose defense of the divinity of Christ led him to be exiled five times — for 17 of his 45 years as a bishop! Use this day to focus on the Eastern Church that celebrates him, and/or on the detachment from worldly possessions that he esteemed in his *Life of Anthony*!

On **May 2**, we remember the passing of **Caspar Johann Rinkel** (1826-1906), the Dutch priest who served as the tenth Dutch Old Catholic bishop of Haarlem. He was elected bishop three times over three years, refusing to be consecrated, but finally consenting to be consecrated in 1873 with Joseph Hubert Reinkens by the bishop of Deventer Hermann Heÿkamp. 16 years later, he signed the 1889 Declaration of Utrecht. In his memory, pray for all humble servants who feel no need to assume positions of power and influence!

On **May 2**, we remember the passing of **Warren Wendel Wiersbe** (1929-2019), the American Baptist pastor and theology professor who has written and published over 150 books, including the 50+ books of his "Be" commentaries on the books of the Bible. In his honor, pause to consider the contribution that you might make to the recorded history and literature of our faith!

On **May 2**, we celebrate the anniversary of the episcopal consecration in 2009 of Bishop **Lynn "Elizabeth" Walker**. Happy anniversary!

On **May 3**, the Church celebrates **Ss. Philip** (c. 80) **and James** (+c. 62). Philip is depicted in iconography holding loaves, due to his role in the feeding of the 5,000 (Jn. 6:5-7). He is a patron saint of queer allies due to his kindness to the non-gender-conforming Ethiopian eunuch (Acts 8:26-40). "James the Lesser" was the "brother of the Lord" and the leader of the Church at Jerusalem. In their honor, pray Eucharistic Prayer I, which mentions them, and reflect on how you're nourishing others and comporting yourself as a sister or brother of the Lord!

On **May 3**, the Church also celebrates **Juana de la Cruz** (1481-1534), the Spanish Franciscan abbess and mystic authorized to publicly preach—an extraordinary permission in that age. Famous for crossdressing, she insisted that she was conceived as a man but that God changed her gender in the womb. She suggested that Christ becomes what the seeker needs: father, mother, husband, wife, friend. Her beatification was quashed by the Roman Church for nearly five centuries before Pope Francis declared her venerable in 2015. Due to her genderbending life and theology, she is a special protector of the queer community. Find new ways to stand in solidarity with all who defy binary gender roles!

If you serve a Latino community, **May 3** is *el día de la santa cruz* (the day of the Holy Cross) and *el día de los albañiles* (Bricklayer's Day) in Latin America. For the former, people decorate crosses and bring them to church for a special blessing: Consider how you might share a cross with your congregants and/or have a crafty congregant lead an activity in which community members can make their own crosses for display at home or to be given as gifts! For the latter, consider a blessing of all who work in building-related trades (e.g., architects, engineers, contractors, concrete workers, builders, painters, electricians, plumbers, HVAC technicians, drywall installers, etc.) and/or a blessing of their tools and/or machinery!

On **May 3**, we remember the passing of **Catherine Mowry LaCugna** (1952-1997), the feminist theologian and author of *God For Us*, who sought to make the doctrine of the Trinity relevant to the everyday lives of believers. She died of cancer at age 44, while teaching systematic theology at Notre Dame. In her memory, consider the place of the Trinity in your own spirituality!

On **May 3**, we remember the passing of **Gardeopatra Quijano** (1918-2003), a prominent Independent Catholic and member of the Philippine Independent Church who is regarded as the first feminist fiction writer in the Cebuano language. A Visayan dentist and teacher, she advocated for the education of women during a time when many girls did not attend school. She later served as President of WOPIC (Women of the Philippine Independent Church) from 1975 to 1977. In her memory, consider how you might better advocate for those who do not yet fully enjoy the rights possessed by others!

On **May 3**, the Ukrainian Autocephalous Orthodox Church Canonical celebrates the birth in 1962 of **Oleh Kulyk**, who became Patriarch Moses of Kyiv. In a spirit of ecumenism, pray for him and for the people he serves!

On **May 3**, the Syriac Orthodox Church celebrates the birth in 1965 of **Sa'id Karim**, who became Patriarch Ignatius Aphrem II of Antioch and All the East. In a spirit of ecumenism, pray for him and for the people he serves!

On **May 3**, we celebrate the birth in 1972 of **Jayme Mathias**, the former Roman Catholic pastor, high school president and elected official who pastors Holy Family Catholic Church, in Austin, Texas. The publisher of 12 books on Independent Catholicism and the creator of the third iteration of a database of Independent Sacramental Movement clergy, he has gathered Independent Catholic clergy for regular in-person and virtual opportunities, including a virtual summer school for over 100 clergy and lay persons in 2020. He publishes *Extraordinary Catholics*, a bimonthly, English/Spanish magazine shared in Independent Catholic communities throughout the U.S. Consider how the Spirit might be calling you to help bridge the many "islands" of our movement!

May 3 is also **World Press Freedom Day**, a day to honor the journalists and other media professionals who share information as a public good. Pray for and lift up those who struggle to report truth amid competing forces!

On **May 4**, the Church celebrates **St. Florian** (250-304), the Roman military commander and firefighter who is a patron of firefighters, chimney sweeps and soapmakers. Pray for the women and men at your local firehouse who stand ready to serve and protect—and find a suitable way to share with them your gratitude!

On **May 4**, we remember the passing of **Cornelio Fabro** (1911-1995), the Italian Stigmatine priest and scholastic philosopher who founded the Institute for Higher Studies on Unbelief, Religion and Cultures. Part of the scholastic revival of Thomism, he also studied anthropocentrism, analyzed the relationship of Kierkegaard's thought to Christian philosophy, and critiqued "progressive" theology. In his memory, find a way to probe the skepticism, the existentialism, and the culture of unbelief that are associated with modern philosophy!

May 4 is **National Day of Prayer** in the U.S., a day when the U.S. Congress asks us to "turn to God in prayer and meditation." The U.S. President is required by law to sign a proclamation encouraging Americans to pray on this day. Pause for a moment today to honor the spirit of this day!

On **May 5**, we remember the passing of **Nicolaas Nelleman** (1722-1805), the second Dutch Old Catholic bishop of Deventer. With the archbishop of Utrecht and bishop of Haarlem, he co-signed a letter to Italian Roman Catholic bishop Scipione de'Ricci concerning the Roman church's condemnation of Gallicanism and Jansenism. As a titular bishop for 25 years, he had no jurisdiction and resided outside of Deventer. In his memory, consider the various titular leaders in our world who bear titles but exercise little leadership among others!

On **May 5**, the Ukrainian Greek Catholic Church (in union with Rome) celebrates the birth in 1970 of **Major Archbishop Sviatoslav Shevchuk**. In a spirit of ecumenism, pray for him and for the 4.5 million Ukrainian Greek Catholics he serves!

On **May 5**, we celebrate the anniversary of the presbyteral ordination in 2012 of **Leslie A. Aguillard**, a priest of the Ascension Alliance. Pray for her and for the people she serves!

In some places, **May 5** is *cinco de mayo*, the day on which some Mexicans and Mexican Americans celebrate the victory of the Mexican Army over the French at the 1862 Battle of Puebla. This day, largely promoted by beer companies, is admittedly more popular in the United States than in Mexico, but, if it's a significant day for your community, find some way to celebrate it—perhaps with Mexican food, drink, music and decorations!

On **May 6**, the Church celebrates **St. Benedicta** (+550), the sixth-century nun, mystic and lover of St. Galla of Rome, who begged St. Peter to allow the couple to enter heaven together. As foretold by St. Peter in a vision, she died 30 days after Galla. In her memory, pray for all who seek to be together with their beloved—in life and death!

On **May 6**, we remember the passing of **Cornelius Jansen** (1585-1638), the Dutch Roman Catholic bishop of Ypres in Flanders (modern-day Netherlands), who taught scripture at Louvain and is now known as the father of the theological movement of Jansenism. 75 years after his death, the opposition to his Augustinian theology became the litmus test for obedience to the Roman papacracy, by the Jesuits who enjoyed political and theological power in the church at that time. In his memory, pray for all who insist on rigid conformity by others to their own theologies and worldviews—and to all who suffer as a result!

On **May 6**, we celebrate the birth in 1939 of **Kenneth Hartley Blanchard**, the American author best known for co-authoring *The One Minute Manager*. The CSO (Chief Spiritual Officer) of his own company, he also co-authored *Lead Like Jesus: Lessons from the Greatest Leadership Role Model of All Time*. In his honor, consider the ways in which you need to grow as you endeavor to…lead like Jesus!

May 6 is **National Nurse Day** in the U.S., an opportunity to thank God for the important role of nurses in our society. Take a moment today to express gratitude to the professionals who help nurse us to health!

Sunday, May 7, 2023
FIFTH SUNDAY OF EASTER
(white)

It's the Easter season: The **paschal candle** remains in close proximity to the ambo!

The thread in today's scriptures: The Johannine Jesus suggests that he will take care of us, even preparing a place for us (Jn. 14:3). Like Jesus and like the seven men in today's first reading (Acts 6:1-7), we are called to care for others. In this way, we show that we are "a chosen race, a royal priesthood, a holy nation, a people set apart" (1Pet. 2:9), and we reflect God's justice, kindness and unfailing love to those in need (Ps. 33:5)!

Holy humor: There are all sorts of heaven jokes! Try one or two of the following, then segue into the Johannine Jesus' message of preparing a place for us in God's house!

- A man died and went to heaven, and Saint Peter welcomed him into the Pearly Gates and led him down golden streets filled with mansions on both sides. Finally, they reached their destination: a little hut! The man asked Saint Peter why he was getting a hut when there were so many mansions he could live in. Saint Peter replied, "Buddy, I tried to do the best I could with the money you shared with us!"

- A lawyer and a priest entered heaven at the same time. Saint Peter welcomed them both and showed them to their new homes. The lawyer received a huge mansion with great landscaping and several large fountains. He was overjoyed at the sight. The priest was excited, too, imagining that, if the lawyer received such a home, the home that God had prepared for the priest, who had dedicated his entire life to God, must be absolutely incredible! Saint Peter took the priest to…a shabby, old apartment, surrounded by several other apartments, and with several cars in the parking lot. Saint Peter said, "Here we are: This is where you'll be living!" The priest exploded: "Are you kidding me? I've served God my whole, entire life, and I get this apartment, when that lawyer got such a great mansion?" Saint Peter sighed and replied, "I'll be honest: We get thousands and thousands of priests up here, but she's the first lawyer we've ever gotten!"

- [For the following joke, feel free to substitute the names of other players and teams. Note: A joke like this presumes some background knowledge of the football players and teams mentioned.] NFL quarterback Peyton Manning of the Denver Colts arrived in heaven, and God was showing him to his new home: a modest little house with a faded Colts flag in the window. God said, "Peyton, this is yours for eternity!" Peyton was certainly grateful the place in heaven, but he also noticed the house directly in front of his: It was a three-story mansion with a blue and red sidewalk, a fifty-foot flagpole with an enormous New England Patriots flag, and with Patriots curtains in all the windows. So, Peyton said, "God, I'm not trying to sound ungrateful, but I'm an all-pro quarterback and hall of famer with several NFL records — so how can Tom Brady get a better house than me?" God chuckled and replied, "Peyton, that's not Tom's house. It's mine!"

Looking for a visual aid for your homily or object lesson? Consider two interlocking magic rings! You can buy them at any magic shop. Hold them separately and explain that one ring represents God, and the other ring represents us. "Magically" interlock the rings, and ask which ring is inside which ring: Is the top ring inside the bottom ring, or is the bottom ring inside the top ring? Both rings are inside one another, in the same way that we are in God, and God is in us (Jn. 14:10)! Now, as you magically separate the rings, talk about how it is that some people try to live their lives apart from God, perhaps thinking that they can leave God at the church and come back the next Sunday to "reconnect" with God. That's not how it is! Magically connect the rings again, and speak of how it is that we carry God with us throughout the week. Why? Because God is in us, and we are in God! [Note: The gospel message of Jesus being in us, and us in Jesus (Jn. 14:20), is repeated next Sunday. If you don't preach this message today, you can save it for next week!]

It's May, the traditional month of Mary! Consider a **May Day crowning of Mary**. Add to the pageantry by inviting First Communicants to wear their white suits and dresses. Invite all to bring flowers from their gardens to honor Mary!

On **May 7**, we remember the passing of **Agnellus of Pisa** (c. 1195-1236), the Italian Franciscan friar considered the founder of the Franciscan Order in England. The first Franciscan minister provincial in England, he saw the growth of the order to 43 friaries in the English province before his death. Pause to consider how you are helping to grow the presence of Independent Catholicism in our world!

On **May 7**, we remember the passing of **Diether von Isenburg** (c. 1412-1482), the German cleric whose election as archbishop of Mainz was not confirmed by Pius II or Emperor Frederick III due to his unceasing desire to reform the Church. The archbishop selected by the pope captured Mainz, killed 400 citizens and exiled 400 others, including Johannes Gutenberg. When the papist archbishop died 13 years later, Diether was again elected archbishop and confirmed by the reform-minded Sixtus IV. Pray today for those praying and pleading for patience amid suffering!

On **May 7**, we remember the passing of **Franz von Sickingen** (1481-1523), the German knight who provided his castles as a refuge for Martin Luther and other reformers, shielding them from the attacks of the Dominicans of Cologne. In his memory, find a way to show your care and concern for those who are persecuted!

On **May 7**, we remember the passing of **Tadeusz Ryszard Majewski** (1926-2002), who served as the first bishop of the Polish Old Catholic Church for 20 years. Ordained by the Old Catholic Mariavite Church, he served as the bishop of Warsaw for over ten years before being elected bishop of the national church. In 1998, he enjoyed a private conversation with his compatriot, John Paul II. He neglected to convene regular synods of the church, causing the Polish Old Catholic Church to lose government recognition, which ultimately led to the election of his successor in 1995. In his memory, pray for all our sisters and brothers of the Polish Old Catholic Church!

On **May 7**, we remember the passing of **Jean Vanier** (1928-2018), the Canadian philosopher, theologian and humanitarian who founded *L'Arche*, an international federation of communities for people with developmental disabilities and those who assist them. He authored over 30 books on religion, tolerance, disability and normality and is credited with saying, "We must do what we can to diminish walls, to meet each other. Why do we put people with disabilities behind walls?" In his honor, consider the ways in which you erect and/or tear down the walls that separate us from the most determined among us—and commit yourself to honoring them by replacing such words in your vocabulary as "disabled" and "disability," with more chosen words, like "determined" and "special abilities"!

On **May 8**, the Church celebrates **St. Julian of Norwich** (1342-1416), the medieval English anchoress known for her mystical *Revelations of Divine Love*. Always celebrated near Mother's Day, she celebrated "Mother Jesus" and shared genderbending visions of an omnigendered God. Believed to be the first Catholic to write at length of God as Mother, she famously said, "As truly as God is our Father, so truly is God our Mother!" Pray for all who help us to imagine God in new and more inclusive ways!

On **May 8**, we remember the passing of **Josip Juraj Štrosmajer** (1815-1905), the Croatian politician and bishop who was a vocal opponent of unlimited papal power and of purported papal infallibility. He left the First Vatican Council after making a three-hour speech deemed heretical by many in attendance. He promoted religious unification through the use of a single Slavonic rite for Catholic and Orthodox churches. In his memory, consider how you are promoting unity and/or being prophetic!

On **May 8**, we remember the passing of **Maria Franciszek Rostworowski** (1874-1956), the Polish Old Catholic Mariavite bishop known for his charity work throughout Europe, Asia, and Africa. In his memory, consider the extent of your own charity!

May 8 is a **Time to Remember Lost Lives from World War II**, a commemoration on Victory in Europe Day of the more than 50 million lives lost during World War II.

On **May 10**, the Church celebrates **St. Damien de Veuster** (1840-1889), who dedicated his ministry to those who suffered leprosy and were exiled to Moloka'i. Consider your own stance toward the "lepers" of your family, community, and/or society, and commit yourself to a concrete act of reaching out to and assisting them!

On **May 10**, we remember the passing of **Józef Padewski** (1894-1951), the Polish National Catholic Church bishop who was brutally tortured and murdered as a political prisoner during the communist occupation of Poland. In his memory, pray for all modern-day martyrs!

On **May 10**, we remember the passing of **Walker Percy** (1916-1990), the American author known for his philosophical novels and his exploration of "the dislocation of [the human person] in the modern age." He and his wife, Mary Bernice, converted to Catholicism together, and his career as a Catholic writer began nearly ten years later with an article in *Commonweal* magazine condemning Southern segregation and demanding a larger role for Christian thought in Southern life. Three months before his death, he made his profession as a secular Benedictine oblate. In his memory, find a way to take a stand against vestiges of segregation that are based on such categories as race, religion, economic status, sex, sexuality and gender identity!

On **May 10**, we celebrate the birth in 1966 of **Teresa Forcades**, the Catalan Benedictine nun and physician known for her outspoken and controversial views on feminism, public health and the Church. Criticized for her advocacy for Catalan independence, she responded, "Criticisms are to be expected. I follow somebody called Jesus, and he had a lot of that." In her honor, pray for your critics!

On **May 10**, we celebrate the birth in 1975 of **Maria Karol Babi**, the Polish Mariavite bishop who leads the Old Catholic Mariavite Church in Poland. In his honor, pray for him and for our sisters and brothers of the Old Catholic Mariavite Church in Poland!

On **May 10**, we celebrate the birth of **Rhee Timbang**, the supreme bishop of the Philippine Independent Church. An advocate for gender equality, he consecrated in 2019 the first woman bishop in the church's 117-year history. Pray for him and for the more than one million Independent Catholics he serves!

On **May 11**, we remember the passing of **Yves René Marie Simon** (1903-1961), the French moral and political philosopher who was recognized as one of the world's "most original and distinguished political theorists." More openminded than many Thomists and scholastic philosophers, Simon ardently defended the compatibility of Thomistic virtues and moral action with liberal, Western democracy, arguing that French Catholics erred in believing that their Catholic faith supported adherence to monarchs. In his memory, pray for all who find themselves in monarchical churches that reflect more the vision and structures of the ancient and medieval Roman Empire, than the reign of God!

On **May 11**, we remember the passing of **Salomão Barbosa Ferraz** (1880-1969), the Anglican priest who founded the Free Catholic Church and was consecrated to the episcopacy by Carlos Duarte Costa. Salomão was later received into the Roman church by John XXIII, named a titular bishop, and participated in the Second Vatican Council. He was a husband and the father of seven children — a rare example of a legitimate, married bishop in the Roman church at that time. In his honor, pray for the reconciliation of churches, that we might all recognize our oneness in Christ!

On **May 11**, we celebrate the birth in 1946 of **Leslie A. Aguillard**, a priest of the Ascension Alliance. Pray for her and for the people she serves!

On **May 12**, the Church celebrates **Ss. Nereus and Achilleus**, the first-century eunuch chamberlains of Emperor Domitian's niece, Flavia Domitilla. They were later banished with her to the island of Ponza and beheaded. In their honor, pray for all who serve others and "stick out their necks" for them!

On **May 12**, we remember the passing of **Joris-Karl Husymans** (1848-1907), the French novelist, civil servant and art critic who abandoned Catholicism but became famous for his portrayal of French Satanism and for a trilogy detailing the spiritual journey of an autobiographical character who converted to Catholicism and learned to accept suffering.

In his memory, pray for all who struggle with the great mystery of human suffering!

On **May 12**, we remember the passing of **George Eglinton Alston Dix** (1901-1952), the British Benedictine monk, liturgical scholar, and Anglican papalist who advocated for reunion of the Church of England with the Roman church. In contrast with traditional Roman Catholic theology on the form and matter of the Church's sacraments, he argued in his 1945 work, *The Shape of the Liturgy*, that the four-action "shape" of the liturgy (offertory, prayer, fraction and communion) matters more than the words that are said. Pause today to thumb through his works and reflect on your own views of church and liturgy!

On **May 12**, we remember the passing of **Erik Homburger Erikson** (1902-1994), the German-American developmental psychologist and psychoanalyst known for his theory of psychological development and his coining of the phrase "identity crisis." In his memory, pray for all who suffer from mistrust, shame, guilt, inferiority, role confusion, isolation, stagnation and/or despair!

On **May 12**, we celebrate the birth in 1962 of **Daniel Fernando**, a prominent Independent Catholic and member of the Philippine Independent Church who has served as governor of the Philippine province of Bulacan since 2019. A renowned actor, he debuted in the controversial erotic thriller "Scorpio Nights" and has since appeared in a dozen movies and 16 television shows. In his honor, consider the "transferable skills" from politics, film and television that might enhance your life and ministry!

May 12 is **International Nurses Day**, an opportunity to thank God for the important role of nurses in our world. Take a moment today to express gratitude to the professionals who help nurse us to health!

May 12 is also **U.S. Military Spouse Appreciation Day**. Find a suitable way to thank those who love and support all who protect and defend us!

On **May 13**, the Church celebrates **Our Lady of Fatima**, the 1917 apparition of Mary to shepherd children in 20th-century Portugal. Faithful to her command to pray for sinners, find a moment today to pray the rosary!

On **May 13**, we remember the passing of **Cornelius Johannes Barchman Wuytiers** (1692-1733), who served as the eighth archbishop of Utrecht. Consecrated by Roman Catholic bishop Dominique-Marie Varlet, he succeeded an archbishop who served for only six months and died, according to the Roman Church, due to divine vengeance. Though suffering a harsher condemnation than his predecessor, Cornelius received more than 100 letters of congratulation, signed by more than 2,000 clergy—including all the Roman Catholic bishops who had congratulated his predecessor. He welcomed into his archdiocese 31 Carthusians and 14 Cistercians who refused to sign *Unigenitus*, and he led his chapter through the election of a bishop of Haarlem, who died before consecration. In his memory, consider how you provide a refuge for the persecuted!

On **May 13**, we remember the passing of **Apolinario Mabini y Maranan** (1864-1903), a prominent Independent Catholic and member of the Philippine Independent Church who wrote the constitutional plan for the First Philippine Republic. A Filipino political philosopher and revolutionary, he served as the first prime minister of the Philippines in 1899. In his memory, consider how you might enhance your own leadership skills!

On **May 13**, we remember the passing of **Jaroslav Jan Pelikan** (1923-2006), the American Lutheran pastor and scholar of medieval intellectual history, Christianity, and Christian doctrine. He authored more than 30 books, including his five-volume *The Christian Tradition: A History of the Development of Doctrine*, and his later works crossed from the scholarly realm into popular reading. Late in life, he "returned" to the Orthodox Church that he discovered through his study. In his memory, pause and consider Jesus and/or Mary through the centuries!

On **May 13**, we celebrate the birth in 1952 of **Edward James Ford**, the American Old Catholic bishop who became the head of the North American Old Roman Catholic Church in 2007. In his honor, pray for him and for the people he serves!

On **May 13**, the Lutheran World Federation celebrates the anniversary of the election in 2017 of President **Musa Panti Filibus**. In a spirit of ecumenism, pray for him and for the 74 million Lutherans he serves!

The second Saturday of May is **World Migratory Bird Day**. Pause today to watch and listen to the marvelous winged creatures around you!

Sunday, May 14, 2023
SIXTH SUNDAY OF EASTER
(white)

It's the Easter season: The **paschal candle** remains in close proximity to the ambo!

Be careful with the exclusive language of today's gospel: We should not presume that only men love God! Perhaps you might proclaim the last two lines in the third person plural: "Those who have my commandments and observe them are the ones who love me. And those who love me will be loved by my Father, and I will love them and reveal myself to them."

The thread in today's scriptures: In today's first reading, Philip, James and John proclaim Christ and are the source of joy for many (Acts 8:8), allowing others to "cry out to God with joy" (Ps. 66:1) and to proclaim what God had done for them (Ps. 66:16). What are Christians to do? "Sanctify Christ in your hearts" (1Pet. 3:15), proclaim Christ (Acts 8:5), and show your love of Christ by carrying out his commands (Jn. 14:15)!

Holy humor: The story is told of the blind man, the paraplegic, and the deaf man who were looking for healing and who had heard of a famous healer who lived on a mountaintop. The blind man went up the trail using his white cane. At the top of the mountain, the healer healed him, he threw his cane off the mountain, and he came back down the mountain. The paraplegic made the difficult trek up the mountain in his wheelchair. At the top of the mountain, the healer healed him, he threw his wheelchair off the mountain, and he came back down the mountain. The deaf man saw what the other two had done. He climbed the mountain with his sign language interpreter — and yes, you know where this is going — at the top of the mountain, the healer healed him, he threw his sign language interpreter off the mountain, and he came back down the mountain! [Segue into the many healings that were taking place in today's first reading — a cause of great joy for many people — and how the early apostles were following Jesus' command to preach, heal and baptize in his name!

Looking for a visual aid for your homily or object lesson? Consider a yoke! [A parish carpenter can easily cut two half-circles into a 2x8 board for this.] Begin your homily by holding up the yoke and saying, "This is what married life is like! Literally." Explain that conjugal (or "married") life comes from a Latin root that literally means that you walk "with the yoke" of another person. In marriage, we're yoked together! Now, transition to today's gospel: The Johannine Jesus says, "If you love me, you will keep my commandments" (Jn. 14:15, repeated in Jn. 14:21). Ancient rabbis used the yoke as a symbol of God's law — and those who resisted God's law were branded as "stiff-necked" — like oxen who try to resist the yoke! Fortunately, in the synoptic gospels, Jesus boiled down 613 biblical mandates into two primary ones: Love God, and love your neighbor. Jesus' yoke is definitely easier and lighter than the Mosaic Law (Mt. 11:30)! In this context, the pseudonymous author of 1Peter might be understood to mean that if we shoulder the "yoke" of Jesus' law, he, like the driver of oxen, will "lead us to God" (1Pet. 3:18)!

On **the second Sunday of May**, U.S. society celebrates **Mother's Day**. Each of us has a mother and various mother figures in our lives: Let's celebrate them today!

- Involve women in all liturgical ministries today!
- Incorporate intercessions for mothers — living and deceased.
- Share a special blessing for mothers and mother figures (e.g., stepmothers, godmothers, aunts, teachers, coaches), lead all present in an applause, and share with all mother figures a red, long-stemmed rose or some other symbol of your community's love for and gratitude to them!
- For the intellectually-curious, note that the ancient Greeks celebrated Cybele — the mother of Greek gods — with a spring festival, and/or share a brief lesson on Mother Jarvis' concern that, prior to Mother's Day, there was no day in the U.S. to honor women.

On **May 14**, when it doesn't fall on a Sunday, the Church celebrates **St. Matthias** (+c. 80), the man chosen from 120 disciples to replace Judas Iscariot (Acts 1:18-26). Pray Eucharistic Prayer I, which mentions him, and use this day to reflect on how you are forming your own "replacements." Identify the people who could one day do what you currently do, and empower them in their education and formation!

On **May 14**, we remember the passing of **Dominique-Marie Varlet** (1678-1742), the Roman Catholic bishop of Babylon who, without the permission of the Roman papacracy, shared valid lines of apostolic succession with four archbishops of Utrecht. Take a moment today to thank God for the tremendous courage and pastoral sensitivity of this giant in the Independent Catholic movement!

On **May 14**, we remember the passing of **John Moynihan Tettemer** (1876-1949), the American former Passionist monk and Roman Catholic priest made famous for his posthumous 1951 autobiography, *I Was a*

9

Monk. He left the Roman church, married, fathered three children, and served as a bishop in the Liberal Catholic Church. The foreword to his autobiography described him as an "expert mountain-climber, skater, skier, and tennis-player, chess enthusiast, voracious reader of everything new in non-fiction and anything exciting in murder mysteries, a stickler for accuracy and for the correct use of words, vigorous individualist and champion of justice and American democracy…who loved God through [others]." In his memory, reach out to support someone who has made a similarly-difficult life decision!

On **May 14**, we celebrate the anniversary of the founding in 2013 of **Our Lady of the Angels Catholic Community** in Kingman, Arizona. Happy anniversary!

On **May 15**, the Church celebrates **St. Isidore the Farmer** (c. 1070-1130, not to be confused with St. Isidore of Seville, who is celebrated on April 4). In honor of the patron saint of farmers, share a prayer for all who raise and harvest the foods we all enjoy!

On **May 15**, we remember the passing of **Peter Maurin** (1877-1949), the French social activist and co-founder of the Catholic Worker Movement who "indoctrinated" Dorothy Day with such ideas as Catholic Worker farms and "houses of hospitality" for the poor. In his memory, consider your own stance toward the poor and those most in need!

On **May 15**, we remember the passing of **Gedeón G. Quijano** (1910-1989), a prominent Independent Catholic and member of the Philippine Independent Church who served as governor of the Philippine province of Misamis Occidental for over 20 years (1946-1967). The son of PIC bishop Juan P. Quijano, he was recruited into the U.S. Army and served as a doctor. After completing his public service, he moved to Salisbury, North Carolina, where he worked as a physiatrist in a V.A. hospital and advocated for citizenship and benefits for the Filipinos who fought alongside U.S. troops in World War II. In his memory, consider how you might better advocate for others!

On **May 15**, we remember the passing of **Gloria Anzaldúa** (1942-2004), the American scholar of feminist, queer and Chicana cultural theories. A native of the Mexico/Texas border, she incorporated her experiences of marginalization into her works. Raised with a self-described "folk Catholicism with many pagan elements," she thwarted patriarchal structures in Catholicism through her devotion to folk Catholic female icons like Our Lady of Guadalupe and indigenous Nahuatl/Toltec divinities. In her memory, consider how your own experiences of privilege and/or of marginalization have made you the marvelous creation you are!

On **May 15**, we celebrate the birth in 1956 of **Chung Hyun Kyung**, the South Korean lay Presbyterian theologian whose research interests have included feminist and ecofeminist theologies, Christian-Buddhist interfaith dialogue, and the theologies and spiritualities of Asia, Africa and Latin America. Pause today to learn something new about another theological or spiritual tradition!

May 15 is **International Day of Families**, an opportunity to focus on meeting the needs and challenges of families. Pray for the families closest to you and consider ways in which you might be of assistance to them!

May 15 is also **U.S. Peace Officers Memorial Day**, an opportunity to honor the local, state and federal peace officers who have been killed or disabled in the line of duty. Search the internet for the wreath-laying ceremonies, candlelight vigils and Blue Masses nearest you!

On **May 16**, we remember the passing of **Johann Jacob van Thiel** (1843-1912), the Dutch priest and seminary rector who served as the eleventh Dutch Old Catholic bishop of Haarlem. He represented the Dutch Old Catholic Church at the Old Catholic Congresses of 1871 and 1872. He corresponded with theologians in several countries, and he promoted the spread of Old Catholicism into France—for which he received an honorary doctorate from the University of Bern in 1903. For 20 years, he served on the Rotterdam-Petersburg Committee, which tried to reunite the Eastern and Western churches, and he played a significant role in admitting the Mariavite Church to the Union of Utrecht in 1909. For five years, he published *De Oud-Katholiek* (*The Old Catholic*) magazine, and he co-founded *Cor Unum et Anima Una* to publish various writings. He promoted congregational singing and liturgy in the vernacular, and he mediated disputes between clergy. In his memory, consider how you might more actively promote harmony and growth within the Church!

On **May 16**, we remember the passing of **A. Philip Randolph** (1889-1979), the American activist and civil rights leader who helped organize the 1963 March on Washington, at which Martin Luther King Jr. delivered his "I Have A Dream" speech. In his memory, consider how you help to speed the fulfillment of a society that sees beyond skin color!

On **May 17**, we remember the passing of **Mary Chase Walker** (1828-1899), the American suffragette who served as the first teacher at the first public school in San Diego County, California. In her memory, pray for all who serve the students in our public schools!

On **May 18**, the Church celebrates **St. John I** (+526), the elderly pope imprisoned by an Arian king. Pray in a special way for the elderly, the imprisoned, and those who are persecuted by others!

On **May 18**, we remember the passing of **Nicolaas Prins** (1858-1916), the Dutch priest who served as the twelfth Dutch Old Catholic bishop of Haarlem. He advocated for the vernacular in liturgy, and, after 25 years of priestly ministry, he celebrated his first Dutch mass in 1908. Four years later, he was consecrated bishop of Haarlem, an office in which he served for less than four years. In his memory, consider the ways in which you help others to better understand our faith and liturgy!

On **May 18**, we remember the passing of **Jeannette Rankin** (1880-1973), the first woman to hold federal office in the United States. To this day, she is the only woman from Montana to be elected to Congress. In her memory, pray for all who are breaking "glass ceilings"!

On **May 18**, we celebrate the birth in 1962 of **Frank Bellino**, pastor of St. Michael Catholic Parish in San Antonio, Texas. Pray for him and for the people he serves!

On **May 19**, we remember the passing of **Alcuin of York** (c. 735-804), the Northumbrian scholar, mathematician and poet in Charlemagne's court later named an abbot and "the most learned person anywhere to be found." Because of his homoerotic poetry and letters, and his affection for certain monks, he is considered a patron saint of the gay community. He penned several works, including the famous *Life of St. Willibrord*, important in the Old Catholic tradition. In his memory, reacquaint yourself with his *Life of St. Willibrord*!

On **May 19**, we remember the passing of **William Ewart Gladstone** (1809-1898), the British prime minister who enjoyed the majestic traditions of Roman Catholicism but opposed the authoritarianism of the pope, the church's hostility toward liberalism, and its refusal to distinguish between secular allegiance and spiritual obedience. During the 1870 Vatican Council, he opposed the purported universal jurisdiction of the bishop of Rome, and he encouraged British Catholics to reject the idea of purported papal infallibility. The sale of 150,000 copies of his pamphlet alleging that Roman Catholics had "no mental freedom" sparked a reply by John Henry Newman. In his memory, pray for all who espouse mental freedom and the values Gladstone cherished!

On **May 19**, we remember the passing of **Max Ferdinand Scheler** (1874-1928), the German "first man of the philosophical paradise" who developed Husserl's phenomenology and greatly influenced contemporary philosophy. Karol Wojtyla (John Paul II) defended his doctoral dissertation on Scheler, who suggested that philosophical knowledge cannot be achieved without sharing in the primal essence of love, which opens us to other "beings-of-value." In Scheler's memory, pause to consider the values and "disvalues" (negative values) that currently direct your life—and the value that you might be attaching to the realization of lower values at the expense of higher values!

On **May 19**, we remember the passing of **Walerian Kierzkowski** (1905-1979), the Polish bishop who administered the diocese of Wroclaw for the Polish Catholic Church in Poland. In his memory, pray for our sisters and brothers of the Polish Catholic Church in Poland!

On **May 19**, we remember the passing of **Soliman Ganno** (1931-1989), who served as seventh supreme bishop of the Philippine Independent Church for only two years before his death. The first dean of the church's national cathedral, he challenged adherents to advocate for the marginalized. His heart failure at the altar of the national cathedral prevented him from seeing the fulfillment of the vision that he outlined for the renewal of his church. In his memory, pray for all who are frustrated in the realization of their dreams!

On **May 19**, we remember the passing of **Jacques Ellul** (1912-1994), the French philosopher, sociologist and lay theologian who was a noted Christian anarchist and who authored 58 books and a thousand articles during his lifetime. A dominant theme of his work was the threat that technology poses to religion and human freedom. In his memory, consider the ways in which technology limits your freedom and the freedom of those whom you love!

On **May 19**, we celebrate the birth in 1929 of **Harvey Cox**, the American theologian who served as a professor at the Harvard Divinity School. Author of the 1965 bestseller, *The Secular City*, he later focused on liberation theology, God's preference for the poor, and Jesus' liberating message. In his honor, reacquaint yourself with one of his many works!

On **May 20**, the Church celebrates **St. Bernardine of Siena** (1380-1444), the orphaned "apostle of Italy" who cared for plague victims, preached devotion to the Holy Name of Jesus, and hosted "bonfires of vanities" to burn unnecessary luxuries. In his memory, encourage acts of care for "untouchables," share a lesson on the IHS Christogram, and/or encourage congregants to share with those in need the extra food in their pantries and the extra clothes in their closets!

On **May 20**, we celebrate the passing of **Crispin Beltrán** (1933-2008), a prominent Independent Catholic and member of the Philippine Independent Church who served as a congressman in the Toiling Masses

Party and was known as the "Grand Old Man of Philippine Labor." A staunch critic of President Gloria Macapagal-Arroyo, he was imprisoned in 2006-2007 on disputed charges of plotting to overthrow her government. In his memory, pray for all who are persecuted by their enemies!

On **May 20**, we celebrate the anniversary of the ordination in 2022 of **Stephen Rodriguez**, a deacon at Holy Family Catholic Church in Austin, Texas. Pray for him and for the people he serves!

Sunday, May 21, 2023
THE ASCENSION OF OUR LORD
(white)

Consider when you'll celebrate the Solemnity of the Ascension: If you celebrate it on the 40th day of Easter, know that many people may be unable to join you for a Thursday liturgy. By transferring the celebration to this Sunday, all will be able to celebrate this mystery of our faith!

It's the Easter season: The **paschal candle** remains in close proximity to the ambo!

For the intellectually-curious, there are various lessons today!

- Provide a brief lesson on the ascension in scripture: it's not contained in the earliest version of Mark, it can only be inferred in Matthew, and it may have taken place as soon as Easter Day in Luke's account. Also, be sure to note that the Acts of the Apostles, which begins with an ascension account, was written by Luke!

- Anthropologist Joseph Campbell pointed out that, even if the risen Christ blasted off from the earth at the speed of light, he'd still be in the Milky Way nearly 2,000 years later! What are more mature understandings that we might have of this mystery, rather than a merely simplistic conception of the resurrected Christ ascending to be atop the "bowl" of the heavens in the ancient cosmology?

Note the exclusive language of today's first reading: Why should we presume that there were no women among the "men of Galilee"—since Jesus' mother and other women were among Jesus' disciples?

You'll need to **choose which form of the second reading you'll use**: Ephesians 1, which speaks of Christ being seated at God's right hand in heaven, or Ephesians 4, which says that Christ descended into the lower regions of the earth before ascending "far above all the heavens."

Note: The introductory line of today's second reading is misleading. The Letter to the Ephesians is a pseudonymous letter, written in Paul's name and spirit, but not written by Paul. Rather than confuse your listeners, begin the proclamation with, "A reading from the Letter to the Ephesians"!

The thread in today's scriptures: Matthew concludes his gospel with the risen Christ's admonition to baptize and teach others to observe his commandments (Mt. 28:19-20; note the connections to last Sunday's scriptures), and we hear the ascension account of Luke's second volume (Acts1:1-11). The psalmist sings a prophecy of the ascension of the messiah to his throne (Ps. 47:2-9), and the pseudonymous author of the Letter to the Ephesians affirms that God "worked in Christ, raising him from the dead and seating him at God's right hand in the heavens" (Eph. 1:20).

Holy humor: The story is told of the priest who was speaking with the small children of her congregation. Before bidding them farewell, she asked if any of the children had any questions for her. Little Rebecca was eager to share what she had discovered this week. She asked, "Do you know why God created the world with only one hand?" The priest was a bit surprised. "God only created the world with one hand?" Little Rebecca continued, "Yes! God created the world with God's left hand — and do you know why?" Deciding to play along, the priest asked, "And just how do we know that God created the world with God's left hand?" Little Rebecca was quick to answer: "Because Jesus was…sitting on God's right hand!" [Segue into today's celebration of Jesus' ascension into heaven.]

Looking for a visual aid for your homily or object lesson? Consider a depiction of ancient cosmology and/or the cross! Ancient depictions of the universe (indeed until some 500 years ago) suggested that the heavens were like an inverted bowl over the flat plate of the earth. So, too, it's time to see this mystery of faith anew. Instead of thinking of Christ as "somewhere up there" (an admittedly androcentric conception by people on any side of the earth), open your eyes: Christ is hidden in the faces of those around you! Medieval mystics suggested that the two beams of the cross lift our attention "vertically" toward God and "horizontally" toward those around us: Consider how this feast has traditionally taken our eyes in a "vertical" direction when, perhaps more appropriately, this celebration should take our eyes in a "horizontal" direction — in the direction of the presence of Christ around us!

The school year is winding down, and some families may be traveling next weekend for Memorial Day: Be sure to have an **end-of-year blessing for all students — and all who serve them** — in thanksgiving for the past year of learning and growth, and asking for God's blessing over them during the summer break! Also, find a fitting way to **celebrate the graduates in your community** — perhaps by inviting them to wear their caps and gowns to mass, sharing scholarships with them, and/or having a reception with cake and punch to honor them!

On **May 21**, when it doesn't fall on Sunday, the Church celebrates **St. Christopher Magallanes** (1869-1927) **and Companions**, the 22 priests and 3 laypersons martyred during anticlerical government reforms in Mexico (1915-1928). Magallanes was killed without trial — and after absolving his executioner. Take a moment today to pray for your enemies; better yet, find a way to reach out to them in love!

On **May 21**, we remember the passing of **Jane Addams** (1860-1935), the American activist who co-founded the American Civil Liberties Union. In her memory, pray for all who actively work for civil rights!

On **May 21**, we remember the passing in 2022 of **Rosemary Radford Ruether**, the American feminist scholar and Catholic theologian who, despite sanction by the Vatican, has been an outspoken advocate for the ordination of women in the Roman church. As a director of Catholics for Choice, she has advocated for allowing women to follow their Spirit-inspired consciences. In her honor, consider what you are doing to advance Jesus' and Paul's vision of a "discipleship of equals"!

May 21 is **World Day for Cultural Diversity**, an opportunity to honor the diversity of cultural expressions in our world. Find a suitable way to esteem the diversity in your community!

On **May 22**, the Church of Italy celebrates the **Madonna of Montevergine**, an image of Mary credited with rescuing a male gay couple from homophobic violence in 1256, thus beginning a long tradition of "ancestral gay pride" processions to her shrine in Montevergine, Italy. She is a matron saint of the gay community in Italy. In her honor, consider how you follow in the footsteps of "she who gives everything and forgives everything"!

On **May 22**, we remember the passing of **St. Constantine I** (272-337). Known as "Constantine the Great" and "the Equal to the Apostles," he reunited the Roman Empire and is now considered a saint in the Orthodox tradition. For centuries, it was believed that he experienced a radical conversion leading to a personal crusade to convert his empire to his mother's religion. Pray today for all civil leaders who have been sympathetic to our Christian/Catholic beliefs and traditions!

On **May 22**, the Church celebrates **St. Rita of Cascia** (c. 1381-1457), a victim of domestic abuse, who, as an Augustinian nun, shared the sufferings of Jesus. Pray for all victims of domestic violence—and promote acts of charity for organizations that assist them!

On **May 22**, we remember the passing of **Victor Marie Hugo** (1802-1885), the French poet, novelist and dramatist who wrote *Les Misérables*. He is considered one of France's greatest and best-known writers, and his likeness is on French currency. Largely raised by his Catholic mother, he received a Catholic Royalist education. As a young man, his views became increasingly anti-Catholic and anti-clerical, particularly in light of the Church's indifference to the plight of the working class. The Catholic press responded with 740 published attacks on *Les Misérables*. In his memory, pray for and/or connect with those who cherish the Church's message of social justice—even if they have challenges with the clericalism, structures and stances of the Church!

On **May 22**, California celebrates **Harvey Milk Day**. A pioneering LGBTQIA+ rights activist and the most famous gay elected official in California, Harvey Milk (1930-1978) is memorialized in two Oscar-winning movies. A martyr for LGBTQ and human rights, he is remembered for his words: "Hope will never be silent."

May 22 is **World Biological Diversity Day**, an opportunity to examine our relationship to the natural world and to highlight nature-based solutions to climate, health issues, food and water insecurity, and sustainable livelihoods. Plants provide 80% of our diet, and fish provide 20% of our protein. We thank God for the biological diversity that allows us to be who we are!

On **May 23,** we remember the passing of **Laurentius Surius** (1523-1578), the German Carthusian hagiographer and church historian known for his collection of the acts of the Church councils and the lives of the saints. In his memory, consider how you are capturing and telling the stories of your community and its saints!

On **May 23,** we remember the passing of **Franz von Baader** (1765-1841), the German Catholic philosopher, theologian, physician and mining engineer who revived the Scholastic school as a means of countering growing empiricism and atheism in Europe. He is known for introducing to academia the works of Meister Eckhart, the Dominican who suffered the inquisitorial process and was condemned for heresy by the Roman church. In his memory, explore the mystical works of Meister Eckhart, whom von Baader attempted to popularize!

On **May 23**, we remember the passing of **Wynn Wagner, III** (1951-2018), the musician, software developer and HIV/AIDS philanthropist who brought attention to the Independent Catholic movement through his many books on religion. An archbishop of the North American Old Catholic Church and pastor of St. Mychal Judge Old Catholic Church in Dallas, Texas, he was known outside Independent Catholic circles as an author of vampire fiction and gay romance.

On **May 23**, the Romanian Greek-Catholic Church (in union with Rome) celebrates the birth in 1930 of **Major Archbishop Lucian Mureşan**. In a spirit of ecumenism, pray for him and for the 504,000 Romanian Greek-Catholics he serves!

On **May 24**, the Church celebrates **St. Joanna**, a woman healed by the Lucan Jesus (Lk. 8:2-3) and who later accompanied him and supported his ministry and travels. She witnessed his resurrection with Mary Magdalene and Mary the mother of James (Mt. 28:8-10). Her husband, Chuza, managed the household of Herod Antipas, the ruler of Galilee. The Orthodox tradition celebrates her as one of eight myrrh bearers for Jesus. In her memory, pray for all who support the continued ministry of Jesus in our world!

On **May 24**, we remember the passing of **Georges Darboy** (1813-1871), the archbishop of Paris who argued for the episcopal independence of the French church and strongly opposed purported papal infallibility at the First Vatican Council. He stirred controversy by suppressing the Jesuits in his diocese, and Pius IX refused him the cardinal's hat due to his liberal writings. He was among the hostages who were executed when the Paris Commune was overthrown in 1871. In his memory, pray for all victims of violence, oppression, and passive-aggression!

On **May 24**, we remember the passing of **Ambrose St. John** (1815-1875), the Roman Catholic priest and soulmate of St. John Henry Newman, who was 14 years his senior. For 32 years, they were inseparable, and, when Newman's "earthly light" died, Newman wrote, "I have always thought no bereavement was equal to that of a husband's or wife's, but I feel it difficult to believe that anyone's sorrow can be greater than mine!" Newman insisted in his will that he be buried in St. John's grave. In 2008, in preparation for Newman's beatification, the Vatican tried to exhume his remains, to separate them from his lover—only to discover that all their remains had decomposed and were thus not separable. Lift up those whose inseparable love is a light in our world!

On **May 24**, we remember the passing of **Nicolaus Spit** (1853-1929), who served as the seventh Dutch Old Catholic bishop of Deventer for 34 years. As a young priest, he oversaw the construction of a new church in Egmond, before moving to Rotterdam where he supported his pastor's publication of *De Oud-Katholiek* magazine. After being consecrated titular bishop of Deventer, with no jurisdiction, he continued his ministry in Rotterdam. He served as co-consecrator of Franciszek Hodur of the Polish National Catholic Church and of Jan Maria Michał Kowalski of the Old Catholic Church of the Mariavites. His episcopal motto was "I have place my trust in you" (Ps. 72:28). His final years were characterized by hearing loss and visual impairment. In his memory, consider how you place your trust in God despite infirmity and human frailty!

On **May 24**, we remember the passing of **Maria Szymon Bucholc** (1893-1965), the Polish Old Catholic Mariavite bishop of the Silesian-Łódź diocese. In his memory, pray for our sisters and brothers of the Old Catholic Mariavite Church in Poland!

On **May 24**, we remember the passing of **Stormé DeLarverie** (1920-2014), the biracial, American "drag king" and civil rights icon often credited with being the spark that stirred to action the "Saints of Stonewall" in New York City on June 28, 1969. She is referred to as the "guardian of lesbians in the Village" and as "the Rosa Parks of the gay community." In her memory, consider how you are stirring others to action on matters of social justice and civil rights!

May 24 is **Emergency Medical Services for Children Day in the U.S.**, an opportunity to celebrate emergency medical service providers and all who provide specialized emergency care for others.

On **May 25**, the Church celebrates **St. Bede the Venerable** (c. 672-735), **St. Gregory VII** (c. 1015-1085), and **St. Mary Magdalene de'Pazzi** (1566-1607). Bede challenges us to consider how we are recording history. Gregory VII was a reformer who, because of his disputes with the emperor, is a model for getting along with those who think very differently from us. Mary Magdalene de'Pazzi developed a love of prayer from an early age (a model for children!) and can be lifted up as a model of prayer, penance, eucharistic devotion, and love for the poor!

On **May 25**, we remember the passing of **Rosa Bonheur** (1822-1899), the famous 19th-century French painter, queer pioneer and feminist icon who honored what she called the "androgyne Christ." Raised in Saint-Simonianism, a French utopian Christian-socialist movement that advocated equality for women and prophesied the coming of a female messiah, she defied gender norms and advocated for gender equality. In her memory, consider how you love and support those who defy gender norms!

On **May 25**, the Anglican Church commemorates **Randall Davidson** (1848-1930), the longest-serving archbishop of Canterbury since the Reformation, who revised the *Book of Common Prayer* and led the church through World War I and such ecumenical efforts as the 1920 Lambeth Conference. Reflecting on his life, he described himself as "a funny old fellow of quite mediocre, second-rate gifts and a certain amount of common sense—but [who] tried to do [his] best." In his memory, consider how you do your best to use your gifts to God's glory!

On **May 25**, we remember the passing of **Robert Georg Heinrich Tüchler** (1874-1952), the violinist and Roman Catholic Barnabite priest who served as the second bishop of the Austrian Old Catholic Church for 14 years. A World War I military chaplain, he was personally attacked, and Old Catholics were made to feel like second-class citizens belonging to a sect. He imitated Roman Catholic liturgy and dress—which wasn't kindly received by all clergy. He established the Old Catholic *Diakonie*, which tended to those most in need. In his memory, pray for all our sisters and brothers of the Austrian Old Catholic Church!

On **May 25**, the Roman Catholic Church celebrates the birth in 1953 of **Francesco Moraglia**, the Latin Patriarch of Venice. In a spirit of ecumenism, pray for him and for the Roman Catholics he serves!

May 25 is **African Day**, an opportunity to learn about the struggles of African communities for liberation and development. Find a way to support our sisters and brothers on the world's poorest and second-largest continent!

May 25 is also **National Missing Children's Day in the U.S.**, an opportunity to focus on child safety and to pray for the 400,000 children on our national registry of missing children.

On **May 26**, the Church celebrates **St. Philip Neri** (1515-1595), the Italian priest and "third apostle of Rome" who founded the Congregation of the Oratory for secular priests. In his memory, consider the ways in which you support and encourage the clergy around you!

On **May 26**, the Church celebrates **St. Peter Sanz** (1680-1747), the Catalan Dominican friar and bishop who was tortured and beheaded by imperial authorities in China. Pray for all who suffer the cruelty of others!

On **May 26**, we remember the passing of **Georg Hermes** (1775-1831), the German Catholic theologian whose works were posthumously condemned by the Roman church but were later championed by his students who joined the Old Catholic Church. Their efforts were in vain, and the condemnation of his works was reiterated by Pius IX—only solidifying their opposition to the oppressive papacracy of the Roman church. In his memory, pray for all who are harshly judged, even after death!

On **May 26**, we remember the passing of **Jan Maria Michał Kowalski** (1871-1942), the Mariavite bishop who led the Mariavite Church and the Old Catholic Mariavite Church for over 25 years. After serving as a Roman Catholic priest for three years, he discovered the Mariavite Church and led the effort to win Vatican approval for the private revelations of Feliksa Kozłowska. When the Vatican condemned Mariavitism, he established the Mariavite Church as a recognized church in the Russian empire. In 1909, he established union with Utrecht and was consecrated an Old Catholic bishop by the archbishop of Utrecht. After the death of Kozłowska in 1921, he became the leader of the Old Catholic Mariavite Church, translated the scriptures into Polish, and published the revelations of Kozłowska. He spearheaded numerous reforms in the church, including communion under both forms, the abolition of clerical celibacy, and the ordination of women. In his memory, pray for all reformers who attempt to bring to birth contemporary manifestations of the early Church!

On **May 27**, the Church celebrates **St. Augustine of Canterbury** (+c. 604), the first bishop of Canterbury: Pray today for our sisters and brothers of the Anglican tradition!

On **May 27**, we remember the passing of **John Calvin** (1509-1564), the French priest, theologian and reformer who wrote commentaries on most books of the Bible, championed the absolute sovereignty of God in matters of salvation, and championed new forms of liturgy and church governance. In his memory, grow in wisdom by increasing your knowledge of God and yourself!

On **May 27**, we celebrate the anniversary of the episcopal consecration in 2007 of Bishop **Robert Ortega**, archbishop of the Charismatic Old Catholic Church. Happy anniversary!

Sunday, May 28, 2023
PENTECOST
(red)

We're still in the Easter season: The **paschal candle** remains in close proximity to the ambo—and is removed from the sanctuary at the conclusion of today's Mass. Consider carrying it out of your worship space as part of the procession during the hymn of sending forth!

Think through the **Pentecost décor** of your worship space!

- Decorate your worship space with splashes of **red**!
- Be sure your **Pentecost vestments** are ironed or steamed—and that they coordinate with any other shades of red in your worship environment.
- Consider **banners** with images of the fire and/or dove that represents the Holy Spirit.
- Consider **floral arrangements** that symbolize the diversity of the persons who experienced the Pentecost event, with a variety of flowers of differing shapes, sizes and colors. Consider flowers with intriguing, flame-shaped and/or flame-colored blooms.
- Bring to mind the appearance of the Holy Spirit as a rushing wind by creating **ribbon banners** on portable stands lining your outer aisles, by placing banners outdoors, and/or by hanging bells and/or chimes in trees. When making ribbon banners, always vary the colors, widths and lengths of the ribbons.
- As always, **decorate the entrance to your worship space and even outdoors**, so that the spirit of the celebration is obvious to congregants as they approach your worship space! Also, don't forget the look of other spaces, like your Blessed Sacrament chapel, parish hall and classrooms!
- **Invite congregants to wear red**, or, if you have a multicultural community, invite congregants to dress in native dress, and proclaim the scriptures—particularly the first reading—in a more multilingual way!

There is no more appropriate way to celebrate the coming of the Holy Spirit than with the **sacrament of Confirmation**: Consider planning well in advance for a celebration of Confirmation on this special day!

The Church shares four "great sequences" each year: Today's is the *Veni, Sancte Spiritus*. Consider having a gifted cantor sing or chant a setting of this, before segueing into the Gospel Acclamation!

192

The thread in today's scriptures (for the Mass during the Day): Luke shares the story of the coming of the Spirit at Pentecost (Acts 2:1-11). John tells a different story, of how the Johannine Jesus breathed forth the Spirit on his friends on Easter night (Jn. 20:19-23). Both point to the same truth: The Spirit is present and active in Christ's Church, endowing us with gifts (1Cor. 12:3-7) and renewing the face of the earth (Ps. 104:30) through those who've received the gift of the Spirit!

Holy humor: You've likely heard the joke about how you make holy water, right? How do you make holy water? You take water, and you...boil the hell out of it! But have you heard what you get when you mix holy water and...vodka? What do you get when you mix holy water and vodka? A holy...spirit! [Segue to how it is that this day celebrates a different type of holy spirit: God's sustaining spirit in our world!]

Looking for a visual aid for your homily or object lesson? Consider a glass of milk, a bottle of chocolate syrup, and a tall spoon! Hold up the glass of milk, and tell your listeners "This glass of milk is...you!" Everyone knows the taste of milk. Invite forward an altar server, have him/her taste the milk, and tell you what it tastes like. It tastes like...milk! Now hold up the chocolate, and say "This chocolate is...the Holy Spirit!" (Your listeners can now guess where this is going!) Pour the chocolate into the glass, and have the altar server taste the milk again. What does it taste like? (Be sure to prepare your altar server in advance, so that s/he is not confused.) Because the chocolate pierced the milk and settled on the bottom of the glass, the milk still tastes like...milk. What do you have to do to the chocolate? You have to stir it up! In the same way, we all receive the Spirit in the sacraments of the Church...but we ourselves need to "stir up" the Spirit! As you stir the chocolate into the milk, list a few ways listeners can "stir up" the Spirit in their lives (e.g., prayer, reading scripture, going to church, performing good works). Finally, ask the altar server to taste the milk one last time. What does it taste like? Chocolate milk! End with these words: "Sisters and brothers, we've all received the Spirit. If your life tastes like milk, it's time to...stir up the Spirit!"

On Pentecost, we refresh the special dismissal that we heard during the Easter Octave: Be sure your deacon knows how to **chant the double Alleluia of the dismissal**.

After today, we return to Ordinary Time — beginning with the 10th Week in Ordinary Time this week — but we won't see the color green on a Sunday until June 18.

It's **Memorial Day** weekend: Include prayers for all who made the ultimate sacrifice for our freedom!

On **May 28**, we remember the passing of **Vicente Sotto** (1877-1950), a prominent Independent Catholic and co-founder of the Philippine Independent Church in Cebu, Philippines. A journalist and dramatist, he authored various anti-friar works and was known as the publisher and editor of the fiery *Ang Suga* and *El Pueblo*. As a senator, he was the principal author of the Sotto Law, which guaranteed freedom of press. At his death, Philippine president Carlos Garcia proclaimed, "Vicente Sotto was a rock of Gibraltar in character because of the ruggedness of his conviction, the indomitability of his soul, the sublimity of his courage, and the depth of his faith in the ultimate triumph of justice....His march saw no retreat, and his soul of steel knew no surrender. He marshaled his efforts and used his influence to secure and safeguard for the press the fullest measure of freedom." In his memory, consider how you are helping others on their journey toward greater independence and freedom!

On **May 28**, we celebrate the anniversary of the episcopal consecration in 2003 of Bishop **Thomas Abel**, bishop of the Catholic Church of America and pastor of Santo Niño Catholic Church in Las Vegas, Nevada. Happy anniversary!

On **May 29**, we remember the passing of **Andrew Greeley** (1928-2013), the Roman Catholic priest, sociologist and novelist who interpreted American Catholicism through his research and fiction. Greeley's explicit treatment of sex and sexuality, as well as of the Roman church's sexual abuse scandal, earned him the scorn of critics. In his memory, pray for all whose words and actions are not always charitably received by those they love!

On **May 29,** the Syro Malabar Catholic Church (in union with Rome) celebrates the anniversary of the installation in 2011 of **George Alencherry** as Major Archbishop of Ernakulam-Ankamali. In a spirit of ecumenism, pray for him and for the 5.1 million Syro Malabar Catholics he serves!

May 29 is **International Day of United Nations Peacekeepers**, an opportunity to celebrate the nearly 90,000 young people who are deployed in United Nations peace operations.

On **May 30**, the Church celebrates **St. Joan of Arc** (1412-1431), the courageous, cross-dressing teenager who stubbornly defined gender rules and led the French army to victory at age 17. The subject of over 10,000 books, plays, paintings and films, she is a queer icon, a girl-power hero, and the matron saint of France and of the transvestite community. She was killed by her church for exercising her God-given right to wear men's clothing. Pray for and show your solidarity to all who defy traditional gender norms to live as the persons God created them to be!

On **May 31**, the Church celebrates the **Visitation of Mary**: Repeat Elizabeth's words as you pray the second Joyful Mystery of the rosary!

On **May 31**, the Church celebrates **St. Petronilla**, the Roman woman believed to be the daughter of St. Peter the Apostle. Legends suggests she was so beautiful that St. Peter locked her in a tower to keep her from eligible men. She is one of the 140 colonnade saints at St. Peter Basilica in Vatican City. In her memory, pray for all women who continue to be oppressed!

May 31 is **World No Tobacco Day**, an opportunity to draw attention to the preventable deaths and diseases caused by the tobacco epidemic.

On **June 1**, the Church celebrates **St. Justin** (c. 100 – c. 165), the early apologist who used philosophy to shed light on the mysteries of our faith: Honor him with a brief refresher of his defenses of our beliefs!

On **June 1**, we remember the passing of **Alfred Loisy** (1857-1940), the French priest, professor and prolific writer considered the founder of Roman Catholic modernism. A critic of traditional views of biblical interpretation, he was excommunicated by Pius X and dismissed from the Catholic Institute of Paris. He famously observed that "Jesus came proclaiming the Kingdom—and what arrived was the Church." In his memory, consider how focused you are on proclaiming God's reign versus building...church!

On **June 1**, we remember the passing of **Karl Paul Reinhold Niebuhr** (1892-1971), the Reformed theologian and ethicist who has been called the most influential American theologian of the 20th century. He battled with religious liberals over the optimism of their Social Gospel and with conservatives over their naïve view of scripture and their narrow definition of "true religion." He frequently wrote on the intersection of religion, politics and public policy. In his memory, find a moment today to reacquaint yourself with his life and works!

On **June 1**, we remember the passing of **Thomas Berry** (1914-2009), the Catholic Passionist priest, cultural historian and eco-theologian—or "geologian," as he preferred to be called—who was a leading voice in eco-spirituality. A leader in the tradition of de Chardin, he advocated for an interdependent "communion of subjects" in an evolving universe, something that cannot be achieved without the assistance of political, economic, educational and religious systems. In his memory, consider your own stance toward the earth from which we were created!

June 1 is **Global Day of Parents**, an opportunity to thank parents for their commitment, selfless love and countless sacrifices. Reach out to and thank your parents and the many parent figures in your life!

On **June 2**, the Church celebrates **Ss. Marcellinus and Peter** (+c. 304), the third-century Roman priest and exorcist venerated by the Church after their martyrdom at the hands of Severus. In their memory, pray Eucharistic Prayer I, which mentions them, and pray for those "martyrs" who witness to God's love through their generous sharing of self!

On **June 2**, we remember the passing of **Anthony de Mello** (1931-1987), the Indian Jesuit priest and psychotherapist who drew from mystical traditions of the East and the West for his works on spirituality. In his memory, dust off his works and enrich your preaching and teaching!

On **June 2**, we celebrate the birth in 1957 of **Gregory A. Boyd**, the American theologian, pastor and author who is a leading voice in the Neo-Anabaptist movement for Christian pacifism and a non-violent understanding of God. He writes widely on Christianity and politics, debunking the myth of a "Christian nation." In his honor, consider your own notions of God's purported violence and the place of peace in Jesus' liberating message!

On **June 3**, we remember the passing of **Johann van Santen** (1772-1858), the Dutch priest who served as the fourteenth archbishop of Utrecht. He led the last efforts of the church of Utrecht to reconcile with the Roman Church, ultimately refusing to sign a formulary demanded by Alexander VII. Likened by many to Martin Luther, for his stand against the Roman papacracy, he purportedly said, "I must obey God and my conscience, even if the Pope and the whole Church are misinformed. Is Catholic unity to be maintained by perjury?" In his memory, consider the extent to which you obey God and your conscience over others!

On **June 3**, the Church celebrates **St. Charles Luwanga** (1860-1886), the Ugandan catechist and chief royal page who was burned alive with 44 other royal pages for refusing to have sex with their 18-year-old king after their conversion to Christianity. An 1885 photo shows many of them the year before they were executed. The first to die, Joseph Mukasa, was the first Black Catholic martyr in Africa. The youngest martyr, 14-year-old St. Kizito, is a patron saint of children and of primary schools. Uganda now celebrates Martyrs Day, a national holiday, in their memory. Pray for all who feel forced to commit acts against their wills— and for their abusers!

On **June 3**, we remember the passing of **Charlotte Grace O'Brien** (1845-1909), the Irish Protestant philanthropist and activist who protected female immigrants to the U.S. from robbery and prostitution, and who exposed the deplorable conditions of emigrant ships, lodging houses and dock slums. She established Our Lady of the Rosary Mission for the Protection of Irish Immigrant Girls, failing to enlist the support of Roman Catholic clergy due to her Protestant background. In her memory, consider your own stance and hospitality to those who have more recently arrived in our nation!

Sunday, June 4, 2023
THE MOST HOLY TRINITY
(white)

Decorate your worship space with a white that matches your vestments, and integrate Trinitarian symbols (e.g., the triangle, or three interlocking figures). Be careful to avoid heretical images of the Trinity: To depict an old man, Jesus, and a bird pushes congregants toward tritheistic notions!

The thread in today's scriptures: God reveals God's self to Moses as "the Lord, the Lord, a merciful and gracious God, slow to anger and rich in kindness and fidelity" (Ex. 34:6), and Daniel shares a hymn of praise to the God of our ancestors (Dan. 3:52). Paul shares a Trinitarian farewell (2Cor. 13:14), and John shares his theology of God loving the world so much that God shared with us God's only Son, "that everyone who believes in him might not perish but might have eternal life" (Jn. 3:16).

Holy humor: [Warning: This joke takes some practice to ensure its smooth delivery.] The story is told of how the pope some centuries ago had decided to expel all Jewish people from Rome. Naturally, there was an uproar from the Jewish community. So the pope made a deal: He would have a religious debate with the rabbi of the Jewish community; if the rabbi won, the Jewish people could stay; but if the pope won, the Jewish people would have to leave. The very smart rabbi chosen to debate the pope had one simple request: To make it more interesting, neither side would be allowed to talk! The pope agreed. The day of the great debate came, and the rabbi sat opposite the pope. The pope raised his hand and showed three fingers [raise three fingers of your right hand], and rabbi looked back at the pope and raised one finger [raise one finger of your left hand]. The pope waved his fingers in a circle around his head [wave your right hand in a horizontal circle], and the rabbi pointed to the ground where he sat [point to the ground with your left hand]. The pope pulled out a host and a chalice of wine [hold up a chalice in your right hand], and the rabbi pulled out an apple [hold up an apple in your left hand]. Exasperated, the pope stood up and said, "I give up! You're too good! Your people can stay!" [Put down the chalice and apple.] Afterwards, the cardinals asked the pope what happened. The pope said, "First, I held up three fingers to represent the Trinity [raise three fingers of your right hand], and he responded by holding up one finger [raise one finger of your left hand] to remind me that there was still one God common to both our religions. Then I waved my finger around me to show him that God was all around us [wave your right hand in a horizontal circle], and he responded by pointing to the ground and showing that God was also right here with us [point to the ground with your left hand]. I pulled out the host and the wine to show that God absolves us from our sins [hold up the chalice in your right hand], and he pulled out an apple to remind me of our original sin [hold up the apple in your left hand]. He had an answer for everything! What could I do?" [Put down the chalice and apple.] Meanwhile, the Jewish community crowded around the rabbi and asked him what happened. "Well," said the rabbi, "First he said to me that we had three days to leave [raise three fingers of your right hand], so I told him that not one of us was leaving [raise one finger of your left hand]. Then he told me that this whole city would be cleared of Jews [wave your right hand in a horizontal circle], and I let him know that we were staying right here. [point to the ground with your left hand]." "And then?" asked a woman. "I don't know," said the rabbi. "He took out his lunch [hold up the chalice in your right hand], so I took out mine [hold up the apple in your left hand]!" [Segue into the theological complexities with which we've surrounded the Trinity and the many and varied perspectives that exist on the Trinity.]

Looking for a visual aid for your homily or object lesson? Consider involving all present in the very Catholic symbol that is…the sign of the cross! Ask listeners how many times in their lives they've made the sign of the cross. Every time we do so, we express our belief in the great mystery of how God created, redeemed and continues to sustain us and our world!

June is here! **For the intellectually-curious**, share a brief lesson on the double etymology of this month: Juno was the Roman goddess who was the patroness of marriage and of women's well-being; June was also the month in which the ancient Romans celebrated their *juvenis*, their young people! Give a June nod to the married couples, women, and/or young people of your community!

For the intellectually-curious, share a lesson on solid Trinitarian theology, definitions from Trinitarian theology, and Trinitarian heresies. Many missals commit the heresy of tritheism by depicting the Father, Son and Holy Spirit as an old man, Jesus, and a bird. How far this is from the *mysterium tremendum et fascinans* for which we use the codename "God"!

On **June 4**, we remember the passing of **Henri Loos** (1813-1873), the Dutch priest who served as the fifteenth archbishop of Utrecht. Together with his successor, he was one of two archbishops of Utrecht after 1724 whose orders *were* recognized by the Roman Church—but he was not invited to the Vatican Council. Loos served as the archbishop of Utrecht during the first two Old Catholic Congresses in Munich in 1871 and in Cologne in 1872. In his memory, pray for all who continue to experience exclusion at the hands of others!

On **June 4**, we remember the passing of **Maurice Blondel** (1861-1949), the French philosopher who attempted to establish a relationship between philosophical reasoning and Christian belief. Though associated with the modernists, he was denied a teaching post because his philosophy was too Christian. He influenced later *ressourcement* theologians, like Henri de Lubac. In his memory, reflect on how you synthesize faith and reason!

On **June 4**, we remember the passing of **Tomas Millamena** (1947-2014), the tenth supreme bishop of the Philippine Independent Church, who led a church of 1.5 million adherents and decried military surveillance, harassment, and arrest of his clergy. He participated in numerous peace talks throughout the Philippines and in Oslo. After his death, one observer noted that, in the same way that his body fought cancer, he battled "against social cancer—and for national liberation, justice, equality, social upliftment and lasting peace." In his memory, consider your own role in fighting various social cancers!

On **June 4**, the Armenian Apostolic Church celebrates the anniversary of the enthronement in 2013 of Boghos Manousian as **Patriarch Nourhan Manougian of Jerusalem**. In his honor, pray for him and for the 9 million people he serves!

June 4 is **World Day for Child Victims of Aggression**, an effort to spotlight the plight of children who suffer physical, mental and emotional abuse or who are recruited and used in war, killing, sexual violence, abduction, attacks on schools and hospitals, and denial of humanitarian access. Pray for the victims of the darkest urges of humanity that seek to exploit the most vulnerable!

On **June 5**, the Church celebrates **St. Boniface** (c. 675-754), the Anglo-Saxon monk who evangelized Germany. According to one legend, people came to believe in him when he chopped down an oak tree dedicated to Thor—and wasn't immediately struck down by lightning. In his honor, reflect on the "sacred cows" that are presumably immune from question or criticism in our own faith tradition, to see if you, too, might grow in a deeper understanding of our faith and our world!

On **June 5**, we remember the passing of **Stefan Hugo Karl Török** (1903-1972), the German-Austrian Roman Catholic Redemptorist priest who served as the third bishop of the Austrian Old Catholic Church for 25 years. He helped students of Jewish descent to find refuge during World War II, and he communicated with Austrian Roman Catholic bishops with the hope of improved relationships between their churches. In his honor, pray for all our sisters and brothers of the Austrian Old Catholic Church!

On **June 5**, we remember the passing of **Mary Ann Shadd** (1823-1893), the American-Canadian anti-slavery activist who was the first Black woman to attend law school in the United States. She later became the first Black woman publisher in North America. In her memory, pray for all Black Americans who continue to face—and break down—barriers!

On **June 5**, our Jewish sisters and brothers celebrate **Shavuot**, the traditional "Pentecost" pilgrimage festivals that marked the summer grain harvest and the giving of the Torah on Mount Sinai.

June 5 is also **World Environment Day**, an opportunity to highlight awareness and action to protect our environment!

On **June 6**, the Church celebrates **St. Norbert** (c. 1080-1134), the German nobleman-turned-priest whose near-death experience of lightning transformed his life. Consider how your life might change if you had a similar near-death experience—and begin to live in that way today!

On **June 6**, we remember the passing of **Jeremy Bentham** (1748-1832), the English philosopher and social reformer regarded as the founder of modern utilitarianism. He defined the right as that which provides the greatest happiness for the greatest number of people. He advocated individual and economic freedoms, the separation of church and state, freedom of expression, equal rights for women, and the right to divorce. For fear of being hanged as a sodomite, he wrote unpublished essays on the decriminalizing of homosexual acts and on biblical evidence for

Jesus' homosexuality. In his memory, consider how much happiness you are creating for others!

On **June 6**, we remember the passing of **Karl Josef von Hefele** (1809-1893), the Roman Catholic bishop and German theologian known for his seven-volume work on the Church's councils. At the advent of the First Vatican Council, he published his *Causa Honorii Papae*, which argued for the moral and historical impossibility of purported papal infallibility, based on his vast knowledge of Church history. At the council, he voted against the promulgation of the proposed dogma. In his memory, spend a bit of time researching the complex contexts from which purported papal infallibility and other dogmas of the Church arose!

On **June 6**, we remember the passing of **Carl Gustav Jung** (1875-1961), the Swiss psychiatrist and psychoanalyst who influenced the fields of psychiatry, anthropology, archaeology, literature, philosophy and religious studies. He delved into individuation and coined such terms as synchronicity, the collective unconscious, extraversion and introversion. In his memory, dust off a few works on human personality and consider the correlations of various personality traits with religious behaviors!

On **June 7**, we remember the passing of **Alan Turing** (1912-1954), the British computer scientist and World War II codebreaker considered a patron saint of the gay community: His codebreaking saved more than 14 million lives and shortened World War II by two years, and he committed suicide after being convicted of homosexuality and sentenced to chemical castration. Nearly 60 years after his death, Queen Elizabeth granted him a posthumous pardon, clearing the way for the pardons of some 50,000 other men convicted under the same law. In his memory, pray for all who help to save lives by breaking the "code" of violence against the LGBTQIA+ community!

On **June 7**, we remember the passing of **Josef Brinkhues** (1913-1995), who served as the seventh bishop of the German Old Catholic Church for 20 years. Shortly after his presbyteral ordination, he was drawn into World War II, serving as a sergeant and medic. In his memory, pray for all who find themselves in difficult circumstances!

On **June 7**, we celebrate the founding in 2005 of the **Reformed Catholic Church International**, currently led by Bishop Doreen C. Noble. Happy anniversary!

On **June 8**, we remember the passing of **Henri Arnauld** (1597-1692), the Roman Catholic bishop of 42 years who ultimately chose to support his brother, Antoine, suffering the displeasure of Louis XIV when he refused to sign the Formulary of Submission for the Jansenists. He attempted to stall the tempest caused by the Archbishop of Paris' insistence that the nuns of Port-Royal-des-Champs sign the formulary, suggesting that they resist or take refuge in subtleties. In his honor, consider how you shield and protect others!

On **June 8**, we remember the passing of **Gerard Manley Hopkins** (1844-1889), the English Jesuit priest whose posthumous fame established him as one of the leading Victorian poets. In his memory, discover his sonnets of desolation!

On **June 8**, we remember the passing of **Emily Davison** (1872-1913), the English suffragette who fought for the right of women to vote in Britain. In her memory, pray for all continue to be denied the right to vote!

On **June 8**, we celebrate the birth in 1928 of **Gustavo Gutiérrez Merino**, the Peruvian Dominican priest, philosopher and theologian regarded as one of the formulators of liberation theology. Focusing the movement on love of neighbor, particularly love of those who suffer poverty as a result of unjust social structures, he lifted up the ministry of Jesus to the rejected and despised as a model for the contemporary Church. In his memory, consider whether your words and actions manifest a "preferential option for the poor"!

On **June 9**, the Church celebrates **St. Ephrem the Syrian** (c. 306-373), the fourth-century, Syriac-Aramean deacon especially venerated by the Eastern Church. He is the patron saint of spiritual directors and spiritual leaders. In his memory, pray for all who have provided you spiritual direction throughout the years — and for the necessary gifts to help others discern the presence and activity of God in our world!

On **June 9**, we remember the passing of **Theodore van der Croon** (1668-1739), who served as the ninth archbishop of Utrecht. Consecrated by Roman Catholic bishop Dominique-Marie Varlet, he was the publisher of a number of works in Dutch and Latin. Church historian C.B. Moss described van der Croon as "a man of particularly gentle disposition." In his memory, consider how others will describe you at your passing — and what you might do today to be found more praiseworthy!

On **June 9**, we remember the passing of **Victoria Woodhull** (1838-1927), the American suffragette considered by many as the first woman to run for president in 1872. In her memory, pray for all pioneers who blaze trails and help to show what is possible!

On **June 10**, we remember the passing of **Carl Gustav Adolf von Harnack** (1851-1930), the Baltic German Lutheran theologian and church historian who drew attention to the Greek influence that forever changed the direction of Christianity. He rejected the historicity of the Gospel of John, criticized the Apostles' Creed, and promoted the Social Gospel. In his memory, pause to critically reflect on those aspects of your faith that you may not have questioned in the past!

Sunday, June 11, 2023
THE BODY AND BLOOD OF CHRIST
(white)

Decorate your worship space with a white that matches your vestments. Incorporate eucharistic symbols, like wheat and grapes and/or a loaf of bread and a cup!

The Church shares four "great sequences" each year: Today's is the *Lauda Sion*. Consider having a gifted cantor sing or chant a setting of this, before segueing into the Gospel Acclamation!

The thread in today's scriptures: God fed our ancestors with manna—bread from heaven (Deut. 8:3), and the psalmist praises God, who fills us with "the best of wheat" (Ps. 147:14). Paul tells us the bread and cup we share are a symbol of our unity and a participation in the body and blood of Christ (1Cor. 10:16-17). The Johannine Jesus shares his "Bread of Life" discourse.

Holy humor: Have you heard the story of the Last Supper? On the night before he died, Jesus was enjoying his last supper with his friends. And he took bread, blessed it, broke it, gave it to his friends, and said, "This is my body." Then he took a cup of wine, and, giving thanks, he said, "This is my blood." And then he opened a jar of mayo…and Judas said, "I'm gonna stop you right there!" [Say, "Wait, I'm going to stop right there. Today's celebration of the Body and Blood of Christ isn't about bread, wine and mayo. It's about bread and wine: the body and blood of Christ!" Segue into the eucharistic motifs of each reading.]

Looking for a visual aid for your homily or object lesson? Consider a loaf of bread and a chalice! Hold up the bread when you speak of manna, wheat, bread, or the body of Christ, and hold up the chalice when you speak of the cup or of the blood of Christ!

Consider hosting a traditional *Corpus Christi* **procession** on this day! It could be as simple as a procession around the inside or outside of your worship space after the Prayer after Communion. Use a host that was consecrated at today's mass, to make clear how our adoration of the Eucharist outside mass flows from our liturgical action. Have your altar servers lead the procession with incense, cross and candles!

In honor of this Solemnity, consider having **a blessing of your community's eucharistic ministers!**

On **June 11**, when it doesn't fall on a Sunday, the Church celebrates **St. Barnabas**, who, due to his missionary endeavors, was considered an "apostle" by St. Luke. He parted ways with Paul over issues of circumcision and observance of the Mosaic law. In his honor, pray Eucharistic Prayer I, which mentions him, and highlight the diversity of the Christian/Catholic community and the need to sometimes "agree to disagree" with those we love!

On **June 11**, we remember the passing of **Antoni Pietrzyk** (1934-1989), the Polish Old Catholic priest of the Krakow-Częstochowa diocese of the Polish Old Catholic Church. In his memory, pray for our sisters and brothers of the Polish Old Catholic Church!

On **June 12**, we remember the passing of **James S. Tinney** (1941-1988), the American historian, journalism professor and pastor of an LGBTQ church in D.C., who wrote on religious and political movements and African-American history. He founded the first scholarly journal on Black Pentecostalism, and he broke the silence about LGBTQ people in the church in his work, *Homosexuality as a Pentecostal Phenomenon*. In his memory, consider the ways in which you might break the silence on taboo subjects!

On **June 12**, we remember the passing of **James Farl "J.F." Powers** (1917-1999), the novelist and short-story writer who often drew inspiration from developments in the contemporary Roman Catholic church. In his memory, consider the inspiration that you draw from contemporary events—and the ways in which you might help to interpret those events through the lens of our Catholic faith!

On **June 12**, the Czechoslovak Hussite Church celebrates the birth in 1958 of **Patriarch Tomáš Butta**. In a spirit of ecumenism, pray for him and for the 39,000 people he serves!

On **June 12**, we remember the deaths in 2016 of the **Orlando Martyrs**, the 49 people killed and 53 wounded in a massacre at the Pulse gay bar. Because the deadliest act of violence against LGBTQ people in U.S. history occurred during the club's "Latin Night," many of the victims were Latinx—and many were "outed" as a result. Pray for all who find a safe space in the dance floors that unite people of diverse generations, languages, races and socioeconomic levels—and for all who violate such places!

June 12 is **World Day Against Child Labor**, an opportunity to advocate for the one in four children worldwide—more than 150 million children—engaged in labor to the detriment of their health and development.

On **June 13**, the Church celebrates **St. Anthony of Lisbon**—or Padua, if you prefer (1195-1231), the Portuguese Franciscan renowned for his preaching and charity toward the poor. He is invoked to find lost items ("Tony, Tony, look around: Something's lost and must be found"), and, in many places, a traditional blessing of St. Anthony loaves is hosted in his memory. In his memory, consider your own stance toward the poor and "lost"!

On **June 13**, we remember the passing of **Martin Buber** (1878-1965), the Austrian-born Jewish philosopher nominated seven times for the Nobel Peace Prize and best known for distinguishing I-Thou and I-It relationships. A translator of Hasidic lore, he emphasized the Hasidic ideal of living in the unconditional presence of God, with no distinction between daily habits and religious experience. In his memory, pause to consider how you treat people as objects and/or the ways in which you sometimes fail to have a heightened sense of God's presence and activity in your life!

On **June 13**, we celebrate the anniversary of the episcopal consecration in 2018 of Bishop **Doreen C. Noble**, presiding bishop of the Reformed Catholic Church International. Happy anniversary!

On **June 13**, we celebrate the founding in 2005 of **St. Stanislaus Polish Catholic Church** in St. Louis, Missouri as an Independent Catholic community. The community is currently led by Father Przem, Mother Annie Watson, Father David Jacobi, Father Jonathan Batchelor and Deacon Donna Nachefski. Happy anniversary, St. Stan's!

On **June 13**, the Eritrean Orthodox Tewahedo Church celebrates the anniversary of the enthronement in 2021 of **Patriarch Qerlos**. In a spirit of ecumenism, pray for him and for the 3 million people he serves!

On **June 14**, we remember the passing of **Emmeline Pankhurst** (1858-1928), the English activist who organized the UK suffragette movement leading to the right of women to vote in Great Britain. In her memory, pray for all who advocate for women's rights!

On **June 14**, we remember the passing of **Gilbert Keith "G.K." Chesterton** (1874-1936), the English writer, poet, biographer, philosopher and lay theologian best known for his reasoned apologetics, his fictional priest-detective, Father Brown, and his biographies of such figures as St. Francis of Assisi and St. Thomas Aquinas. In his memory, familiarize yourself with his works and reflect on how you might bridge his words to your life!

On **June 14**, we remember the brutal murder of **Benjamin "Benjie" Bayles** (+2010), the 43-year-old Filipino activist and lay leader of the Philippine Independent Church who became a national symbol for the 1,200+ extrajudicial killings and even more "disappearances" suffered by the Filipino people in recent history. He courageously denounced abuses and human rights violations by the Philippine army. In his memory, consider your own courage in speaking out against the many human rights abuses in our world!

On **June 14**, we celebrate the anniversary of the episcopal consecration in 2008 of Bishop **Ronald Stephenson**, diocesan bishop of the Holy Trinity Diocese. Happy anniversary!

On **June 14**, we celebrate the founding in 2014 of the **Convergent Christian Communion**, currently led by Bishop Kenneth von Folmar. Happy anniversary!

June 14 is **World Blood Donor Day**, an opportunity to highlight the global need for safe blood and blood products. When is the last time you donated blood? In an act of self-diffusive love, Jesus gave of his blood for others. Will you?

June 14 is also **U.S. Flag Day**, a symbol of American unity.

On **June 15**, we remember the passing of **Evelyn Underhill** (1875-1941), the English Anglo-Catholic writer and pacifist known for her numerous works on religion and mysticism. Due to her 1911 work, *Mysticism*, she was one of the most widely-read writers on the subject in the first half of the 20th century. In her memory, reflect on your own stance toward the mystical elements of life and religion!

On **June 15**, we remember the passing of **Maria Filip Feldman** (1885-1971), the Polish-German bishop of the Old Catholic Mariavite Church. In his memory, pray for our sisters and brothers of the Old Catholic Mariavite Church!

On **June 15**, we celebrate the birth in 1937 of **Kisan Baburao "Anna" Hazare**, the Indian social activist who has led grassroots movements to fight corruption in India. In his honor, pray for all who advocate for greater transparency in governments and large organizations!

On **June 15**, the Syro-Malankara Catholic Church (in union with Rome) celebrates the birth in 1959 of **Major Archbishop-Catholicos Moran Mor Baselios Cleemis**. In a spirit of ecumenism, pray for him and for the 500,000 Syro-Malankara Catholics he serves!

June 15 is **World Elder Abuse Awareness Day**, an opportunity to spotlight the exploitation, abuse and neglect of those with greater life experience. Wear purple, light your community in purple, and reach out to and listen to the stories of the elders around you!

On the Friday after the Solemnity of the Body and Blood of Christ — the Church celebrates the **Solemnity of the Most Sacred Heart of Jesus**. For a deeper understanding of this mystery, challenge yourself to read Karl Rahner's more mature, contemporary views on this very medieval devotion. After all, what we celebrate is the mystery of Jesus' love!

On **June 16**, we remember the passing of **Johannes Tauler** (c. 1300-1361), the German Dominican priest, theologian and mystic. A disciple of Meister Eckhart and a medieval Christian universalist, he was known for his sermons, which were widely disseminated. Pause to consider how you might better share your words and thoughts with others!

On **June 16**, we remember the passing of **Peter Joseph Elvenich** (1796-1886), the German Catholic theologian and philosopher who defended the condemned works of his teacher, Georg Hermes. His work was in vain, he was removed from his teaching post, and, after the Vatican Council, he affiliated himself with the Old Catholic Church. In his memory, pause to consider how you are defending those who lack a voice in our world!

On **June 16**, we remember the murder of **Joselito Agustín** (1976-2010), the Filipino radio journalist and lay leader of the Philippine Independent Church who was gunned down for speaking against and jeopardizing the political futures of mayoral candidates in Bacarra, Ilocos Norte, Philippines. He courageously spoke out in favor of worker rights and against government corruption. In his memory, pray for the many prophets in our world who continue to speak truth to power!

On **June 16**, we celebrate the birth in 1970 of **David Oliver Kling**, bishop of the Community of Saint George and host of Sacramental Whine podcast. Pray for him and for the people he serves!

On **June 16**, the Southern Baptist Convention celebrates the anniversary of the installation in 2022 of President **Bart Barber**. In a spirit of ecumenism, pray for him and for the 15 million Baptists he serves!

On **June 17**, we celebrate the birth in 1959 of **Don Davidson**, a priest who has served the Independent Catholic movement for nearly 40 years. Pray for him and for the people he serves!

On **June 17**, the Ukrainian Autocephalous Orthodox Church Canonical celebrates the anniversary of the installation in 2005 of Oleh Kulyk as **Patriarch Moses of Kyiv**. In a spirit of ecumenism, pray for him and for the people he serves!

On **June 17**, we celebrate the anniversary of the episcopal consecration in 2014 of Bishop **Michael Beckett**, presiding bishop of the Unified Old Catholic Church. Happy anniversary!

Sunday, June 18, 2023
ELEVENTH SUNDAY IN ORDINARY TIME
(green)

The thread in today's scriptures: God chose the Israelites as God's chosen people (Ex. 19:2-6), and Jesus chose 12 apostles (Mt. 10:2-4) to heal and preach. We are not like the crowds that gathered around Jesus — "sheep without a shepherd" (Mt. 9:36). Instead, we recognize that "we are God's people, the sheep of God's flock" (Ps. 100:3), reconciled to God through Christ (Rom. 5:6-11)!

Holy humor: Perhaps you've heard this joke before. Jesus and his friends walked into a bar, where Jesus said to the bartender, "13 waters, please." And then he turned and winked at his apostles! [Segue into today's gospel of Jesus choosing 12 apostles.]

Looking for a visual aid for your homily or object lesson? Draw attention to your eyelashes and those of your listeners! The English word "reconciliation" comes from the Latin roots *re* (meaning "again") and *concilium* (meaning "eyelash"). When the bishops of the Church meet in a council (*concilium*), they are literally eyelash-to-eyelash with one another. Similarly, though we turn our back on God and others through sin, through reconciliation we are brought eyelash-to-eyelash again with God and others!

On **the third Sunday of June**, U.S. society celebrates **Father's Day**!

- Incorporate intercessions for father — living and deceased!
- Share a special blessing for fathers and father figures (e.g., stepfathers, godfathers, uncles, teachers, coaches), lead all present

in an applause for them, and share with them a keychain, a parish koozie, or some other symbol of your community's love of and gratitude for them!

On **June 18**, when it doesn't fall on a Sunday, the Church celebrates **St. Marina the Monk**, the fifth-century monk who, as a young lady, shaved her head and donned men's clothing to prevent her father from marrying her off. She and her father joined a monastery together, and, after her father died ten years later, "Father Marinos" was accused of impregnating an innkeeper's daughter and was expelled from the monastery for several years to raise the child. Finally readmitted to the monastery, her identity was not revealed until the monks were preparing her body for her funeral. She is a matron saint of the trans community and of transgender parents. She is memorialized in the award-winning 2018 Lebanese film "Morine." In her memory, pray for all who courageously defy the gender binary!

On **June 19**, the Church celebrates **St. Romuald of Ravenna** (c. 950-1027), the self-indulgent young man who became a monk after the death of his father in a duel. In his honor, consider the place of solitude, meditation and contemplative prayer in your life!

On **June 19**, we remember the passing of **Lambert de Jong** (1825-1867), the Dutch priest who served as the ninth Dutch Old Catholic bishop of Haarlem. Archbishop of Utrecht Henri Loos refused to recognize his election by the clergy of Haarlem and did not attend his consecration two years later by the bishop of Deventer. De Jong's consecration was never reported to the government, causing some doubts about the legality of his acts as bishop and prolonged disputes between the church of Haarlem and the archbishop of Utrecht after de Jong's death two years later. In his memory, pray for all who are engaged in disputes!

On **June 19**, we remember the passing of Lord Acton, **John Emerich Edward Dalberg** (1834-1902), the English Catholic historian, politician and writer known for his remark, "Powers tends to corrupt, and absolute power corrupts absolutely. Great [people] are almost always bad [people]." Lord Acton succeeded John Henry Newman as editor of a Roman Catholic paper, sharing his wealth of historical knowledge. Though Roman Catholic, he was hostile to ultramontane pretensions. His independence of thought brought him into conflict with the Roman church's hierarchy, which censured his paper. In his memory, pray for all who foster Independent Catholic thought in our world!

On **June 19**, we remember the passing of **Fernand Portal** (1855-1926), the French priest who attempted to reconcile the Catholic Church and the

Anglican communion. In his memory, consider how you might better be an instrument of reconciliation!

On **June 19**, we remember the passing of **Donald Boisvert** (1951-2019), the Canadian Anglican priest, religion professor and gay theologian who authored various works on gay spirituality. He was known for saying, "Saints simply assume the risks more often than the rest of us do." In his memory, reacquaint yourself with his works!

On **June 19**, we celebrate the founding in 2005 of the **Reformed Catholic Church**, currently led by Bishop Christopher Carpenter. Happy anniversary!

June 19 is **International Day for the Elimination of Sexual Violence in Conflict**, an opportunity to raise awareness of the trafficking and sexual violence connected to war, terrorism, violent extremism and organized crime.

On **June 19**, **Juneteenth** is celebrated in Texas: an opportunity for us to show our solidarity with our African-American sisters and brothers who have endured far too many injustices throughout history!

On **June 20**, we remember the passing of **Bartholomew Johann Bijeveld** (1713-1778), the first Dutch Old Catholic bishop of Deventer for 20 years. To ensure the continuation of apostolic succession in the Netherlands, he was appointed and consecrated a titular bishop with no jurisdiction by Utrecht archbishop Peter Johann Meindaerts. He, in turn, co-consecrated Meindaerts' successor in 1768. In his memory, pray for all who consent to help lead and guide God's people!

On **June 20**, the Greek Melchite Catholic Church (in union with Rome) celebrates the birth in 1946 of **Patriarch Youssef Absi**. In a spirit of ecumenism, pray for him and for the 1.5 million Greek Melchite Catholics he serves!

June 20 is **World Refugee Day**, an opportunity to raise awareness of the plight of the more than 80 million people in our world who have been forcibly displaced from their homes and homelands.

On **June 21**, the Church celebrates **St. Aloysius Gonzaga** (1568-1591), a patron saint of youth. He died serving victims of the plague. In his honor, host a special blessing of youth, that they might be inspired by the lives of the saints in the same way that the young Aloysius was!

On **June 21**, we remember the passing of **Tomasz Gnat** (1936-2017), the Polish American bishop who led the Polish National Catholic Church in the United States and Canada. In his memory, pray for our sisters and brothers of the Polish National Catholic Church!

On **June 21**, we celebrate the birth in 1979 of **Gregory Godsey**, the American Independent Catholic bishop who serves as presiding bishop of the Old Catholic Churches International. He created the second iteration of a database of clergy of the Independent Sacramental Movement, and he published *Convergent Streams*, a quarterly that he branded as the premier ISM magazine, for seven years. Pray for him and for the people he serves!

On **June 21**, the Greek Melchite Catholic Church (in union with Rome) celebrates the anniversary of the election in 2017 of **Youssef Absi** as Patriarch of Antioch, Alexandria and Jerusalem. In a spirit of ecumenism, pray for him and for the 1.5 million Greek Melchite Catholics he serves!

June 21 is the **summer solstice**, the day of the year with the most sunlight in the northern hemisphere.

On **June 22**, the Church celebrates **St. Paulinus of Nola** (353-431) and **Ss. John Fisher** (1469-1535) **and Thomas More** (1478-1535). Paulinus and his wife, Therasia, gave their family's riches to the poor and lived an active/contemplative life by serving the lost and wayward who occupied the first floor of their two-story "monastery." Thomas More and John Fisher were known for their integrity in the court of Henry VIII. On this day, consider the privilege you enjoy (e.g., education, resources, relationships) — and how it is that you're using that privilege to advance God's reign!

On **June 22**, we remember the passing of **John Joseph Keane** (1839-1918), the American Roman Catholic archbishop of Dubuque, Iowa, who, as bishop of Richmond, Virginia, founded African-American schools and churches, despite opposition. He built relationships with Protestants, aligned with the progressive wing of the Roman Catholic hierarchy, and served as the first rector of The Catholic University of America in Washington, D.C. — until conservatives demanded his resignation ten years later. In his memory, pray for all who persevere despite opposition!

On **June 22**, we remember the passing of **Yves Marie-Joseph Congar** (1904-1995), the French Dominican priest and theologian best known for his influence on ecumenism at the Second Vatican Council and for reviving theological interest in the Holy Spirit. He promoted the role of laity in the Church, criticized the Roman Curia and its clerical pomp, advocated for a "collegial papacy," and encouraged openness to ideas from the Eastern Orthodox Church and Protestantism. Following the publication of an article in support of the worker-priest movement in France, he was barred from teaching and publishing, and his book, *True and False Reform in the Church*, was forbidden. In his memory, pray for all who follow the promptings of the Spirit and advocate for the ideas espoused by Congar!

June 23 is **Public Service Day**, an opportunity to spotlight the value and virtue of public service and to celebrate public servants and all who pursue careers in the public sector. Pray for and find a way to support all who work for the common good!

On **June 24**, the Church celebrates the **Solemnity of the Nativity of St. John the Baptist**. Decorate your worship space with large, clear vases of water (turned slightly more blue with food coloring), and pray Eucharistic Prayer I, which mentions him. For the intellectually-curious, share a lesson on the timing of this celebration, six months before Christmas Eve. Challenge congregants to be heralds of the king! If you haven't recognized your Proclaimers of the Word recently, today might be an appropriate day to share with them a special blessing and a token of your appreciation for their ministry!

On **June 24**, we remember the passing of **Johann Jacob van Rhijn** (+1808), the Dutch priest who served as the twelfth archbishop of Utrecht. During his leadership, Napoleon ruled the Netherlands and tried to end the independence of the church of Utrecht—perhaps even ordering the death of Rhijn, who died by poisoning. In his memory, pray for all who might wish you harm!

On **June 24**, we remember the deaths of the 32 **UpStairs Lounge martyrs** who died in the 1973 New Orleans arson that was the deadliest attack on the American LGBTQIA+ community prior to the 2016 Orlando Pulse massacre. Four bodies were never identified or claimed by relatives, and several homophobic churches refused to perform funerals for the deceased. In memory of this tragic day, pray for all who seek refuge from a hostile world—and for all who continue to persecute them!

On **June 24**, the Roman Catholic Church celebrates the anniversary of the appointment of **Pierbattista Pizzaballa** as Latin Patriarch of Jerusalem. In a spirit of ecumenism, pray for him and for the Roman Catholics he serves!

June 24 is **World Day of Prayer for Priests**. Pray for all priests!

Sunday, June 25, 2023

TWELFTH SUNDAY IN ORDINARY TIME

(green)

For the next 13 Sundays, our second reading will come from Paul's Letter to the Romans. For the intellectually-curious, share a brief lesson on the dating, audience and context of this letter, as well as its structure and themes!

Be mindful of the exclusive language in today's second reading (repeated from the second reading of the First Sunday of Lent): An inclusive proclamation might read, "Death came to all people [not men], inasmuch as all sinned."

The thread in today's scriptures: Sin and death entered the world through one man (Rom. 5:12), and the sinfulness of humanity leads people to wish us harm—just as Jeremiah's enemies wished him harm (Jer. 20:10-13). Like Jeremiah, we sometimes bear insult and shame as well (Ps. 69:8), but, like Jeremiah, we also trust that God "rescue[s] the life of the poor from the power of the wicked" (Jer. 20:13). The Matthean Jesus—who would ultimately suffer insults and death at the hands of others—tells us not to fear those who wish us physical harm (Mt. 10:28): We are worth more than the sparrows that God protects (Mt. 10:31)!

Holy humor: Have you heard the story of the sparrow that collided with the biker? One day a biker was riding his Harley Davidson down the highway, when a sparrow hit his helmet. In his mirror, he saw the poor little creature bounce on the pavement behind him. Feeling guilty, the biker stopped to pick up the unconscious bird. He took the sparrow home and put it in a cage with some bread and water. The next day, the sparrow woke up. The sparrow saw the bars of the cage. The sparrow saw the bread and the water. And the sparrow put his head between his wings and cried, "Oh no, I killed that biker!" [Segue to how it is that God rescues the lives of the poor, just as the biker rescued the sparrow, then to the gospel story of sparrows.]

Looking for a visual aid for your homily or object lesson? Do you have a parakeet? This is the perfect Sunday to bring him/her to church! If not, grab a small, decorative bird from a craft store, to visually drive home the point that "[we] are worth more than many sparrows" (Mt. 10:31)!

On **June 25**, when it doesn't fall on a Sunday, the Church celebrates **St. Febronia of Nisibis** (284-304), the Greek woman who was martyred for refusing to renounce her faith and marry the nephew of the Roman emperor Diocletian. She is one of the 140 colonnade saints at St. Peter Basilica in Vatican City. In her memory, pray for all who resist relationships of convenience!

On **June 25**, we remember the passing of **Abraham von Franckenberg** (1593-1652), the Silesian mystic, poet and hymn writer who drew inspiration from alchemy, the Kabbalah and medieval mysticism. Many of his writings focused on unity with God through denial of self and all worldly things. In his memory, consider the sources that you incorporate into your own spirituality and the additional sources that might help you better grow in your relationships with God and others!

On **June 25**, we remember the passing of **Johann Bon** (1774-1841), the Dutch priest who served as the seventh Dutch Old Catholic bishop of Haarlem. He was the only 19th-century bishop of Haarlem not to be excommunicated by the Roman church. Elected in 1815, he was not consecrated until 1819 due to the Napoleonic Wars. In his memory, pray for patience and perseverance for those whose dreams are delayed!

On **June 25**, we celebrate the birth in 1960 of **Thomas Paul Schirrmacher**, who serves as Secretary-General of the World Evangelical Alliance. In a spirit of ecumenism, pray for him and for the 600 million Evangelicals he serves!

On **June 25**, we celebrate the anniversary of the installation of **Rhee Timbang** as supreme bishop of the Philippine Independent Church in 2017. An advocate for gender equality, he led his church to consecrate its first woman bishop in the church's 117-year history, in 2019. Pray for him and for the one million Independent Catholics he serves!

On **June 26**, we remember the passing of **Hans Urs von Balthasar** (1905-1988), the Swiss theologian who was considered one of the most important Catholic theologians of the 20th century and who died before being elevated to his cardinalate in the Roman Catholic Church. He is best known for his works on theological aesthetics, theodramatics of the paschal mystery, his theo-logic on the relationship of Christology to ontology, and his 15-volume systematics. In his memory, take a moment to see what wisdom from his works might enrich your life and ministry!

On **June 26**, we celebrate the anniversary of the founding in 2019 of **St. Michael Catholic Parish**, a community of the Unified Old Catholic Church in San Antonio, Texas. Happy anniversary!

On **June 26**, we celebrate the anniversary of the presbyteral ordination in 2019 of **Frank Bellino**, pastor of St. Michael Catholic Parish in San Antonio, Texas. Pray for him and for the people he serves!

214

June **26** is **World Day against Drug Abuse and Trafficking**, an opportunity to raise awareness of the many adverse effects of illicit drugs on personal health, local community wellness, and global peace.

June **26** is also **World Day to Support Torture Victims**, an opportunity to raise awareness of all forms of cruel, degrading and inhuman treatments that persist despite global prohibition of torture. Pray for the hundreds of thousands of people alive today—an estimated 400,000 in the U.S. alone—who have been victims of torture!

On **June 27**, the Church celebrates **St. Cyril of Alexandria** (c. 375-444), who advanced the view that Mary is the Mother of God (*theotokos*), over the archbishop of Constantinople's "Nestorian" view that Mary is the Mother of Christ (*Christotokos*). Cyril inspired the Chalcedonian teaching on the two natures (viz., human and divine) of Christ. On this day, reflect on the great diversity of high and low Christologies and Mariologies throughout the Church, and challenge yourself to see Christ and/or Mary from a different perspective!

On **June 27**, we remember the passing of **Gerhoh of Reichersberg** (1093-1169), the canon, provost and Gregorian reformer known as one of the most distinguished theologians of 12th-century Germany. Held in high esteem by Eugene III, Gerhoh lost favor when he initially hesitated to support Alexander III and was forced to flee Rome. In his memory, consider how your own support or lack of support of others has led to friction and tension!

On **June 27**, we remember the passing of **Peter Ludwig Berger** (1929-2017), the Austrian-born American sociologist and Protestant theologian known for his work in the sociology of knowledge and religion. His co-authored work, *The Social Construction of Reality*, is considered one of the most influential texts in the sociology of knowledge, and his religious works explored the secularization and desecularization of a pluralistic, relativistic world. In his memory, deepen your own knowledge of the mutual influence of sociology and religion!

On **June 28**, the Church celebrates **St. Iraneus** (c. 130 - c. 202), the second-century Greek bishop who helped bring Christianity to present-day southern France. According to tradition, he received the faith from Polycarp, who, in turn, received it from John the Evangelist. Iraneus regarded all four now-canonical gospels as essential, and he countered Gnosticism with his three pillars of orthodoxy: scripture, tradition, and apostolic succession. In his memory, pray for those who shared the faith with you—and for those who handed on the faith to them!

On **June 28**, we remember the passing of **Mortimer Jerome Adler** (1902-2001), the American Aristotelian/Thomistic philosopher and author of *How to Think About God*, whose spiritual journey took him from the Jewish religion to the Episcopal Church to the Roman Catholic Church — which he resisted for many years due to its limited views on such issues as abortion. In his memory, pray for those on winding spiritual paths who might welcome the refreshing waters of Independent Catholicism!

On **June 28**, we celebrate the birth in 1950 of **Gary Robert Habermas**, the American New Testament scholar, philosopher of religion, and apologist who has catalogued and communicated trends among scholars in New Testament studies and the historical Jesus. The author of several works, he has frequently lectured on the resurrection of Jesus. In his honor, update your own knowledge of the trends in New Testament studies and/or in studies of the historical Jesus!

On **June 28**, we remember the sacred resistance that occurred at the Stonewall Inn in New York City. The "**Saints of Stonewall**" battled an unjust system, performing the miracle of transforming shame and self-hatred into the pride now annually celebrated throughout the U.S. and the world. In their memory, consider how you contribute to the great miracle of turning shame into pride today!

On **June 28**, we celebrate the birth in 1974 of **Lawman Chibundi**, the Zambian, former Roman Catholic priest who serves as a police chaplain and as pastor of Rabbouni Catholic Community in Louisville, Kentucky. An enthusiastic preacher, he found himself unable to deny people the sacraments for which they yearned, thus bringing to birth a vibrant Independent Catholic community where those marginalized by other churches "can simply be." Pray for him and his congregation — and for all who seek to faithfully follow Jesus, the rabbouni!

On **June 29**, the Church celebrates the **Solemnity of Ss. Peter** (+c. 64-68) **and Paul** (+c. 62-64), two preeminent figures in the early Church! Pray Eucharistic Prayer I, which mentions them, and meditate today on the greatness — but also the great humanness — of both saints!

On **June 29**, we remember the passing of **Henry of Ghent** (c. 1217-1293), the Italian "Solemn Doctor" and scholastic philosopher who sided with secular priests in their disputes with mendicants at the University of Paris — particularly on the issue of mendicants needing to confess to their parish priests, rather than to the priests of their orders. Henry had a hand in the creation of the 219 condemnations that were shared by the bishop of Paris. In his memory, pray for all misguided yet zealous defenders of "orthodoxy"!

On **June 29**, we remember the passing of **Alois Pašek** (1869-1946), the Czech Old Catholic bishop who led the Old Catholic Church in Czechoslovakia from 1922-1946. In his memory, pray for our sisters and brothers of the Old Catholic Church in the Czech Republic!

On **June 29,** we remember the passing of **Elizabeth Martínez** (1925-2021), the American Chicana activist best known for her book, *500 years of Chicano History in Pictures.* In her memory, pray for all who help to foster pride in their history!

On **June 29**, our Islamic spiritual siblings celebrate **Eid Al-Adha**, their annual celebration of the absolute devotion of Abraham (the prophet Ibrahim) to God (Allah). Pray for the 1.8 billion Muslims with whom we share this common ancestor of faith!

On **June 30**, the Church celebrates the **first martyrs of the Roman church**—those who were killed in 64 A.D., when Nero needed a scapegoat to assume the blame he was receiving for a fire that broke out in Rome. According to the stories that were shared, some were crucified, others were covered in animal skins and torn apart by dogs, and still others were tied to posts and set on fire. In their memory, consider your own courage for professing our faith!

On **June 30**, we remember the passing of **Raymond Lull** (c. 1232 - c. 1315), the Majorcan mathematician, philosopher and secular Franciscan credited with the first major work of Catalan literature. A pioneer of computational theory, he had a considerable influence on Leibniz. In his memory, consider the ways in which you are being pioneering, and/or challenge yourself in this respect!

On **July 1**, the Church celebrates **Bl. Junípero Serra** (1713-1784), the Franciscan friar who established the California missions, traveling thousands of miles on foot despite a leg injury. Lift him up as a model for overcoming obstacles in life!

On **July 1**, we remember the passing of **Jemima Wilkinson** (1752-1819), the American Quaker preacher who woke from a 1776 near-death experience as a genderless evangelist named the Public Universal Friend. Shunning birth name and gendered pronouns, the Friend donned androgynous clothes and preached throughout the northeastern United States, attracting many followers to the Society of Universal Friends. A non-binary saint and important figure in trans history, the Friend challenges us to ask how well we love and accept all who refuse to be defined by the gender binary!

On **July 1**, we remember the passing of **Antonio Rosmini** (1797-1855), the Italian priest and philosopher who founded the Institute of Charity, pioneered the concept of social justice, and was a key figure in Italian Liberal Catholicism. The Jesuits opposed his *Constitution of Social Justice* and *Of the Five Wounds of the Holy Church*, which were condemned. Leo XIII condemned 40 propositions in his work—a decision reversed by the Congregation for the Doctrine of the Faith in 2001. In his memory, reacquaint yourself with the works of "the only contemporary Italian author worth reading"!

On **July 1**, we remember the passing of **Pauli Murray** (1910-1985), the American lawyer, civil rights activist and women's rights activist, who was the first African-American woman to be ordained as an Episcopal priest in 1977. Jailed for refusing to sit in the back of a segregated Virginia bus in 1938, she organized restaurant sit-downs 20 years before the famous events in Greensboro, and her writings were used by the NAACP to win *Brown v. Board of Education*. A matron saint of the lesbian and transgender communities, she remarked that she was a man trapped in a woman's body. Her canonization was fast-tracked by the Episcopal Church. In her memory, find new ways to stand in solidarity with those who don't conform to the gender binary!

July 1 is **Canada Day**, the anniversary of the 1867 formation of the Canadian Confederation of Nova Scotia, New Brunswick, Ontario and Quebec. Pray for all who are celebrating "milestones" toward liberation!

Sunday, July 2, 2023
THIRTEENTH SUNDAY IN ORDINARY TIME
(green)

Be mindful of the exclusive language in today's gospel, which could just as easily be rephrased, "Whoever receives a righteous person because he or she is righteous will receive a righteous person's reward" or "Whoever receives the righteous because they are righteous will receive the reward of the righteous." It's also problematic to presume that only men can take up the cross and find or lose their lives!

The thread in today's scriptures: Because of her hospitality (2Kgs. 4:8-11 & 14-16), the Shunamite woman experienced the goodness of the Lord (Ps. 89:2). We, too, are called to die to sin (Rom. 6:11) and to ourselves (Mt. 10:39), and to hospitably receive others (Mt. 10:40-42)!

Holy humor: Do you know any good prophet jokes? Share two or three, then segue into today's scriptures! A few examples follow:

- How do you know that God is rich? Because back in Israel, God made…a prophet!
- Why didn't Jesus start a charity? Because charities are…not-for-prophets!
- Did you hear about Jesus' personal trainer? He was making a big prophet!
- What happens if you buy a goat for $10, name it Jesus, and sell it for $15? You just made…a prophet!
- Why couldn't Elisha join the [insert the name of a 501(c)(3)] or the [insert the name of another 501(c)(3)]? Because they're…non-prophet organizations!
- I talked to an atheist today. Turns out he's part of a non-prophet organization! [Or, turns out he supports non-prophet organizations!]
- Why are less and less people buying into religion? Prophets are down!
- I started a figurine company that specializes in miniature statues of Jesus. We make…a small prophet!
- What do you call a person who can predict the number of fish a boat will catch? A net prophet!
- What happened when they started selling faulty jet packs to fortune tellers? The prophets went through the roof!

Looking for a visual aid for your homily or object lesson? Consider a mask! In today's first reading, the Shunamite woman receives the prophet Elisha (2Kgs. 4:8-11), and the Matthean Jesus tells us "Whoever receives a prophet…will receive a prophet's reward" (Mt. 10:41) — but do you know where the English word "prophet" comes from? The ancient Greeks invented theater and various theatrical genres, including comedy, tragedy and satire. They created a Greek word, prophenein, for the act of "speaking through a mask." Invite an altar server to put on the mask and to speak through it. Who's talking: the mask or the altar server? In the same way, a prophet is a "mask" through which God speaks to our world! We are all baptized prophets: Are you allowing God to speak through you, to those around you?

July is here! **For the intellectually-curious**, share a brief lesson on the etymology of this month, named after Julius Caesar (100-44 B.C.), the Roman dictator after whom the Julian calendar was named. Speak of the difficulties presented by this calendar, which led to the Church's institution of the Gregorian calendar and the Church's attempt to (incorrectly) date it to the birth of Jesus of Nazareth. July and August are the two months named after Roman emperors, which, when inserted into the Roman calendar, caused the seventh (September), eighth (October), ninth (November) and tenth (December) months of the year to become the ninth, tenth, eleventh and twelfth months we now know!

On **July 2**, we remember the passing of **John Sebastian Marlowe Ward** (1885-1949), the English author and antique collector who served as archbishop of the Orthodox Catholic Church in England. A writer on Freemasonry and esotericism, he authored the controversial *Psychic Powers of Christ* and shared various "prophesies." After suffering a legal and media campaign, he and his religious community moved to Cyprus, where he died three years later. In his memory, pray for all who dwell at the margins of our Catholic tradition!

On **July 2**, we remember the passing of **Eliezer "Elie" Wiesel** (1928-2016), the Romanian-born Holocaust survivor, writer, political activist and Nobel Laureate who strongly defended human rights and drew attention to victims of oppression. In his memory, consider how you might better be a messenger of peace, atonement and human dignity!

On **July 2**, we celebrate the birth in 1962 of **Carmelita "Menchie" Aguilar Abalas**, a prominent Independent Catholic and member of the Philippine Independent Church who has served as mayor of Mandaluyong, Philippines since 2016, succeeding her husband and father-in-law. She has shown tremendous leadership during the COVID-19 pandemic in the Manila metropolitan area. In her honor, consider how you model for others during challenging times!

On **July 3**, the Church celebrates **St. Thomas the Apostle** (+c. 53), the twin known for his doubts and the only apostle believed to evangelize outside the Roman Empire. Pray Eucharistic Prayer I, which mentions him, push yourself beyond your comfort zone, and encourage those with doubts!

On **July 3**, we remember the passing of **Sydney Eckman Ahlstrom** (1919-1984), the American historian who specialized in the religious history of the United States. In his memory, thumb through his work, *A Religious History of the American People*, to remember aspects of American religious history you may have forgotten!

On **July 3**, we remember the passing of **Bernard Häring** (1912-1998), the German priest and moral theologian who authored 80 books and 1,000 articles, and who achieved notoriety with his three-volume work, *The Law of Christ*. As a young priest, he was conscripted into the German army and, though forbidden by Nazi authorities, shared sacraments with soldiers. As a *peritus* at Vatican II, he was part of the commission that prepared the pastoral constitution *Gaudium et spes*. In his memory, reacquaint yourself with his dialogical approach to moral theology, which esteems the ways in which God awakens and speaks to our conscience!

On **July 3**, we celebrate the birth in 1945 of **Thomas Mapfumo**, the Zimbabwean musician and political activist whose music supported the revolution in Zimbabwe, leading to his imprisonment and exile. In his honor, pray form him and for all who fight oppressive governments!

On **July 3**, we celebrate the birth in 1946 of **Jean-Luc Marion**, the French Catholic theologian who writes on modern and contemporary philosophy and religion. A student of Derrida and known for his work, *God Without Being*, Marion philosophizes on such concepts as love, self-love, self-idolatry, intentionality and gift. In his honor, pause to consider how your love of others may be nothing more than your love of your own ideas as expressed in the "chance cause" of others!

On **July 3**, we celebrate the birth in 1962 of noted Dutch Old Catholic priest and theologian **Angela Berlis**, who was one of the first women ordained by the Old Catholic Church of Germany. A professor on the theological faculty of the University of Bern, she widely writes on Old Catholicism, church history, ecumenical theology, and women and gender studies. Let her know of your appreciation for her significant contributions to theology and the Church!

On **July 4**, we celebrate the birth in 1946 of **Roy Agullana Cimatu**, a prominent Independent Catholic and member of the Philippine Independent Church who serves as the Philippine Secretary of Environment & Natural Resources. The former chief of staff of the Philippine Armed Forces and special envoy to the Middle East, he has spearheaded "the Battle for Manila Bay," an effort to rehabilitate the polluted Manila Bay. In June 2020, he was tasked with overseeing the nation's COVID-19 response in Cebu City. In his honor, consider the projects that you might step up to and lead!

On **July 4**, the Chaldean Catholic Church (in union with Rome) celebrates the birth in 1948 of **Catholicos-Patriarch Louis Raphaël Sako**. In a spirit of ecumenism, pray for him and for the 640,000 Chaldean Catholics he serves!

On **July 4**, the Assyrian Church of the East celebrates the birth in 1975 of David Royel who became **Catholicos-Patriarch Awa III** of Iraq. In a spirit of ecumenism, pray for him and for the people he serves!

On **July 4**, the U.S. celebrates **Independence Day**: Pray the proper contained in the Proper of Saints, lift up human freedom, and reflect on the *e pluribus unum* ("from many, one") theme of the second Prayer over the Gifts during today's mass. Celebrate this day with a barbecue and with games for kids!

On **July 4**, the Latin American Church celebrates **Our Lady Refuge of Sinners** (a feast celebrated by dioceses of California on July 5 and by the U.S. Church on August 13). The "New Eve" and *Refugium Peccatorum* is the patroness of California and parts of Mexico: If you serve a *Latino* community, pray the Litany of Loreto, which invokes her!

On **July 5**, the Church celebrates **St. Anthony Zaccaria** (1502-1539) and **St. Elizabeth of Portugal** (c. 1271-1336). Anthony was the doctor-turned-priest who popularized the 40-hour devotion of Eucharistic exposition and established three religious orders to reform society and abuses in the Church. Isabel, the wife of the king of Portugal, was known for her peacemaking skills and is a patron saint of Third Order Franciscans. Consider your own commitment to peacemaking and the reform of Church and society!

On **July 5**, we remember the passing of **Aurelio Tolentino y Valenzuela** (1869-1915), a prominent Independent Catholic and co-founder of the Philippine Independent Church in Pampanga, Philippines. A prominent writer and dramatist, he founded the first workers' cooperative in the Philippines, and he co-founded the Katipunan, the secret society that set in motion the Philippine revolution. His 1903 drama *Kahapon, Ngayon at Bukas* featured the tearing of an American flag on stage, which infuriated Americans in the audience and led to his arrest for sedition and rebellion. In his memory, consider how your words and actions might be inciting the ill will of others!

On **July 5**, we remember the passing of **Helmut Richard Niebuhr** (1894-1962), one of the most important Christian ethicists of 20th-century America. The younger brother of Reinhold Niebuhr, he was part of the neo-orthodox school of American Protestantism and was one of the main sources of the "Yale School" of postliberal theology. In his memory, find a moment today to reacquaint yourself with his life and works!

On **July 5**, we remember the passing of **William Reed "Bill" Callahan** (1931-2010), the Jesuit priest whose advocacy for social justice, LGBTQ Catholics, and the ordination of women led to his expulsion from the Roman church in 1991. He founded the Quixote Center, Priests for Equality, and Catholics Speak Out, ministering to dissident Catholics and "following the example of Jesus, who was never willing to shut up."

In his memory, pray for the modern-day prophets who model the necessary courage to stand up against powerful religious institutions!

On **July 6**, we remember the passing of **Jan Hus** (c. 1372-1415), the Czech priest, theologian and philosopher who called out simony and spoke against the sale of indulgences. Excommunicated, he was arrested and brought before the Council of Constance where he proclaimed, "I would not for a chapel of gold retreat from the truth!" He sang psalms as he was burned at the stake for "heresy." Consider your own courage and willingness to question the practices of the Church that may run contrary to gospel values!

On **July 6**, we remember the passing of **William George Ward** (1812-1882), the English mathematician and Anglican priest who was stripped of his degrees for urging the union of the Anglican Church and the Roman Catholic Church. John Henry Newman followed him into the Roman Church, and Ward dedicated himself to ethics, metaphysics, moral philosophy, supporting papal infallibility and attacking Döllinger, Montalembert and Liberal Catholicism. In his memory, pray for the various "rotweilers" who attack you!

On **July 6**, the Church celebrates **St. Maria Goretti** (1890-1902), the patroness of teenage girls and rape victims. Use this day to advocate for self-determination and against sexual abuse!

On **July 6**, we celebrate the anniversary of the founding in 1945 of the **Catholic Apostolic Church in North America** (CACINA). Happy anniversary!

On **July 6**, we remember the passing of **Marsha P. Johnson** (1945-1992), the African-American, gay liberation and transgender rights activist credited with throwing one of the first objects that incited to action the "Saints of Stonewall" in New York City on June 28, 1969. The co-founder of a ministry to homeless drag queens, gay youth and trans women, she is considered a matron saint of the trans community. In her memory, consider how you are stirring others to action and caring for the most marginalized in our society!

On **July 6**, we remember the passing of **Maksymilian Rode** (1911-1999), a Roman Catholic priest who edited an underground magazine and organized secret education during the World War II German occupation of Poland. Arrested and sent to a concentration camp, he was released by American troops nearly nine months later. After a 1951 clash with his archbishop, his renown led to his being named vicar general of the Polish Old Catholic Church. He served as bishop of the church for six years until his ouster by a secret meeting of clergy convened by his successor. In his memory, pray for all who serve and advocate for others despite the most difficult circumstances!

On **July 6**, the Roman Catholic Church celebrates the anniversary of the installation in 2013 of Manuel José Macário do Nascimento Clemente as **Manuel III**, the Latin Patriarch of Lisbon. In a spirit of ecumenism, pray for him and for the Roman Catholics he serves!

On **July 7**, we celebrate the founding in 2005 of the **Progressive Catholic Church International**, currently led by Bishop Barry Frier. Happy anniversary!

On **July 8**, the Church celebrates **Ss. Priscilla and Aquila**, the first-century married couple in the New Testament deemed "fellow workers in Christ Jesus" by Paul (Rom. 16:3). Aquila was traditionally listed among the 70 or 72 disciples sent out by Jesus, and Priscilla is thought by many to have been an early presbyter in the Church. Paul credited them with instructing Apollos, an important first-century evangelist. In their memory, pray for all couples who work together to support contemporary expressions of the Jesus movement!

On **July 8**, we remember the passing of **Eugene III** (c. 1080-1153), the pope who confirmed the privilege granted by Sergius I to the cathedral chapter of Utrecht, allowing it to elect its own bishop without the permission or oversight of the pope. Consider how you empower others to make decisions and exercise "local control"!

On **July 8**, we remember the passing of **Joseph René Vilatte** (1854-1929), the Frenchman later known as Mar Timotheus I, who lived on the fringes of various religious traditions and is often referred to as the first Independent Catholic bishop in the U.S. Ordained by the Episcopal Church, he ministered to the Belgian Catholics in Wisconsin who had broken from the Roman church and who had sympathies more aligned with the Old Catholic Church. As Metropolitan of North America for the Malankara Orthodox Syrian Church, he built the small St. Louis Cathedral in Green Bay. When asked how one might define Independent Catholics, he replied that, in contrast to Roman Catholics, "we are Catholics without qualification." In his memory, seek to be less denominational and more *catholic* — more universal and inclusive — in your love for God and others!

On **July 8**, we remember the passing of **Joseph Kardas** (1898-1958), the Polish-American bishop who led the Polish National Catholic Church in the United States. In his memory, pray for our sisters and brothers of the Polish National Catholic Church in the United States!

Sunday, July 9, 2023

FOURTEENTH SUNDAY IN ORDINARY TIME

(green)

The thread in today's scriptures: The Matthean Jesus refers to himself as "meek and humble of heart" (Mt. 11:29), fulfilling Zechariah's prophecy that the messiah would be "meek, and riding on an ass" (Zec. 9:9). With an eye toward the lowly, the Lord "lifts up all who are falling and raises up all who are bowed down" (Ps. 145:14). Following the example of the meek and lowly, let us therefore "put to death the deeds of the body" (Rom. 8:13) and put on the spirit of Christ (Rom. 8:9)!

Holy humor: The story is told of the meek bus driver who had an interesting passenger on his route. The passenger was seven feet tall and built like a professional wrestler. He would step onto the bus, glare at the driver, and say, "Big John doesn't pay!" Then he'd go sit in the back of the bus—without paying! The meek bus driver didn't say anything for weeks. He didn't dare argue with Big John! Finally, by the end of the summer, the bus driver worked up the courage to confront Big John. The next morning, Big John stepped onto the bus, glared at the bus driver, and said, "Big John doesn't pay!" And the meek bus driver stammered, "And why doesn't Big John have to pay?" With a surprised look on his face, Big John replied, "Big John has a bus pass!" [Segue into how being meek doesn't mean that we allow ourselves to be a doormat for others, but means identifying with the poor, the humble, the powerless and the marginalized—the anawim for whom God has a special love!

Looking for a visual aid for your homily or object lesson? Consider a sword or a spear! The prophets had visions of instruments of war being turned into instruments of peace: Zechariah speaks of God banishing horses, chariots and warriors' bows (Zec. 9:10), and Proto-Isaiah suggested that God's reign would result in the beating of swords into plowshares and spears into pruning hooks (Is. 2:4). Instead of living according to the flesh (Rom. 8:13) and bringing death and destruction to this world, may we "proclaim peace to the nations" (Zec. 9:10)!

On **July 9**, we remember the passing of **Angelus Silesius** (c. 1624-1677), the German Franciscan priest, physician, mystic and poet who converted from Lutheranism, studied medieval mystics, wrote 55 pamphlets on Catholicism, and explored themes of mysticism, quietism and pantheism in 1,676 poems in German couplets. His words were popularized in 18th-century Lutheran, Catholic and Moravian hymns. In his memory, consider how you might better help others to lift up their hearts in prayer!

On **July 9**, the Church celebrates **St. Augustine Zhao Rong** (1746-1815) **and Companions**—the 87 Chinese Catholics and 33 Western missionaries who lost their lives for failing to renounce their Christian faith between 1648 and 1930. Consider your own commitment to your Church and your ministry!

On **July 9**, we remember the passing of **Gisbert Cornelius de Jong** (+1824), the third Dutch Old Catholic bishop of Deventer for nearly 20 years. Like his predecessors, he served as a titular bishop with no jurisdiction, and he resided outside of Deventer, as a pastor in Rotterdam. In his memory, pray for the many titular leaders in our world who are "more hat than cattle"!

On **July 9**, we remember the passing of **Jaime Luciano Balmes y Urpiá** (1810-1848), the Spanish metaphysician, theologian and sociologist deemed the Prince of Modern Apologetics. In his memory, consider your own willingness to contribute to the apologetics of the Independent Catholic movement!

On **July 9**, we remember the passing of **Alice Paul** (1885-1977), the American activist who led the National Woman's Party. In her memory, pray for all who continue the fight for women's rights!

On **July 9**, we remember the passing of **Piotr Bogdan Filipowicz** (1933-1998), the Polish Old Catholic bishop who led the Old Catholic Church in the People's Republic of Poland from 1965-1993. In his memory, pray for him and for our sisters and brothers of the Old Catholic Church in the People's Republic of Poland!

On **July 10**, we remember the passing of **Peter Anson** (1889-1975), the English former Anglican Benedictine who authored 40 books, including *Bishops at Large*, an unflattering work on the multiplication of sheepless shepherds in the Independent Catholic movement. In his memory, reflect on how we might help shift our movement from the wandering bishops (*episcopi vagantes*) of the past, to the vibrant ministries to which the Sprit is calling us!

On **July 11**, the Church celebrates **St. Benedict of Nursia** (c. 480 – c. 547), the hermit-turned-monk who established the fundamentals of monastic life. The opening line of his rule says, "Listen carefully." In his memory, reflect on how it is that the English words "listen" and "silent" contain the same letters, and consider how silence and solitude might assist you in your own journey of spiritual growth!

July 11 is **World Population Day**, an opportunity to focus on world population trends and issues. Our world population is expected to reach 8.5 billion by 2030, 9.7 billion by 2050, and 10.9 billion by 2100: What are we doing to protect our planet's resources for future generations?

On **July 12**, we remember the passing of **Jean Charlier de Gerson** (1363-1429), the French scholar, educator, reformer and poet who served as chancellor of the University of Paris and was one of the most prominent theologians at the Council of Constance. He championed conciliarism as a means to overcome the competing claims of rival popes, and he defended Joan of Arc and her supernatural vocation. In his memory, consider how you're bringing people together and defending their dignity and rights!

On **July 12**, we remember the passing of **Desiderius Erasmus** (1469-1536), the Dutch Catholic priest and Christian humanist who was the greatest scholar of the northern Renaissance. Though faithful, he was critical of the abuses of the Roman church, and he raised questions that would be influential in the Protestant Reformation and Catholic Counter-Reformation. In his memory, we pray for all who abuse the power and positions they currently enjoy.

On **July 12**, we celebrate the birth in 1997 of **Malala Yousafzai**, the Pakistani activist and human rights activist who became the youngest Nobel Prize laureate at age 17 for her work on human rights and women's education. In her honor, pray for all who advance women's rights throughout the world!

On **July 13**, the Church celebrates **St. Henry** (973-1024), the childless German king and Holy Roman Emperor invoked against infertility. Lift up in prayer those who struggle to bring to birth the families they desire!

On **July 13**, we remember the passing of **Henri Johann van Buul** (1795-1862), the Dutch priest who served as the eighth Dutch Old Catholic bishop of Haarlem for 18 years. Consecrated without the consent of King William II, he was denied recognition and a salary from the government for eight years. In his memory, pray for all who suffer the petty grievances of others!

On **July 13**, we remember the passing of **Wilhelm Emmanuel von Ketteler** (1811-1877), the German theologian and bishop of Mainz whose social teachings influenced Leo XIII's *Rerum novarum*. He opposed the formulation of purported papal infallibility as inopportune, and he proposed the founding of prayer societies for the reconciliation of Catholics and Protestants. In his memory, pray that unity might one day be restored to the Body of Christ!

On **July 13**, we remember the passing of **Joseph Langen** (1837-1901), the German priest and theologian who was excommunicated with Döllinger and others for not accepting the dogma of purported papal infallibility. As an Old Catholic priest, he published various works on scripture and the New Testament world and was famous for the sound scholarship of his *History of the Church of Rome*. He was instrumental in the German Old Catholic Church and contributed to the Old Catholic *International Theological Journal*. In his memory, consider your own possible contributions to scholarship!

On **July 13**, we remember the passing of **Kate Sheppard** (1848-1934), the New Zealander suffragette who fought for civil rights by organizing petitions and public meetings. In her memory, pray for all who continue to organize people for the purpose of creating change!

On **July 14**, the Church celebrates **St. Kateri Tekakwitha** (1656-1680), the first Native American to be canonized. Scarred by smallpox, Kateri was embarrassed by her appearance, and she died at age 24, after years of self-mortification. She is the patroness of ecology and the environment, of people in exile, and of Native Americans. Find a way today to better advocate for those in exile and for our spiritual siblings of Native American traditions!

On **July 14**, we remember the passing of **Sally Miller Gearhart** (1931-2021), the American lesbian separatist and activist who fought anti-gay policies alongside Harvey Milk. She founded a women-only refuge in the Redwood Forest and wrote various influential works, including a classic of lesbian science fiction about a women-only society. One of the first openly-lesbian tenure-track professors at a major American university in 1983, she was "a disrupter who rejected the church and the 'patriarchy,' but knew the Bible through and through." In her memory, discover her life and works!

On **July 15**, we remember the passing of **Anselm of Laon** (+1117), the French theologian who helped pioneer biblical hermeneutics and co-wrote a "gloss" on the scriptures—an interlineal and marginal incorporation of scriptural interpretations—which is hailed as one of the great intellectual achievements of the Middle Ages. Known for expelling Peter Abelard from his cathedral school in 1113, Anselm's style of writing inspired the theological "handbooks" of Peter Abelard and Thomas Aquinas. In his memory, increase your knowledge of biblical hermeneutics throughout the centuries!

On **July 15**, the Church celebrates **St. Bonaventure** (c. 1217-1274), the Franciscan philosopher and theologian who was captivated by medieval,

Pseudo-Dionysian suggestions that God is self-diffusive Good—goodness that just keeps overflowing, like a cup of coffee, resulting in all that exists. In his memory, reflect on and share God's self-diffusive goodness!

July 15 is **World Youth Skills Day**, an opportunity to focus on equipping young people with the necessary skills to support themselves and their families.

Sunday, July 16, 2023

FIFTEENTH SUNDAY IN ORDINARY TIME

(green)

You'll need to **choose whether you'll proclaim the shorter form of today's gospel, or the longer form**, which includes an additional 14 verses of the Matthean Jesus' explanation of the Parable of the Sower. (Remember: Rather than risk boring your listeners with this long narrative, you can always summarize Jesus' explanation in your homily!)

The thread in today's scriptures: God's word descends like rain upon the earth, "making it fertile and fruitful, [and] giving seed to the one who sows" (Is. 55:19). Jesus' Parable of the Sower (Mt. 13:1-9), found in the synoptic gospels, is paraphrased by the response of the psalm: "The seed that falls on good ground will yield a fruitful harvest" (Lk. 8:8). Growth is sometimes a seemingly long, painful process, leaving us "groaning in labor pains" (Rom. 8:22), until we at last bear "the firstfruits of the Spirit" (Rom. 8:23)!

Holy humor: The story is told of the young man who went to a party, hoping to meet his one true love. First, he met a tall, lithe, beautiful blond. She played with him in the same flirty way that she did with every other guy there, and, in the middle of their conversation, she excused herself and went over to the bar, where she began a conversation with another guy. The young man then saw a vivacious red-head, who possessed an amazing sense of humor. They immediately hit it off—but all she could do was crack jokes, so his interest in her quickly withered. He moved on to a petite, exotic brunette, with whom he felt he could share his most intense, passionate feelings—but when he let slip a word that was apparently politically incorrect, he received the most severe tongue-lashing in his life. Finally, he saw a sweet, kind girl over in the corner. He fell deeply in love with her, and she with him. And they married and lived happily ever after some 30% of the time, or 60% of the time, or sometimes even 100% of the time! Let anyone with ears listen! [Segue into how there are different types of people in this world—and how that's the essence of Jesus' message, too: Different people were going to receive Jesus' words in different ways!]

Looking for a visual aid for your homily or object lesson? Be like the prodigal sower, throwing out handfuls of invisible "seeds" over your listeners' heads! Help your listeners visualize the different types of soil upon the seeds fall. Then ask with which type(s) of "soil" their hearts are filled!

On **July 16**, when it doesn't fall on a Sunday, the Church celebrates **Our Lady of Mount Carmel**. Recall the beautiful symbolism of the scapular in her honor: of our call and challenge to hold Christ and the saints close to our hearts!

On **July 16**, we remember the passing of **Marie Norbert Helmut Maas** (1918-1992), the German archbishop of the Extrajudicial Mariavite Order in Germany. In his memory, pray for our sisters and brothers of the German Mariavite Church!

On **July 16**, we remember the passing of **Stephen Richards Covey** (1932-2012), the American educator and author known for his bestsellers, including *First Things First*, *Principle-centered Leadership*, and *The Seven Habits of Highly Effective People*. In his memory, consider your own mission in life, the many roles you juggle, and ways in which you might schedule greater effectiveness into your life and ministry!

On **July 16**, the Roman Catholic Church celebrates the birth in 1948 of **Manuel José Macário do Nascimento Clemente**, the Latin Patriarch of Lisbon. In a spirit of ecumenism, pray for him and for the Roman Catholics he serves!

On **July 16**, we celebrate the birth in 1951 of **Dušan Hejbal**, the Czech bishop who led the Old Catholic Church in the Czech Republic. In his honor, pray for him and for our sisters and brothers of the Old Catholic Church in the Czech Republic!

On **July 17**, we remember the passing of **Leon Grochowski** (1886-1969), who served for 16 years as the first bishop of the Poland diocese of the Polish National Catholic Church in the U.S. and Canada. After being arrested by the tsarist government in Poland for organizing a student riot, he emigrated to the U.S., where he was ordained by Francis Hodur, whom he succeeded as bishop of the PNCC. During his leadership, he promoted unity between the PNCC and the Roman Catholic Church. In his memory, pray for all our sisters and brothers of the Polish National Catholic Church!

On **July 17**, we celebrate the birth in 1948 of **Stanisław Bosy**, the Polish Old Catholic priest who administered the Wrocław diocese of the Polish Catholic Church in Poland. In his honor, pray for him and for our sisters and brothers of the Polish Catholic Church in Poland!

On **July 18**, the Church celebrates **St. Camillus de Lellis** (1550-1614), a patron saint of hospitals, nurses and the sick. In his memory, reach out to someone in need of healing and health!

On **July 18**, we remember the passing of **Nancy Ledins** (1932-2017), who made headlines as the first transgender Roman Catholic priest after gender confirmation surgery on Holy Thursday 1979. A former Precious Blood priest, army chaplain in Vietnam, and doctor of psychology, she halted her ministry to the Roman Church but later served a Baptist church in North Carolina. In her memory, pray for all who build rigid "boxes" around the Church's sacraments—and for all who break them!

On **July 19**, the Church celebrates **St. Macrina the Younger** (c. 330 - 379), the early Christian nun who lived a chaste and humble life, devoting herself to prayer and spiritual education. She is one of the 140 colonnade saints at St. Peter Basilica in Vatican City. In her memory, consider your own stance toward prayer and spiritual education!

On **July 19**, we remember the passing of **Margaret Fuller** (1810-1850), the American journalist whose work, *Woman in the Nineteenth Century*, is considered the first major feminist book in the United States. In her memory, pray for all who lift up the gifts of women!

On **July 19**, we celebrate the birth in 1962 of **Benjamín "Benhur" de Castro Abalos, Jr.**, a prominent Independent Catholic and member of the Philippine Independent Church who served as mayor of Mandaluyong, Philippines (1998-2016) immediately after his father, Benjamín Abalos, Sr. (1988-1998), and before his wife, Carmelita "Menchie" Aguilar Abalas (since 2016). In his honor, consider how you are preparing your successors in life and ministry!

On **July 20**, the Church celebrates **St. Apollinaris** (+c. 175), the patron saint of those suffering from epilepsy and gout—the causes of pain and fear in far too many lives. Pray for and reach out to those affected by such maladies!

On **July 20**, the Church formerly celebrated **St. Wilgefortis**, the fictitious saint of 14th-century legends whose popularity in some placed rivaled the Virgin Mary. To avoid being married to a pagan king, she…grew a beard!

Known as Uncumber in England and Librada ("liberated") in Spain, she is an intersex protector of women who wish to be liberated or "uncumbered" from abusive husbands. Crucified by her angry father, she is pictured in iconography as a bearded woman on a cross.

On **July 21**, the Church celebrates **St. Praxedes** (+165), an early Christian saint who, during an age of persecution, buried the bodies of Christians and distributed their goods to the poor. She is one of the 140 colonnade saints at St. Peter Basilica in Vatican City. In her memory, pray for all who engage in the corporal works of mercy!

On **July 21**, the Church also celebrates **Daniel the Prophet**, the hero of lion den fame (Dan. 6). Daniel is a patron saint of sexual minorities due to the "favor and tender love" he enjoyed from the chief eunuch Ashpenaz, who oversaw the castrated men, homosexual men, and intersex folk who served the royal court. He is also a special saint of the gay community owing to his vision of a supernatural man whose "hand touched [him] and made [his] hands and knees shake" (Dan. 10:10). In his memory, pray for all who find themselves in "lion dens"!

On **July 21**, the Church also celebrates **Ss. Symeon and John of Emesa**, sixth-century Syrian hermits who were joined in *adelphopoiesis*, a ceremony of same-sex union, and lived together in the desert for 29 years. After a tearful split due to Symeon's desire to move to Emesa, Symeon became known as the "holy fool of Emesa," the patron saint of holy fools and puppeteers. They are patron saints of LGBTQIA+ Christians persecuted for their self-identity. In their memory, lift up and encourage the "holy fools" in your life!

On **July 21**, we remember the passing of **Peter Lombard** (c. 1096-1160), the scholastic theologian and bishop of Paris who authored the *Four Books of Sentences*, which became the medieval textbook of theology. His view on marriage as consensual and needing to be consummated had a significant impact on the Church's later interpretations of the sacrament. In his memory, thumb through a summary of his lengthy *Sentences*!

On **July 22**, the Church celebrates **St. Mary Magdalene** (or St. Mary of Magdala), the "apostle to the Apostles": Find a way today to share the inclusive love of the Church with our sisters who have been the backbone of the Church for centuries — and help to empower them for ministry!

On **July 22**, we remember the passing of **David Wojnarowicz** (1954-1992), the American artist and AIDS activist who caused controversy by expressing the holiness and intensity of the gay experience through the religious symbols of his Roman Catholic childhood. A frequent target of the religious right during the 1980s culture wars, he is best known for the

2010 national uproar over his video "Fire in the Belly," which used an ant-covered crucifix to symbolize the suffering and sacredness of AIDS patients. After pressure from religious and political conservatives, the video was removed from a Smithsonian Institution exhibit, sparking protests and charges of censorship. In his memory, pray for all creative spirits who feel censored!

On **July 22**, the Jacobite Syrian Christian Church celebrates the birth in 1929 of **Catholicos Baselios Thomas I of India**. In a spirit of ecumenism, pray for him and for the 1.2 million people he serves!

On **July 22**, the Armenian Apostolic Church celebrates the birth in 1948 of **Boghos Manousian**, who became Patriarch Nourhan Manougian of Jerusalem. In his honor, pray for him and for the 9 million people he serves!

On **July 22**, the Romanian Orthodox Church (recognized by the Ecumenical Patriarch of Constantinople) celebrates the birth in 1951 of **Dan Ilie Ciobotea**, who became Patriarch Daniel of Romania. In a spirit of ecumenism, pray for him and for the 17 million Romanian Orthodox Catholics he serves!

On **July 22**, we celebrate the birth in 1961 of **Ezio Maria Scaglione**, the Italian Old Catholic bishop who is ordinary of the Italian diocese of the Old Catholic Church in the Republic of Poland. In his honor, pray for him and for our sisters and brothers of the Old Catholic Church in the Republic of Poland!

Sunday, July 23, 2023
SIXTEENTH SUNDAY IN ORDINARY TIME
(green)

You'll need to **choose whether you'll proclaim the shorter form of today's gospel, or the longer form**, which includes an additional 14 verses with the synoptic Parable of the Mustard Seed, the quelle Parable of the Yeast, and the Matthean Jesus' explanation of the Parable of the Weeds. Remember: Your listeners will likely thank you for shorter narratives, upon which you can always expand in your homily!

The thread in today's scriptures: God is "lenient to all" (Wis. 12:16), which is revealed in the Matthean Jesus' suggestion that the wheat and weeds are allowed to grow together until the time of the harvest (Mt.

13:24-30). Good news for the "weeds": God is "good and forgiving, abounding in kindness to all who call upon [God]" (Ps. 85:5), and we can always count on the assistance and intercession of the Spirit (Rom. 8:26)!

Holy humor: There once was a boy named Eric, who thought he was a grain of wheat. That's right: a grain of wheat! And there was nothing that Eric's family could say, to convince him that he was a human being and not a grain of wheat. When he saw birds, Eric would panic and run away, thinking that, because birds eat grains of wheat, he was in mortal danger! Fortunately, Eric got help, and, after months of therapy and psychiatric help, Eric seemed to be cured of thinking that he was a grain of wheat. His family was thrilled: He finally recognized that he was a human being! Until one day, when Eric and his cousin were walking in the countryside and saw a chicken. Eric panicked and ran! When his cousin caught up to him, he asked Eric, "Why did you panic and run away? I thought you knew that you aren't a grain of wheat anymore!" Breathless, Eric replied, "I know that I'm not a grain of wheat—but did the chicken know that?" [Segue into how it is that we really can't know whether another person is "a grain of wheat" or its similar-looking counterpart, darnel. Leave the judgment and separation of "wheat" and "weeds" to God—and be like God: "abounding in kindness to all" (Ps. 86:5)!

Looking for a visual aid for your homily or object lesson? Hold up large pictures of wheat and darnel (for images, google "wheat and tares"). How difficult (and time-consuming!) would it be for you to weed the wheat field? Rather than engage in that task yourself, leave it to the good judgment of God! If you're preaching on the Parable of the Mustard Seed, consider sharing a mustard seed with everyone present, so that each person can hold a mustard seed in his/her hand and reflect on just how small a mustard seed is!

On **July 23**, when it doesn't fall on a Sunday, the Church celebrates **St. Bridget** (+c. 525), the patroness of Europe and of widows: Reach out to a widow or widower, and share with him/her God's love!

On **July 23**, we remember the passing of **Charlotte Forten Grimké** (1837-1914), the African-American anti-slavery activist. Her diaries before the end of the Civil War are among the few earliest writings by free Black women. In her memory, consider how you are chronicling your own life!

On **July 23**, we celebrate the birth of Father **Günter Esser**, the Director of Old Catholic Studies at the University of Bonn, who was part of conversations in 2006 with a small group of U.S. "Old Catholic" clergy that discussed the (im)possibility of union with Utrecht. Take time today to delve more deeply into the rich tradition of Old Catholicism and to pray about how we might continue to grow in our relationship with one another!

The fourth Sunday of July is **Parents' Day** in the U.S., an opportunity to let our parents — and the many parent figures in our lives — know of our love and affection for them!

On **July 24**, the Church celebrates **St. Sharbel Makhlūf** (1828-1898), the Lebanese Maronite Catholic monk known for his holiness. Devotion to him is popular throughout Mexico: If you serve a Mexican community, be sure to send congregants home with an(other) image of him!

On **July 24**, the Russian Orthodox Church celebrates **St. Boris** (+1015), the prince and military commander who, with his brother, was one of the first two saints canonized by the Russian Orthodox Church in 1071. A patron saint of the gay community, Boris deeply loved and was murdered with his servant, George the Hungarian. When assailants stabbed Boris, George, who "was loved by Boris beyond reckoning," threw himself on the prince and was murdered for his defense of his soulmate. Their love is memorialized in several icons. In their memory, consider your own love and defense of others!

On **July 24**, we remember the passing of **Johann Hermann Berends** (1868-1941), who served as the eighth Dutch Old Catholic bishop of Deventer for 12 years. A lecturer in church history, he served as president of the Dutch synod in 1936. After the 1931 Bonn Agreement, he was one of the first Old Catholic bishops to participate in the consecration of an Anglican bishop. In his memory, consider how you show your support for our sisters and brothers of other communions!

On **July 24**, we remember the passing of **Mary Church Terrell** (1863-1954), the African-American activist who was among the first African-American women to earn a college degree. She fought for civil rights and suffrage throughout her life, helping to found the National Association of Colored Women. In her memory, pray for all who overcome barriers to fight for the rights of others!

On **July 24**, we remember the passing of **Joseph Leo Cardijn** (1882-1967), the Belgian cardinal who earlier in life founded the Young Christian Workers. Imprisoned during World War II and becoming increasingly aware of social inequalities, he dedicated his life to social activism and bringing the Gospel to the working class. In his memory, pause to consider your own efforts on behalf of social justice and the working class!

On **July 24**, we remember the passing of **Lawrence Edward Boadt** (1942-2010), the American Paulist priest and scripture scholar who authored *Reading the New Testament* and other works. He advocated for improved relationships between Christians and Jews. In his memory, explore more deeply the world inhabited by our ancient Hebrew and Jewish ancestors!

On **July 24**, we celebrate the birth in 1940 of **Stanley Hauerwas**, the American theologian and ethicist who has written on a diverse range of subjects and who was named "America's Best Theologian" by *Time* magazine in 2001. A fierce critic of capitalism, militarism and fundamentalism, he often draws from a number of theological perspectives, including Methodism, Anabaptism, Anglicanism and Catholicism. In his honor, consider the sources that shape your own theology and help you to critique the systems that surround us!

On **July 25**, the Church celebrates **St. James the Greater** (+44), one of Jesus' close friends and a witness of some of Jesus' greatest signs. He is the patron saint of Spain, Nicaragua and Guatemala, and his shrine in Spain was a popular pilgrimage destination in the Middle Ages. He was invoked during the Crusades as *Santiago Matamoros* (St. James the moor-slayer): Make an inclusive gesture today to reach out to our Muslim sisters and brothers!

On **July 25**, we remember the passing of **Thomas à Kempis** (1380-1471), the German/Dutch canon who followed Geert Groote and wrote *The Imitation of Christ*, one of the most popular and best-known Christian devotional books. Consider how you are imitating Christ!

On **July 25**, we remember the passing of **Paolo Miraglia-Gulotti** (1857-1918), the Sicilian Roman Catholic priest excommunicated for his "incredible, audacious and obstinate scandals." After attending the 1897 International Old Catholic Congress, he joined the Independent Catholic movement and founded the Italian National Catholic Church. When the International Old Catholic Bishops Conference refused to consecrate him, he appealed to Joseph René Vilatte, who consecrated him in Piacenza, Italy. Facing various criminal charges, he fled to Switzerland, England, France, then Massachusetts, where he was charged with obtaining alms under false pretense and writing vicious letters to women. He died three years later outside Chicago, Illinois. In his memory, pray for all who are trying to outrun rather checkered pasts!

On **July 25**, we celebrate the birth in 1946 of **Bayani Flores Fernando**, a prominent Independent Catholic and member of the Philippine Independent Church who has served in the Philippine House of Representatives since 2016. A mechanical engineer, businessman and politician, he served as mayor of Marikina (1992-2001) and now chairs the Metropolitan Manila Development Authority. In his honor, consider how you might better organize people and resources — as all politicians do, but for the sake of the gospel!

On **July 26**, the Church celebrates Mary's parents, **Ss. Joachim and Anne**. Bring attention to the Protogospel of James and its stories about them, and invoke them as patron/matron saints of grandparents! In some places, St. Anne is also invoked as the saint who can help a single woman find a suitable spouse. The traditional rhyme to her is: "Saint Anne, Saint Anne, help me find a man!"

On **July 26**, we remember the passing of **Joachim Vobbe** (1947-2017), who served as the ninth bishop of the German Old Catholic Church for 15 years. A Roman Catholic priest for five years, he continued his pastoral ministry after incardinating into the Old Catholic tradition. As bishop, he ordained the first two women priest for his church in 1996. He wrote various pastoral letters — on the ordination of women, the turn of the millennium, and the seven sacraments. In his memory, pray for our sisters and brothers of the German Old Catholic Church!

On **July 26**, the Jacobite Syrian Christian Church celebrates the anniversary of the appointment of **Catholicos Baselios Thomas I of India** in 2002. In a spirit of ecumenism, pray for him and for the 1.2 million people he serves!

On the evening of **July 26** our Jewish spiritual siblings celebrate **Tisha B'Av**, their annual commemoration of the destruction of both temples (in 586 B.C. and 70 A.D.), the expulsion of Jews from Spain (1492) and the beginning of the Roman Catholic inquisition. Reflect on these events and, rather than reach out to Jewish friends today, keep in mind their tradition of not greeting anyone on this sad day.

On **July 29**, the Church celebrates **Martha, Mary and Lazarus**. A model for active ministry, Martha is a matron saint of homemakers, domestic servants, laundry workers, hotel-keepers, cooks, dieticians and single laywomen. Mary and Lazarus were added more recently to this day's celebration. Likely due to confusion with Jesus' mother and the likes of Mary Magdalene, little is told of Mary, though John suggests it was Mary who anointed Jesus' feet (Jn. 11:2). The Eastern Orthodox Church celebrates her as a myrrh-bearer — one of the women who went to anoint Jesus' body. Mary and Martha formed a non-traditional family in an era of great pressure toward heterosexual marriage, thus leading some scholars to suggest that they were a lesbian couple living with the gay Lazarus. For years, legends suggested that Lazarus was the first bishop of Marseilles, France, before dying (for a second time) in the second century. In their honor, pause to consider how well you strike an active/contemplative Martha/Mary balance in your own life!

On **July 29**, we remember the passing of **Maria Andrzej Jałosiński** (1904-1986), the Polish Old Catholic Mariavite bishop of the Silesian-Łódź diocese in Poland. In his memory, pray for him and for our sisters and brothers of the Old Catholic Mariavite Church in Poland!

On **July 29**, our Islamic sisters and brothers celebrate the start of **Muharram**, the second-holiest month for Muslims, when warfare is forbidden. How are you fasting from "warring" words and actions?

Sunday, July 30, 2023
SEVENTEETH SUNDAY IN ORDINARY TIME
(green)

You'll need to **choose whether you'll proclaim the shorter form of today's gospel, or the longer form**, which includes an additional six verses with the Parable of the Net.

The thread in today's scriptures: Let's talk about the things we treasure! Solomon could have asked for anything from God, including wealth and/or a long life for himself; instead he showed that treasured wisdom and understanding beyond all else (1Kgs. 3:12). God's law is to be treasured, since it is "more precious than thousands of gold and silver pieces" (Ps. 119:72 & 127). The reign of God is like a treasure buried in a field, or a pearl of great price (Mt. 13:44-46). What do you treasure? Do you treasure the fact that "all things work for good for those who love God", and/or that, having been foreknown, predestined and called by Christ, you will be justified and glorified by God?

Holy humor: There are innumerable genie jokes: Tell your favorite as a way to segue into today's first reading on God giving Solomon one wish. Need help? Try one of the following:

- Three men found themselves on a deserted island with a magic lamp. A genie appeared and said that, since he could only grant three wishes, he would give each a wish. The first man said, "I really miss my family and friends. I just want to go home." And, poof! He was gone. The second man heard what the first had said and similarly said, "I miss my family and friends, too. I just want to go home." And, poof! He was gone. Now alone, the third man said, "It sure is lonely here. I wish my friends were still here!" Poof!

- A husband and wife in their early 70's were celebrating their 50th wedding anniversary. Knowing that his wife loved antiques, the man bought her an old, brass oil lamp. When she unwrapped it, a genie appeared, thanked them for releasing him from the lamp, and offered to give them one wish each. The wife went first: She wished for an all-expenses-paid, first-class cruise around the world. Poof! She instantly held in her hand the tickets for the entire journey, including meals and shopping! It was now her husband's turn: Despite their good times together, he wished for…a wife 50 years younger than himself. Poof! Instantly, he turned 122 years old!

- A genie appeared to a young engineer and promised her anything she asked for. Being an engineer, she asked for a bridge from California to Hawaii. The genie said, "That's impossible. Think of the logistics! How will the supports reach the bottom of the Pacific Ocean? Think of all the concrete and steel you'd need. It's impossible! Ask me for another wish." The engineer paused. "Well, I really don't understand men at all. Help me to understand men!" Pausing pensively, the genie replied, "Would you like that bridge to be two-lane or four-lane?"

Looking for a visual aid for your homily or object lesson? Consider a genie's lamp, a large pearl, and/or a treasure chest! God's appearance to Solomon resembles the stories of genies appearing and promising to fulfill wishes. The treasure chest and pearl are images from today's gospel.

On **July 30**, when it doesn't fall on a Sunday, the Church celebrates the "golden-worded" **St. Peter Chrysologus** (c. 400/06 – c. 450), known for his 176 extant homilies: Consider the way in which you're recording and sharing your own "golden words" of inspiration!

On **July 30**, we remember the passing of **Rudolf Karl Bultmann** (1884-1976), the German Lutheran theologian who was a prominent voice in the liberal Protestant Christian movement and a major figure in early-20th-century biblical studies. Bultmann attempted to demythologize the New Testament and disregard historical analysis of Jesus' life in favor of the "thatness" of Jesus (i.e., *that* Jesus existed, preached and died). In his memory, reflect on some of the myths that you might continue to cling to with respect to Jesus!

July 30 is also **World Friendship Day**, an opportunity to celebrate our special bonds with other people. Let your friends know that you love and appreciate them!

July 30 is also **World Day against Trafficking Persons**, an opportunity to raise awareness of this grave violation of human rights. Many victims find themselves unable to get help, experiencing traumatic post-rescue experiences, and revictimized and punished for crimes they were forced to commit. Consider ways in which you might support victims and combat human trafficking!

On **July 31**, the Church celebrates **St. Ignatius of Loyola** (1491-1556), the founder of the Jesuits and the author of *Spiritual Exercises*: Find some time and space to "retreat" today and focus on spiritual exercises meaningful to you!

On **July 31**, we remember the passing of **Marinus Kok** (1916-1999), the Dutch priest and seminary professor who served as the twentieth archbishop of Utrecht from 1970 to 1981. He led efforts to resume communion between the Old Catholic Church and the Mariavite Church after 35 years of estrangement, and he traveled to Poland for the 1972 consecration of Mariavite bishop Stanislaw Kowalski. In his memory, consider how you might build bridges with those who've burned bridges in the past!

On **July 31**, we remember the passing of **Jerzy Szotmiller** (1933-2011), the Polish Old Catholic bishop of the Krakow-Częstochowa diocese of the Polish Catholic Church in Poland. In his memory, pray for our sisters and brothers of the Polish Catholic Church in Poland!

On **July 31**, we remember the passing of **Warren Gamaliel Bennis** (1925-2014), the American scholar and author widely regarded as a pioneer in the field of leadership studies. He suggested that future challenges will be best met by institutions that are less hierarchical and more democratic and adaptive. In his memory, pause to consider the experience, self-knowledge and personal ethics you bring to your life and ministry—and the ways in which you might grow in each!

On **July 31**, we remember the passing of **Patrick Leuben Mukajanga** (1976-2021), the Ugandan pastor and LGBTQ activist who founded the Saint Paul's Voice Centre of Uganda (SPAVOC), which fights for LGBTQ equality and access to AIDS/HIV services. In his memory, consider how you might better support marginalized communities in foreign lands!

In **August**, we remember the passing of **Callixtus III** (+c. 1180), the abbot elected "antipope" of the Roman church in 1168. Emperor Frederick played the rival popes as pawns against one another, finally uniting the empire under Alexander III with the condition that Callixtus III be given an abbacy and that all cardinals previously named by him be incorporated into the College of Cardinals. The occasion was celebrated with a feast in honor of Callixtus III by Alexander III. In his memory, consider ways in which you might make peace with your enemies!

On **August 1**, the Church celebrates **St. Alphonsus Liguori** (1696-1787), the lawyer whose lost case propelled him to found the Redemptorists, a community of priests dedicated to preaching, hearing confessions, and administering the sacraments: Consider ways in which you and your community might improve your own "Redemptorist" mission!

On **August 1**, we remember the passing of **Peter Paul Brennan** (1941-2016), the American Independent Catholic bishop who served the Old Catholic Confederation, the Ecumenical Catholic Diocese of the Americas, the African Orthodox Church, and the Order of Corporate Reunion. He succeeded Roman Catholic archbishop Emmanuel Milingo as president of Married Priests Now! He died without appointing a successor for the Order of Corporate Reunion, which subsequently divided. In his memory, pause to consider your own succession planning efforts, to ensure that others are equipped with the necessary knowledge and skills to do what you do!

On **August 1**, we celebrate the birth in 1949 of **Bruno Forte**, the noted Italian Roman Catholic theologian and archbishop who oversaw the preparation of "Memory and Reconciliation," which led to John Paul II's famous liturgy of asking God's forgiveness for 2,000 years of sins by the Roman church. Known for his works on Trinitarian theology and his defense of Jesus' historical resurrection, he is considered "one of the more noted theological minds in the Italian hierarchy." In his honor, pause to consider—and ask forgiveness for—the sins you have committed against others!

On **August 1**, we celebrate the birth in 1955 of **Emilie M. Townes**, the African-American Christian social ethicist and theologian who was the first Black woman to be elected president of the American Academy of Religion in 2008. She is the author of various works on womanist ethics, spirituality and justice. In her honor, take a moment today to deepen your own knowledge of womanist theology!

On **August 2**, the Church celebrates **St. Eusebius of Vercelli** (+c. 370) and **St. Peter Julian Eymard** (1811-1868). Eusebius advocated for the divinity of Christ and of the Holy Spirit, and urged merciful treatment of repentant bishops who had signed the Arian creed: Consider your own stance toward and (in)ability to forgive the repentant. Peter Julian, the "apostle of the Eucharist," dissuaded sculptor Auguste Rodin from giving up art: Consider how you're encouraging others in the development and sharing of their gifts—and of their understanding and reception of the Eucharist!

On **August 2**, we remember the passing of **Gioacchino Ventura dei Baroni di Raulica** (1792-1861), the Italian Jesuit and Theatine orator and philosopher known for his eloquence and his papal funeral orations. He advocated for the separation of church and state, and his diatribe against monarchs and for the union of religion and liberty earned a spot on the *Index of Forbidden Books*. In his memory, pray for all who continue to stand against theocracy and autocracy!

On **August 2**, we remember the passing of **Wacław Maria Innocenty Gołębiowski** (1913-1985), the Polish Old Catholic Mariavite bishop who served as supreme bishop of the Old Catholic Mariavite Church in Poland. In his memory, pray for our sisters and brothers of the Old Catholic Mariavite Church!

On **August 3**, the Church celebrates **St. Lydia**, the "seller of purple" in the New Testament, who offered her home to Paul and his companions and who baptized her entire household in response to Paul's preaching (Acts 16:14-15). She is considered the first European Christian convert. In her memory, wear a splash of purple and pray for all converts to the faith!

On **August 3**, the Church traditionally celebrated **St. Nicodemus**, the Pharisee and member of the Sanhedrin thrice mentioned in the Gospel of John (3:1-21, 7:50-51 & 19:39-42). After visiting Jesus at night, he reminded his colleagues that people deserve to be heard before judgment is passed against them. According to John, Nicodemus provided the spices for Jesus' burial. Because the gospel of his night visit to Jesus was proclaimed on Trinity Sunday, Johann Sebastian Bach and others composed cantatas memorializing Nicodemus. John Calvin later coined the term "Nicodemite" to describe crypto-Protestants who feared punishment for proclaiming their true beliefs in predominantly-Catholic settings. Nicodemus became a model of rebirth in American Christianity, and Martin Luther King, Jr. used him as a metaphor for the need for the U.S. to be "born again" with social and economic equality. In Nicodemus' memory, pray for all individuals and systems struggling to experience rebirth!

On **August 3**, we remember the passing of **Mary Flannery O'Connor** (1925-1964), the American novelist whose writings reflected her Catholic faith. She examined questions of morality and ethics, and highlighted the acceptance or rejection of characters with limitations and imperfections. In her memory, take a few moments to expand your knowledge of her works!

On **August 3**, the Salvation Army celebrates the anniversary of the installation in 2020 of **General Brian Peddle**. In a spirit of ecumenism, pray for him and for the 1.6 million people he serves!

On **August 4**, when it doesn't fall on a Sunday, the Church celebrates **St. John Marie Vianney** (1786-1859), the patron saint of parish priests! He was internationally known for transforming his community of Arx, France, and 20,000 would come to visit him each year, causing him to spend 16 to 18 hours each day in the confessional. In his memory, pray for your parish priests, and consider how you are transforming your community and serving the needs of those around you!

On **August 5**, we remember the passing of **Franciszek Rowiński** (1918-1990), the American bishop of the Polish National Catholic Church. In his memory, pray for our sisters and brothers of the Polish National Catholic Church!

Sunday August 6, 2023

TRANSFIGURATION OF THE LORD

(green)

The thread in today's scriptures: Jesus' transfiguration, where "his face shone like the sun and his clothes became white as light" (Mt. 17:2) was prefigured in Daniel's vision of the Ancient One, "[whose] clothing was snow bright" (Dan. 7:9). We pray for the day when all people might see God's glory (Ps. 97:6) and be "eyewitnesses of [Christ's] majesty" (2Pet. 1:16) — and when it might be said of us: "This is my child, my beloved, with whom I am well pleased" (2Pet. 1:17, Mt. 17:5)!

Holy humor: Woodrow Wilson once observed, "If you want to make enemies, try to change something!" Cite a few examples of our "Catholic" resistance to change — then segue into the "change" in today's gospel! Note how our faith should change and "transfigure" us!

Looking for a visual aid for your homily or object lesson? Try a bottle of bleach or a Transformers toy. Both speak of change and transformation!

August is here! **For the intellectually-curious**, share a brief lesson on the etymology of this month, named after Augustus Caesar (63 B.C. to 14 A.D.), the Roman emperor (and grandnephew of Julius Caesar) who ruled the Roman empire during the first half of Jesus' life. July and August are the two months named after Roman emperors, which, when inserted into the Roman calendar, caused the seventh (September), eighth (October), ninth (November) and tenth (December) months of the year to become the ninth, tenth, eleventh and twelfth months we now know!

On **August 6**, the Church celebrates the **Transfiguration of the Lord**. Luke's account is the only story that speaks of the disciples napping after their journey up the mountain: Stop to consider whether you're getting enough rest these days, whether you're seeing Christ transfigured in otherwise-ordinary moments of your day, and how you've "come down the mountain" after the mountaintop experiences in your life!

On **August 6**, we remember the passing of **Jacqueline-Marie-Angélique Arnauld** (1591-1661), the Abbess of the Abbey of Port-Royal des Champs, who was instrumental in the reform of several monasteries. Raised by Cistercian nuns, she desired to be the superior of a convent from a young age and was named coadjutrix to the abbess at age 12. Her biography was largely the story of her community's heroic resistance in the face of tribulations caused by the Roman church. In her memory, pray for all who display courage in the face of resistance and obstacles!

On **August 6**, we remember the passing of **John Neale** (1818-1866), the English Anglican priest, scholar and hymnwriter who penned *A History of the So-called Jansenist Church of Holland*, with its account of the Brothers of the Common Life. In his memory, renew your acquaintance with his works!

August 6 and **August 9** are the anniversaries of the bombings by U.S. forces of Hiroshima and Nagaski. Pray for world peace!

On **August 7**, the Church celebrates **St. Sixtus II** (+258) **and Companions** and **St. Cajetan**. Sixtus II was bishop of Rome for less than a year before his martyrdom, but is known for reconciling the Western church of Europe and the Eastern churches of Africa on the issue of baptism. Stop today to consider how you are bringing together and reconciling others! Cajetan founded the Theatines, an order of clerics who performed works of charity, promoted reception of the sacraments, and called clergy to their vocations in a time when many hierarchs in the Church were morally compromised. Pause to consider the example that you're providing others!

244

August 7 is also **Purple Heart Day**, an opportunity to honor all who were wounded in battle or made the ultimate sacrifice of their lives for our freedom.

On **August 8**, the Church celebrates **St. Dominic of Guzmán** (1170-1221), founder of the Dominican Order, whose friars preached the goodness of the body in contrast to the Albigensian belief that matter — and specifically the body — is evil. His order became synonymous with the torture and deaths of the Inquisition. Pray for the self-righteous who persecute others, and find ways to reinforce the goodness of the body and its functions in a world that continues to look askew at things created good by God!

On **August 8**, we remember the passing of **Antoine Arnauld** (1612-1694), the French Roman Catholic patristic theologian, philosopher and mathematician who was one of the leading intellectuals at Port-Royal-des-Champs. He attracted controversy by pointing out the relaxed morals of the Jesuits of his day and by suggesting that frequent communion was a deviation from the ancient Christian practice of celebrating the eucharist on the Lord's Day alone. For more than 20 years, he couldn't appear publicly in Paris. In his memory, pray for outcasts of every kind and those who are scorned — particularly in your family and among those you know!

On **August 8**, we remember the passing of **Augustin Theiner** (1804-1874), the German priest, theologian and historian who had access to several sources while serving as prefect of the Vatican's secret archives during the First Vatican Council. His book against the Jesuits was forbidden in the papal states, and he was deposed from his office for communicating the previously-secret order of business of the Council of Trent to opponents of purported papal infallibility. Despite these acts and his later correspondence with Old Catholic scholar Johann Friedrich, he was buried adjacent to St. Peter's Basilica, in the German cemetery for those who served the Roman church. In his memory, pray for all the "insiders" of other churches who help us to better know and understand the inner workings of those institutions!

On **August 8**, we remember the passing of **Maria Tymoteusz Kowalski** (1931-1997), the Polish Old Catholic Mariavite bishop who served as supreme bishop of the Old Catholic Mariavite Church in Poland. In his memory, pray for him and for our sisters and brothers of the Old Catholic Mariavite Church in Poland!

On **August 8**, we remember the passing of **Raymond Edward Brown** (1928-1998), the American Sulpician priest and prominent biblical scholar known for his studies of the Johannine community and of the life and death of Jesus. The historical investigation of the Bible was forbidden by the Roman church in 1893, but authorized in 1943, and Brown became one of the first Catholic scholars to apply historical-critical analysis to the Bible at that time. He opposed literalism and was scorned by traditionalists who suggested that he denied the inerrancy of scripture and cast doubt on the historical accuracy of numerous articles of the Catholic faith, including the virginal conception of Jesus. In his memory, explore his works and/or reflect on the elements of scripture that may be more fantastical than historical!

On **August 8**, we remember the passing of **Wiesław Skołucki** (1937-2015), the Polish bishop of the Wrocław diocese of the Polish Catholic Church in Poland. In his memory, pray for our sisters and brothers of the Polish Catholic Church in Poland!

On **August 8**, we celebrate the birth in 1949 of **Franz Segbers**, the noted German Old Catholic theologian and social scientist who writes widely on globalization and Christian social ethics. In his honor, discover some of his works!

On **August 9**, the Church celebrates **Bl. John of La Verna** (1259-1322), the Italian Franciscan friar and noted preacher known for his homoerotic visions of kissing and being kissed by Jesus. Far beyond tolerating the spirituality of this patron saint of the gay community, the *Fioretti* and his Franciscan Order lifted him up as an example of paradigmatic intimacy and union with Christ. Pause to consider your own relationship with Christ!

On **August 9**, we remember the passing of **Pierre d'Ailly** (1351-1420), the French cardinal, theologian, astrologer and chancellor of the University of Paris who supported conciliarism as a way to depose rival popes and end the Great Schism. In his memory, work to overcome division and help others to see the value of collective wisdom!

On **August 9**, the Church celebrates **Edith Stein** (1891-1942). Also known as **St. Teresa Benedicta of the Cross**, Edith was raised in an observant Jewish family. She is known for converting to atheism, then to Catholicism, before dying in Auschwitz. Pray today for those whose doubts and beliefs are taking them in various directions, and for all who continue to extinguish tremendous light in this world!

On **August 9**, we celebrate the birth in 1937 of **Justo L. González**, the Cuban-American Methodist historian and theologian known for his contributions to the development of Hispanic theology and Latin-American theology. His two-volume work, *The Story of Christianity*, is a popular text on Church history. In his honor, enrich your preaching and teaching with his thought!

On **August 9**, the Salvation Army celebrates the birth in 1957 of **General Brian Peddle**. In a spirit of ecumenism, pray for him and for the 1.6 million people he serves!

On **August 9**, we celebrate the birth in 1959 of **Sylwester Bigaj**, the Polish-Canadian Old Catholic bishop of the Canadian diocese of Polish National Catholic Church. In his honor, pray for him and for our sisters and brothers of the Polish National Catholic Church!

August 9 is **World Indigenous Peoples' Day**, an opportunity to demand inclusion and equity for our indigenous sisters and brothers in all social and economic systems.

On **August 10**, the Church celebrates **St. Lawrence** (225-258), whose words to those roasting him to death ("Turn me over; I'm done on this side") has made him the patron saint of…comedians! Pray Eucharistic Prayer I, which mentions him, consider how you employ humor in your ministry, and search for a joke to tickle the funny bones of those around you!

On **August 11**, the Church celebrates **St. Clare of Assisi** (1194-1253), the contemplative whose purported act of bilocation resulted in her renown as the matron saint of television: Consider how much time you spend watching television—and how you might better use technology to "bilocate" and reach more people!

On **August 11**, we remember the passing of **Nicholas of Cusa** (1401-1464), the German cardinal, philosopher, theologian, mathematician, astronomer and prolific writer hailed as the "first modern thinker." As bishop, he enacted reforms in his diocese—some of which were nullified by papal decree—and he discouraged pilgrimages to the "bleeding hosts" of Wilsnack. In his memory, consider what reforms might be necessary in your life and in the life of your community!

On **August 11**, the Church of England celebrates **John Henry Newman** (1801-1890), the Anglican priest and Roman Catholic cardinal who was an important and controversial figure in 19th-century England. Despite rampant speculation that he was gay, he was canonized by the Roman Church in 2019. For 32 years, he lived with his "earthly light," Fr. Ambrose St. John, who was 14 years younger than him; the two were inseparable and share the same grave. In 2008, in preparation for his beatification, the Vatican tried to exhume his remains, to separate them from his lover—only to discover that all their remains had decomposed and were thus not separable. Many consider him to be the most learned Catholic thinker of the English-speaking world. His episcopal motto was *Cor ad cor loquitur* (Heart speaks to heart). In his memory, learn a bit about his works or listen to a recording of his hymns "Lead, Kindly Light" and "Praise to the Holiest in the Height."

On **August 11**, we remember the passing of **Tadeusz Zieliński** (1904-1990), the American bishop of the Polish National Catholic Church in the United States and Canada. In his memory, pray for our sisters and brothers of the Polish National Catholic Church!

On **August 11**, we remember the passing of **Abdias de la Cruz** (1931-2019), the sixth supreme bishop of the Philippine Independent Church who unseated his predecessor and then struggled for the entire six years of his service to maintain unity and win the legal battle that ensued. He defended his central office from a violent takeover by the defenders of his predecessor, who retaliated by seizing parishes in four cities. In his memory, pray for your enemies and those who persecute you!

On **August 11**, we celebrate the birth in 1975 of **Vlastimil Šulgan**, the Slovak Old Catholic bishop who leads the Old Catholic Church in Slovakia. In his honor, pray for him and for our sisters and brothers of the Old Catholic Church in Slovakia!

On **August 12**, we remember the passing of **Francisco de Vitoria** (c. 1486-1546), the Spanish philosopher, theologian and jurist who founded the School of Salamanca. He is remembered for his contributions to just war theory and international law. In his memory, take a moment to reacquaint yourself with the Church's social teachings on just war.

On **August 12**, the Church celebrates **St. Jane Frances de Chantal** (1572-1641), the wealthy widow whose newly-formed congregation admitted women refused by other congregations due to their health or age. Consider your own biases against those who enjoy less health and/or vigor, and find a way to let them know they are loved and appreciated!

On **August 12**, we remember the passing of **José Garvida Flores** (1900-1944), a prominent Independent Catholic and member of the Philippine Independent Church. A patriot and prolific Ilokano poet and playwright, he composed "Philippines, Beloved Philippines", which is sung in churches throughout the archipelago. He edited a newspaper that he co-published with the church's second supreme bishop. In his memory, consider how you are using the power of words to inflame the hearts of others to love!

On **August 12**, we remember the passing of **Walter Jackson Ong** (1912-2003), the Jesuit language professor, philosopher and religious historian who explored the impact on human consciousness of the shift from orality to literacy. In his memory, consider the written records generated and maintained by your community, and challenge yourself to better capture your history through "craft literacy" — like the scribes of old!

On **August 12**, we remember the passing of **Teunis Johann Horstman** (1927-2014), the Dutch priest who served as the sixteenth Dutch Old Catholic bishop of Haarlem for seven years. At the 1971 Old Catholic theological conference, he advocated for the ordination of women, which was approved 27 years later at the 1998 diocesan synod. After a ten-year struggle to unite three parishes, he was consecrated bishop. His memoirs focus on his 15 years of pastoral ministry as a parish priest in Egmond. In his memory, pray for all who struggle to unite others!

August 12 is **International Youth Day**, an opportunity to raise awareness of cultural and legal issues surrounding the young people who are a driving force of change in our world!

Sunday, August 13, 2023
NINETEENTH SUNDAY IN ORDINARY TIME
(green)

The thread in today's scriptures: Our ancient ancestors prayed to see God and to see God's kindness (Ps. 85:8). God appeared to the ancient Israelites, giving them the law and its promises, the patriarchs, and ultimately the messiah (Rom. 9:4-5). God appeared to Elijah in a whisper (1Kgs. 19:12-13). And Peter recognized, through his friend's ability to walk on water, that he was truly in the presence of the Son of God (Mt. 14:33)!

Holy humor: There once was a boy who hated going to school because all the kids there made fun of him for not being good at anything. You can imagine what this did to his self-esteem and how many nights he lay awake, crying in his bed. But he prayed to God and asked God to give him an incredible talent, so that the kids would no longer make fun of him for not being good at anything. And it happened: the boy was given the ability to walk on water! His mind was blown: He was so happy! He now had something that he could show others, and they could no longer make fun of him for not being good at anything! Right? The next day, we went to the local swimming pool, where several of his classmates were swimming. And what did he do? He walked onto the water, right out to them in the deep end of the pool! And what did the other kids say? They burst out laughing and shouted, "Look at him! He can't even swim!" [Segue into what it would mean to defy nature's laws and have the necessary buoyancy in the soles of your feet to do the impossible: to walk on water. But this story made sense to the evangelist: If Jesus is Lord, then Jesus must have had power over nature — and this might have been one of the ways in which Jesus' friends recognized him as the Son of God! Eventually move from today's stories of ancient people experiencing God, to how it is that your listeners might experience God today!]

Looking for a visual aid for your homily or object lesson? Does your worship space have a projector and screen? There are many images in today's scriptures: a heavy wind rending mountains and crushing rocks, an earthquake, a fire, a man hiding his face in his cloak, a man walking on water, and another man attempting to do the same! If you don't have a projector and screen, try your best to visually represent some of these images: hiding your face in your chasuble or dalmatic, pretending to walk on water, and/or pretending to slowly sink into the waters!

On **August 13**, when it doesn't fall on a Sunday, the Church celebrates **Ss. Pontian** (+235) **and Hippolytus** (+235): Pontian was a bishop of Rome exiled by the emperor, and Hippolytus was a bishop — known for the invaluable information we now have from the *Apostolic Tradition* — who, ironically, led a schism against Pontian, whose day he now shares! Pray for reconciliation with those who seem most against you!

On **August 13**, the U.S. Church also celebrates **Our Lady Refuge of Sinners** (a feast celebrated by the Church of Latin America on July 4). She is the patroness of California. If you serve a *Latino* community, pray together the Litany of Loreto, which invokes her!

On **August 14**, the Church celebrates **St. Maximilian Kolbe** (1894-1941), the polish Franciscan who volunteered to die in place of a stranger at Auschwitz. Invoke the patron saint of prisoners on behalf of those who are incarcerated, and consider how you're doing with respect to the corporal work of mercy of visiting the imprisoned!

On **August 15**, the Roman Church celebrates the **Solemnity of the Assumption of Mary** — the last dogma proclaimed by the bishop of Rome. This day is not universally celebrated by Independent Catholics due to its tie to the Roman church's novel proclamations of purported "papal infallibility" and universal jurisdiction of the pope — the same issues that filled bishops and priests of the 1800's with a desire to return to the beliefs of the ancient—or Old—Catholic Church. Pause today to consider the extent to which your Mariology—your views on Mary—are rooted in the beliefs of the ancient Church and/or are influenced by the novelties introduced by hierarchs of more-recent memory! If you celebrate the Assumption, call to mind the German custom of blessing fruits and herbs on this day by decorating your worship space with baskets overflowing with ripe fruits and vegetables, calling to mind Mary's fertility. Fill pots with pungent herbs that stimulate the senses. Leave them in place through the Queenship of Mary on August 22.

On **August 15**, we remember the passing of **Hermann of Wied** (1477-1552), the German archbishop of Cologne who pushed for the punishment of Martin Luther, then, after a quarrel with the papacy, broke from Roman church. The people of Cologne failed to support his reforms and theological innovations, leaving him deposed and excommunicated in the last year of his life. In his memory, pray that more people might experience Saul/Paul conversions and come to embrace those they previously persecuted!

On **August 15**, we celebrate the birth in 1967 of Bishop **Christopher Carpenter**, presiding bishop of the Reformed Catholic Church. Pray for him and for the people he serves!

On **August 16**, the Church celebrates **St. Stephen of Hungary** (c. 975-1038), the founder and first king of Hungary, who established Christianity there. He is the patron saint of kings, masons, and children who are dying. In his honor, consider how you might be the hands and heart of Christ for the thousands of children who daily die—and for their heartbroken families!

On **August 16**, we remember the passing of **John Courtney Murray** (1904-1967), the Jesuit theologian known for his advocacy for religious freedom, his efforts to reconcile Catholicism and religious pluralism, and his key role in persuading bishops at Vatican II to adopt *Dignitatis humanae*, the Council's declaration on religious liberty. He had previously helped to draft the 1943 *Declaration on World Peace*, he promoted a close post-war constitutional agreement between the Roman church and the German state, and, in 1954, the Vatican forbade him from writing on religious freedom. In his memory, re-read *Dignitatis humanae* and/or consider your own stance toward issues of religious pluralism and freedom!

On **August 17**, the Church celebrates **St. Juliana** (+c. 270), the Christian saint who, along with her brother, was tortured for her refusal to renounce Christ. She is one of the 140 colonnade saints at St. Peter

Basilica in Vatican City. In her memory, pray for all who hold fast to Christ despite persecution!

On **August 17**, the Church celebrates **St. Beatrice of Silva** (c. 1424 - 1492), the Portuguese woman who founded the monastic Order of the Immaculate Conception of Our Lady in Spain. She is one of the 140 colonnade saints at St. Peter Basilica in Vatican City. In her memory, pray for all women who lead and guide our church!

On **August 17**, we remember the passing of **Henri Brémond** (1865-1933), the French Jesuit priest and philosopher suspended for attending the funeral of his friend, modernist George Tyrrell. He authored several books on Catholicism, including his renowned *A Literary History of Religious Sentiment in France*. Several of his books explored his interest in English topics, including English public schools, the evolution of Anglican clergy, and the psychology of John Henry Newman. In his memory, reacquaint yourself with the life and works of Brémond!

On **August 17**, we remember the passing of **Ruth First** (1925-1982), the South African anti-apartheid activist who wrote against apartheid. She was tried for treason, exiled, and later assassinated. In her memory, pray for all who fight racism!

On **August 18**, we remember the passing of **Walafrid Strabo** (c. 808-849), the Alemannic Benedictine monk known for his exposition on the mass and the psalms, and for his rhymed poems on scripture, theology, rulers of his day, and, most famously, his garden. In his memory, incorporate poetry into your prayer and/or pause for the meditative exercise of creating your own poem!

On **August 19**, we remember the passing of **Blaise Pascal** (1623-1662), the French mathematician, physicist, inventor, writer and Catholic theologian who died before reaching his 40th birthday. By age 23, he self-identified as a Jansenist Catholic, and his famous *Provincial Letters* are set in the conflict between the Jansenists and the Jesuits. Because of his chronic poor health, he pleaded with his sister, Jacqueline, not to enter the Jansenist convent at Port-Royal-des-Champs. Later, he frequently visited the convent and donated her share of their inheritance to the community there. In his memory, pray for and find a way to support the expressions of religious life that exist outside of mainstream religions!

On **August 19**, the Church celebrates **St. John Eudes** (1601-1680), who founded seminaries to equip future priests with the necessary knowledge and skills to help people grow in their relationship with God and others. Reflect on how you're empowering others and helping them to grow in their knowledge and skills for ministry in the Church!

On **August 19**, we remember the passing of **Johann Friedrich** (1836-1917), the Catholic priest and German theologian who was an early leader in the Old Catholic movement. As secretary to the leading German cardinal at the First Vatican Council, he played an important role in opposing the dogma of purported papal infallibility by supplying historical and theological material for opposing bishops. He was excommunicated in 1871 but continued to serve as a priest and professor. In 1874, he established the Old Catholic theological faculty at the University of Bern. In his memory, reach out to those who continue to exercise their ministry outside the churches they once loved!

On **August 19**, we remember the passing of **Dick Gregory** (1932-2017), the American civil rights activist and comedian who advocated for civil rights through his comedic writings. In his memory, consider how you might more creatively advocate for the rights of others!

On **August 19**, we remember the passing of **Robert Wood** (1923-2018), the American congregational minister known as the first member of the clergy to picket for LGBTQ rights in the early 1960s. His groundbreaking book, *Christ and the Homosexual*, urged churches to welcome homosexuals, recognize same-sex marriage and ordain gay clergy. In his memory, consider how you help to bridge and bring Christ to those most marginalized by our society!

On **August 19**, we celebrate the birth in 1944 of **Jack Canfield**, the American author and motivational speaker who co-authored the bestselling *Chicken Soup for the Soul* series. More than 500 million copies have been sold of his 250 books. In his honor, infuse your teaching and preaching with a story or two from his works!

On **August 19**, we celebrate the birth in 1948 of **Susan Brooks Thistlethwaite**, the American theologian, activist, biblical translator and former president of the Chicago Theological Seminary who served as a columnist on religion and public life for *The Washington Post* for six years. In her honor, reacquaint yourself with her works!

On **August 19**, the Coptic Catholic Church (in union with Rome) celebrates the birth in 1955 of **Patriarch Ibrahim Isaac Sidrak of Alexandria**. In a spirit of ecumenism, pray for him and for the 175,000 Coptic Catholics he serves!

On **August 19**, the Philippine Independent Church celebrates the birth in 1966 of **Emelyn Dacuycuy**, the first woman consecrated bishop by the church in its 117-year history. She shared, "Gender is just a social construct, a way of ordering society and ascribing values. As a spiritual community, however, we must see beyond gender. We must see God's people as Jesus sees them—children of God and heirs of God's eternal reign." In her honor, pause to consider how you are helping to empower our sisters for ministry at all levels of our Church and society!

On **August 19**, the Ancient Church of the East celebrates the anniversary of the installation in 2022 of **Catholicos Patriarch Yacob III Daniel of Baghdad and Basra**. In a spirit of ecumenism, pray for him and for the people he serves!

August 19 is **World Humanitarian Day**, an opportunity to celebrate the aid workers who uplift humankind!

August 19 is also **National Aviation Day** in the U.S. Celebrated on Orville Wright's birthday, it's an opportunity to revel in all things aeronautical!

Sunday, August 20, 2023

TWENTIETH SUNDAY IN ORDINARY TIME

(green)

Don't gloss over today's tremendous scriptural message for Independent Catholic communities: Unlike other "catholic" communities that are not truly catholic (or universal) and that seek to exclude certain persons, most Independent Catholic communities share the inclusive love of God manifested in today's scriptures!

The thread in today's scriptures: Even foreigners will be brought to God's holy mountain, since God's house is "a house of prayer for all peoples" (Is. 56:7). The psalmist affirms this: All nations will praise God and know God's salvation (Ps. 67:2-5)! Paul confirms this as well: "God delivered all to disobedience, that God might have mercy upon all" (Rom. 11:32)! And Matthew shares Mark's story of Jesus not denying the request of the Canaanite woman: Even though she wasn't Jewish, she had faith—and, because of that, Jesus healed her daughter (Mt. 15:21-28, Mk. 7:24-30)!

Holy humor: In 2005, the *Guardian* recognized the following joke as the funniest religious joke of all time. Have you heard it before? It's a joke about Baptists, told by Emo Phillips, who says: "Once I saw this guy on a bridge about to jump. I said, 'Don't do it!' He said, 'Nobody loves me.' I said, 'God loves you. Do you believe in God?' He said, 'Yes.' I said, 'Me, too!' I asked, 'Are you a Christian?' He said, 'Yes.' I said, 'Me, too!

Protestant or Catholic?' He said, 'Protestant.' I said, 'Me, too! What franchise?' He said, 'Baptist.' I said, 'Me, too! Northern Baptist or Southern Baptist?' He said, 'Northern Baptist.' I said, 'Me, too! Northern Conservative Baptist or Northern Liberal Baptist?' He said, 'Northern Conservative Baptist.' I said, 'Me, too! Northern Conservative Baptist Great Lakes Region, or Northern Conservative Baptist Eastern Region?' He said, 'Northern Conservative Baptist Great Lakes Region.' I said, 'Me, too! Northern Conservative Baptist Great Lakes Region Council of 1879, or Northern Conservative Baptist Great Lakes Region Council of 1912?' He said, 'Northern Conservative Baptist Great Lakes Region Council of 1912.' I said, 'Die, heretic!' And I pushed him over." [Segue into how it's easy to fall into us/them dichotomies, loving those who are like us and demonizing those who are different from us. Does God show such distinctions? No! God loves all people, and, for God, all means…all!]

Looking for a visual aid for your homily or object lesson? Consider a big, warm embrace! Every time you speak of God's inclusive love in today's scriptures, put your arms out, as if you were giving a bear hug to an invisible person in front of you. That's how God is: loving and embracing all people!

On **August 20**, when it doesn't fall on a Sunday, the Church celebrates **St. Bernard of Clairvaux** (1090-1153), the French abbot who founded 70 monasteries and wrote numerous theological and spiritual classics. Because of his devoted, passionate friendship with Irish archbishop Malachy of Armagh, whom he covered in kisses when he visited from afar, Bernard is a special saint of the gay community. After his death, the French believed that they would undergo a gender metamorphosis if they passed under "St. Bernard's rainbow." Consider how you might better show love and affection to those close to you!

On **August 20**, we remember the passing of **Geert Groote** (1340-1384), the Dutch deacon and popular preacher who co-founded the Brothers of the Common Life and was a key figure in *Devotio Moderna*. He taught the virtues of piety and joy to all who flocked to the nearly 100 communities of his Windesheim Congregation for clergy, which played an important role in education and in the transcribing and printing of books. Pause to consider how you might grow in charism, attract more people to the Lord's work, and help them to grow in their relationship with God and with one another!

On **August 20**, we remember the passing of **Erwin Kreuzer** (1878-1953), the fifth bishop of the German Old Catholic Church. Like most German bishops at the time, he swore an oath of episcopal allegiance to Adolf Hitler, "bearing [his] solemn witness to the fact that our Church knows itself to be intimately allied with the people." Despite a severe heart attack in 1946 and clear signs of Parkinson's disease, he remained in office through his death seven years later. In his memory, pray for all who find themselves in unholy alliances!

On **August 21**, we remember the passing of **Alexander of Hales** (c. 1185-1245), the "Irrefutable Doctor," who played a key role in the development of medieval Scholasticism and the Franciscan School. He quoted Aristotle, cited works not frequently cited by others, and he shared his agreement and disagreement with such theological authorities as Anselm and Augustine. He also formulated the question that became a focal point of philosophical and theological inquiry: Would Christ have become incarnate if humanity had never sinned? In his memory, reacquaint yourself with his life and works!

On **August 21**, we remember the passing of **Noël Alexandre** (1639-1724), the French Dominican theologian and ecclesiastical historian who was the pensioned preacher to King Louis XIV. Later banished and deprived of his pension for his opposition to *Unigenitus*, his works are still valued by students of Church history. In his memory, pray for those who suffer loss as a result of their beliefs!

On **August 21**, the Church celebrates **St. Pius X** (1835-1914), who, despite his conservative tendencies, lowered the age of reason from 12 to 7, making him the patron saint of First Communicants. Reflect on how you might better eliminate barriers to the sacraments of the Church, particularly for the youngest among us!

On **August 21**, we celebrate the birth in 1949 of **John Okoro**, the Roman Catholic priest, military chaplain and psychotherapist who served as the sixth bishop of the Austrian Old Catholic Church for seven years. His episcopal motto was "With God all things are possible." In his honor, pray for all our sisters and brothers of the Austrian Old Catholic Church!

On **August 21**, the Armenian Apostolic Church celebrates the birth in 1951 of **Ktrij Nersessian**, who became Catholicos Karekin II of All Armenians. In a spirit of ecumenism, pray for him and for the nine million people he serves!

August 21 is **World Senior Citizen Day**, an opportunity to raise awareness of issues affecting older adults!

On **August 22**, the Church celebrates the **Queenship of Mary**: Pray the fifth glorious mystery of the rosary, and reflect on the place of Mary in your own theology and Mariology!

On **August 23**, the Church celebrates **St. Rose of Lima** (1586-1617), the patroness of South America, Central America, and the Philippines. She disfigured herself when others complimented her beauty. In her honor, pray for and reach out to those who struggle with their physical appearance!

On **August 23**, we remember the passing of **Maria Franciszka Kozłowska** (1862-1921), the Polish nun excommunicated by the Roman Church after devotion to her private revelations swept Poland. Her *Great Work of Mercy* spurred Mariavitism and led to the rise of the Mariavite Church and the Old Catholic Mariavite Church, movements perceived as a threat by those suspicious of the spiritual guidance of women. She faced many attempts to discredit and undermine her work. In her memory, pray for all who remain faithful despite the setbacks and obstacles they face!

August 23 is **World Day for Slave Trade Abolition**, a day to remember the atrocities perpetrated by the transatlantic slave trade.

On **August 24**, the Church celebrates **St. Bartholomew**, the first-century apostle who was skinned alive and beheaded for his faith. Pray Eucharistic Prayer I, which mentions him, consider how much "skin in the game" you have with respect to the faith, and pray for those whose suffering is extremely difficult to endure!

On **August 24**, we remember the passing of **Gerard Shelley** (1891-1980), the British linguist and translator for prisoners of war who was ordained by the Old Roman Catholic Church in Great Britain in 1950 and became its third archbishop three years later. He lived with the Oblates of St. Joseph and translated several Russian works to English. In his memory, consider how you "translate" the gospel message for others!

On **August 24**, we remember the passing of **Bayard Rustin** (1912-1987), the African-American civil right leader who strengthened Martin Luther King Jr.'s leadership and teaching about non-violence. He was a chief organizer of the 1963 March on Washington. Openly gay, he was known as "Brother Outsider" and is considered a patron saint of the gay community. He famously said, "We need, in every community, a group of angelic troublemakers." In his memory, consider your own calling as an "angelic troublemaker"!

On **August 24**, we remember the passing of **Elisabeth Kübler-Ross** (1926-2004), the Swiss-American psychiatrist and pioneer in near-death studies. Her groundbreaking work, *On Death and Dying*, outlined the five stages of grief. In her memory, pray for and find a meaningful way to minister to someone who is approaching the great mystery of death!

On **August 25**, the Church celebrates **St. Louis King of France** (1214-1270) and **St. Joseph Calasanz** (1556-1648). Crowned at age 12, Louis dedicated his reign to the promotion of justice and peace, feeding and housing the poor, and negotiating peace with England. He tried to prevent the private wars that plagued his country, and he introduced the presumption of innocence in criminal procedure. In his memory, consider the ways in which you might better promote justice and peace in our world. Joseph was the Spanish priest who founded the Pious School to provide free education to the children of the poor. Together with St. Camillus de Lellis, he served Christ in the "distressing disguise" of plague victims, and his religious order, the Piarists, were last of the religious Orders of solemn vows approved by the Church. As a new school year dawns, find a way to contribute in his memory to the education of those in need!

On **August 25**, we remember the passing of **Hubert Augustus Rogers** (1887-1976), the bishop of the African Orthodox Church who was named coadjutor archbishop of the North American Old Roman Catholic Church in 1942 by Carmel Henry Carfora, whom he succeeded in 1958. During an era of segregation, Rogers was the first Black man to lead a predominantly-White Independent Catholic jurisdiction in the U.S. In his memory, consider how you might help our sisters and brothers from diverse backgrounds to grow in their relationship with God and others through the rich tradition of Independent Catholicism!

On **August 26**, the Church celebrates the **Black Madonna of Czestochowa**. A famous Polish Catholic icon attributed to St. Luke, she is one of dozens of medieval European Black Madonnas. Through syncretism, her image was assumed into *Santería* as Erzulie Dantor, a Haitian vodou goddess known as the defender of lesbians—thus providing an LGBTQ overtone to a traditional Catholic image. In her honor, reach out to those who might need to hear the scriptural affirmation, "I am black and beautiful" (Song of Songs 1:4)!

On **August 26**, the Philippine Independent Church celebrates **Our Lady of Balintawak**, an image of Mary from a revolutionary's dream, who saw her dressed as a Filipina farmer, in the white, blue and red colors of the Filipino flag, crying, "Liberty! Liberty!" and leading by the hand a boy dressed as a Katipunan guerilla. As a result of the vision, the revolutionaries chose not to return to Manila and were kept safe from capture. In honor of this day, imagine ways in which you might help to inculturate images of Mary and Jesus in ways that are meaningful to the people you serve!

On **August 26**, we remember the passing of **William James** (1842-1910), the philosopher and "Father of American psychology" whose work influenced several 20th-century intellectuals. His renowned work, *The Varieties of Religious Experience*, suggests that religious experience should take precedent over religious institutions, and that "over-belief" in things that can't be proven helps us to live fuller, better lives. In his memory, seek out an opportunity today to share with someone of your own religious experiences!

August 26 is **Women's Equality Day**, the day on which women were given the right to vote in the U.S. in 1920. Find a way to spur conversation and action on the obstacles that continue to keep us from recognizing the equality of all!

Sunday, August 27, 2023

TWENTY-FIRST SUNDAY IN ORDINARY TIME

(green)

The thread in today's scriptures: God builds up strength within us (Ps. 138:3), making us like Jesus' friend Rocky (or "Peter," if you prefer; Mt. 16:18), who recognized the messiah and was promised "the keys to the kingdom of heaven" (Mt. 16:19). The keepers of keys, like Shebna and Eliakim in today's first reading (Is. 22:19-23), are able to open and shut doors; they can lock people and/or things in, and they can let them loose (Mt. 16:19). No one can know the mind of the Lord (Rom. 11:34), but Paul cracks open the door (or pulls back the curtain) just enough to reveal that all things are "from him and through him and for him" (Rom. 11:36).

Holy humor: The thousands of jokes that place Saint Peter at the pearly gates are rooted in today's gospel. Try a joke or two about Peter at the Pearly Gates, then segue into today's scriptures! Here are a few possibilities:

- A young couple was killed in an accident on the day before their wedding. When they arrived at the Pearly Gates, they asked Saint Peter if they could be married in heaven. "No problem," said Saint Peter. Years passed, and they still weren't married—when they ran into Saint Peter and asked him about the wedding. "Everything is being arranged," he assured them. Several more years passed, and they still weren't married — when they met Saint Peter again. They reminded him about the wedding and said, "We know that in heaven, time is of no consequence, but we have been waiting years now to get married." Saint Peter replied, "I'm sorry. All the arrangements for your wedding were made the day you arrived. There's only one thing that's keeping us from celebrating your wedding: We're waiting for a priest!" (Ouch!)

- A man died and approached the Pearly Gates, where Saint Peter told him heaven was getting crowded, so he had to test people with a point system. If the man got to 100 points, he could enter heaven. So the man told Peter that he gave to the poor, and Peter marked him down for 3 points. The man thought again, then said that he tithed. Peter added one point. The man, desperately searching his memory, finally said that he never cussed. Peter added a half point. By now, the man was frustrated and said, "At this rate, I'll only get into heaven by the grace of God!" And Peter replied, "Come on in!"

- At the Pearly Gates, Saint Peter asked the men to form two lines: "All the hen-pecked husbands — all the men whose wives tell them what to do — are on this side, and all other men are over here." The men formed two lines — but Saint Peter noticed that one hen-pecked man was in the wrong line. He said to the man, "Excuse me, but I said all hen-pecked men are supposed to be over in that other line." "I know," said the man, "but my wife told me to stand here!"

- A teacher, a doctor, and a lawyer all die and end up at the Pearly Gates. Saint Peter meets them and says, "It's good to have you here, but we're a little overcrowded today. You'll each have to answer one question before I can let you in." Peter turns to the teacher and asks, "What was the name of the famous ship that hit an iceberg and sank in the early 1900's?" The teacher smiles and says, "That's easy. The Titanic!" Peter lets her in. He turns to the doctor and asks, "How many people died on the Titanic?" The doctor says, "Now that's a tricky question, but I just saw a documentary on it. The answer is 1,503." Peter lets the doctor in, too. Then Peter turns to the lawyer and says, "Name them."

Looking for a visual aid for your homily or object lesson? Try a set of keys! We all carry them. Today, they provide a great visual on how we're able to open and shut doors — how we're able to "bind" and "loose"!

On **August 27**, when it doesn't fall on a Sunday, the Church celebrates **St. Monica** (c. 331-387), who suffered a promiscuous, alcoholic husband and a son whose lifestyle greatly pained her. Pray for and reach out to distressed spouses and parents!

On **August 27**, we remember the passing of **Hélder Pessoa Câmara** (1909-1999), the Brazilian archbishop and advocate of liberation theology who championed human rights and democracy during the country's military regime. He once said, "When I give food to the poor, people call me a saint; when I ask why they are poor, people call me a communist." In his memory, consider your own words and actions on behalf of the poor and marginalized!

On **August 27**, we celebrate the birth in 1952 of **Miguel Ángel Ruiz Macías**, the Mexican spiritual writer who uses the pen name "Don Miguel Ruiz" for his works on indigenous Mexican spirituality. In 2018, he was named one of the 100 Most Spiritually Influential People, and his bestseller, *The Four Agreements*, was a *New York Times* bestseller for more than a decade. In his honor, enrich your teaching and preaching with insights from indigenous religious traditions!

On **August 28**, the Church celebrates **St. Augustine of Hippo** (354-430), one of the four great fathers of the Western Church, who suggested that, contrary to the teaching of the Eastern Church, we all bear the consequences of the sin of Adam and Eve. A sexually-active, bisexual youth, he shared sex-negative views but argued that God created intersex people. On this day, consider the wisdom of the Eastern tradition—and the consequences of Augustine's views on the development of such Western novelties as infant baptism and limbo!

On **August 28**, we remember the passing of **Paul Marie Marc Fatôme** (1873-1951), the French bishop who led the Mariavite Catholic Church in France. In his memory, pray for our sisters and brothers of the Mariavite Catholic Church!

On **August 28**, the Serbian Orthodox Church (recognized by the Ecumenical Patriarch of Constantinople) celebrates the birth in 1930 of **Miroslav Gavrilović**, who became Patriarch Irinej of Serbia. In a spirit of ecumenism, pray for him and for the 12 million Serbian Orthodox Catholics he serves!

On **August 28**, we celebrate the birth in 1957 of **Ai Weiwei**, the Chinese artist and activist who actively criticizes the Chinese Government for its stances against democracy and human rights. In his honor, pray for all who fight for human rights throughout the world!

On **August 28**, we celebrate the anniversary of the presbyteral ordination in 2010 of **Elaine Groppenbacher**, the Pastoral Associate of Guardian Angels Ecumenical Catholic Community in Tempe, Arizona. Pray for her and for the people she serves!

On **August 29**, the Church commemorates **the Passion (formerly "the Beheading") of St. John the Baptist**: Consider the gifts and actions of this greatest of persons (Lk 7:28), which drew to him so many persons desirous of his baptism of repentance!

On **August 29**, we remember the passing of **Elmer Talmadge Clark** (1886-1966), the American Methodist executive who brought attention to various Independent Catholic communities and clergy as part of his 1937 survey of the historical, theological and psychological background of 300 religious groups in *The Small Sects in America*. In his memory, acquaint yourself with other Independent Catholic clergy and communities near you!

On **August 29**, we remember the passing of **Wayne Walter Dyer** (1940-2015), the American motivational speaker and self-help author whose first work, *Your Erroneous Zones*, was one of the bestselling books of all time. He distinguished between religion and spirituality and famously wrote: "I don't think that Jesus was teaching Christianity; Jesus was teaching kindness, love, concern, and peace. What I tell people is don't be Christian, be Christ-like. Don't be Buddhist, be Buddha-like." In his memory, find a concrete way today to be more Christ-like!

On **August 29**, we celebrate the birth in 1950 of Bishop **Theodore Feldmann**, a bishop of the Ascension Alliance. Pray for him and for the people he serves!

August 29 is **International Day against Nuclear Tests**, a day to highlight the global need for bans on nuclear weapon tests and use.

On **August 30**, we remember the passing of **Don Richard Riso** (1946-2012), the American author on the Enneagram's nine impressionistic sketches of personality types and their implications for spirituality. In his memory, consider the broad strokes of your own personality and the degree to which you manifest various healthy and unhealthy personality traits!

On **August 30**, we celebrate the birth in 1976 of Father **Robert W. Caruso**, author of *The Old Catholic Church*. Reacquaint yourself with his work, and pray for our sisters and brothers of the Union of Utrecht of Old Catholic Churches!

August 30 is **World Day of Victims of Enforced Disappearances**, an opportunity to raise awareness of the many people throughout our world who involuntarily "disappear" through arrest, detention and abduction—a crime against humanity.

On **August 31**, the Church celebrates **St. Joseph of Arimathea**, the wealthy disciple who, in all four canonical gospels, assumed responsibility for the burial of Jesus after his crucifixion. Medieval traditions tied him to Britain as the first keeper of the Holy Grail. In his memory, consider how you are caring for Christ in others!

On **August 31**, we celebrate the birth in 1948 of Bishop **Mark Elliott Newman**, presiding bishop of the Catholic Apostolic Church of Antioch. Pray for him and for the people he serves!

On **August 31**, we celebrate the birth in 1970 of **Queen Rania**, the queen consort of Jordan. Since marrying the King of Jordan, she has advocated for education and children's welfare. In her honor, pray for all those who use their platform to advocate for those who can't advocate for themselves!

August 31 is **International Overdose Awareness Day**, an effort to raise awareness of an issue while acknowledging the grief of those left behind and without wanting to stigmatize those who have died.

On **September 1**, we remember the passing of **Izidor Guzmics** (1786-1839), the Hungarian theologian known for his Hungarian translations of ancient writers and for his work, *On Religious Unity among Christians*. He also founded a school and built an asylum for 150 children. In his memory, pray for Christian unity, and consider how you're serving the children of your community!

On **September 1**, we remember the passing of **Gregorio Aglípay y Labayán** (1860-1940), the Filipino priest and revolutionary who was excommunicated by the Roman church for serving as vicar general of the revolutionary army. He served as the first supreme bishop of the Philippine Independent Church, which grew to over one million adherents during his lifetime. After unsuccessfully campaigning for president of the Philippines in 1940, he married at age 79, the year before his death, to set an example for his clergy. In his memory, pray for our sisters and brothers in the Philippines who continue to honor his life and legacy!

On **September 1**, we celebrate the anniversary of the episcopal consecration in 2004 of Bishop **David Oliver Kling**, bishop of the

Community of Saint George and host of Sacramental Whine podcast. Happy anniversary!

On **September 1**, we celebrate the founding in 2014 of the **Unified Old Catholic Church**, currently led by Bishop Michael Beckett. Happy anniversary!

On **September 2**, we remember the passing of **Johann Nikolaus von Hontheim** (1701-1790), the priest and professor who used the pseudonym Febronius to denounce papal pretensions, papal absolutism in Germany, and the interference of the Roman church in the affairs of the empire. Threatened with censure and excommunication, he was forced to retract what he wrote — then to say that he had done so of his own free will. In his memory, pray for the victims of bullying and all who must act anonymously for fear of reprisals!

On **September 2**, we remember the passing of **Viktor Frankl** (1905-1997), the Austrian neurologist and Holocaust survivor whose bestselling *Man's Search for Meaning* encourages readers to find meaning — and a reason to continue living — in even the most brutal forms of existence. In his memory, consider the hope and meaning that you share with others!

Sunday, September 3, 2023

TWENTY-SECOND SUNDAY IN ORDINARY TIME

(green)

The thread in today's scriptures: In a world where people seek to harm others through violence, reproach and derision (Jer. 20:8), we should expect to suffer, just as Jeremiah (Jer. 20:7) and Jesus suffered (Mt. 16:21). If we learn to deny ourselves (Mt. 16:24) and offer ourselves as a living sacrifice (Rom. 12:1), our souls will be satisfied "as with the riches of a banquet" (Ps. 63:5)!

Holy humor: Begin with a pun on sacrifice, then segue into today's scriptures! Here are a few examples:

- Why did God ask Abraham to sacrifice his 12-year-old son, Isaac? Because if he had waited another year or two, for Isaac to become a teenager, it would no longer have been a sacrifice!
- My ex- said that relationships are all about sacrifice — and still she screamed when she saw the bloody goats on the altar!

- In order to make a relationship work, you have to make a lot of sacrifices — which is why I keep a large number of goats in my backyard!
- My friend, who lives with his parents, adopted a goat the other day, but his mother said he'd have to get rid of it. As long as he lives with his parents, I guess he'll have to make sacrifices!
- Today, I was told that I'll never achieve great things if I never make sacrifices. Anyone know where I can buy some cheap chickens?
- "I've made a lot of sacrifices to get to where I am today," said the Aztec high priest!
- Did you hear about the stage performer who did live sacrifices of celebrities during his act? I gave him five stars!
- When my husband cooks, he treats me like a goddess. Everything is either a burnt offering or a bloody sacrifice!

Looking for a visual aid for your homily or object lesson? Consider a clown nose! People made fun of Jeremiah, causing him to say, "All the day, I am an object of laughter; everyone mocks me" (Jer. 20:7). And perhaps Peter thought that following Jesus was going to be fun and easy. Ha! Following Jesus more likely results in the sad clown's tears, than the painted smiles of circus clowns!

September is here! **For the intellectually-curious**, note that the remaining months of the calendar year are named for the seventh (*septem*), eighth (*octo*), ninth (*novem*) and tenth (*decem*) months of the Roman calendar! Four months remain this year: Are you accomplishing the goals you had for 2023?

This is **Labor Day weekend**: Expect lower mass attendance than usual. Consider planning a barbeque, picnic, or "white party" for those desirous of building community!

On **September 3**, when it doesn't fall on a Sunday, the Church celebrates **St. Gregory the Great** (c. 540-604), the mayor of Rome who gave half his fortune to the poor, and the other half for the establishment of seven monasteries. His name is associated with reforms: of the calendar, church governance, clerical behavior, and liturgy. Consider your own vocation to reform!

On **September 3**, the Church also celebrates **St. Phoebe**, the deaconess and "helper of many" mentioned in Romans 16:1. A notable member of the church in Cenchreae, she was entrusted by Paul to deliver his letter to the Romans. She is the only named deaconess in the canonical scriptures. In her memory, pray for all women who are preparing to share in the Church's ordained ministries!

On **September 4**, the U.S. celebrates **Labor Day**: Pray the Proper Mass for Labor Day or the Mass "for the Sanctification of Human Labor," pray for those currently without employment, and thank the volunteers of your community for their labor of love!

On **September 4**, the Church celebrates **St. Candida the Elder**, the Italian woman who converted to Christianity after hosting St. Peter and being cured of an illness by him. A matron saint of Naples, she is one of the 140 colonnade saints at St. Peter Basilica in Vatican City. In her memory, pray for all those who are leading others to Christ!

On **September 4**, we remember the passing of **Gilbert de la Porrée** (c. 1085-1154), the scholastic logician and theologian from Poitiers (present-day France) whose commentary on Boethius was widely misinterpreted as a Trinitarian heresy. Brought to trial before Eugene III, Gilbert aptly defended his works, and his knowledge of scriptures eclipsed that of his prosecutor, Bernard of Clairvaux — but he was forced to edit parts of his work to express the official position of the Roman church. In his memory, consider the ways in which others might misunderstand you — or that you might misunderstand others!

On **September 4**, we remember the passing of **Johann Baptist von Hirscher** (1788-1865), the German priest and theologian whose works on moral theology were censured as part of the Roman church's reaction against rationalistic morality. His catechism advanced the teaching of religion in Germany and gave rise to lively discussions, requiring him to vigorously defend it. His book, *The Notion of a Genuine Mass*, was included on the *Index of Forbidden Books* for its relegation of sacrifice to the background. Accused of being "an enemy of Rome and everything Roman," of opposing celibacy and the breviary, and of promoting a German national church, he continued to defend himself through the publication of pamphlets. Those closest to him knew him as a holy, zealous catechist with pure intentions, who spurred a religious awakening in Baden. In his memory, pause to consider how you are contributing to the spiritual and religious awakening of those around you!

On **September 4**, we remember the passing of **Henri-Marie de Lubac** (1896-1991), the French Jesuit who played a key role in shaping the Second Vatican Council and is now considered one of the most influential Catholic theologians of the 20th century. His *Meditations on the Church* had a profound influence on *Lumen gentium*. Pius XII's *Humani* *generis* is believed to be directed at de Lubac and other theologians of the "new theology," which respected lay competencies and addressed contemporary concerns through patristic sources. After three of his books were condemned, de Lubac turned conservative, co-edited a journal with Joseph Ratzinger, and was named a non-bishop cardinal of the Roman church by John Paul II. In his memory, pray for all whose prophetic spirit is dulled by the vicissitudes of life!

On **September 5**, the Church celebrates **St. Teresa of Calcutta** (1910-1997), who dedicated her life to the poorest of the poor. The United Nations marks this day as **International Day of Charity**. Consider your own stance toward the poor, and find a unique way today to recognize your relationship to our sisters and brothers with much less means!

On **September 6**, we remember the passing of **Henri Theodore Johann van Vlijmen** (1870-1954), the Dutch priest who simultaneously served as a pastor in Haarlem and as the thirteenth Dutch Old Catholic bishop of Haarlem. After the 1931 Bonn Agreement, he was one of the first Old Catholic bishops to participate in the consecration of an Anglican bishop. He served as bishop for nearly 30 years, concluding his service in 1945. In his memory, pray for all who have dedicated several years of their lives to the service of God's people!

On **September 6**, we remember the passing of **Margaret Sanger** (1879-1966), the American activist who founded the first birth control clinic in the United States, which later became Planned Parenthood. In her memory, pray for all women who lack access to birth control and resources for reproductive health!

On **September 6**, we remember the passing of **Joachim Jeremias** (1900-1979), the renowned German Lutheran theologian and scholar of Near Eastern and New Testament studies. The author of several publications, he attempted to reconstruct the historical context of Jesus and to provide a deeper understanding of Jesus' life and teachings. In his memory, update your own understanding of the New Testament context in which Jesus lived and ministered!

On **September 6**, we celebrate the birth in 1959 of Bishop **Edmund N. Cass**, a longtime bishop in the Independent Catholic movement. Pray for him and for the people she serves!

On **September 7**, the Church celebrates **St. Theofredus**, the third-century soldier and martyr. In Renaissance art, he and St. Maurice were depicted as a same-sex couple, gazing into one another's eyes, with hands almost touching. In their memory, pray for all same-sex couples who model the love of Christ to our world!

On **September 7**, we remember the passing of **Carl Bean** (1944-2021), the American activist and pastor of the LGBTQ-affirming Unity Fellowship Church. A Motown and disco singer, he created the gay liberation song "I Was Born This Way," which hit #15 on the Billboard Charts and inspired a similarly-titled song by Lady Gaga. In his memory, reach out to those who might need to hear the affirmation that God loves them just the way God created them!

On **September 8**, the Church celebrates **the birth of Mary**. Consider a unique way to celebrate this day, perhaps with a small birthday cake and/or prayer of gratitude to God for the birth of Jesus' mother!

On **September 8**, we remember the passing of **Sergius I** (c. 650-701), the pope who consecrated Willibrord as bishop to the Frisians and — very significantly — extended to him the special privilege of allowing Utrecht to elect his successors without the permission or oversight of the pope. Consider how you equip, support and empower others to spread the Word as co-workers in the Lord's vineyard!

On **September 8**, we remember the publication in 1713 of *Unigenitus*, the papal bull condemning 101 propositions of Pasquier Quesnel as "false, captious, ill-sounding, offensive to pious ears, scandalous, pernicious, rash, injurious to the [Roman] Church and its practices, contumelious to Church and State, seditious, impious, blasphemous, suspected and savoring of heresy, favoring heretics, heresy, and schism, erroneous, bordering on heresy, often condemned, heretical, and reviving various heresies, especially those contained in the famous propositions of Jansen." (They really pulled out the thesaurus for that sentence!) *Unigenitus* became a litmus test for obedience to the Roman papacracy, as it purportedly warned against "false prophets…[who] secretly-spread evil doctrines under the guise of piety and introduce ruinous sects under the image of sanctity." In memory of this day, pray for all within the Independent Catholic tradition who, inspired by those who've gone before us, have risked the ill perceptions of others in order to help the People of God to grow in holiness!

September 8 is **International Literacy Day**, an opportunity to raise awareness of the nearly 800 million non-literate adults and young people in our world.

On **September 9**, the Church celebrates **St. Peter Claver** (1581-1654), the Spanish Jesuit who preached missions to plantation owners and ministered to the needs of African slaves in Colombia. Consider new ways to share God's love with oppressors and the oppressed!

On **September 9**, we remember the passing of **Henry Parry Liddon** (1829-1890), the Anglican theologian who communicated with Old Catholic and Russian Orthodox clergy in an attempt to create closer bonds between them and the Anglican Church. Intriguingly known for his pulpit oratory and his defiance to modern thought and scholarship, he was a pioneer in ecumenical relations. In his memory, consider how your own words and actions contribute to ecumenism in our world!

On **September 9**, the Church of Jesus Christ of Latter-day Saints celebrates the birth in 1924 of President **Russell Marion Nelson**. In a spirit of ecumenism, pray for him and for the 16 million Mormons he serves!

On **September 9**, we celebrate the birth in 1948 of **Maria Bernard Kubicki**, the Polish Old Catholic Mariavite bishop of the Silesian-Łódź diocese of the Old Catholic Mariavite Church in Poland. In his honor, pray for him and for our sisters and brothers of the Old Catholic Mariavite Church in Poland!

On **September 9**, we celebrate the founding in 2009 of **St. Anthony of Padua Catholic Community** in Centreville, Virginia, currently led by Fathers Jason Lody and Julian Garcia. Happy anniversary, St. Anthony!

Sunday, September 10, 2023
TWENTY-THIRD SUNDAY IN ORDINARY TIME
(green)

Reflect the coming of Autumn in **your worship environment**!

- Consider switching out your medium green vestments of Summer Ordinary Time, for **yellow-green vestments** that reflect the changing season! Be sure they match the décor of your worship space — and that they're ironed or steamed!

- **Incorporate elements from the natural world** into your evolving Ordinary Time décor: first fruits from the harvest, colored leaves, and other signs of the season.

- As you change the shade of green, **change the shape and placement of fabric** as well. If you started Ordinary Time with simple vertical fabric, try changing to a draped placement or a series of smaller widths of fabric hung together on a large rod.

- Complement with **green plants containing yellow-green leaves**.

Be mindful of the exclusive language in today's first reading: "You, son of man, I have appointed a watchman" could just as easily be rephrased, "I have appointed you a sentinel." To avoid the suggestion that only men sin, you might change all instances of the third person singular (he/him/his), to the third person plural (they/them/their). In the gospel, "your brother" could just as easily be "another person," and the many instances of "he" might just as easily be "the person" or "he or she"!

The thread in today's scriptures: We're challenged to speak with others about their faults (Mt. 18:15) and to warn the wicked of their ways (Ez. 33:7-9). "Love does no evil" (Rom. 13:10)! And when God speaks to us through others about our own faults, we're challenged not to harden our hearts (Ps. 95:8). May we open our hearts and our ears to Paul's warnings, to follow God's commandments (Rom. 13:9)!

Holy humor: A man got a job as a night watchman at a factory. There had been a lot of thefts by the workers on the night shift, and so every morning when the night shift workers passed through his gate, it was his job to check their bags and pockets to make sure that nothing was being stolen. Things were going along very well the first night on the job until a man pushing a wheelbarrow of newspapers came through his gate. Aha, he thought, that man thinks he can cover up what he's stealing beneath all that newspaper! So he removed the paper, only to find…nothing. Still he felt that the man was acting strangely, so he questioned him about the paper. The man replied, "I get a little extra money from the newspapers I recycle, so I go into the lunchroom and pick up all the ones people have thrown away." The guard let him pass, but decided to keep a close eye on him. The next night it was the same, and the night after that. Week after week, it went on. The same guy would push the wheelbarrow of newspapers past the guard's checkpoint. The guard would always check and find nothing. A month later, the guard discovered that he had been fired. "Fired?" he asked his supervisor, in total surprise. "Why? What did I do?" His supervisor replied, "It was your job to make sure that no one stole anything from this plant, and you have failed. So you're fired." "Wait a minute," the guard said. "What do you mean that I failed. Nobody ever stole anything from this place while I was on guard!" "Oh, really," his boss answered. "Then how do you explain the fact that we're missing 30 wheelbarrows?" [Segue to the message of today's scriptures of watchfulness and being on the lookout for evil!]

Looking for a visual aid for your homily or object lesson? Consider a spyglass or a pair of binoculars! Like the sentinel (Ez. 33:7), we're on the lookout for evil. And just as the sailor calls out the sight of land ("land ho!"), and just as the sentinel warns of approaching enemies, we're called to warn others of encroaching evil ("evil ho")!

U.S. society celebrates **Grandparents' Day** today: Mark this day with special prayers for all grandparents, living and deceased, and share a special blessing and gift with all grandparents in attendance! Even better, invite grandparents to bring their grandchildren to Mass today, and take photos after Mass of grandparents with their grandkids! Print and share free copies of the photos next Sunday!

On **September 10**, we remember the passing of **Mary Wollstonecraft** (1759-1797), the English philosopher known for her book, *A Vindication of the Rights of Woman*. Considered one of the original feminist philosophers, she argued that the inferiority of women was not natural, but was due to a lack of education and opportunity. In her memory, pray for all who have been deprived of access and opportunity!

On **September 10**, we celebrate the birth in 1943 of **Neale Donald Walsch**, the American actor, screenwriter, and author of the longtime international bestseller, *Conversations with God*. Raised Catholic, he informally studied comparative religion and attempted to unify all theologies to help people relate to God from a modern perspective. In his honor, reflect today on how you are "one with God and one with life," in a shared global state of being!

On **September 10**, we celebrate the birth in 1951 of **Sarah Coakley**, the English Anglican priest and theologian whose works focus on systematic theology, the philosophy of religion, the philosophy of science, patristics, feminist theory, and the intersections of law and medicine with religion. In her honor, reacquaint yourself with her works!

On **September 10**, we celebrate the birth in 1958 of Bishop **Michael Beckett**, presiding bishop of the Unified Old Catholic Church. Pray for him and for the people he serves!

September 10 is **World Suicide Prevention Day**, an opportunity to reach out to those experiencing pain and hopelessness. Long stigmatized by the Church, one million of our sisters and brothers die of suicide each year, and 20 times more attempt suicide. Spread word of the National Suicide Prevention Hotline: (800) 273-8255.

On **September 11**, we remember the passing of **Frederick Ebenezer John Lloyd** (1859-1933), the Welsh Independent Catholic bishop consecrated by Joseph René Vilatte and Paolo Miraglia-Gulotti, who succeeded Vilatte as the primate and metropolitan of the American Catholic Church. He led the church during 13 years of growth, consecrating John Churchill Sibley for missionary activity in England. In his memory, pray for all who assist us in extending the legacy of our lives and ministries!

On **September 11**, the **National Day of Mourning and Remembrance** in the U.S., we remember the many victims who died in the terrorist attacks of 2001, including **Mychal Judge**, the Roman Catholic Franciscan priest and chaplain of the New York Fire Department who rushed into the twin towers and was killed by falling debris after anointing a fallen firefighter. As a result, he was designated Victim 0001, the first recorded casualty of that day. Many firefighters loved him for his memory of their names, birthdays, interests and family members. Openly gay, he is one of the patron saints of the gay Catholic community. Find someone today with whom you might share his words: "If no one told you today that they love you, let me tell you: I love you!"

On **September 12**, we remember the passing of **Claude Beaufort Moss** (1888-1964), the English Anglican theologian and ecumenist who authored *The Old Catholic Movement: Its Origin and History*. In his memory, thumb through his works for insights into the church of our Old Catholic sisters and brothers!

On **September 12**, we remember the passing of **John Shelby Spong** (1931-2021), the American Episcopal bishop and theologian who challenged Christians to rethink traditional doctrines. One of the first American bishops to ordain women and LGBTQIA+ persons, he described his life as a journey from the literalism and conservative theology of his childhood, to an expansive view of Christianity. In 1998, he published his 12 points for the reform of Christianity. In his memory, pause to consider how popular, literal interpretations of scripture fail to honestly address the situations of modern believers!

On **September 13**, the Church celebrates "golden-tongued" **St. John Chrysostom** (347-407), a head and reformer of the Eastern church. How much do you know about the rich traditions of the Eastern church? Take a moment today to increase your knowledge of this saint and his heritage!

On **September 13**, we remember the passing of **Dante Alighieri** (c. 1265-1321), the Italian poet who composed a *comedia* later considered divine — the most important poem of the Middle Ages. His depictions of heaven, purgatory and hell have influenced imaginations to the present day. In his memory, pause to consider the influences on your own ideas of the afterlife!

On **September 13**, we remember the passing of **William Farel** (1489-1565), the French theologian who invited John Calvin to remain in Geneva, causing the city to become the "Protestant Rome," a refuge for persecuted reformers of the Church. Farel dedicated his life to the formation of missionaries. Pray for all missionaries and for all who help prepare them for ministry, and consider your own role in empowering others to preach the Good News!

On **September 13**, the Assyrian Church of the East celebrates the anniversary of the installation in 2021 of David Royel as **Catholicos-Patriarch Awa III** of Iraq. In a spirit of ecumenism, pray for him and for the people he serves!

On **September 14**, the Church celebrates the **Exaltation of the Cross**: Lift high the cross as the symbol of our redemption!

On **September 15**, the Church celebrates **Our Lady of Sorrows**. Pray the sorrowful mysteries of the rosary for all whose hearts are pierced by suffering!

On **September 15**, we celebrate the birth in 1955 of **John Mack**, the Polish-American bishop of the Buffalo-Pittsburgh diocese of the Polish National Catholic Church. In his honor, pray for him and for our sisters and brothers of the Polish National Catholic Church!

September 15 is **International Day of Democracy**, an annual opportunity to reflect on the state of democracy in the world.

September 15 is also **National POW/MIA Recognition Day** in the U.S., an opportunity to remember all who are prisoners of war or missing in action—and for those who grieve their absence.

This is a week of celebrating freedom in Latin America: **September 15** is **Independence Day in Costa Rica, El Salvador, Guatemala, Honduras and Nicaragua**. **September 16** is **Independence Day in Mexico**. **September 18** is **Independence Day in Chile**. If you serve a *Latino* community and/or have congregants who descend from these nations, find a fitting way to celebrate their *fiestas patrias*! Invite people to wear traditional dress and to share traditional foods. Decorate with *papel picado* and traditional decorations. Play traditional music. Share the *grito*. They will appreciate your desire to honor their culture and heritage!

On **September 16**, the Church celebrates **Ss. Cornelius** (+253) **and Cyprian** (+258). Cornelius advocated for welcoming back to the Church repentant individuals who had previously renounced their faith, and

Cyprian spent much of his life in hiding due to persecution. Pray Eucharistic Prayer I, which mentions them, and consider your own stance toward those who express contrition!

On **September 16**, we remember the passing of **Michael Baius** (1513-1589), the Belgian theologian and leader of the anti-scholastic reaction of the 16th century, whose presence at the Council of Trent was not allowed before intervention by the King of Spain. His positions on St. Augustine's theology brought him into conflict with Rome, and 79 of his propositions were condemned by Pius V. Despite this and subsequent condemnations, he retained his professorship and was named chancellor of the University of Louvain. His name is most often associated with Cornelius Jansen, the young Blaise Pascal, and the theologians of Port-Royal-des-Champs. In his memory, pray for all who inspire others to think "outside the box"!

On **September 16**, we celebrate the birth in 1988 of **Grzegorz Wyszyński**, the Polish bishop who leads the Polish diocese of the National Catholic Church. In his honor, pray for him and for our sisters and brothers of the National Catholic Church in Poland!

September 16 is **World Ozone Layer Day**, an opportunity to raise awareness of the depletion of the ozone layer and to promote ways to preserve it.

September 16 is also **National CleanUp Day** in the U.S., an opportunity for us to show our care for Mother Earth!

Sunday, September 17, 2023
TWENTY-FOURTH SUNDAY IN ORDINARY TIME
(green)

Be mindful of the exclusive language in today's scriptures! In the first reading, because the preceding sentence is in the second person, "Could anyone refuse mercy to another like himself, can he seek pardon for his own sins?" might just as easily be rephrased, "Could you refuse mercy to another like yourself, can you seek pardon for your own sins?" In the gospel, "my brother" might just as easily be "another person"!

The thread in today's scriptures: Kind and merciful and rich in compassion (Ps. 103:8), God doesn't deal with us according to our sins (Ps. 103:10), but instead pardons our iniquities (Ps. 103:3) and puts our transgressions far from us (Ps. 103:12). We're called to be kind, merciful, compassionate and forgiving as well (Mt. 18:21-35). Just as the Quelle Jesus suggests (Mt. 6:12), we're called to "forgive [our] neighbor's injustice, so that when we pray, our own sins will be forgiven" (Sir. 28:2). As Paul suggests, we don't forgive others for our sake alone (Rom. 14:7-8), we do it "for the Lord" who is the Lord of all (Rom. 14:9)!

Holy humor: The story is told of the boy who prayed every night for a new, red bicycle—until he realized that's not how God works. So, he stole a bicycle and prayed for God's forgiveness instead! [Share the disclaimer that your listeners shouldn't steal, but that the essential truth in the joke is that God is rich in mercy and forgiveness! Segue to the themes of today's scriptures.]

Looking for a visual aid for your homily or object lesson? Consider a measuring cup or a bushel basket! We use measuring cups to measure out ingredients: they're a visual reminder that the measure of forgiveness that we use with others will be measured back to us. And our ancestors carried bushel baskets that served a dual measuring purpose: they would measure with them the grain they sold to others—but they'd also use them to measure the items that they purchased from others! The same measure that we use for others is the measure we receive!

Today is **Catechetical Sunday**: If you have a religious education program, host a blessing for all teachers and students!

On **September 17**, we remember the passing of **Hildegard of Bingen** (1098-1179), the German Benedictine abbess, writer, composer and mystic who created the oldest surviving morality play. Named a Doctor of the Church in 2012, she is considered the founder of scientific natural history in Germany. Because of her love for Richardis von Stade, the nun who served as her personal assistant, Hildegard is considered a matron saint of the lesbian community. The love story of the two and Richardis' inspiration of Hildegard was captured by the 2009 film, "Vision." In her memory, pray for all who inspire your creativity and productivity!

On **September 17**, we remember the passing of **Heinrich Bullinger** (1504-1575), the Swiss pastor who was one of the most influential theologians during the 16th-century Reformation of the Church. Nearly 12,000 letters to and from him exist. In his memory, consider how you are reaching out and staying in touch with friends old and new!

On **September 17**, the Church celebrates **St. Robert Bellarmine** (1542-1621), who prayed for his opponents during a time of deep division in the Church. Honor him by thinking through non-defensive ways in which you might articulate your own beliefs with those who have differing views!

On **September 17**, we remember the passing of **Kartini** (1879-1904), the Indonesian activist who advocated for women's rights and education. In her memory, pray for all who fight for women's rights!

On **September 17**, we remember the passing of **Adrienne von Speyr** (1902-1967), the Swiss Catholic physician, writer, theologian, mystic and stigmatist who authored over 60 books on spirituality and theology. She was the inspiration for much of the work of the Jesuit priest Hans Urs von Balthasar. In her memory, reach out to the women whose lives and faith have inspired you!

September 17 is **U.S. Constitution Day** and **U.S. Citizenship Day**, opportunities to reflect on our responsibilities as U.S.—and global—citizens!

On **September 18**, we celebrate the birth in 1955 of **Antoni Kopka**, the American bishop who led the Polish National Catholic Church in the United States and Canada. In his honor, pray for him and for our sisters and brothers of the Polish National Catholic Church!

On **September 19**, the Church celebrates **St. Januarius** (+305), the Italian bishop credited with preventing the eruption of Mount Vesuvius. Consider the ways in which you might help prevent "eruptions" in the relationships that are boiling around you!

On **September 19**, the Roman Church celebrates the apparition in 1846 of **Our Lady of La Salette**, a vision of Mary during an era of several purported apparitions. It inspired John Vianney, John Bosco and Joris-Karl Huysmans and led to the 1852 founding of the Missionaries of Our Lady of La Salette. Consider the ways in which you enflesh the prayer, conversion, reconciliation and commitment celebrated on this day!

On **September 19**, we remember the passing of **Stephen Kaminski** (1859-1911), the Prussian organist who led the Polish Independent Catholic Church in the U.S. He infamously occupied St. Paul Roman Catholic Church in South Omaha, Nebraska, defending it with six revolvers and two carbines. His 1898 consecration by Joseph René Vilatte is a case study in simony: Vilatte agreed to consecrate him for $5,000, but, after a bankruptcy and the loss of his home and cathedral, Vilatte consecrated Kaminski for $100 in cash and promissory notes for a few hundred dollars more. Kaminski's consecration by Vilatte led to the latter's excommunication by the Syriac Orthodox Patriarch of Antioch. Kaminski's death in Buffalo, New York led to the creation of the Polish

National Catholic Church, which was a member of the Union of Utrecht of Old Catholic Churches from 1907 to 2003. In his memory, consider the lessons we might learn from the more checkered parts of our history!

On **September 19**, we remember the passing of **Étienne Gilson** (1884-1978), the French philosopher and scholar of medieval philosophy who viewed Thomism as a revolt against Scholasticism. He is perhaps the only Thomist philosopher whose work and reputation have not suffered from the decline in interest in medieval philosophy since the 1960's. In his memory, reacquaint yourself with a chapter or two of his writings on the philosophy of St. Bonaventure and/or St. Thomas Aquinas!

On **September 20**, we remember the passing of **Paschal III** (c. 1110-1168), the cardinal and "antipope" who, consecrated by the bishop of Liège, challenged the reign of Alexander III. To gain the support of the emperor, he hosted a magnificent celebration of the canonization of Charlemagne. In his memory, pray for all whose political motivations have shaped and continue to shape Church history!

On **September 20**, we remember the passing of **Pierre de La Broue** (1644-1720), the French bishop, doctor of theology and court preacher who opposed the papal bull *Unigenitus*. He called for a general council of the Church to discuss the matter. The founder of two seminaries, he was known for his charitable works. In his memory, pray for all theologians of the Church who draw the attention of bishops to the errors of their ways!

On **September 20**, the Church celebrates **Ss. Andrew Kim Dae-gŏn** (1821-1846), **Paul Chong Ha-sang** (1795-1839) **and 101 Companions**, who represent the 8,000 Catholics martyred in Korea between 1839 and 1867. Consider your own willingness to lay down your life for your beliefs!

On **September 20**, we remember the passing of **Basil Christopher Butler** (1902-1986), the English Benedictine priest and internationally-respected scripture scholar who defended the traditional priority of the Gospel of Matthew [celebrated tomorrow] and became the pre-eminent English-speaking voice at the Second Vatican Council. He wrote on spirituality, contemplative prayer, ecumenism, and the Church Fathers, and he contributed, often in fluent Latin, to many of the Council's documents. In his memory, thumb through the documents of Vatican II — particularly *The Dogmatic Constitution on Divine Revelation*, which Butler considered to be the foundation for all other Vatican II documents!

On **September 21**, the Church celebrates **St. Matthew**, the first-century tax-collector-turned-apostle to whom the first gospel is attributed. In his honor, pray Eucharistic Prayer I, which mentions him, and flip through the Gospel of Matthew and refamiliarize yourself with its themes and stories—and find one on which to reflect in a deeper way today!

On **September 21**, we remember the passing of **Arthur Schopenhauer** (1788-1860), the German philosopher most known for his philosophical pessimism. He affirmed asceticism, self-denial and the world-as-appearance, he fervently opposed slavery, and he condemned "those devils in human form, those bigoted, church-going, strict sabbath-observing scoundrels" for how they "treat their Black brothers [and sisters] who, through violence and injustice, have fallen into their devil's claws." In his memory, reflect on how you are standing in solidarity with the oppressed!

On **September 21**, we remember the passing of **Luigi Taparelli** (1793-1862), the Italian Jesuit who coined the term "social justice" and whose social teachings influenced Leo XIII's 1891 encyclical, *On the Condition of the Working Classes*. In his memory, consider how your own words and actions promote social justice in our Church and in our world!

On **September 21**, we remember the passing of **Henri Nouwen** (1932-1996), the Dutch Catholic priest and theologian who wrote widely on psychology, pastoral ministry, spirituality, social justice and community. Because of his struggles with accepting his own homosexuality in his private journals and conversations, he is one of the patron saints of the gay community. He coined the concept of the "wounded healer" and retired from academia to work with individuals with intellectual and developmental disabilities. In his memory, consider how your "growing edges" might be great gifts to your own ministry as a wounded healer!

On **September 21**, we celebrate the birth in 1935 of **Benjamín Abalos, Sr.** (1935-), a prominent Independent Catholic and member of the Philippine Independent Church who served as mayor of Mandaluyong, Philippines (1988-1998), and as chair of the Philippine Commission on Elections (2002-2007). An outstanding trial judge, he lost various elections before and after his time of public service. In his honor, pray for all who are tempted to give in after defeat!

On **September 21**, we celebrate the birth in 1979 of noted Dutch Old Catholic priest and theologian **Peter-Ben Smit**, who has authored and edited several books and articles and who leads the annual summer school in Old Catholic theology at Utrecht University. Let him know of your appreciation for his impactful scholarship!

On **September 21**, we celebrate the anniversary of the episcopal consecration in 2019 of **Anthony Green**, Pastor of St. John of God Parish in Schenectady, New York and Auxiliary Bishop for Diocese of Little Portion of the Catholic Apostolic Church in North America (CACINA). Pray for him and for the people he serves!

September 21 is **International Day of Peace**, a day of non-violence and cease-fire.

On **September 22**, the Church celebrates **St. Maurice**, the third-century soldier and martyr, often depicted as a Black knight in shining armor. In Renaissance art, he and St. Theofredus were depicted as a same-sex couple, gazing into one another's eyes, with hands almost touching. In their memory, pray for all same-sex couples who model the love of Christ to our world!

On **September 22**, we remember the passing of **Josse van Clichtove** (c. 1472-1543), the Flemish priest, theologian and humanist who was entrusted with the task of collecting and summarizing all the charges against Martin Luther. Pray today for all who store up grievances against others!

On **September 22**, we remember the passing of **Tyler Clementi** (1992-2010), the American student at Rutgers University who committed suicide at age 18 after his roommate made public a secret recording of Tyler kissing another man. His death brought national attention to the issue of cyberbullying and the struggles facing LGBTQ youth. In his memory, raise awareness of the great work of the Trevor Project and its 24-hour national help line (866 4U TREVOR) for LGBTQIA+ youth!

On **September 22**, we remember the passing of **John McNeill** (1925-2015), the American Jesuit scholar, theologian and psychotherapist who inspired countless LGBTQ people of faith and their allies. His ministry to gay Catholics in the 1970s contributed to the birth of Dignity. He was silenced by the Vatican and expelled from the Jesuit Order after his 1976 groundbreaking book, *The Church and the Homosexual*. He authored books on LGBTQ spirituality and traveled to Rome in 2011 to ask Benedict XVI to condemn violence against LGBTQ people. In his obituary, the *National Catholic Reporter* named him a "patron saint of LGBT Catholics." In his memory, pray for all who are silenced by others!

On **September 23**, the Church celebrates **St. Thecla**, the early Greek follower of the Apostle Paul. She encouraged other women to follow in her footsteps, and she is one of the 140 colonnade saints at St. Peter Basilica in Vatican City. In her memory, pray for all who lead others in their pursuit of the apostolic life!

On **September 23**, we remember the passing of **Antonio Francisco Xavier Alvares** (1836-1923), the Goan Roman Catholic priest who joined the Malankara Orthodox Syrian Church as Mar Julius I, was elevated to metropolitan, and who consecrated Joseph René Vilatte. Interested in the education and health of Goans, he created a college and an English school, and he published pamphlets on the treatment of cholera and the cultivation of cassava. He opened his home to the poor and to those who suffered from leprosy and tuberculosis. In his memory, consider how you are contributing to the education and health of others!

On **September 23**, the Church celebrates **St. Pius "Padre Pio" of Pietrelcina** (1887-1968), the Capuchin priest who purportedly bore the stigmata until his death, when—intriguingly—the wounds of Christ were no longer visible. Consider how you and others "bear the marks of Christ" (Gal 6:17) in various ways!

On **September 23**, we remember the passing of **Joseph Zawistowski** (1918-2001), the American bishop of the Western Diocese of the Polish National Catholic Church. In his memory, pray for our sisters and brothers of the Polish National Catholic Church!

On **September 23**, the Czechoslovak Hussite Church celebrates the anniversary of the installation in 2006 of **Patriarch Tomáš Butta**. In a spirit of ecumenism, pray for him and for the 39,000 people he serves!

September 23 is the **autumn equinox**, the day on which the sun crosses the equator on its journey south!

Sunday, September 24, 2023
TWENTY-FIFTH SUNDAY IN ORDINARY TIME
(green)

For the next four Sundays, the second reading will come from Paul's Letter to the Philippians. For the intellectually-curious, take a moment to share of the dating, audience and context for this letter, as well as its structure and themes!

Be mindful of the exclusive language in today's scriptures (repeated from the proclamation of Deutero-Isaiah at the Easter Vigil): Because most of the reading is in the second person, "Let the scoundrel forsake his way, and the wicked man his thoughts; let him turn to the Lord for mercy" might just as easily be rephrased, "Forsake your wicked ways, and turn to the Lord for mercy."

The thread in today's scriptures: Not only is God "generous in forgiving" (Is. 55:7), as we heard last Sunday (Ps. 103:1-12), but "[God's] thoughts are not [our] thoughts" (Is. 55:8). We see this in today's gospel, where all the workers in the vineyard are treated equally (Mt. 10:1-16). The Lord is indeed "compassionate to all" (Ps. 145:9 — even to the latecomers in the Lord's vineyard! And for those already in the vineyard: Continue your "fruitful labor" (Phil. 1:21) and "conduct yourselves in a way worthy of the gospel of Christ" (Phil. 1:27)!

Holy humor: A mother was preparing pancakes for her young sons when the boys began arguing over who would get the first pancake. Their mother saw an opportunity for a lesson! She told her sons, "If Jesus were sitting here, he'd say that the first will be last, and the last will be first. In fact, he'd probably say, 'Let my brother have the first pancake. I can wait.'" The younger boy turned to his older brother, and said, "You be Jesus!" [Segue into the human tendency to put ourselves first and to compare what we have to others, then to the themes of today's scriptures.]

Looking for a visual aid for your homily or object lesson? Consider a bunch of grapes! Ancient cultures regarded grapes as sacred and as a symbol of abundance (see Num. 13:23). How are you contributing "fruitful labor" to God's abundant harvest? And what is your attitude to those who labor with you in the Lord's vineyard — and to those who are still standing outside the vineyard?

Today is **Priesthood Sunday**, a special day to honor the priesthood in the U.S. Don't wait until your priests transfer or retire to celebrate them!

On **September 24**, our Jewish spiritual siblings celebrate **Yom Kippur**, the holiest day of the year, which focuses on a day-long fast and time of prayer for atonement and repentance.

On **September 25**, we remember the passing of **Francisco Suárez** (1548-1617), the Spanish Jesuit priest, philosopher and theologian who was one of the leading figures of the School of Salamanca and is regarded as one of the greatest scholastics after Aquinas. His work bridged the scholasticisms of the Renaissance and Baroque phases, and it influenced Leibniz, Schopenhauer and Heidegger. In his memory, reacquaint yourself with his thought and/or the main currents of the Salamanca School!

On **September 25**, we remember the passing of **John Ireland** (1838-1918), the American Roman Catholic archbishop of Saint Paul, Minnesota known for his progressive stances on education, immigration and church/state relations. Though remembered for his acrimonious relations with Eastern Catholics, he promoted progressive social ideals and the Americanization of Catholicism. In 1890, he was viewed as "bold and outspoken" when he preached on racial justice, saying, "The color line must go; the line will be drawn at personal merit." In his memory, pause to consider the social ideals you espouse!

On **September 25**, we remember the passing of **M. Scott Peck** (1936-2005), the American psychiatrist known for his bestselling *The Road Less Traveled* and *People of the Lie.* He explored the notion of discipline as key for emotional, psychological and spiritual health, and he expounded on such concepts as balance, delayed gratification, acceptance of responsibility and dedication to truth. In his memory, read a chapter or two from one of his works and use it as fodder for self-reflection!

On **September 25**, we remember the passing of **Wangari Maathai** (1940-2011), the Kenyan activist who was the first African woman to win the Nobel Peace Prize. She is known for her focus on environmental protection and women's rights. In her memory, pray for those who continue the fight for the rights of women!

On **September 25**, we remember the passing of **Virginia Ramey Mollenkott** (1932-2020), the trailblazing feminist biblical scholar and queer theologian whose 13 books liberated countless LGBTQ lives. She shook the religious world with her groundbreaking 1978 book, *Is the Homosexual My Neighbor?* In 2001, she published her award-winning work, *Omnigender: A Trans-religious Approach.* Raised evangelical and struggling with gender nonconformity, she went from attempting suicide, to being able to declare, "Hallelujah, I'm queer!" In her memory, reach out to someone who might be struggling and in need of a helping hand!

On **September 25**, we celebrate the birth in 1956 of **Miroslav Volf**, the Croatian Protestant "theologian of the bridge" who has attempted to bring Christian theology to bear on culture, politics and economics. Volf has explored dialogues between different faiths, denominations and ethnic groups. In his honor, consider the bridges you're building and/or burning!

On **September 26**, the Church celebrates **Ss. Cosmas and Damian**, the third-century brothers who practiced medicine and wouldn't accept money for their services. They are the patron saints of twins, confectioners, the blind, and of many medical professions (e.g., physicians, nurses, dentists). Pray Eucharistic Prayer I, which mentions them, and find a fitting way to honor their memory and those who continue their legacy. If your community has ties to the Franciscan tradition, call these saints to mind through your display of the San Damiano Crucifix.

On **September 26**, we remember the passing of **Frederick William Faber** (1814-1863), the English hymn writer and theologian known for his work, *Faith of Our Fathers*. An Anglican vicar, he followed his hero, John Henry Newman, into the Roman church. He was joined by 11 men who formed a religious community that called itself the Brothers of the Will of God. In his memory, pray for all who continue to be inspired to leave behind their former religious affiliations and to found new communities that seek to realize the will of God!

On **September 26**, we remember the passing of **George Santayana** (1863-1952), the Spanish-American philosopher, poet and novelist known for his aphorisms. With a fond spot in his heart for the Catholic values, practices and worldview with which he was raised, he described himself as a "Catholic atheist." In his memory, pray for and/or reach out to someone who may no longer self-identify as Catholic, but who still shares a fondness for our Catholic values and/or traditions!

On **September 26**, we remember the passing of **Gerhard Anselm van Kleef** (1922-1995), the Dutch priest and seminary rector who served as the fifteenth Dutch Old Catholic bishop of Haarlem for 20 years. The son of Old Catholic theologian Bastiaan Abraham van Kleef, he was ordained in 1946. History was made at his episcopal consecration in 1967, when Theodore Zwartkuis was the first Roman Catholic bishop to attend an Old Catholic episcopal consecration. In his memory, consider how you might reach out in a gesture of acceptance to those who feel condemned or excluded by others!

September 26 is **World Day for the Total Elimination of Nuclear Weapons**. Pray for global nuclear disarmament!

On **September 27**, the Church celebrates **St. Vincent de Paul** (1581-1660), who provided for the physical needs of the poor. Cold weather is coming: Plan a clothing drive or a collection of canned goods and imperishable foods in his honor, to benefit a local food pantry or St. Vincent de Paul Society!

On **September 27**, we celebrate the birth in 1943 of **Marie André Le Bec**, the French Old Catholic Mariavite bishop who leads the French province of the Old Catholic Mariavite Church. In his honor, pray for him and for our sisters and brothers of the Old Catholic Mariavite church in France!

On **September 27**, we celebrate the birth in 1987 of **Stephen Rodriguez**, a deacon at Holy Family Catholic Church in Austin, Texas. Pray for him and for the people he serves!

September 27 is **World Tourism Day**, an acknowledgement of the social, cultural, political and economic value that tourism provides and the way in which it contributes to sustainable development.

On **September 28**, the Church celebrates **St. Wenceslaus** (c. 911-935), the duke who evangelized pagan Bohemia (present-day Czech Republic) and was murdered by his brother. The song, "Good King Wenceslas" is based on the legend of him going out into the snow on the Feast of St. Stephen to give alms to the poor. His page, Podiven, followed him with bare feet, stepping in the miraculously-warm footprints of the saint. Because Wenceslas "truly loved [Podiven] during his lifetime" and, after the murder of Wenceslas, Podiven "was often overcome by grief, sorrowing for days on end," they are patron saints of the gay community. Pray for all who continue to be the hands and heart of Christ, helping those in need!

On **September 28**, the Church also celebrates **St. Lawrence Ruiz** (1594-1637) **and Companions**. Lawrence was a married father of three who fled from Manila to Japan and refused to trample Catholic images and adhere to the state religion of Japan. He and 231 Catholics were martyred in Japan during the 16th and 17th centuries. Consider the ways in which you "trample" the image of God in others and in creation!

On **September 28**, we remember the passing of **Ferdinand Marcos, Sr.** (1917-1989), a prominent Independent Catholic and member of the Philippine Independent Church who served as the tenth president of the Philippines (1965-1986). Raised as an Independent Catholic, he converted to Roman Catholicism in 1954, in order to marry his wife, Imelda Marcos. Espousing an ideology of "constitutional authoritarianism," he ruled as a dictator under martial law from 1972 to 1981. He was one of the most controversial leaders of the 20th century, and his rule was infamous for its corruption, extravagance and brutality. He was removed from power during the People Power Revolution of 1986, when he fled to Hawaii. He and his wife hold the Guinness World Record for "Greatest Robbery of a Government." In his memory, consider the ways in which you might be a negative role model and/or influence others in a negative way!

On **September 28**, we celebrate the birth in 1956 of **Barb Fichter**, who serves St. Martin of Tours Catholic Community in Saint Alans, Vermont. Pray for her and for the people she serves!

September 28 is **World Rabies Day**, the acknowledgement of a preventable disease from which 60,000 people die each year in our world.

September 28 is also **World Maritime Day**, an opportunity to reflect on and honor the international shipping industry.

On **September 29**, the Church celebrates the **Archangels Michael, Gabriel and Raphael**. They are the three biblical archangels: Michael, who led the angels in fighting the dragon (Satan) and hurling it to the earth (Rev. 12:7-9), Gabriel, who appeared to Zechariah and Mary (Lk. 1:19-20 & 26-38), and Raphael, who disguised himself as a human to heal Tobit and free Sarah from a demon (Tob. 12:15). Many people are captivated by the idea of angels and other heavenly beings. For the intellectually-curious, share a lesson on heavenly beings, the rise of angels in ancient religions, the symbolism of such numbers as seven, and the lack of agreement on the names of the other four archangels!

On **September 29**, we remember the election of **Innocent III** (died after 1180), the cardinal and "antipope" supported by Roman barons over Alexander III. A cardinal successfully bribed the guards of his castle, and he and his supporters were imprisoned for life in a monastery. In his memory, pray and/or perform an act of charity for our sisters and brothers in prison!

On **September 29**, we remember the brutal murder of **FannyAnn Eddy** (1974-2004), the Sierra Leonean LGBTQ rights activist and founder of the first-of-its-kind Sierra Leone Lesbian and Gay Association. A modern-day martyr on a continent where many LGBTQ people still live in fear, she was known for saying, "Silence creates vulnerability." Her attackers went unpunished. In her memory, raise awareness of the continued violation of rights perpetrated against members of the LGBTQIA+ community!

September 29 is **World Heart Day**, an opportunity to raise awareness to the world's leading cause of death, which claims nearly 19 million lives each year. Consider actions you might take to promote your own heart health—and that of those whom you love!

On the evening of **September 29**, our Jewish spiritual siblings begin their one-week celebration of **Sukkot**, the Feast of Tabernacles (or Booths), when they commemorate the 40 years spent by Moses and the Israelites in the desert after the Exodus.

On **September 30**, the Church celebrates **St. Jerome** (c. 347-420), the patron saint of scholars and librarians. In his honor, enrich your ministry through the purchase of a new biblical commentary for your personal library!

On **September 30**, the Old Catholic Church celebrates the anniversary of the consecration in 1725 of **Cornelius Johannes Barchman Wuytiers** as the eighth archbishop of Utrecht, by Bishop Dominique-Marie Varlet of the Roman church. This was the second of four consecrations performed by Varlet without the permission of Rome. Pray in a special way today for those who bravely and tenaciously follow their beliefs — despite the consequences!

On **September 30**, we remember the passing of **Johann Jakob Herzog** (1805-1882), the Swiss-German Protestant theologian known for his writings on reformers, his studies of the Waldensians, and his editing of the *Encyclopedia of Religious Knowledge*, which later came to include articles on Independent Catholic bishops. In his memory, consider ways in which you might increase your own religious knowledge!

On **September 30**, we remember the passing of **Antoni Klawiter** (1836-1913), the Polish insurrectionist who served as a Roman Catholic priest in Chicago and Pittsburgh. He co-founded St. Stanislaus Roman Catholic Church in St. Louis, Missouri. After being driven from various parishes, largely for alienating those he served, he pastored an Independent Catholic parish in Buffalo, New York, which led to his excommunication by the Roman Church. After a few more failed attempts to pastor communities, he joined the Polish National Catholic Church in 1897. Four years later, he moved to Canada, where he ministered for the last 12 years of his life. In his memory, pray for all who are not entirely aware of the impact of their words and actions on others!

On **September 30**, we remember the passing of **Monika Konrad Hildegard Hellwig** (1929-2005), the German-born British theologian who left religious life to pursue her academic career. As the research assistant to a Vatican official, she was one of the few women permitted to enter Vatican II as an observer. The author of many books, she co-signed a controversial letter in support of Charles E. Curran, who was barred from teaching Roman Catholic theology due to his dissent on the church's teachings on such issues as contraception and homosexuality. In her memory, reacquaint yourself with one of her works!

On **September 30**, the Romanian Orthodox Church (recognized by the Ecumenical Patriarch of Constantinople) celebrates the anniversary of the installation in 2007 of Dan Ilie Ciobotea as **Patriarch Daniel of**

Romania. In a spirit of ecumenism, pray for him and for the 17 million Romanian Orthodox Catholics he serves!

Sunday, October 1, 2023
TWENTY-SIXTH SUNDAY IN ORDINARY TIME
(green)

Be mindful of the exclusive language in today's scriptures: The first reading suggests that only men are wicked. Since the reading begins in the second person, simply continue with the second person throughout (e.g., "But if you turn from the wickedness you have committed, and do what is right and just, you shall preserve your life"). And the instance of "his own interests" in the second reading might just as easily be rephrased, "his or her own interests."

You'll have to **choose which form of today's second reading you'll use**: the shorter form, or the longer form, which adds the six verses of the Philippians hymn that we hear each Good Friday.

The thread in today's scriptures: Echoing last Sunday's gospel (Mt. 20:1-16), Ezekiel notes that sometimes it seems that "the Lord's way is not fair" (Ez. 18:25). It's not fair that tax collectors and prostitutes would enter heaven ahead of the scribes and Pharisees (Mt. 21:31-32) — except that sometimes the "virtuous" turn away from virtue (Ez. 18:26), like the second son in today's gospel (Mt. 21:30), and sometimes those who seem "bad" turn from their sins and the iniquity they've committed (Ez. 18:27), like the first son in today's gospel (Mt. 21:28-29). Yes, God "shows sinners the way" (Ps. 25:8). Which do you more closely resemble: the selfish (Phil. 2:3) son who didn't go to the vineyard, or the son who completed his father's joy by being of the same mind and love as his father (Phil. 2:2)?

Holy humor: Comedy is difficult! Sometimes we tell good jokes that go flat, and sometimes the groaners are the best and most memorable. Illustrate this with a "bad" joke or two (or three) from the following, then segue into today's message on how the "good" is sometimes bad and the "bad" is sometimes good!

- Does anyone need an ark? I Noah guy!
- How does Moses make his tea? Hebrews it!
- How do you make holy water? You boil the hell out of it!
- What do you call a man who can't stand? Neil!
- Why aren't shrimp more generous? Because they're shellfish!

- What does a nosey pepper do? It gets jalapeño business!
- What does a baby computer call her father? Data!
- What did the buffalo say when his son left? Bison!
- What did the symphony director name his twin daughters? Anna one, Anna two!
- I bought some shoes from a drug dealer. I don't know what he laced them with, but I was tripping all day!
- What do you call a bear without teeth? A gummy bear!
- What does a zombie vegetarian eat? Grrraaaiinnnns!
- Why shouldn't you play poker in the jungle? Too many cheetahs!
- What do you call a person with no body and no nose? Nobody kn-knows!
- I used to work at a calendar factory—but I got fired because I took a couple of days off!
- Don't believe atoms: They make up everything!
- What's the best part of living in Switzerland? I don't know, but the flag is a big plus!
- Ever try to eat a clock? It's time-consuming!
- Did you hear about the circus fire? It was in tents!
- What do I have if I have a deer with no eyes? I have a no-eye deer!

Looking for a visual aid for your homily or object lesson? Use your hands to symbolize the goodness and badness of the two sons of today's gospel! Hold your left hand high (at the top of an invisible circle) when you speak of the "good" son who told his father that he would go to the family's vineyard, and hold your right hand low (at the bottom of the "circle") when you speak of the "bad" son who said that he wouldn't go. But wait, was the "good" son really good? Did he go to the vineyard? No. [Move your left hand in a circular motion to the place of the other.] And was the "bad" son really bad? Did he go to the vineyard? Yes! [Move your right hand in a circular motion to the top.] Yes, sometimes the "good" is bad, and the "bad" is good! And, if you use the long form of today's second reading, you can trace Christ's path in a circle: starting at the top, with Christ being in the form of God, begin tracing a circle downward (counterclockwise, so that it appears clockwise to your listeners) when you speak of him humbling himself and taking human likeness, then complete the tracing of the circle to the top, as you speak of him being exalted above all things. Saint Bonaventure loved speaking of this "circle" that Christ traced, from the heavens to earth and back to the heavens again!

On **October 1**, we remember the passing of **Johann Baptista Baltzer** (1803-1871), the German Catholic priest and theologian who traveled to

Rome in an attempt to prevent the condemnation of Anton Günther's writings. The Holy See subsequently suspended him and asked him to resign his professorship. Baltzer was a strenuous opponent of purported papal infallibility and later promoted the Old Catholic movement in Silesia. In his memory, pray for all who promote and defend Independent Catholicism in our world!

On **October 1**, the Church celebrates **St. Thérèse of the Child Jesus** (1873-1897), the "Little Flower," who was the youngest of five daughters—all of whom became nuns. Don't be so ageist: Pray that God might continue to manifest God's self in the vocations of the young!

On **October 1**, we remember the passing of **Romano Guardini** (1885-1968), the noted Italian-German academic whose *The Spirit of the Liturgy* was a major influence on the Liturgical Movement in Germany, and, by extension, on the liturgical reforms of Vatican II. In his memory, reacquaint yourself with his works and/or with the liturgical documents that continue his liturgical legacy!

On **October 1**, we celebrate the birth in 1957 of **Harald Rein**, the German priest and theologian who has served as the seventh bishop of the Swiss Old Catholic Church since 2009. His works have highlighted practical theology, parish management, and ecumenical relations between the Old Catholic, Anglican and Orthodox churches. His episcopal motto is *Nec laudibus, nec timore*—that we should not be motivated by praise or fear. In his honor, consider how praise and/or fear motivate various aspects of your life!

On **October 1**, we celebrate the birth in 1965 of **Anthony Green**, Pastor of St. John of God Parish in Schenectady, New York and Auxiliary Bishop for Diocese of Little Portion of the Catholic Apostolic Church in North America (CACINA). Pray for him and for the people he serves!

October 1 is **International Day of Older Persons**, an effort to raise awareness of the need to create societies that embrace people of all ages!

October 1 is also **World Vegetarian Day**, an opportunity to focus on the health and environmental benefits of eco-friendly lifestyles.

On **October 2**, the Church celebrates **Guardian Angels**: Incorporate an image into the décor of your narthex or devotional chapel. For the intellectually-curious, share a lesson on the history of and scriptural basis for this belief!

On **October 2**, we remember the passing of **Zeger-Bernard van Espen** (1646-1728), the Belgian canonist who argued for conciliarity, supported the tenets of Gallicanism, and championed secular power over religious authority. He pronounced the validity of the consecration of the archbishop of Utrecht by a single bishop and without prior authorization from the Holy See, which led to his condemnation by the University of Leuven. He died while in hiding with a Jansenist community in Amersfoort, Netherlands.

On **October 2**, the birthday of Mahatma Gandhi, we also celebrate **International Day of Nonviolence**, a day established by the United Nations in 2007 to promote education and public awareness of nonviolence. In honor of this day, reflect on how your words, actions and preaching espouse this universal value!

October 2 is **World Habitat Day**, an opportunity to reflect on the state of shelter in our communities and in our world.

The first Monday in October is **Child Health Day**, an acknowledgement of the care that children need in order to grow into strong, healthy adults.

On **October 3**, the Anglican Church commemorates the passing of **George Bell** (1883-1958), the Anglican theologian, dean of Canterbury, member of the House of Lords, and pioneer of the ecumenical movement. A proponent of nuclear disarmament, he dreamed of a post-war Europe united under Christian values. In his memory, find a concrete way to advance Christian unity!

On **October 3**, we remember the martyrdom of **Alberto Ramento** (1936-2007), the ninth supreme bishop of the Philippine Independent Church, who empowered laity, enhanced the church's stewardship efforts, established a concordat with the Church of Sweden, and approved the ordination of women within the church. Known as "the bishop of the poor, peasants and the oppressed," he campaigned against human rights violations and famously remarked, "I know [the government is] going to kill me next. But never will I abandon my duty to God and my ministry for the people." He was brutally stabbed to death while asleep in his home. In his memory, pray for all courageous modern-day prophets and martyrs!

On **October 4**, the Church celebrates **St. Francis of Assisi** (c. 1182-1226), the patron saint of ecology. Due to his love for an unnamed companion, he is also a special saint of the queer community. Pray his "Canticle of Brother Sun" and thank God for all creation. And be on the lookout: Many churches have a blessing of pets today!

On **October 4**, we remember the passing of **Wessel Gansfort** (1419-1489), the Frisian theologian, pre-Reformation reformer and "learned light of the world" who spoke against magical and superstitious conceptions of the sacraments, the paganization of the papacy, and the supremacy of ecclesiastical tradition. When Sixtus VI offered him a bishopric, he asked instead for a copy of the Hebrew scriptures, which he read aloud to the bemusement of his fellow monks. Consider what you might do to be perceived as a "learned light" by those around you!

On **October 4**, we remember the passing of **Jacqueline Pascal** (1625-1661), the French nun who vehemently opposed the Roman church's attempt to compel assent for the condemnation of Jansenism. Her brother, Blaise Pascal, was instrumental in her conversion to Jansenism but strongly opposed her decision to join the convent of Port-Royal-des-Champs. Shortly after being compelled to provide her assent to *Unigenitus*, she died on her 36th birthday. In her memory, pray for all who find themselves in situations where they feel forced to do what they do!

On **October 4**, we remember the passing of **Catherine Booth** (1829-1890), the British missionary and co-founder of the Salvation Army who worked for women's equality in the Church. A powerful preacher, she addressed women's equal right to speak, and she used her gifts to inspire change in converts and alcoholics. In her memory, consider how you empower others to use their voices!

On **October 4**, we remember the passing of **Joseph Tomczyk** (1935-1995), the American bishop who shepherded the Canadian Diocese of the Polish National Catholic Church. In his memory, pray for our sisters and brothers of the Polish National Catholic Church!

On **October 5**, the Church celebrates **Bl. Francis Xavier Seelos** (1819-1867), the German Redemptorist immigrant to the U.S. who refused the bishopric of Pittsburgh to be a missionary throughout the U.S. In his honor, consider saying "no" to certain goods, so that you can say "yes" to even greater goods!

October 5 is **World Teacher Day**, an opportunity to celebrate all educators!

On **October 6**, we remember the passing of **St. Bruno of Cologne** (c. 1030-1101), the renowned teacher at Reims, advisor of his former student, Urban II, and the founder of the Carthusian Order. Depicted in iconography with a skull in his hand, he refused an archbishopric and vowed to renounce secular concerns. In his honor, contemplate your own death and how you will use your remaining days and years to grow in your relationship with God and others!

On **October 6**, we remember the passing of **Jean du Vergier de Hauranne** (1581-1643), the French Catholic priest who served as Abbot of Saint-

Cyran and as spiritual director of the nuns at Port-Royal-des-Champs. He introduced to France the thought of his friend, Cornelius Jansen, and was imprisoned for his view that contrition (and not the less-perfect "attrition") could save a person. In his memory, pray for those who might misunderstand you, your intentions, and/or your desire to help others grow in their relationship with God and others!

On **October 6**, the Church celebrates **Bl. Marie-Rose Durocher** (1811-1849), the Canadian "saint of Beloeil" and reluctant co-foundress of the Sisters of the Holy Names of Jesus and Mary. Her last years were marked by poverty, trials, sickness and slander. Pray and reach out to those who similarly suffer!

On **October 6**, we celebrate the birth in 1958 of **Miguel De La Torre**, the Southern Baptist professor who has written over 30 books on social ethics and Latinx Studies. He achieved notoriety in 2005 when he was forced to resign his tenure over his article "When the Bible is Used for Hatred," which satirized James Dobson's outing of SpongeBob SquarePants. He continues to comment on ethical issues, Hispanic religiosity, LGBTQ civil rights, and immigrant rights. In his honor, consider your own willingness to speak a prophetic word against the powers that be!

October 6 is **Shmini Atzeret**, the "eighth day" celebrated by our Jewish spiritual siblings after their seven-day Sukkot, to mark the end of their annual public reading of the Torah.

On **October 7**, in the midst of this Month of the Holy Rosary, the Church celebrates **Our Lady of the Rosary**. Nothing is more fitting than praying the rosary on this day! Learn new mysteries. If you have a multilingual community, consider bringing the community together for a multilingual experience of the rosary!

On **October 7**, the Church celebrates **Ss. Sergius & Bacchus**, the fourth-century soldiers and martyrs known as patron saints of the military and of gay couples. As officers in Galerius' army, they enjoyed high esteem until they were exposed as "closet Christians." Severely punished, Bacchus died during torture, and Sergius was beheaded shortly thereafter. Their close relationship was characterized by John Boswell as romantic. In their memory, pray for all friends and non-traditional couples who mirror God's love to our world!

On **October 7**, we remember the passing of **Radclyffe Hall** (1880-1943), the English poet and author best known for her groundbreaking lesbian novel, *The Well of Loneliness*, which featured a queer Christ figure as the main character. The work was banned for obscenity in England due to its portrayal of lesbian love and its use of religious arguments to support "inverts" — a 1920s term for LGBTQ people. A devout Catholic, she was nailed to the cross in a satirical cartoon. In her memory, pray for all who are "crucified" for their words and actions!

On **October 7**, we celebrate the anniversary of the episcopal consecration in 1996 of **Mark Elliott Newman**, presiding bishop of the Catholic Apostolic Church of Antioch. Happy anniversary!

Sunday, October 8, 2023
TWENTY-SEVENTH SUNDAY IN ORDINARY TIME
(green)

The thread in today's scriptures: Proto-Isaiah speaks of destruction, outcry and bloodshed in the Lord's vineyard (Is. 5:7), a theme echoed by the psalmist (Ps. 80:12-13 & 16). The Matthean Jesus warns the chief priests and elders that the "bloodshed" in the Lord's vineyard (Mt. 21:35-38) will have consequences: "The kingdom of God will be taken away from you and given to a people that will produce its fruit" (Mt. 21:43). The good news for those who confront evildoers who destroy and kill: We need not be anxious (Phil. 4:6); God "will guard our hearts and minds in Christ Jesus" (Phil. 4:7)!

Holy humor: The story is told of the nuns who started selling flower bouquets to support their convent. Their business quickly grew, since there were no other florists in town — until the Franciscans across the street saw the nuns' success and decided to open their own greenhouse and flower shop! The friars started stealing business from the nuns, so the nuns plotted how they would push the friars out of the community. One night, the nuns snuck into the friars' shop and lit it on fire — but the firefighters quickly extinguished it, leaving it with little damage. The nuns tried to tarnish the friars' reputation with rumors and gossip, but customers saw through it, and the rumors dissipated. Finally, the nuns contracted Hugh, a local thug who had a knack for destruction. He drove his truck into the friars' flower shop, took his weed-whacker to everything in sight, and dowsed the place with herbicide. The friars had no option but to close their business. And the moral to this story is: Hugh and only Hugh can prevent florist friars! [Segue into the destruction and bloodshed in today's scriptures, by those wishing harm to others.]

Looking for a visual aid for your homily or object lesson? Consider pruning shears and/or a hoe! Both are alluded to by Proto-Isaiah (Is. 5:6), and both can be symbols of life-giving cultivation and of destruction!

On **October 8**, when it doesn't fall on a Sunday, the Church celebrates **St. Pelagia the Penitent**, the 4th- or 5th-century actress and harlot described as "immodestly bareheaded" and followed by a "worldly crowd" until she repented after hearing a sermon on hell and heaven. She died as a result of her extreme asceticism and is one of the 140 colonnade saints at St. Peter Basilica in Vatican City. In her memory, pray for all who hear the Word of God and act!

On **October 8**, we celebrate the birth in 1930 of **Faith Ringgold**, the American artist who participated in many feminist protests and incorporated feminist ideals into her art. In her honor, pray for her and for all who use their artistic talents to promote women's rights!

On **October 8**, we celebrate the birth in 1940 of **Thomas Moore**, the American psychotherapist and former monk who has authored a number of popular spiritual works, including his bestselling *Care of the Soul* and *Soul Mates*. His books and lectures have covered such topics as spirituality, religion, ecology, imagination, mythology and archetypal psychology. In his honor, reflect on one of his works as a spiritual exercise!

On **October 8**, we celebrate the birth in 1954 of **Kerry S. Walters**, the prolific, American author and priest of the American National Catholic Church. A professor emeritus of philosophy at Gettysburg College, he writes on a variety of subjects, including Christian mysticism, pacifism, deism, atheism, and the history of the early United States. His award-winning works include *The Art of Dying and Living*, *Giving up God...to Find God*, *St. Teresa of Calcutta*, and *Oscar Romero: Priest, Prophet, Martyr*. Check out his works, and let him know that we thank God for him, for his scholarship, and for his works!

On **October 8**, we remember the passing of **Gabriel Honoré Marcel** (1889-1973), the French Catholic philosopher and Christian existentialist who wrote over 30 plays and 12 books, including his two-volume *The Mystery of Being*. He paid particular attention to the modern struggle against our dehumanization by technology, and he hosted a weekly philosophical discussion group, where he influenced Ricœur, Levinas and Sartre. In his memory, pause to consider the possibly-dehumanizing impact of technology in your life and in the lives of those around you!

On **October 9**, the Church celebrates **St. Denis of Paris** (+c. 258) and **St. John Leonardi** (1541-1609). Denis (not to be confused with Dionysius the

Aeropagite or Pseudo-Dionysius) is depicted as a decapitated bishop holding his own head and is invoked against headaches, rabies and demonic possessions. Pray for those who suffer these, and for those who are "losing their head" and acting overly emotional or irrational! John Leonardi was a pharmacist's assistant who, after being ordained to the priesthood, gathered laity interested in ministering in hospitals and prisons. They formed the Clerks Regular of the Mother of God, and John died 14 years later of the plague, which he contracted from his ministry to the ill. In his memory, consider how you are being the hands and heart of Christ to those most in need!

On **October 9**, we remember the passing of **Robert Grosseteste** (1175-1253), the English statesman, scientist, scholastic theologian and bishop who has been called the founder of scientific thought in medieval Oxford. He was an original thinker on what today is known as scientific method. In his memory, pray for all who seek to bridge theology to the many great scientific discoveries of our day!

On **October 9**, we remember the passing of **Penny Lernoux** (1940-1989), the American Roman Catholic educator, author and journalist who criticized the Roman church's policies toward Latin America. Drawn to liberation theology, she attempted to relate Christ's teachings to Latin American struggles against economic exploitation and military dictatorship. She focused her last years on the attempts of John Paul II and Joseph Ratzinger to clamp down on dissent and to fortify an authoritarian, pre-conciliar model of the church. In her memory, reacquaint yourself with the tensions between Latin American liberation theologians and the church with which they shared a love/hate relationship!

On the second Monday of October, U.S. society celebrates **Columbus Day**, which is increasingly celebrated as **Indigenous Peoples' Day** in more than 50 U.S. cities. Latin America celebrates this day as *el día de la raza* (the Day of Our People). Find a fitting way to commemorate this day, with an acknowledgement of the sins of the Church in erasing the rich cultures and religions of indigenous people. If debates over critical race theory still rage, speak to the Church's stance on such social sins as racism, discrimination and inequality.

On **October 10**, we remember the passing of **Jules Ferrette** (1828-1904), the French Dominican and Roman Catholic priest who came to the conclusion that the many divisions within Christianity were unnecessary and capable of readjustment. After leaving the Roman church, he was consecrated bishop of Iona by the Syriac Orthodox Patriarch of Antioch, he founded the Catholic Apostolic Church of the West, and he introduced Eastern Orthodoxy to the West. Consider how you might help to "readjust" divisions in the Body of Christ!

On **October 10**, we remember the passing of **Isabelo de los Reyes, Sr.** (1864-1938), the Spanish-Filipino politician, writer and labor leader who announced the formation of the Philippine Independent Church on August 3, 1902. He rallied support of the new church and directed the church's publications, including its catechism, rituals, magazine and numerous devotional and doctrinal texts. Consider how you dedicate your time, talent and treasure to the upbuilding of God's reign!

On **October 10**, we remember the passing of **Vida Dutton Scudder** (1861-1954), the American social reformer, professor, lesbian author and Episcopal saint who was active in the Social Gospel movement and co-founded a settlement house in Boston to reduce poverty, promote Christian socialism and support trade unions. In her memory, consider what you are doing to help reduce poverty in our world!

On **October 10**, we remember the passing of **Isabelo de los Reyes, Jr.** (1900-1971), the Spanish-Filipino supreme bishop who led the Philippine Independent Church for 25 years and died on the same day as his father, 33 years later. He famously rejected the Unitarian views of his father and of the church's founder, forming his own Trinitarian Independent Catholic Church, which later won the rights to the name Philippine Independent Church in 1955. As supreme bishop, he secured apostolic succession for the church and severed its ties to the revolutionary nationalism, rationalism and socialism that previously characterized it. In his memory, consider the ties that you do well to cut, in order to experience greater growth and vitality!

On **October 10**, we celebrate the anniversary of the presbyteral ordination in 2006 of Canon **MichaelAngelo D'Arrigo**, senior pastor of Agape Fellowship of Greater Atlanta and canon to the presiding bishop of the Convergent Christian Communion. Happy birthday!

October 10 is **World Mental Health Day**, an opportunity to raise awareness of mental health issues.

On **October 11**, we remember the passing of **Ulrich Zwingli** (1484-1531), the "soldier of Christ" and *Leutpriester* (people's priest) in Zürich who emphasized the authority of the Bible, questioned Lenten fasting, noted the corruption of Roman Catholic hierarchy, and promoted clerical marriage. In his memory, pray for all "soldiers of Christ" who courageously question the practices of our Catholic tradition!

On **October 11**, we remember the passing of **Félix Antoine Philibert Dupanloup** (1802-1878), the French priest, prolific writer, and "Apostle to Youth" who very vocally opposed purported papal infallibility during the First Vatican Council. He was known for his imposing height, eloquence, zeal and charity, and his fiery rhetoric contributed to the canonization of St. Joan of Arc. In his memory, consider how your own preaching and teaching embody the energy, the powerful voice, and the impassioned gestures for which Félix was famous!

On **October 11**, we remember the passing of **Adalbert Schindelar** (1865-1926), who served as the first bishop of the Austrian Old Catholic Church for two years. He helped organize the 1909 Old Catholic Congress in Vienna. In his memory, pray for all our sisters and brothers of the Austrian Old Catholic Church!

On **October 11**, the Church celebrates **St. John XXIII** (1881-1963), the bishop of Rome who sought to model the Good Shepherd and who advocated for opening the "windows" of the Roman church, to allow in "fresh air." In his honor, thumb through the documents of Vatican II, and find a few fresh insights to enliven your ministry and your liturgy!

On **October 12**, we remember the passing of **Luis de Molina** (1535-1600), the Spanish Jesuit priest and scholastic who stirred controversy and debate through his staunch defense of free will in the debate over human liberty and God's grace. Molinism was the precursor of Jansenism, a lightning rod issue with respect to submission to the authority of the Roman papacracy. In his memory, pause to consider your own views on grace and freedom!

On **October 12**, we remember the passing of **Ram Manohar Lohia** (1910-1967), the Indian activist who worked toward Indian independence from British rule. In his memory, pray for all who suffer the negative effects of colonialism — and all who seek to liberate them!

On **October 12**, we remember the passing of **Matthew Shepard** (1976-1998), the modern gay martyr whose death at the University of Wyoming sparked national awareness of anti-LGBTQ violence and contributed to the 2009 Matthew Shepard Hate Crimes Prevention Act. A cultural icon and patron saint of the gay community, he has inspired countless artistic works. In his memory, consider how you might better stand in solidarity with those who decry violence against others!

October 12 is **World Day for Natural Disaster Risk Reduction**, an opportunity to reflect on how we can reduce loss of life, livelihood and health due to natural disasters.

On **October 13**, we remember the passing of **Calixto Zaldívar** (1904-1979), a prominent Independent Catholic and member of the Philippine Independent Church who served as a legislator, as governor of Antique, as a justice of the Philippine Supreme Court, and as president of the Philippine Independent Church's National Lay Organization. He wrote a famous dissenting opinion that the 1973 martial law constitution of Ferdinand Marcos was not in force because it was not validly ratified by the Filipino people. Pray for all who serve in the executive, legislative and judicial branches of government!

On **October 14**, we celebrate the birth in 1952 of **Joris Vercammen**, the Roman Catholic priest who joined the Old Catholic Diocese of Utrecht and was named Archbishop of Utrecht in 2000. Pray today for Archbishop Emeritus Vercammen and for all our sisters and brothers of the Old Catholic tradition!

Sunday, October 15, 2023
TWENTY-EIGHTH SUNDAY IN ORDINARY TIME
(green)

We're nearing the end of Fall Ordinary Time: Does **your worship environment** reflect this? (Please don't say that you have same worship environment you had in June!)

- Consider transitioning to a **darker green** in your décor and vestments, to mirror the darkening days of this season. Be sure the greens match — and that your vestments are ironed or steamed!
- Among the plants in your worship space, intersperse tall pottery vases of **dried grasses or willow branches** that reflect nature's changes.
- Incorporate **fruits of the harvest** — particularly those grains that call to mind the sifting of "wheat" and "chaff" that will occur in the final judgment.
- Harvested **squash and pumpkins** can add variety — but be sure to clean pumpkins with a solution of water and bleach, to slow deterioration.
- **Experiment with textures, small prints, discrete woven patterns, and fabrics with a sheen**.
- Complement with **green plants possessing deeper green leaves**.

You'll need to **choose which form of today's gospel you'll proclaim: the shorter form, or the longer form**, which adds four verses on the man not properly dressed for the wedding banquet.

The thread in today's scriptures: More destruction! But this time, God is destroying death — "the veil that veils all peoples, the web that is woven over all nations" (Is. 25:7)! Now God is feeding God's people with "rich food and choice wine: juicy, rich food and pure, choice wine" (Is. 25:6). The psalmist echoes this image of God spreading a table before us (Ps. 23:5), as does the Matthean Jesus with his image of the king's wedding banquet for his son (Mt. 22:2, with its images of destruction). Knowing abundance himself (Phil. 4:12), Paul believed that his God would "fully supply whatever [we] need" (Phil. 4:19). Will we be counted among those worthy to enter the wedding feast (Mt. 11:13)?

Holy humor: Before walking into the toy store, the mother pulled her children aside. She said, "Repeat after me: 'The Lord is my shepherd...' [Put your hand to your ear, so as to encourage your listeners to repeat after you] 'I shall not want!'" [Segue into today's message that God provides for us, fully supplying whatever we need (Phil. 4:19).]

Looking for a visual aid for your homily or object lesson? Consider a loaf of bread and a bottle of wine, the symbols of the elements with which God nourishes us in the Eucharist, or, if you're preaching on the longer form of the gospel, consider a piece of attire (e.g., a tie and/or suit coat, or pearls and an evening gown) symbolic of being "appropriately dressed" for the wedding banquet!

On **October 15**, when it doesn't fall on a Sunday, the Church celebrates **St. Teresa of Jesus** (1515-1582), the mystic and Carmelite reformer who modeled her life on the poor and crucified Christ. In her honor, go deeper into your own "interior castle" and consider how you might grow in your own "way of perfection"!

On **October 15**, the Old Catholic Church celebrates the anniversary of the consecration in 1724 of **Cornelius van Steenoven** as the seventh archbishop of Utrecht, by Bishop Dominique-Marie Varlet of the Roman church. This was an historic day: the first of four consecrations performed by Varlet without the permission of Rome! Pray in a special way today for our sisters and brothers of the Old Catholic Church, who trace the succession of their archbishop back to these consecrations by Varlet!

On **October 15**, the Bulgarian Orthodox Church (recognized by the Ecumenical Patriarch of Constantinople) celebrates the birth in 1945 of **Simeon Nikolov Dimitrov**, who became Patriarch Neophyte of Bulgaria.

In a spirit of ecumenism, pray for him and for the 11 million Bulgarian Orthodox Catholics he serves!

On **October 15**, the Indian Orthodox Church celebrates the anniversary of the installation in 2021 of **Catholicos Baselios Marthoma Mathews III**. In a spirit of ecumenism, pray for him and for the 2.5 million people he serves!

October 15 is **International Day of Rural Women**, an opportunity to raise awareness of the importance of gender equality in fighting extreme poverty, hunger and malnutrition.

On **October 16**, the Church celebrates **St. Hedwig of Silesia** (1174-1243) and **St. Margaret Mary Alacoque** (1647-1690). Living 500 years apart, both are known today as protectors of orphaned children. Find a way today to honor the little ones for whom God shows a particular solicitous concern!

On **October 16**, we remember the passing of **Joseph Leycester Lyne** (1837-1908), the Anglican Benedictine monk known as Ignatius of Llanthony, who reintroduced monasticism into the Church of England — a controversial move that led to his being barred from preaching. Unable to be ordained in his faith tradition, he received priestly ordination from Independent Catholic bishop Joseph Vilatte and he hoped to establish an "Old Catholic" church in England. In his memory, consider how you might fulfill some of the deep longings of your heart!

On **October 16**, we celebrate the anniversary of the founding in 2016 of **St. John of God Parish**, a community of the Catholic Apostolic Church in North America (CACINA) in Schenectady, New York, Texas. Happy anniversary!

October 16 is **World Food Day**, an opportunity to raise awareness of food insecurity in our communities and in our world.

October 16 is also **National Boss' Day** in the U.S., an opportunity to express our appreciation for those for whom we work!

On **October 17**, the Church celebrates **St. Ignatius of Antioch** (+c. 140), the apostolic father who emphasized the humanity and divinity of Christ, and advocated for Church unity. Pray Eucharistic Prayer I, which mentions him, and consider how you're bringing greater unity (or not) to the Church!

On **October 17**, we remember the passing of **Helmut Gollwitzer** (1908-1993), the Bavarian Lutheran theologian and author who was part of the Confessing Church movement that resisted the efforts of the Nazi regime to control the Church. The diary of his experiences as a prisoner of war in Russia for four years became a bestseller in Germany, and the president of West Germany referred to it as "a great historical document." Gollwitzer later became a pacifist, opposing nuclear weapons, the arms race, and the Vietnam War. In his memory, pray the peace prayer attributed to St. Francis, meditating on how Gollwitzer and so many others have been instruments of peace—and how it is that you, too, might better bring pardon and hope to situations of injury and despair!

October 17 is **International Day for the Eradication of Poverty**, an opportunity to reflect on and address the many forces that perpetuate poverty in our communities and in our world.

On **October 18**, the Church celebrates **St. Luke** (+84): Incorporate a large Book of the Gospels into today's décor. If you haven't already, on this physician's feast, consider celebrating a White Mass, with a special recognition and blessing of all who work in medical professions!

On **October 18**, the Old Catholic Church celebrates the anniversary of the consecration in 1739 of **Petrus Johannes Meindaerts** as the tenth archbishop of Utrecht, by Bishop Dominique-Marie Varlet of the Roman church. This was the fourth of four consecrations performed by Varlet over the course of 15 years, without the permission of Rome. Meindaerts, who served as bishop for nearly 30 years, would later consecrate three other bishops to ensure the apostolic succession of the Old Catholic Church. Pray in a special way today for all who have the foresight to think about the legacy they are creating in this world—and for those who fail to do so!

On **October 18**, we remember the passing of **Lucy Stone** (1818-1893), the American activist who advocated for abolition and women's rights. She helped form the American Woman Suffrage Association. In her memory, pray for all who continue the fight for women's rights!

On **October 19**, the Church celebrates **Ss. John de Brébeuf** (1593-1649), **Isaac Jogues** (1607-1646) **and Companions**. They were Jesuit priests misunderstood and martyred by early indigenous Americans. Pray for and reach out to those persons you find most difficult to understand and share with them the merciful, compassionate face of Christ!

On **October 19**, we remember the passing of **Walter Slowakiewicz** (1911-1978), the American bishop who served as the fourth bishop of the Eastern Diocese of the Polish National Catholic Church. In his memory, pray for our sisters and brothers of the Polish National Catholic Church!

On **October 20**, the Church celebrates **St. Paul of the Cross** (1694-1775), founder of the Passionists, a religious congregation that takes a fourth vow of spreading memory of Jesus' passion. Consider how you lift up the suffering of Jesus as a model for all who follow in his footsteps on the path to redemption!

On **October 20**, we remember the passing of **Philip Schaff** (1819-1893), the German Protestant theologian whose "Mercersburg theology" was deemed heretical for being too pro-Catholic. He spent most of his life in the U.S., teaching at Union Theological Seminary, chairing the committee that translated the American Standard Version of the bible, and translating Johann Herzog's encyclopedias. A promoter of Christian unity, he urged Leo XIII to abandon papal infallibility in favor of the reunion of Christianity. In his memory, pause to consider your own role in bringing God's reign to our world!

On **October 21**, we remember the passing of **Paul Scriptoris** (c. 1460-1505), the German Franciscan mathematician and Scotist whose work on Scotus was the first book created with a printing press in Tübingen. He was banished for lecturing against transubstantiation, and he died in exile. In his memory, pause to learn about alternative perspectives in Eucharistic theology than the ancient Greek metaphysical categories of transubstantiation!

On **October 21**, we celebrate the birth in 1957 of **Kittredge Cherry**, the American priest of Metropolitan Community Church and author of LGBTQIA+ spirituality. The creator of the QSpirit website, she has advocated for LGBTQIA+ issues to the National Council of Churches and World Council of Churches. In her honor, consider how you might better help others to experience Christ's love through the Church!

On **October 21**, we celebrate the anniversary of the episcopal consecration in 2006 of **Alan Kemp**, Chief Executive Officer of the Ascension Alliance. Happy anniversary!

Sunday, October 22, 2023
TWENTY-NINTH SUNDAY IN ORDINARY TIME
(green)

For the next five Sundays, the second reading will come from Paul's First Letter to the Thessalonians—the first extant writing currently contained in the New Testament! For the intellectually-curious, take a moment to share of the dating, audience and context for this letter, its structure and themes, and the fact that the Second Letter to the Thessalonians is likely pseudonymous (attributed to Paul and written in his spirit, even if not written by him)!

The thread in today's scriptures: Give to God that which belongs to God! God anointed Cyrus and subdued the nations before him (Is. 45:1); God gets the credit, even though Cyrus didn't know or acknowledge God (Is. 45:4 & 5)! Those of us who do know and acknowledge God—those of us who are chosen by God, like the Thessalonians (1Thes. 1:4)—"give the Lord glory and honor…[and] the glory due God's name" (Ps. 96:7-8). The Matthean Jesus likewise encourages us to give "to God what belongs to God" (Mt. 22:21).

Holy humor: You've likely heard this joke before. There was a man who was extremely grateful to God for the many gifts that God had given him—but he was always wondering what would be an appropriate gift to put in the collection basket on Sunday mornings. Finally, he came up with what he thought would be the ideal solution: He decided to throw all the money he made that week into the air and allow God to take all the money that God wanted—and he would keep the rest! [Clarify that this is probably not an ideal solution for gifting back to God a bit of what God has given us, and segue into the belief that everything we are and everything we have belongs to God—and is meant to be shared!

Looking for a visual aid for your homily or object lesson? Consider a large coin—perhaps an old Eisenhower silver dollar or a JFK half-dollar! Hold it up when you speak of today's gospel message.

It's **World Mission Sunday**: Consider having a special collection to support a concrete missionary endeavor, and invite congregants to be "missionaries" from afar through their support of the Church's missions!

Pastoral Care Week begins today: Pray for and recognize the spiritual caregivers in your midst!

On **October 22**, we remember the passing of **Paul Johannes Tillich** (1886-1965), the German-American philosopher and Lutheran theologian who is regarded as one of the most influential theologians of the 20th century. His works introduced theology and modern culture to popular audiences, and his three-volume *Systematic Theology* helped theologians explore the symbols of Christian revelation as answers to the problems of human existence raised by contemporary philosophy. In his memory, "brush up" on your knowledge of Tillich's life and works!

On **October 22**, the Roman church celebrates **St. John Paul II** (1920-2005), a conservative voice barring our sisters from the ministries enjoyed by women in the early Church. Find a way today to promote conversation on the place of women in the ordained ministries of the Church — both during the first quarter of the Western Church's history and in Independent Catholicism today!

On **October 22**, we celebrate the birth in 1976 of Canon **MichaelAngelo D'Arrigo**, senior pastor of Agape Fellowship of Greater Atlanta and canon to the presiding bishop of the Convergent Christian Communion. Happy birthday!

On **October 23**, the Church celebrates **St. Anicius Manlius Severinus Boëthius** (c. 477-524), the sixth-century Roman senator and philosopher whose *Consolation of Philosophy* expounded on human nature, virtue, evil, justice and free will — and became one of the most popular and influential works of the Middle Ages. As a translator of Aristotle, Boethius became an intermediary between classical antiquity and the following centuries. In his memory, dust off his conversations with Lady Philosophy!

On **October 23**, the Church celebrates **St. John of Capistrano** (1386-1456), the Italian Franciscan who attracted so many people that he had to preach outdoors! Think through ways in which you might extend the reach of your ministry. John is also the patron of those involved in the legal profession: Consider hosting a Red Mass and/or praying for judges, lawyers, law school professors, law students and elected officials!

On **October 23,** we remember the passing of **Luigi Nazari di Calabiana** (1808-1893), the Italian senator and Roman Catholic archbishop of Milan who led Italian opposition to the innovation of purported papal infallibility. A century after his death, it was revealed that he secretly consecrated Thomas Mossman of the Order of Corporate Reunion. In his memory, pray for our allies and friends in the Roman church!

On **October 23** we remember the passing of **Tom Hayden** (1939-2016), the American social and anti-war activist who fought for civil rights in the 1960s. In his memory, pray for all those who experience systemic oppression and those who fight for their rights!

On **October 23**, we remember the passing of **Francis A. Sullivan** (1922-2019), the American Jesuit theologian best known for his writings on ecclesiology and in defense of the Roman Catholic magisterium. His research on Pauline charisms was incorporated into *Lumen gentium*, and his students included Avery Dulles, Joseph Komonchak, Richard McBrien and William Levada. He questioned John Paul II's assertion in *Ordinatio sacerdotalis* that the prohibition of women's ordination has been infallibly taught, and he emphasized consensus among theologians as a criterion by which it might be determined that a doctrine is universally taught by the Church. In his honor, consider your own role in helping to define the ecclesiology of the Independent Catholic movement!

On **October 24**, the Church celebrates **St. Anthony Mary Claret** (1807-1870), the Spanish weaver and printer who was named archbishop of Santiago, Cuba, where he confronted racism, slavery and anti-Christian persecution. Pray and show solidarity today with those who suffer racism, work for unjust wages, and/or are persecuted for their faith!

On **October 24**, we remember the passing of **Rosa Parks** (1913-2005), the African-American civil rights activist whose refusal to give up her bus seat to a white passenger led to a federal court ruling that bus segregation was unconstitutional. In her memory, pray for all who fight the good fight!

On **October 24**, the Greek Orthodox Patriarchate of Alexandria and all Africa (recognized by the Ecumenical Patriarch of Constantinople) celebrates the anniversary of the installation in 2004 of Nikolaos Horeftakis as **Pope and Patriarch Theodore II of Alexandria**. In a spirit of ecumenism, pray for him and for the 1.4 million Greek Orthodox Catholics he serves!

On **October 24**, the Armenian Catholic Church (in union with Rome) celebrates the anniversary of the enthronement in 2021 of **Catholicos-Patriarch Raphaël Bedros XXI Minassian**. In a spirit of ecumenism, pray for him and for the 758,000 Armenian Catholics he serves!

On **October 24**, the Armenian Catholic Church (in union with Rome) celebrates the anniversary of the enthronement in 2021 of **Catholicos-Patriarch Raphaël Bedros XXI Minassian**. In a spirit of ecumenism, pray for him and for the 758,000 Armenian Catholics he serves!

October 24 is **United Nations Day**, a commemoration of the founding of the United Nations in 1945.

October 24 is also **World Development Information Day**, an opportunity to raise awareness of the challenges hindering world development.

On **October 25**, the Church celebrates **St. Dorcas** (also known by her Aramaic name, Tabitha), the early disciple of Jesus mentioned in Acts 9:36-43. A resident of the port city of Joppa, in present-day Tel Aviv, she was known for her "good works and acts of mercy," including the sewing of clothes for the poor. After her death, Peter reportedly raised her from the dead. In her memory, consider your own stance toward those with fewer resources!

On **October 25**, we remember the passing of **Geoffrey Chaucer** (c. 1342-1400), the English author widely regarded as "the Father of English Literature" and the greatest English poet of the Middle Ages. The creator of "The Canterbury Tales," Chaucer esteemed Christianity, even while recognizing that the Church contained some venal, corrupt individuals. In his memory, share with another person your understanding of the difference between Christianity and the Church!

On **October 25**, we celebrate the birth in 1932 of **Phyllis Trible**, the American biblical scholar whose research has focused on feminist biblical interpretation of the Hebrew scriptures. With a deep respect for biblical texts and a commitment to equality for women, she engages in rhetorical criticism of the interpretations of biblical texts. In her honor, reacquaint yourself with her works!

On **October 26**, we remember the passing of **Elizabeth Cady Stanton** (1815-1902), the American writer who campaigned for women's rights alongside Susan B. Anthony. She wrote *The Women's Bible*, which viewed scripture as a reflection of the culture in which it was written. In her memory, reacquaint yourself with her life and legacy!

On **October 27**, we remember the passing of **Miguel Serveto** (c. 1509-1553), the Spanish theologian, physician, cartographer and humanist who first described pulmonary circulation. Regarded as the first Unitarian martyr, Serveto was burned at the stake for denying Catholic Trinitarian and Christological theology, and aversion to his death spurred the idea of religious tolerance in Europe. In his memory, renew your own commitment to religious tolerance, ecumenism and interreligious dialogue!

On **October 27**, we remember the passing of **James Hillman** (1926-2011), the American psychologist and author who wrote widely on archetypal psychology. His bestselling work, *The Soul's Code*, suggests that the soul is revealed in imagination, fantasy, myth and metaphor—but also in psychopathology (literally, the "speech of the suffering soul"). In his memory, consider the ways in which you might better allow your soul to "speak" and breathe life into our world!

On **October 27**, we remember the brutal murder of **Allen R. Schindler, Jr.** (1969-1992), the American Navy petty officer and radioman whose death on Navy Day in a public toilet in Nagasaki, Japan stirred debate concerning LGBT members of the military and culminated in the 1993 "Don't ask, don't tell" bill. In his memory, consider how you call out homophobia and other social sins!

On **October 27**, we celebrate the birth in 1963 of **Armando Leyva**, the Mexican former Roman Catholic priest who pastors St. Matthew Ecumenical Catholic Church in Orange County, California. The suffragan bishop for Hispanic affairs in the Ecumenical Catholic Communion, he has brought together a network of 17 highly-trained, bilingual clergy serving seven missions in California.

On **October 27**, the Armenian Apostolic Church celebrates the anniversary of the installation in 1999 of Ktrij Nersessian as **Catholicos Karekin II of All Armenians**. In a spirit of ecumenism, pray for him and for the nine million people he serves!

On **October 27**, the World Evangelical Alliance celebrates the anniversary of the election in 2020 of **Secretary-General Thomas Paul Schirrmacher**. In a spirit of ecumenism, pray for him and for the 600 million Evangelicals he serves!

On **October 28**, the Church celebrates **Ss. Simon and Jude**, two first-century apostles about whom we know very little. St. Jude is invoked as the patron saint of hopeless causes and occupies a preeminent space in the canon of Mexican saints. St. Simon the Zealot, according to one tradition, preached and was martyred in Persia along with St. Jude. Pray Eucharistic Prayer I, which mentions them. If you serve a *Latino* community, be sure to share a prayer card or medal with St. Jude's image!

On **October 28**, we remember the passing of **Libert Froidmont** (1587-1653), the theologian and scientist who corresponded with René Descartes and posthumously published Cornelius Jansen's *Augustinus*. As a theologian, he chaired the scriptural studies department at Louvain, and, as a physicist interested in meteors, he sought to co-opt, rather than reject, new scientific discoveries. In his memory, consider your own stances toward science and emerging views on the human person and on the world we inhabit!

On **October 28**, the Old Catholic Church celebrates the anniversary of the consecration in 1733 of **Theodorus van der Croon** as the ninth archbishop of Utrecht, by Bishop Dominique-Marie Varlet of the Roman church. This was the third of four consecrations performed by Varlet without the permission of Rome. Pray in a special way today for all who continue to generously share the gift of the Spirit and the sacraments of the Church for the sake of God's holy people!

On **October 28**, we remember the passing of **Hermann Heÿkamp** (1804-1874), who served as the fifth Dutch Old Catholic bishop of Deventer for over 20 years. A priest in Leiden, Delft and Rotterdam, he served as a canon in the metropolitan chapter and as the dean of south Holland. Like his predecessors, he served as a titular bishop with no jurisdiction. The year after his death, his nephew, Johann Heÿkamp was elected archbishop of Utrecht. In his memory, consider how you are preparing others for life and ministry!

On **October 28**, we remember the birth in 1957 of **Scott W. Hahn**, the American Roman Catholic theologian who, influenced by *Opus Dei*, converted from Presbyterianism and became an ardent and conservative apologist for the Roman church. He is the author of various works and is a regular guest on EWTN. On this day, pray that the Spirit might similarly inflame the hearts of those who contribute to the upbuilding of the Independent Catholic movement in our world!

On **October 28**, we celebrate the anniversary of the presbyteral ordination in 1981 of Father **Joseph C. Spina**, pastor of Ss. Francis & Clare Catholic Community in Wilton Manors, Florida. Happy anniversary!

Sunday, October 29, 2023

THIRTIETH SUNDAY IN ORDINARY TIME

(green)

The thread in today's scriptures: The Matthean Jesus boils down the entire Mosaic Law into two precepts: love God and love others (Mt. 22:34-40). Ideally, we should sing with the psalmist: "I love you, Lord" (Ps. 18:2). And Exodus shares the shocking view that if we don't love others—like aliens, widows and orphans (Ex. 22:21-22)—we risk kindling Gods' wrath, such that our spouses will be widows and widowers, and our children will be orphans (Ex. 22:24)! The way in which we give and/or lend to others also manifests our love for others (Ex. 22:25-27). By loving God and others, we all have the opportunity to be "a model for all the believers" (1Thes. 1:7)!

Holy humor: The story is told of the newly-ordained deacon who came to her new community and preached her first homily, titled, "Love God, and Love Your Neighbor." Everyone enjoyed it. She continued to get to know the people, and, a few weeks later, her pastor invited her to preach again. So, she shared her homily: "Love God, and Love Your Neighbor." Her pastor thought it was odd—but maybe the young deacon was so busy ministering to the needs of the people that she didn't have time to prepare a new homily. The deacon continued to get to know the people, and, a few weeks later, her pastor invited her to preach again. You guessed it: She shared the same homily: "Love God, and Love Your Neighbor." Her pastor patiently endured the homily for a third time, but quickly took her aside after Mass. She smiled and replied: "For weeks now, I've been getting to know this community, and I'd love to preach a new homily. Believe me, I would. But it doesn't seem they've done anything about the first one yet!" [Segue into how easy it is to talk about loving God and others—but how difficult it might be to prove that our love for God and/or others is actually growing from week to week!]

Looking for a visual aid for your homily or object lesson? Use a pattern of some sort! Do you do crafts? If so, you probably have a piece that serves as a model or pattern for other similar pieces? Do you sew clothing? You likely have a pattern that you place on top of the cloth. Do you know how to write? You likely learned by patterning your handwriting on model letters! That's what we're called to be: patterns and models of love (1Thes. 1:7) for those who might become "imitators of us and of the Lord" (1Thes. 1:6)!

Daylight Saving Time ends next Sunday: Be sure to spread word today, letting congregants know to "fall back" and enjoy an extra hour at home, rather than arrive an hour early for Mass!

On **October 29**, we remember the passing of **Godfrey of Fontaines** (+1306-1309), the scholastic philosopher and theologian at the University of Paris who wrote on subjects ranging from moral philosophy to epistemology and metaphysics. The "Venerated Doctor" attacked mendicant orders but defended the novel theory of Thomism, formulated by a mendicant and condemned by the bishop of Paris. In his memory, pause to consider the inconsistencies in your own words and actions!

On **October 29**, we remember **the closure of the convent of Port-Royal-des-Champs** by King Louis XIV in 1709. The convent that sixty years earlier had flourished with 150 nuns had been reduced to 22, all of whom were over the age of 50 and several of whom were now ill. "For the good of the state," 200 soldiers descended on the convent, gave the nuns three hours to pack their belongings and say good-bye, then drove them in separate carriages to the different convents to which they were now scattered and exiled. Shortly thereafter, the convent cemetery was exhumed, the remains of the nuns there were dumped into a mass grave, and the convent was razed. In memory of this somber event, pray for those whose histories have been purposely erased—throughout the centuries and even still today!

On **October 29**, we celebrate the anniversary of the passing of **Luis Fernando Castillo Méndez** (1922-2009), the Venezuelan priest who was the last living bishop consecrated by Carlos Duarte Costa. He served as Patriarch of the National Catholic Apostolic Church of Brazil and was persecuted by the Roman church and tortured with hot irons by the Venezuelan government, to make him deny that he was a Catholic bishop. Pray today for all who are persecuted for serving the people of God as Independent Catholics!

On **October 30**, we remember the passing of **Gustav Adolf** (1594-1632) who was named a Roman Catholic bishop at age 34 and a cardinal at age 44. After von Bismarck appointed him Ambassador of the German Empire to the Holy See, Pius IX (who appointed him a cardinal) rejected him due to his public opposition to the pope's ultramontane position. In his memory, pray for all who are suffering the pain of friendships gone bad!

On **October 30**, we remember the passing of **Joseph John Campbell** (1904-1987), the American professor who penned groundbreaking works on comparative religion and mythology. His 1949 book, *The Hero with a Thousand Faces*, pointed to the archetypal hero shared by the "monomyth" of world mythologies. He also drew attention to the various myths surrounding Jesus of Nazareth, noting, for instance, that even if Jesus ascended from the earth at the speed of light, he would still be in our galaxy nearly 2,000 years later. George Lucas credited Campbell for his influence on the Star Wars saga. In Campbell's memory, consider the place of myth in our faith tradition and its many, fascinating stories!

On **October 30**, we celebrate the birth in 1991 of **Artur Robert Wieciński**, the Polish Old Catholic bishop of the Old Catholic community of the Nativity of Christ in Warsaw. He is one of the youngest bishops in Poland. In his honor, pray for him and for the people he serves!

On **October 30**, we celebrate the anniversary of the diaconal ordination in 2021 of Deacon **Elsa Y. Nelligan**, a deacon at Holy Family Catholic Church in Austin, Texas. Happy anniversary!

On **October 31**, we remember the passing of **Pieter John Meindaerts** (1684-1767), the Dutch priest who served as the tenth archbishop of Utrecht. Ordained to the Roman Catholic priesthood in Ireland, where he was arrested on suspicion of being a Jacobite spy, he was later consecrated by Roman Catholic bishop Dominique-Marie Varlet. After the deaths of his consecrator and his three predecessors, he set himself to consecrating others to ensure the survival and longevity of the Old Catholic Church. In 1763, he convened the first synod in Utrecht since 1565, for which many Roman Catholic bishops congratulated him. In his memory, consider how you are working to ensure the survival and longevity of your ministry and legacy!

On **October 31**, we remember the passing of **William Montgomery Brown** (1855-1937), the American Episcopal bishop deposed for heretical teachings, who then became an Independent Catholic. He angered Arkansans by his rejections of many Episcopal practices and his publication of a book supporting the segregation of races. "Bad Bishop Brown" went on to write various works on Marxism, communism and eight volumes on the bankruptcy of Christian supernaturalism. It is said that his ghost haunts his home, which is now a museum in Galion, Ohio. In his memory, pray for all whose memory continues to "haunt" others!

On **October 31**, we remember the passing of **Henry Brandreth** (1914-1984), the Anglican priest and preeminent scholar of *episcopi vagantes*, who was asked to present a report for his church on this threat. His two works on the subject largely condemned abuses of consecration and shared the most comprehensive source of information on wandering bishops. In his memory, find a way to deepen your own knowledge of the episcopacy within the Independent Catholic tradition!

October 31 is **Reformation Day**, a commemoration of Martin Luther's legendary sharing of his 95 theses in time for the many Mass-goers on All Saints Day to read them. In many places, the Evangelical Lutheran Church in American has been extremely kind to our Independent Catholic movement. In a spirit of gratitude, pray for them as they celebrate the 1517 start of much-needed reform in the Body of Christ!

October 31 is **World Cities Day**, an opportunity to address the challenges related to urbanization and sustainable urban development.

November is marked by the Roman Church as **Black Catholic History Month**, an opportunity to spotlight the contributions of Black Americans to our Catholic Church!

On **November 1**, the Church celebrates **All Saints Day**! Consider hosting a heavenly-themed party and costume contest with ribbons for all participants—or minimize the stress by having halos and silver beads that congregants can wear on top of their regular attire. Use the occasion as a way to catechize. Have an All Saints photo booth. Plan some heaven-themed games. Decorate with silver foil stars and clusters of white balloons. Cover furniture with white sheets and cushions. Drape white tulle around the room, with white lights behind for a twinkling effect. Scatter white, silver and clear balloons all over the floor, to give the effect of walking on clouds. Pull out a fog machine, for an additional effect. Provide a smorgasbord of white treats: finger sandwiches on white bread, cauliflower and jicama with ranch dressing, white cheeses and crackers, marshmallows, yogurt-covered nuts, white M&Ms, macadamia nuts, white chocolate pretzels, cloudlike meringue cookies, and, of course, an angel food cake with whipped cream and coconut. You will have created a heavenly memory!

On **November 1**, we remember the passing of **Dale Harbison Carnegie** (1888-1955), the American writer and speaker known for assisting others with their public speaking and interpersonal skills. The renowned author of the bestselling *How to Win Friends and Influence People*, Carnegie believed that the best way to influence other people's behavior is by changing your own behavior toward them. In his memory, reflect on your own interpersonal skills, and consider incorporating suggestions from his works into your life and ministry!

November 1 is **World Vegan Day**, an opportunity to focus on the health and environmental benefits of eco-friendly lifestyles.

On **November 2**, the Church celebrates **All Souls Day**, an outgrowth from the 1274 formulation of Purgatory, a place where our loved ones and friends are purportedly purged of sin. Consider hosting a Mass of remembrance in a cemetery or mausoleum, and invite all families who lost a loved one during this year. Announce this a few weeks in advance with a special envelope (since Catholics are accustomed to offering masses for the dead) onto which congregants can write the names of their beloved departed family members and friends, for inclusion in the intentions of this day. During the presentation of gifts, bring these envelopes forward in a lovely basket, and place them near the altar during the celebration of the Liturgy of the Eucharist. The Church shares four "great sequences" each year: Today's is the *Dies Irae*. Consider having a gifted cantor sing or chant a setting of this, before segueing into the gospel acclamation. Offer a prayer for those who've gone before us, and conclude with the popular words: "Eternal rest grant unto them, O Lord…."

On **November 2**, people throughout Latin America celebrate *el día de los muertos* ("the Day of the Dead") with altars in memory of departed loved ones. They fill these altars with photos, *papel picado* (hand-cut tissue paper), yellow and orange chrysanthemums and marigolds, and foods, drinks and objects that call to mind the lives of their beloved deceased. Incorporate elements into your own celebration of All Souls Day, and point to the *esqueletos* (skeletons that are eating, drinking, playing the guitar, riding bicycles, etc.) as a reminder of the great mystery of our faith: that those who have gone before us are not dead, but are very much alive in Christ. Send congregants home with ideas for their own simple home altars in honor of deceased loved ones!

On **November 2**, we remember the passing of **Geevargese Mar Gregorios** (1848-1902), the Malankara Orthodox Syrian metropolitan and first canonized Christian saint from India. He is known in Independent Catholicism for co-consecrating and sharing apostolic succession with Joseph René Vilatte in 1892. In his memory, consider how generously you share of what you possess!

On **November 2**, we remember the passing of **Kadavil Paulose Mar Athanasius** (+1907), the Jacobite Syrian metropolitan who co-consecrated Joseph René Vilatte in 1892. He bequeathed all his property and assets to found a seminary to teach Syriac and English to clergy. In his memory, consider your own legacy and update your will to reflect your desire to continue support for the Church and its ministries even after being born into eternal life!

On **November 2**, the Eastern Orthodox Church celebrates the anniversary of the installation in 1991 of Aghios Theodoros as **Ecumenical Patriarch Bartholomew I of Constantinople**. In a spirit of ecumenism, pray for him and for the 260 million Eastern Orthodox Catholics he serves!

November 2 is **International Day to End Impunity for Crimes against Journalists**, an opportunity to raise awareness of violence against those who report the truth in a world that sometimes attempts to obfuscate it.

On **November 3**, the Church celebrates **Malachy of Armagh** (1094-1148), the Irish archbishop who became the first native-born Irish saint in the Roman Church. Because of his devoted, passionate friendship with St. Bernard of Clairvaux, who covered him in kisses when he visited from afar, Malachy is a patron saint of the gay community. The two were buried together, wearing each other's clothes. Consider how you might better show love and affection to those close to you!

On **November 3**, we remember the passing of **Julius Joseph Overbeck** (1820-1905), the German Roman Catholic priest who, convinced that the papacy was on the verge of collapse, converted to Eastern Orthodoxy, was received into the Russian Orthodox Church, and became a pioneer of Western Rite Orthodoxy. He built bridges with Old Catholics and persistently labored for the recognition of Western Rite Orthodoxy. In his memory, consider the "bridges" you're building in your life and ministry!

On **November 3**, we remember the passing of **Léon Bloy** (1846-1917), the French novelist and poet who underwent a dramatic conversion from agnosticism to the Catholicism that he ardently defended. Quoted by other novelists and prominently figured in Michel Houellebecq's *Submission*, he denounced "Christian riches ejaculating on misery" and is known for saying, "There is only one tragedy in the end: not to have been a saint." In his memory, pause to consider the ways in which you fail to "surrender…to the poor souls" around you and the ways in which you fail to be a saint!

On **November 3**, we remember the passing of **Herbert Thurston** (1856-1939), the English Jesuit and scholar who wrote 150 articles for the *Catholic Encyclopedia* and 800 other articles in magazines and journals. In his re-editing of Butler's *Lives of the Saints*, he expressed skepticism of the legends and relics of saints. A close friend of George Tyrell, he dismissed the stigmata as a psychosomatic phenomenon and denounced spiritualism's communication with the dead. In his memory, commit yourself to a concrete action to increase your knowledge of our faith!

314

On **November 3**, we remember the passing of **Urs Küry** (1901-1976), the Swiss priest and theologian who served as the third Old Catholic bishop in Switzerland for 27 years. He represented his church at the founding assembly of the World Council of Churches in 1948, and he co-founded the International Old Catholic Theological Conference in 1950. He succeeded his father as head of the Swiss church. In his memory, pray for our sisters and brothers of the Swiss Old Catholic Church!

On **November 4**, the Church celebrates **St. Charles Borromeo** (1538-1584), the doctor of civil and canon law who established seminaries and formulated a code of moral conduct for clergy. Consider ways to focus today on your own continuing education and formation!

On **November 4**, we remember the passing of **Antoine Le Maistre** (1608-1658), the French Jansenist lawyer and author. He was the nephew of Antoine Arnauld, the leading Jansenist theologian in 17th-century France, and of Jacqueline-Marie-Angélique Arnauld, the abbess of Port-Royal-des-Champs. A talented jurist, Antoine withdrew from public affairs, greatly displeasing Cardinal Richelieu, and founded an ascetic group of hermits at Port-Royal. In his memory, lift up in prayer all who dedicate themselves to a contemplative life of prayer!

Sunday, November 5, 2023
THIRTY-FIRST SUNDAY IN ORDINARY TIME
(green)

Note the inclusive themes in today's scriptures for Inclusive Catholics: We do not show partiality like the priest's in Malachi's day (Mal. 2:9), we do not try to burden others (1Thes. 2:9, Mt. 23:4), and many of us have no problem sharing with others the nurturing love of a God that can just as easily be imagined as mother or father (Ps. 131:2, 1Thes. 2:7-8)!

The thread in today's scriptures: Like the scribes and Pharisees in today's gospel (Mt. 23:1-12), the priests in Malachi's day caused people to falter and turn away from God (Mal. 2:8). Rather than be proud and haughty (Ps. 131:1), seeking the praise of others (1Thes. 2:6), may we nourish others with gentle, motherly love (1Thes. 2:6-8)!

Holy humor: A man told his pastor, "I just can't go to church. There are so many hypocrites there!" "Don't let that keep you away," she wisely replied, smiling. "You know there's always room for one more!" [Segue into our human tendency to judge others while overlooking our own faults and shortcomings, as epitomized by the scribes and Pharisees in today's gospel.]

Looking for a visual aid for your homily or object lesson? Hold up a judge's gavel, a symbol of judgment, or struggle to pull out a super-heavy barbell! Malachi and Jesus condemned the religious leaders of their eras for their hypocrisy in judging others and making them carry heavy burdens, without lifting a finger themselves. The irony: Jesus and Malachi suggest that such people will be weighed down with the harshest judgment from God!

It's **Vocation Awareness Week**: What are you doing to promote vocations to the ordained ministries of the Church?

On **November 5**, we remember the passing of **Francisco de Quiñones** (c. 1482-1540), the Spanish Franciscan friar and cardinal responsible for several reforms of the Roman church in Spain, including the formulation of a breviary that was printed in 100 editions over 30 years. His breviary was later banned for its disregard of tradition. In his memory, consider how you are helping others to pray and grow in their daily relationship with God!

On **November 5**, we celebrate the birth in 1931 of **Charles Margrave Taylor**, the Canadian philosopher who has contributed to many philosophical fields, including the philosophy of religion. His work, *A Secular Age*, argues against the diminished influence of religion in light of science and technology, noting that religion continues to grow and diversify in our world. In his honor, consider your own stance toward the intersection of science, technology and religion, and the role of religion in a quickly-evolving world!

On **November 5**, we celebrate the birth in 1968 of **Robert Stanisław Matysiak**, the Polish-German Old Catholic priest who became the first bishop of the National Catholic Church in Germany. In his honor, pray for him and for our sisters and brothers of the National Catholic Church in Germany!

On **November 5**, we celebrate the anniversary of the founding of the **Ascension Alliance** in 2009. Happy anniversary!

On **November 6**, we remember the passing of **Guillaume Fillastre** (1348-1428), the French cardinal, canonist and geographer who was among the first to advocate at the Council of Constance for the abdication of rival popes in favor of conciliarism at the Council of Constance. He kept a diary during the council, which shed light on the quarrels, the precedence of various "nations," and the French king's response to the proceedings. Pause today to consider the ways in which you are helping to record and share history!

On **November 6**, we celebrate the anniversary of the presbyteral ordination in 2021 of **Barb Fichter**, who serves St. Martin of Tours Catholic Community in Saint Alans, Vermont. Pray for her and for the people she serves!

On **November 7**, we celebrate the anniversary of the presbyteral ordination in 1992 of Father **Don Davidson**. Happy anniversary!

On **November 8**, we remember the passing of **Æthelbert of York** (+780), the Northumbrian monk, scholar and Archbishop of York who rebuilt the cathedral and taught many missionaries, including Alcuin, the biographer of Willibrord. He convened a council to depose and exile the Northumbrian king. In his memory, consider how you are contributing to the formation of others!

On **November 8**, we remember the passing of **John Duns** (c. 1265-1308), the Scottish "Subtle Doctor" of the High Middle Ages. Also known as Duns Scotus, he argued for the Immaculate Conception and developed a complex argument for the existence of God. He is also known for such concepts as haecceity, formal distinction, and the univocity of being. In his memory, refresh your knowledge of him and his works!

On **November 8**, we remember the passing of **John Milton** (1608-1674), the English poet and intellectual who created his own non-trinitarian catechism and wrestled with theological themes, including the tension between virtue and vice. Milton was not shy about sharing his dislike for Roman Catholicism and its episcopacy, referring to Rome as Babylon and to its bishops as Egyptian taskmasters. He also saw England as the new Israel, led by the new Moses, Oliver Cromwell. In his memory, consider more creative expressions for your views on our church and world!

On **November 9**, the Church celebrates **St. Matrona** (+492), the fifth-century nun who assumed the identity of Babylas the eunuch and founded a convent in Constantinople where women dressed as men. Their local bishop allowed them to wear the wide, black leather belts and white mantles of men, rather than the woolen girdles and veils of women. For this reason, Matrona is a special saint of the trans community. In her memory, pray for greater acceptance of the many diverse expressions of humanity!

On **November 10**, we remember the passing of **George Alexander McGuire** (1866-1934), the Caribbean Episcopal priest who immigrated to the U.S. and was named chaplain-general of Marcus Garvey's Universal

Negro Improvement Association. He founded and led the African Orthodox Church for 13 years, overseeing congregations in the U.S., Canada, the Caribbean and East Africa. McGuire drew on his knowledge of religion and African history to create foundational documents on Black Independent Catholic theology and ritual. In his memory, consider how you are working to correct vestiges of colonialism and slavery in our world!

On **November 10**, we remember the passing of **Ken Saro-Wiwa** (1941-1995), the Nigerian writer and activist who has spoken against Nigerian environmental devastation due to crude oil extraction since the 1950s. In his memory, pray for all who are working to reverse the effects of environmental degradation!

November 10 is **World Science Day for Peace and Development**, which highlights the significant role of science in our world and promotes public awareness of scientific advances.

On **November 11**, the Church celebrates **St. Martin of Tours** (+397), the soldier who shared his cloak with Christ disguised as a poor man. Consider the persons around you through whom Christ might be appearing "in disguise"! In Mexico, Martin is the patron saint of business owners. Pray for all entrepreneurs who are attempting to support themselves and their families in creative ways!

On **November 11**, we remember the passing of **Lucretia Mott** (1793-1880), the American women's rights activist who co-wrote the Declaration of Sentiments at the first women's rights convention. In her memory, pray for all who continue the fight for women's rights!

On **November 11**, we remember the passing of **Josef Demmel** (1846-1913), the third bishop of the German Old Catholic Church. A Roman Catholic, he left his church and the Benedictine order after the First Vatican Council. After 31 years as an Old Catholic priest, he was elected to lead the German church in 1906, serving through the first years of World War I. In his memory, pray for our sisters and brothers of the German Old Catholic Church!

On **November 11**, we remember the passing of **Tito Pasco y Esquillo** (1930-2008), the eighth supreme bishop of the Philippine Independent Church, who was elected to complete the unexpired term of his predecessor. He made national news for his nationwide campaign to close all U.S. military bases in the Philippines and to remove all nuclear weapons from the archipelago. During his leadership, his churches were designated "peace zones," where warring parties could engage in peace talks, and his supreme council petitioned the Aquino government to resume peace negotiations with the National Democratic Front. In his memory, consider how you might better be an instrument of peace in our world!

On **November 11**, we remember the passing of **Jerome Murphy-O'Connor** (1935-2013), the Irish Dominican priest and New Testament professor considered a leading authority on St. Paul. He made numerous television appearances, and he authored several books, including an archaeological guide to the Holy Land. In his memory, explore more deeply St. Paul's life, writings and theology!

On **November 11**, U.S. society celebrates **Veterans Day**. Freedom is not free: Pray for all who have defended us in the military!

Sunday, November 12, 2023
THIRTY-SECOND SUNDAY IN ORDINARY TIME
(green)

Be sure to **choose which version of the second reading you'll proclaim**: the shorter version, or the longer form, which adds four verses speaking of the dead being raised when Christ comes down from heaven, with those who are living "caught up together with them in the clouds to meet the Lord in the air" (1Thes. 4:17). For the intellectually-curious, note how the parousia in this first extant letter of Saint Paul differs from his vision of Christ's second coming in future works!

The thread in today's scriptures: The liturgical year is drawing to a close, and we begin reflecting on the end times! The author of Wisdom says, "Whoever watches for [Wisdom] at dawn shall not be disappointed…Whoever for her sake keeps vigil shall quickly be free from care" (Wis. 6:14-15), and the psalmist meditates on God "through the night watches" (Ps. 63:6). The Matthean Jesus shares the parable of the ten virgins, concluding, "Stay awake, for you know neither the day nor the hour" (Mt. 25:13). Even Saint Paul suggests that Christ's return is imminent, since "we who are alive [will see]…the coming of the Lord" (1Thes. 4:15)!

Holy humor: Try recasting the parable of the ten virgins in contemporary terms! There were ten teens who went to a party. They all took their cell phones, but only five of them took the adapters and cords needed to charge their phones, too. They all used their phones all night—calling, texting, taking photos and videos, and playing games—and they all looked forward to recording the girls' night karaoke contest in the early morning hours! The party wore on, the batteries of their phones were quickly diminishing, and when the teens who didn't bring their chargers asked if they could borrow the chargers of those who had brought them, those who thought to bring along their chargers said, "No! We have to charge our phones, too!" [Segue into the gospel's message of preparedness—particularly since we know neither the day nor the hour of the Lord's "karaoke contest"!

Looking for a visual aid for your homily or object lesson? Consider a symbol of waking up, like an alarm clock, or a symbol of watchfulness, like a torch. Any tiki torch will work: If you're hosting a backyard party with tiki torches, aren't you going to check, to make sure they have enough oil to last through the end of the party? Otherwise, what will happen? Exactly!

On **November 12**, when it doesn't fall on a Sunday, the Church celebrates **St. Josaphat** (1580-1623), the Lithuanian archbishop who tirelessly worked in an attempt to unite the Western and Eastern Churches. Renew your commitment today to deepening ecumenical relations!

On **November 12**, we celebrate the birth in 1936 of **Sandra Marie Schneiders**, the American professor emerita who has published numerous works on theology, spirituality, feminism and religious life. In her memory, consider the ways in which you might be pouring "new wine" into "old wineskins" by failing to reimagine your life and ministry!

On **November 12**, we celebrate the birth in 1942 of **John F. Haught**, the American systematic theologian who has written widely on physical cosmology, evolutionary biology and Christianity. His many works provide a space for both scientific inquiry and a biblical understanding of God, and he explores the persistence of biblical literalism, which erroneously looks to the Bible as a source of scientific truth. In his honor, consider your own views toward the "science" contained in the scriptures!

On **November 12**, we celebrate the anniversary of the episcopal consecration in 1992 of Bishop **David Strong**, bishop of the Missionaries of the Incarnation and pastor of Spirit of Christ Catholic Community in Tacoma, Washington. Happy anniversary!

November 12 is also **Diwali**, the Hindu "Festival of Lights," a colorful and happy family celebration. Light a candle or lantern and pray for our 1.2 spiritual siblings of the Hindu tradition!

On **November 13**, we remember the passing of **Francis Thompson** (1859-1907), the English poet and mystic who dropped out of medical school to pursue his passion of writing. His poem, "The Hound of Heaven," describes the pursuit of the human person by God and has been described as "one of the most tremendous poems ever written." In his memory, pray using the words of Thompson's "The Hound of Heaven"!

On **November 13**, the Church celebrates **St. Frances Xavier Cabrini** (1850-1917), the first American citizen to be canonized. In honor of the matron saint of immigrants, share a special prayer for all who are attempting to survive and thrive in a foreign land!

On **November 13**, we celebrate the birth in 1963 of **Ayaan Hirsi Ali**, the Somali-born, Dutch-American activist and feminist who has been critical of fundamentalist Islam for its oppression of women. In her honor, pray for her and for all women who experience oppression!

On **November 13**, we celebrate the anniversary of the episcopal consecration in 2022 of Bishop **MichaelAngelo D'Arrigo** of the Convergent Christian Communion. Happy anniversary!

On **November 14**, we remember the passing of **Georg Wilhelm Friedrich Hegel** (1770-1831), the German philosopher who sought to overcome dualisms and whose philosophy of the spirit integrated philosophy, psychology, history, art and religion. Called the "Protestant Aquinas" by Barth, he provided the basis for many great philosophical ideas of the 19th and 20th centuries. In his memory, take a moment to reacquaint yourself with Hegel's life and works!

On **November 14**, we remember the passing of **Michael B. Kelly** (1954-2020), the Australian Independent Catholic bishop, queer theologian, retreat leader and spiritual counselor who co-founded the Rainbow Sash Movement in Australia, which publicly challenges the Roman Church's treatment of gay and lesbian people. After 17 years as a Roman Catholic religious education specialist and campus minister, he was dismissed by his church when he came out in 1993. In his memory, pray for all who feel forced to live in the shadows for fear of revealing who they are!

On **November 15**, the Church celebrates **St. Albert the Great** (c. 1200-1280), the great teacher and mentor who suffered memory loss and dementia before death. Pray in a special way for all who suffer similar maladies — and for all who so lovingly and patiently care for them!

On **November 15**, we remember the passing of **Margaret Mead** (1901-1978), the American cultural anthropologist whose work helped broaden attitudes towards sex and the 1960s sexual revolution. In her memory, pray for all who help open our hearts and minds to new ways of seeing our world!

On **November 15**, we celebrate the birth in 1932 of **Alvin Carl Plantinga**, the American philosopher whose writings on the philosophy of religion include a "free will defense" to refute the argument that a good God could not allow evil in the world. Within the study of theodicy, he is best known for his work, *God, Freedom and Evil*. In his honor, pause today to reflect on your own beliefs with respect to the presence of evil and suffering in our world!

On **November 15**, the Syriac Catholic Church (in union with Rome) celebrates the birth in 1944 of **Patriarch Ignatius Ephrem Joseph III Yonan of Antioch**. In a spirit of ecumenism, pray for him and for the 205,000 Syriac Catholics he serves!

On **November 15**, we celebrate the birth in 1946 of **Rebiya Kadeer**, the Uyghur activist who opposed Chinese occupation of East Turkestan and actively advocates against totalitarianism and religious intolerance. In her honor, pray for all who challenge hostile governments!

On **November 15**, we celebrate the birth in 1974 of Father **Jason Lody**, pastor of St. Anthony of Padua Catholic Church in Centreville, Virginia. Pray for him and for the people he serves!

On **November 15**, we celebrate the anniversary of the presbyteral ordination in 2008 of Father **Jason Lody**, pastor of St. Anthony of Padua Catholic Community in Centreville, Virginia. Happy anniversary!

On **November 16**, the Church celebrates **St. Margaret of Scotland** (1045-1093) and **St. Gertrude the Great** (1256-1302). Margaret raised eight children and lived a life of extraordinary charity that flowed from prayer. Gertrude was a nun whose prayer led to ecstatic, mystical experiences. Pause today to consider the state of your own prayer life. Even better, find some time and space today to focus on growing in your own prayerful relationship with God!

On **November 16**, we remember the passing of **Pierre Nicole** (1625-1695), the great Jansenist theologian whose *Les Imaginaires* suggested that the supposed heretical opinions ascribed to the Jansenists existed only in the imaginations of the Jesuits. Despite his absent-mindedness and social awkwardness, he wrote numerous popular theological works and a 14-volume work of moral theology. In his memory, encourage the gifts of the persons you're tempted to "write off"!

On **November 16**, we remember the passing of **Ignacio Ellacuría** (1930-1989), the Spanish Jesuit priest, philosopher and theologian who was assassinated with other Jesuits by Salvadoran soldiers in the closing years of the Salvadoran Civil War. His work, a significant contribution to liberation theology and liberation philosophy, met with strong opposition from political forces in El Salvador and conservative voices in the Roman Church. In his memory, pray for all modern-day martyrs and all who pour out their lives for the liberation of others!

On **November 16**, we remember the passing of **Maria Roman Nowak** (1931-2013), the Polish Old Catholic Mariavite bishop who led the Lublin-Odlasie diocese. In his memory, pray for our sisters and brothers of the Old Catholic Mariavite Church in Poland!

November 16 is **International Day for Tolerance**, a day for strengthening tolerance by fostering mutual understanding among cultures and peoples.

On **November 17**, we remember the passing of **Giovanni Pico della Mirandola** (1463-1494), the Italian Renaissance nobleman and philosopher known for his manifesto of 900 theses on religion, philosophy, natural philosophy and magic—the first book to be universally banned by the Roman church. The founder of the Christian Kabbalah tradition, his teachings influenced Western esotericism. In his memory, research the works that have been condemned and/or banned throughout history!

On **November 17**, we remember the passing of **Jakob Böhme** (1575-1624), the "first German philosopher," mystic and Lutheran theologian who was made famous by his first, scandalous work, *Aurora*, and later influenced German idealism and Romanticism. Many of his works focused on sin, evil and redemption. Pause today to consider your own views on these theological themes!

On **November 17**, we remember the passing of **André Dreuillet** (1664-1727), the French doctor of theology and bishop of Bayonne who opposed the papal bull *Unigenitus*. He was one of four appellants who called for a general council of the Church to discuss the matter. In his memory, pray for all who encourage conversation and communication!

On **November 17**, we remember the passing of **Rudolph de Landas Berghes** (1873-1920), the Italian Protestant consecrated regionary bishop of Scotland by Arnold Harris Mathew. He immigrated to New York, where he was named rector of an Anglican parish and later vanished when the press questioned his consecration. As archbishop of the Old Roman Catholic Church, he consecrated his successor, Carmel Henry Carfora. He also consecrated—and subsequently banished—Lithuanian separatist Stanislaus Mickiewicz. At age 46, he joined the Roman

Catholic Church and died as an Augustinian postulant less than a year later. In his memory, reflect on the winding path of your own spiritual journey!

November 17 is **World Prematurity Day**, an opportunity to raise awareness to the global crisis of preterm births fueled by the health equity gap.

On **November 18**, we remember the passing of **Adam Marsh** (c. 1200-1259), the English Franciscan theologian and bishop who was "the most eminent master of England" after Grosseteste. The queen's spiritual director, he mediated between the court party and its opposition, rebuking both for their shortcomings, but remaining a friend of all. In his memory, consider which "bridges" you need to mend in order to be "a friend to all"!

On **November 18**, the Church celebrates **St. Rose Philippine Duchesne** (1769-1852), who cared for the Native Americans of St. Louis, Missouri. Pause to consider your own efforts of catechesis and evangelization!

On **November 18**, we remember the passing of **Karl Hugo Prüter** (1920-2007), the Congregationalist minister who became an Independent Catholic bishop and founded Christ Catholic Church. For decades, his church was deemed the world's smallest cathedral by *Guinness Book of World Records*. He also established St. Willibrord Press to publish and distribute Independent Catholic literature. In his memory, recommit yourself to leaving a greater legacy within the Independent Catholic movement!

On **November 18**, the Coptic Orthodox Church of Alexandria celebrates the anniversary of the installation in 2012 of Wagih Subhi Baqi Sulayman as **Pope Tawadros II of Alexandria**. In a spirit of ecumenism, pray for him and for the 22 million people he serves!

Sunday, November 19, 2023
THIRTY-THIRD SUNDAY IN ORDINARY TIME
(green)

Be mindful of the heavily-exclusive language in today's scriptures: The first reading speaks to the qualities and skills that bring value to a single gender. The second verse of the responsorial psalm yields to patriarchal notions of a wife and her children "belonging" to a man, and "thus is the man blessed" could just as easily be rephrased "thus is the one blessed."

You'll need to **choose which gospel you'll proclaim**: the shorter form, or the longer form, which adds three verses on what the servants did with their talents, as well as nine verses on what happened to the servants who received two talents and one talent. If you put yourself in the moccasins of your listeners, you'll likely spare them the extra 12 verses and summarize those verses as part of your homily instead!

The thread in today's scriptures: As we mark the last Sunday in Ordinary Time, we're reminded that the industrious will be rewarded for their labor when the Lord returns to tell us, "Well done, my good and faithful servant" (Mt. 25:21 & 23)! The worthy spouse is more interested in doing good, than in deceptive charm and fleeting beauty (Prov. 31:30). Those who walk in God's way bear fruit (Ps. 128:3) and "eat the fruit of their handiwork" (Ps. 128:2). They are "children of the light and children of the day" (1Thes. 5:5). They are the ones who will hear the Lord say, "Come, share your master's joy" (Mt. 25:21 & 23)!

Holy humor: The story is told of the Texas oil tycoon who walked into a bank in New York City and asked for a loan officer. He told the loan officer he was going to Europe for two weeks and needed to borrow $5,000. Because the man didn't bank there, the loan officer needed a form of security for the loan, so the tycoon handed over the keys and title to his new Ferrari. The loan officer agreed to hold the car as collateral for the loan and apologized for having to charge 12% interest. You can imagine how the loan officer—and even the bank president—laughed at how the southerner used his $250,000 Ferrari as collateral for a $5,000 loan! An employee of the bank then drove the Ferrari into the bank's private underground garage and safely parked it. Two weeks later, the tycoon returned and repaid the $5,000 loan—with the interest of $23. The loan officer said, "Sir, we're happy to have your business, and this transaction has worked out very nicely, but we're a little puzzled: Why would a wealthy person like you bother to borrow $5,000?" And the good 'ole Texan replied, "Where else in New York City can I park my car for two weeks for only $23 and expect it to be there when I return?" [Segue into the investments and industriousness of the people in today's scriptures!]

Looking for a visual aid for your homily or object lesson? Try a bag of coins: They call to mind the image of the industrious person helping the needy (Prov. 31:20), the prosperity of Jerusalem (Ps. 128:5), the thief and those who are of the darkness (1Thes. 5:4-5), and the parable of the coins (Mt. 25:14-30). Recall, though, that a talent may have had as much value as…6,000 days' (or 20 years') wages—perhaps some half-million dollars today. What a responsibility to be given a talent or two!

Thanksgiving is this week: Consider hosting a post-mass **Thanksgiving dinner**, complete with traditional foods!

In preparation for Thanksgiving, consider sharing with each family a laminated card with a beautiful, meaningful **Thanksgiving meal blessing**. Include your community's name and contact information on it. Congregants will use it, then find a special place for it, so that they can use it in future years!

Will your community have an **end-of-year appeal**? After the celebration of Thanksgiving this week, congregants will be receiving end-of-year appeals from a number of non-profit organizations. Consider an appeal, perhaps to launch on Giving Tuesday next week! Also, be thinking about a custom holiday card that you might design and print during the coming days, to be shared during the holidays as a symbol of your appreciation for all who have supported your community throughout this year!

It's **National Bible Week**, a week devoted to encouraging people to read the bible. Explore the bible. Discover a new verse. Read it in different translations. Host a bible discussion. Give the gift of a bible to someone and share with them your favorite verses!

November 19 is **International Men's Day**, an opportunity to acknowledge the positive value of men in our world.

On **November 20**, we celebrate the birth in 1942 of **Daniel A. Helminiak**, the American Roman Catholic priest and theologian who has written widely on such topics as neuroscience, human sexuality, and the psychology of spirituality. He is renowned for his bestseller, *What the Bible Really Says about Homosexuality*, which argues that the Bible does not condemn, but is actually indifferent to, same-sex relationships. In his honor, share a copy of his book with someone who might be in need of a bit of good news on what the Bible *really* says about sexuality!

On **November 20**, we celebrate the birth in 1943 of **Luke Timothy Johnson**, the American Benedictine New Testament scholar and historian of early Christianity. He has written widely on Luke-Acts, the Pastoral Letters, the Letter of James, and the Greco-Roman context of early Christianity. He has voiced his disagreements with the Roman church, including its prohibition of same-sex marriage. In his honor, reacquaint yourself with his scholarship!

On **November 20**, the Russian Orthodox Church (recognized by the Ecumenical Patriarch of Constantinople) celebrates the birth in 1946 of **Vladimir Mikhailovich Gundyayev**, who became Patriarch Kirill of Moscow. In a spirit of ecumenism, pray for him and for the Russian Orthodox Catholics he serves

On **November 21**, the Church celebrates the **Presentation of Mary**, a day observed for centuries despite its lack of scriptural basis. Many artists depict her as a three-year old presenting herself to God. The Latino community, with its high historical infant mortality rate, has tied this act to the traditional *presentación de 3 años*, in which parents present their three-year-old children to the Church. Pray for all parents who thank God for the life of their children—and for the end of the "terrible two's"!

On **November 21**, we remember the passing of **Jean-Baptiste Henri-Dominique Lacordaire** (1802-1861), the French priest, theologian and political activist who reestablished the Dominican Order in post-Revolutionary France and whose liberal Catholic views were not welcomed by the Roman papacracy. He demanded the separation of church and state, challenging French clergy to embrace apostolic poverty over state salaries, and he attacked conservative, government-appointed bishops as ambitious and servile. He was an early advocate for freedom of conscience and freedom of the press—both of which were condemned by Gregory XVI. In his memory, pause to consider how your own words and actions contribute to and/or limit basic human freedoms!

On **November 21**, we remember the consecration in 1897 of **Anthony Stanislas Kozlowski**, who organized the Polish National Catholic Church in Chicago for Polish congregants dissatisfied with their mostly-Irish Roman Catholic bishops. Pray today for those unable to identify with the Church's ministers around them!

On **November 21**, we celebrate the birth in 1957 of **Elsa Y. Nelligan**, a deacon at Holy Family Catholic Church in Austin, Texas. Pray for her and for the people she serves!

On **November 21**, the Polish National Catholic Church celebrates the anniversary of the installation in 2010 of **Prime Bishop Anthony**

Mikovsky. In a spirit of ecumenism, pray for him and for the 26,000 people he serves!

On **November 21**, we remember the death in 2021 of **Robert Bly**, the American poet, essayist and activist whose bestselling work, *Iron John*, made him the leader of the mythopoetic men's movement. He pointed to the predicament of children, particularly boys, who lack models and rites of passage to guide them through life's stages. In his memory, pray for and/or reach out to those trapped between childhood and maturity, and who continue to struggle from having grown up without the love and leadership of a father and/or mother!

On **November 22**, the Church celebrates **St. Cecilia**, the third-century matron saint of musicians. She was martyred for refusing to forsake her vow of virginity and sacrifice to pagan gods. Find a small way today to grow in your own musical ability. If you're not entirely confident in your vocal abilities, ask a gifted friend for a brief vocal lessons! Also, if you haven't recognized your parish's instrumentalists and vocalists recently, this is an opportune day to do so!

On **November 22**, we remember the passing of **Cornelius Diependaal** (1829-1893), who served as the sixth Dutch Old Catholic bishop of Deventer for 18 years. In 1874, he was elected archbishop of Utrecht, which he declined less than two weeks later. The following year, he was consecrated titular bishop of Deventer, with no jurisdiction. He served as a canon of the metropolitan chapter and as dean of south Holland, and he was a co-signer of the 1889 Utrecht Declaration. In his memory, consider your own ability to say "no"!

On **November 22**, we remember the passing of **C.S. Lewis** (1898-1963), the British Anglican writer and theologian whose fiction and Christian apologetics have been read by millions. In his memory, read one of his works and/or consider the written legacy you're leaving!

On **November 22**, we also remember the passing of **Aldous Leonard Huxley** (1894-1963), the English Nobel Prize winning author, philosopher, humanist and pacifist who wrote on mysticism and who illustrated the similarities between Western and Eastern mysticisms. In his memory, reflect on the universality of your own spiritual vision!

On **November 22**, we remember the passing of **Robert Ronald Jan Maria Zaborowski** (1946-2010), the American archbishop and head of the Old Catholic Mariavite Church in North America. In his memory, pray for our sisters and brothers of the Old Catholic Mariavite Church in North America!

On **November 22**, the Greek Orthodox Church of Jerusalem (recognized by the Ecumenical Patriarch of Constantinople) celebrates the anniversary of the installation in 2005 of Ilias Giannopoulos as **Patriarch Theophilus III of Jerusalem**. In a spirit of ecumenism, pray for him and for the 500,000 Greek Orthodox Catholics he serves!

On the fourth Thursday of November, U.S. society celebrates **Thanksgiving**: Find a way to involve your congregants not only in celebrating the abundance they enjoy, but of sharing with others. Encourage a canned food drive to assist those who will hunger during the upcoming holiday season, or volunteer for a community Thanksgiving dinner! For the intellectually-curious, note how the turkey is traditionally a symbol of bounty, a rare treat for early settlers in the New World, and/or point to the nine "turkeys" in today's gospel who lacked an "attitude of gratitude"!

On **November 23**, the Church celebrates **St. Clement I** (c. 35-99), **St. Columban** (c. 543-615), and **Bl. Miguel Agustín Pro Juárez** (1891-1927). Clement I addressed division in the Church and urged Christians to live in love and union. Columban was a monk who urged the Church toward greater holiness. Miguel Agustín was a Jesuit priest murdered by the anticlerical, anti-Christian political regime in Mexico. Consider today your own commitment to unity, holiness and our faith!

On **November 23**, the Church celebrates **Walatta Petros** (1592-1642), the Ethiopian woman who resisted conversion to Roman Catholicism, formed many religious communities, led a successful movement to expel Portuguese Jesuit missionaries from Ethiopia, and performed miracles for those seeking asylum from rulers. After the deaths of her three children, she shaved her head, left her husband and became a nun. She lived "a lifelong partnership of deep romantic friendship" with a noblewoman named Eheta Kristos, who succeeded Walatta as head of their community. Walatta's biography, written 30 years after her death, contains 27 miracles and depicts the earliest-known same-sex relationship of women in sub-Saharan Africa. In her memory, lift up and celebrate the love of all who honor Walatta's love and spiritual legacy!

On the day after Thanksgiving, we celebrate **Native American Heritage Day**, an opportunity to honor our indigenous sisters and brothers and their rich cultural and spiritual heritage!

On **November 24**, we remember the passing of **Maria Michał Sitek** (1906-1970), the Polish Old Catholic Mariavite bishop who served the Old Catholic Mariavite Church in Poland. In his memory, pray for our sisters and brothers of the Old Catholic Mariavite Church in Poland!

On **November 24**, the Armenian Catholic Church (in union with Rome) celebrates the birth in 1946 of **Catholicos-Patriarch Raphaël Bedros XXI Minassian**. In a spirit of ecumenism, pray for him and for the 758,000 Armenian Catholics he serves!

On **November 25**, the Church celebrates **St. Catherine of Alexandria** (c. 287 – c. 305), a saint removed from the canon of saints for lack of historical evidence — but later restored as a gesture of good will to Orthodox Christians. Consider today what gestures you're making — or could be making — to increase ecumenical relations!

On **November 25**, the Greek Orthodox Patriarchate of Alexandria and all Africa (recognized by the Ecumenical Patriarch of Constantinople) celebrates the birth in 1954 of **Nikolaos Horeftakis**, who became Pope and Patriarch Theodore II of Alexandria. In a spirit of ecumenism, pray for him and for the 1.4 million Greek Orthodox Catholics he serves!

November 25 is the **World Day to Eliminate Violence against Women**, which focuses on one of the most widespread, persistent and devastating human rights violations in our world today. Violence against women remains largely unreported due to the impunity, silence, stigma and shame surrounding it. Pray and advocate for an end to this social sin!

Sunday, November 26, 2023
CHRIST THE KING OF THE UNIVERSE
(white)

The Sundays of Summer/Fall Ordinary Time have come to an end: **Decorate your worship space** in white and gold. Be sure your vestments match the environment and are ironed or steamed. Highlight the solemnity of this day with an arrangement of fresh flowers!

The thread in today's scriptures: Ezekiel, the psalmist and the Matthean Jesus imagine God to be like the ancient shepherd-kings, tending the sheep, shepherding them rightly, and separating the sheep from the goats (Ez. 34:11-12 & 15-17, Ps. 23:1, Mt. 32-33). Paul imagines Christ putting all his enemies — including death — under his feet, then "hand[ing] over the kingdom to his God and Father" (1Cor. 15:24). Will you be part of that kingdom? It depends on whether you're counted among the "sheep" or the "goats" (Mt. 25:34-46)!

Holy humor: Have you heard the story of the woman who was walking in the countryside when she saw a shepherd tending a huge flock of sheep? She asked him, "How many sheep do you have there?" The shepherd asked, "Which kind, dear: the white sheep or the black sheep?" She said, "The white ones, for example." He said, "There are about 200 white sheep in this meadow." "And how many black sheep are there?", she asked. "About 200, too." She continued, "And what do they eat?" The shepherd asked, "Which ones, dear: the white sheep or the black sheep?" She said, "I don't know…the white ones." He replied, "They eat the greenest grass." "And the black ones?", she asked. He replied, "The black sheep eat the greenest grass, too." She continued, "And how much wool does each sheep produce?" The shepherd asked, "Which ones, sweetheart? The white sheep or the black sheep?" By this point, the woman was beginning to get annoyed. "The white sheep," she said. He replied, "The white sheep produce an average of 12 pounds of wool each year." "Uh-huh. And the black ones?", she asked. He replied, "And the black ones produce about 12 pounds of wool each year, too." Exasperated, the woman asked: "Why do you always ask me which sheep — the white ones or the black ones — if the answer is always the same for all of them?" The shepherd replied, "Well, that's easy. That's because the white sheep are mine!" "Oh," she said. "I didn't think about that. And whose are the black ones?" And the shepherd replied, "The black ones are mine, too!" [Segue into the scriptural image of God shepherding all "sheep" — and even the "goats," too!]

Looking for a visual aid for your homily or object lesson? Consider a golden crown and a crozier or shepherd's staff! That's the image we have in today's scriptures of the shepherd-king! Invite your listeners to consider how well they're following in the footsteps of the shepherd-king and tending the "sheep" and the "lambs" around them!

On **November 26**, we remember the passing of **Sojourner Truth** (1797-1883), the Black American abolitionist and women's right activist who felt a calling from God to testify to "the hope that was in her." She was instrumental in recruiting Black troops for the Union Army during the Civil War. In her memory, pray for all who continue the fight for civil and women's rights!

On **November 26**, we remember the passing of **Adolf Küry** (1870-1954), the Swiss priest and theologian who served as the second Old Catholic bishop in Switzerland for over 30 years. A professor of church history, canon law and liturgy, he edited the *International Church Journal*. As bishop, he continued his predecessor's work, promoting ecumenism and fostering relations with the Anglican and Orthodox churches. He was succeeded by his son, Urs Küry. In his memory, pray for our sisters and brothers of the Swiss Old Catholic Church!

On **November 26**, we remember the passing of **Bernard Joseph Francis Lonergan** (1904-1984), the Canadian Jesuit philosopher and theologian regarded as one of the prominent Catholic thinkers of the 20th century. In his memory, spend a few minutes reacquainting yourself with his life and works!

On **November 27**, we remember the assassination of **Harvey Milk** (1930-1978), the pioneering LGBTQIA+ rights activist and most famous gay elected official in California. His birthday (May 22) is a state holiday in California, and he is memorialized in two Oscar-winning movies. A martyr for LGBTQ and human rights, he is remembered for his words: "Hope will never be silent."

On **November 27**, we remember the passing of **Louie Crew Clay** (1936-2019), the American Rutgers professor emeritus of English who campaigned for the acceptance of LGBTQ people by Christians and founded Integrity, the national Episcopal LGBTQ organization. He included more than 1,000 people and events in his "Today in LGBTQ History" calendar. In his memory, consider how you might help others to better understand others unlike themselves!

On **November 27**, we celebrate the birth in 1942 of **Robert M. Nemkovich**, the American clergyman who served as the sixth prime bishop of the Polish National Catholic Church. In his honor, pray for him and for our sisters and brothers of the Polish National Catholic Church!

On **November 28**, we remember the passing of **Adrian Johann Broekman** (1724-1800), the Dutch priest and seminary rector who served as the fifth Dutch Old Catholic bishop of Haarlem for over 20 years. His consecration by the archbishop of Utrecht, who was consecrated by the former bishop of Haarlem, brought a full circle to the shared apostolic succession that the two dioceses have since shared. In his memory, consider the ways in which you fail to reciprocate the kindness of others!

On **November 28**, we remember the passing of **Antonina Maria Izabela Wiłucka-Kowalska** (1890-1946), the first Polish woman to receive the sacrament of Holy Orders. The wife of Michał Kowalski, who was consecrated by the archbishop of Utrecht, she served as bishop and high priestess of the Mariavite Catholic Church in Poland. She led the church after her husband's imprisonment in a concentration camp, until her death in 1946. In her memory, pray for all who lead in difficult circumstances!

On **November 28**, we celebrate the birth in 1978 of **Pavel Benedikt Stránský**, the Czech bishop who leads the Old Catholic Church in the Czech Republic. In his honor, pray for him and for our sisters and brothers of the Old Catholic Church in the Czech Republic!

On **November 29**, the Church celebrates **Bl. Bernardo Francisco de Hoyos** (1711-1735), the young Spanish Jesuit priest who vividly wrote of his mystical marriage to Jesus. At age 18, he had a vision of marrying Jesus, where Jesus put a gold ring on his finger and said, "You are mine, and I am yours....You are Bernardo de Jesús and I am Jesús de Bernardo....You and I are one!" In icons, Jesus' sacred heart burns in Bernardo, a patron saint of same-sex marriage. In his memory, lift up all whose love and unity mirror our mystical marriage with Christ!

On **November 29**, we remember the passing of **Dorothy Day** (1897-1980), the American journalist and activist who maintained her social activism after converting to Catholicism. Imprisoned for being a suffragette, she later co-founded the Catholic Worker Movement and edited its newspaper. Pope Francis referred to her as one of four exemplary Americans who built a better future for our world. In her memory, pray for all whose faith calls them to advocate for civil rights!

November 29 is also **International Day of Solidarity with the Palestinian People**. In honor of this day, deepen your knowledge of the post-World War II "Palestine problem" which led to the commemoration of this day!

On **November 30**, we celebrate **St. Andrew** (c. 5-60), referred to as one of Jesus' first disciples (Mt 4:18) and, in another place, as a disciple of John the Baptist who introduced his brother, Peter, to Jesus (Jn 1:40-42). Pause to celebrate the patron saint of those who fish and sing, and consider how you are bringing others to Jesus!

On **November 30**, we remember the passing of **Oscar Wilde** (1854-1900), the Irish poet, novelist and playwright who was one of the most prominent LGBTQIA+ Catholics in his day. Sentenced to two years of prison and forced labor, he wrote of his spiritual journey in a lengthy letter that was posthumously published. In his memory, be inspired by one of the several biographies that celebrate this inaugural honoree of San Francisco's Rainbow Honor Walk!

On **November 30**, we remember the passing of **Johann Josef Demmel** (1890-1972), the sixth bishop of the Old Catholic Church of Germany. His ministry was interrupted by his military service during World War I. He published German works on the sacrament of reconciliation and Old

Catholicism. In his memory, pray for our sisters and brothers of the German Old Catholic Church!

On **December 1**, we celebrate the birth in 1954 of **Medha Patkar**, the Indian social activist who fights for justice for the farmers, laborers and women of India. In her honor, consider how you are bringing God's justice to this world!

December 1 is also **World AIDS Day**. Pray for all who suffer from HIV/AIDS—and for all who care for them!

On **December 2**, we remember the passing of **Jan van Ruysbroeck** (1294-1381), the Augustinian priest and prominent Flemish mystic who penned 12 books on the spiritual life. Pause to consider where you are on the "spiritual ladder"—and what you might do to achieve the next "rung"!

On **December 2**, we remember the passing of **Pasquier Quesnel** (1634-1719), the French theologian banished from Paris for his Jansenist sympathies. The Roman church published a papal bull, *Unigenitus*, to condemn 101 sentences in his devotional commentary on the New Testament. In his memory, pray for all who continue to write and publish in an attempt to foster the devotion of others—and for all who are persecuted by the people they love!

On **December 2**, we remember the passing of **Thomas Forsyth "T.F." Torrance** (1913-2007), the Scottish Protestant theologian who was a pioneer in the study of science and theology and who edited the translations of hundreds of theological writings into English, including Karl Barth's six-million-word *Church Dogmatics*. Torrance was instrumental in drafting a joint statement on the doctrine of the Trinity for an historical agreement between the Reformed and Eastern Orthodox churches. In his memory, consider how generously you are sharing the gifts God has given you for the upbuilding of God's reign in this world!

December 2 is also **World Day for Slavery Abolition**. Deepen your knowledge of the various forms of slavery that persist in our world, and pray for the 150 million children who are still subject to child labor!

And with that, we've come to the end of the Year of Matthew!

If you have any feedback on how we can improve this text for use by you and your community, please call us at (512) 826-0280 or write us at editor@extraordinarycatholics.faith.

Please know of our prayers for you and your community as you seek to create extraordinary celebrations for Extraordinary Catholics!

Important Dates to Remember
& Celebrate in Our Community!

December

_____   _____

_____   _____

_____   _____

January

_____   _____

_____   _____

_____   _____

February

_____   _____

_____   _____

_____   _____

March

_____   _____

_____   _____

_____   _____

April

_____   _____

_____   _____

_____   _____

May

_____   _____

_____   _____

_____   _____

Important Dates to Remember
& Celebrate in Our Community!

June

_____   _____

_____   _____

_____   _____

July

_____   _____

_____   _____

_____   _____

August

_____   _____

_____   _____

_____   _____

September

_____   _____

_____   _____

_____   _____

October

_____   _____

_____   _____

_____   _____

November

_____   _____

_____   _____

_____   _____

Our Plan for Creating Extraordinary Celebrations

November 27 – First Sunday of Advent

_____   _____

_____   _____

December 4 – Second Sunday of Advent

_____   _____

_____   _____

December 11 – Third Sunday of Advent

_____   _____

_____   _____

December 18 – Fourth Sunday of Advent

_____   _____

_____   _____

December 24/25 – The Nativity of Our Lord

_____   _____

_____   _____

January 1 – Mary Mother of God

_____   _____

_____   _____

January 6 – The Epiphany of Our Lord

_____   _____

_____   _____

January 8 – The Baptism of Our Lord

_____   _____

_____   _____

Our Plan for Creating Extraordinary Celebrations

January 15 – Second Sunday in Ordinary Time

_____   _____

_____   _____

January 22 – Third Sunday in Ordinary Time

_____   _____

_____   _____

January 29 – Fourth Sunday in Ordinary Time

_____   _____

_____   _____

February 5 – Fifth Sunday in Ordinary Time

_____   _____

_____   _____

February 12 – Sixth Sunday in Ordinary Time

_____   _____

_____   _____

February 19 – Seventh Sunday in Ordinary Time

_____   _____

_____   _____

February 22 – Ash Wednesday

_____   _____

_____   _____

February 26 – First Sunday of Lent

_____   _____

_____   _____

Our Plan for Creating Extraordinary Celebrations

March 5 – Second Sunday of Lent

_____   _____

_____   _____

March 12 – Third Sunday of Lent

_____   _____

_____   _____

March 19 – Fourth Sunday of Lent

_____   _____

_____   _____

March 26 – Fifth Sunday of Lent

_____   _____

_____   _____

April 2 – Palm Sunday

_____   _____

_____   _____

April 6 – Holy Thursday

_____   _____

_____   _____

April 7 – Good Friday

_____   _____

_____   _____

Our Plan for Creating Extraordinary Celebrations

April 8 – Easter Vigil

_____   _____

_____   _____

April 9 – The Resurrection of the Lord

_____   _____

_____   _____

April 16 – Second Sunday of Easter

_____   _____

_____   _____

April 23 – Third Sunday of Easter

_____   _____

_____   _____

April 30 – Fourth Sunday of Easter

_____   _____

_____   _____

May 7 – Fifth Sunday of Easter

_____   _____

_____   _____

May 14 – Sixth Sunday of Easter

_____   _____

_____   _____

May 21 – Seventh Sunday of Easter

_____   _____

_____   _____

Our Plan for Creating Extraordinary Celebrations

May 28 – Pentecost

_____   _____

_____   _____

June 4 – The Most Holy Trinity

_____   _____

_____   _____

June 11 – The Solemnity of the Most Holy Body and Blood of Christ

_____   _____

_____   _____

June 18 – Eleventh Sunday in Ordinary Time

_____   _____

_____   _____

June 25 – Twelfth Sunday in Ordinary Time

_____   _____

_____   _____

July 2 – Thirteenth Sunday in Ordinary Time

_____   _____

_____   _____

July 9 – Fourteenth Sunday in Ordinary Time

_____   _____

_____   _____

July 16 – Fifteenth Sunday in Ordinary Time

_____   _____

_____   _____

Our Plan for Creating Extraordinary Celebrations

July 23 – Sixteenth Sunday in Ordinary Time

_____   _____

_____   _____

July 30– Seventeenth Sunday in Ordinary Time

_____   _____

_____   _____

August 6 – Transfiguration of the Lord

_____   _____

_____   _____

August 13 – Nineteenth Sunday in Ordinary Time

_____   _____

_____   _____

August 20 – Twentieth Sunday in Ordinary Time

_____   _____

_____   _____

August 27 – Twenty-first Sunday in Ordinary Time

_____   _____

_____   _____

September 3 – Twenty-second Sunday in Ordinary Time

_____   _____

_____   _____

September 10 – Twenty-third Sunday in Ordinary Time

_____   _____

_____   _____

Our Plan for Creating Extraordinary Celebrations

September 17 – Twenty-fourth Sunday in Ordinary Time

_____   _____

_____   _____

September 24 – Twenty-fifth Sunday in Ordinary Time

_____   _____

_____   _____

October 1 – Twenty-sixth Sunday in Ordinary Time

_____   _____

_____   _____

October 8 – Twenty-seventh Sunday in Ordinary Time

_____   _____

_____   _____

October 15 – Twenty-eight Sunday in Ordinary Time

_____   _____

_____   _____

October 22 – Twenty-ninth Sunday in Ordinary Time

_____   _____

_____   _____

October 29 – Thirtieth Sunday in Ordinary Time

_____   _____

_____   _____

November 5 – Thirty-first Sunday in Ordinary Time

_____   _____

_____   _____

Our Plan for Creating Extraordinary Celebrations

November 12 – Thirty-second Sunday in Ordinary Time

_____   _____

_____   _____

November 19 – Thirty-third Sunday in Ordinary Time

_____   _____

_____   _____

November 26 – Christ the King of the Universe

_____   _____

_____   _____

Other notes on our plans for creating extraordinary celebrations"...

Index

Made in the USA
Monee, IL
03 December 2022

19523615R00197